7.1.6.1.2 DC(W)

AF843963

UNITED NATIONS LAW MAKING

Bibliothèque
INSTITUT HENRY-DUNANT
02196

UNITED NATIONS LAW MAKING

Cultural and Ideological Relativism and International Law Making for an Era of Transition

EDWARD MCWHINNEY, Q.C.

Holmes & Meier Publishers
NEW YORK LONDON

Unesco
PARIS

First published 1984
by the United Nations Educational,
Scientific and Cultural Organization,
7 Place de Fontenoy,
75700 Paris, France,
and Holmes & Meier Publishers, Inc.
30 Irving Place, New York, N.Y. U.S.A.

Copyright © 1984 by Unesco
All rights reserved

Book design by Stephanie Barton

Library of Congress Cataloging in Publication Data

McWhinney, Edward.
United Nations law making; cultural and ideological relativism and international law making for an era of transition.

1. United Nations. 2. International law.
3. International relations. I. Title.
JX1977.M42 1984 341′.1 83-22755
Unesco ISBN N°92-3-102147-8
Holmes & Meier ISBN N° 0-8419-0948-2

Manufactured in the United States of America

Contents

Foreword by Unesco ix
Acknowledgments xi
Introduction: Legal Characteristics of an Era of Transition 3

1. HISTORICAL RELATIVISM AND THE *SPATIAL* DIMENSION OF INTERNATIONAL LAW: COMPETING "REGIONAL" SYSTEMS 8
   - Special Systems of International Law: Latin American Regional Internaticnal Law. 9
   - Regional Systems of International Law: Marxist-Leninist International Law, Chinese-Style; International Law of Development. 10
   - Soviet, Socialist International Law 11
   - The Antinomy of Marxist-Leninist Legal Principles and Socialist International Law. 13
   - The Accommodation (Synthesis) of Soviet, Socialist International Law and Classical, Western-based International Law: Peaceful Coexistence 16
   - The Dialectical Development of International Law: Historical Critique of Peaceful Coexistence (Friendly Relations) 19

2. HISTORICAL RELATIVISM AND THE *TEMPORAL* DIMENSION OF INTERNATIONAL LAW: THE "OLD" AND THE "NEW" INTERNATIONAL LAW 21
   - Intertemporal Law: The Classical Formulation: *Island of Palmas* (1928) 24
   - The Institut de Droit International: The Search for a Modern Restatement 25
   - Creative Judicial Legislation: The World Court 27
     - *Namibia* (1971) 27
     - *Western Sahara* (1975) 29
     - *Continental Shelf (Tunisia/Libyan Arab Jamahiriya)* (1982) 34
   - Conclusions 37

3. The International Law-Making Process: Sources of International Law 42
Closed Categories of Formal Sources 42
Hierarchical Ranking of Sources 44
Contemporary Trends in the Sources of International Law 46
International Custom 47
International Conventions (General and Particular) 49
International Legislation: Resolutions of the United Nations General Assembly 55
Judicial Decisions: The International Court of Justice 58

4. The International Law-Making Process: Imperative Principles of International Law 62
Categories of Imperative Principles 62
The General Principles of Law Recognized by Nations 62
Equity 63
Jus Cogens *73*
Contemporary Trends in Sources of International Law 76
Teachings of the Most Qualified Publicists: *Dédoublement Fonctionnel* *78*
"Soft" Law and "Hard" Law 78

5. Law-Making Arenas: Security Council, General Assembly, and International Law Commission 80
United Nations Membership: "Original Members," "Peace-Loving States" 80
United Nations Charter: Limited Treaty or Constitution? 84
Security Council: The Permanent Members' Veto 87
Filling the Gaps in the Charter: General Assembly Legal Innovation 91
International Law Commission: International Legal Codification, "Progressive Development" 96

6. Arenas and Institutions: International Court of Justice and Judicial Policy Making 105
Court Jurisdiction: *Inter Partes* and Advisory Opinion 105
Comparative "Regional" Attitudes to International Adjudication 106
Election of Judges: Political-Legal Factors 109
The Judges as Legal "Honoratiores" 112
Law and Policy: Judicial Self-Restraint and Judicial Activism 114
Court in Transition: Contradictions and Conflicts 116
Institutional Reform within the Court: Special Chambers 123
The Future of Judicial Settlement 129

7. INTERNATIONAL LAW-IN-THE-MAKING: UNITED NATIONS CHARTER REFORM, THE MANILA DECLARATION ON PEACEFUL SETTLEMENT 133
Direct Amendment of the Charter 133
The Special Committee on the Charter of the United Nations and on the Strengthening of the Role of the Organization 135
The Manila Declaration on the Peaceful Settlement of International Disputes 141

8. INTERNATIONAL LAW MAKERS 145
The Secretary-General: Legal Competence and Powers 145
Auxiliary Legal Offices: United Nations Legal Counsel, Codification Division (Office of Legal Affairs) 150
The Sixth (Legal) Committee 153
The Reformed International Law Commission 155

9. IDEOLOGICAL PLURALISM AND CONTEMPORARY INTERNATIONAL LAW VALUES: SELF-DETERMINATION OF PEOPLES, ECONOMIC SOVEREIGNTY 162
Jural Postulates of a Civilization Area and Civilization Period 162
Values and Value Choice 164
  Value Identification 164
  Value Ranking 168
  Value Concretization 168
Contemporary International Law Values: Self-Determination of Peoples, the Decolonization Imperative 170
Contemporary International Law Values: The Economic Sovereignty Imperative, New International Economic Order 177

10. IDEOLOGICAL PLURALISM AND CONTEMPORARY INTERNATIONAL LAW VALUES: PEACE, "ONE WORLD," ENLIGHTENMENT, HUMAN DIGNITY 189
The Peace Imperative: Outlawing the Use of Force 189
The Peace Imperative: Nuclear and General Disarmament 193
The "One World" Imperative: "Common Heritage of Mankind" 195
The Enlightenment Imperative: New World Information and Communications Order 197
The Human Dignity Imperative: Contemporary Antinomies 205
  "Specialists" and "Generalists" in International Legal Negotiations 205
  United Nations Charter-based Principles and Processes 206
  Differing "Regional" Approaches: Eurocentrism and Human Rights 209

11. International Law Making for an Era of Transition 213
Alternative World Order Constructs 213
Evolving United Nations Constitutionalism 216
United Nations Membership: The Credentials Issue 216
General Assembly and Security Council 220
Office of Secretary-General 223
International Court of Justice 224
International Law Commission, Sixth (Legal) Committee, Special Codifying Commissions and Conferences 226
United Nations Expenses: Financial Dues of Member States 227
The Axiological Problem: Value Conflicts, Value Antinomies 228
Operationalism in International Legal Problem Solving 230
Historical Contradictions in Space and Time 230
The Skills of Legal Pragmatism: Problem Solving 232
On Legal "Receptions" and Legal Eclecticism 233
Notes 236
Index 261

Foreword

In 1979 Unesco launched a new collection called *New Challenges To International Law,* with the aim of encouraging critical reflection on international law to see how it can be better adapted to the demands of the contemporary world. The present volume is the third in the collection. Like the two previous volumes, it deals with a dimension of the international normative system which is characteristic of the continual process of adaptation of international law to the changing realities of international relations.

The center of the post-1945 structure of the interstate system is without doubt the United Nations Organization. Conceived to prevent the outbreak of large-scale violence and to resolve the social, economic, and political problems of the community of nations, it soon became a barometer of rising expectations of the peoples represented by governments at the United Nations and of conflictual relations among states, for a variety of reasons, including cultural and ideological ones. The process of transformation of international society manifests itself throughout the law-making activity of the United Nations, in particular in the Security Council, the General Assembly, the International Law Commission, the International Court of Justice, and through the Secretary-General.

Professor Edward McWhinney has undertaken in this book the task of analyzing the processes, arenas, and actors involved in law making in the United Nations for what he calls "an era of transition"—that is, the transition from an old system of world public order to a new one. He has brought to this task the experience of a distinguished career in teaching and writing in international law and in the practice of law, and the wisdom of an adviser to government and to international organizations. Member of the Institut de Droit International, he is a leading authority in the fields of constitutional law and new frontiers in international law. The views expressed are, of course, those of the author alone and do not necessarily reflect the opinions of Unesco.

Unesco is grateful to Professor McWhinney for preparing this volume, which will provide insights to scholars and practitioners on the evolution of the law-making process within the community.

Such a complex subject requires more than an examination of the writings of other scholars and official documents, and Professor McWhinney was able to bring to this task his experience as special adviser to the thirty-sixth, thirty-seventh and thirty-eighth sessions of the General Assembly and his firsthand observations of many of the developments described in this book. Professor McWhinney looks at the empirical evidence concerning the behavior of states and in no way underestimates the conflictual dimension in that behavior; he nevertheless also sees the emergence of a legislative process in the world community and does not hesitate to urge improvements in the law-making capacity of the United Nations. His vision is one of the adaptation of international law to the realities of this era of transition and its enforcement in the collective interests of the emerging world public order.

This vision corresponds to the aim of Unesco in this collection of publications on the new challenges facing international law of today and tomorrow. Unesco hopes this book, like the entire collection, will contribute to a better understanding of the role of law in contemporary international society and its potential in the building of a world order based on justice and solidarity.

Acknowledgments

This study is being published as part of Unesco's series *New Challenges to International Law,* inaugurated in 1979 with Judge Bedjaoui's monograph, *Towards a New International Economic Order.*

The main hypotheses were tested in preliminary form in courses of lectures I gave in French, as Professeur associé in the Faculté de Droit of the Université de Paris I (Panthéon-Sorbonne) in the spring semester of 1982, and in the Collège de France in the spring of 1983, and I owe a special intellectual debt to Claude-Albert Colliard and René-Jean Dupuy, my hosts at these two institutions.

Much of the empirical source material was obtained while I served at the United Nations as special adviser to the thirty-sixth annual session of the General Assembly in the autumn of 1981, and to the thirty-seventh annual session in the autumn of 1982. The manuscript was completed while I was University Research Professor at Simon Fraser University.

Responsibility for the present work is that of the author, and conclusions and recommendations do not necessarily reflect the opinions of any of the institutions, academic or governmental, national or international, with which the author has been associated at various times in recent years.

Université de Paris I (Panthéon-Sorbonne)
Collège de France, Paris
United Nations, New York
Simon Fraser University, Vancouver

E. McW.

UNITED NATIONS LAW MAKING

Introduction: Legal Characteristics of an Era of Transition

We live today in an era of transition in the world community, from an old system of world public order to a new one. What President de Gaulle characterized as the "postwar" era in international relations—bipolarity and the twin political-military blocs or alliances, dominated respectively by the Soviet Union and the United States—is clearly at an end, without, however, the main contours and directions of the new system of world public order that will replace it having yet become clear. From Cold War through coexistence to eventual détente, the patterns of post-1945 international relations had a certain predictability and comfortable assurance, since they were based upon two main players only, the Soviet Union and the United States, each of which was manifestly rational and also relatively conservative in its approach to international decision making. There was a sufficiency of shared values, at least in the peace-keeping area; and there was a common interest in maintaining the World War II political-military settlement, already agreed upon by the wartime Big Three at Yalta in February 1945, even before the war's end, and then confirmed at Potsdam in August 1945. Beyond that, there was a mutual understanding and ability to maintain one's basic interests in the legal-institutional machinery worked out at the Conference on International Organization at San Francisco in 1945, and incorporated in the resulting United Nations Charter. For, in its specific stipulations against the so-called enemy states in Articles 53 and 107 of the new charter, not less than in the special connotation given to "peace-loving states," which was the criterion of United Nations membership—in terms of Article 4 of the charter and in actual political-administrative practice in the early years of the new

United Nations Organization—it was clear that the dominant design was to establish and maintain a postwar world public order system that would reflect as nearly as possible the historic consensus of the fleeting wartime years of the so-called wartime alliance against fascism.

Like all constitutional documents framed in fairly general terms at a particular moment in history, the Charter of the United Nations came to take on a meaning and significance not necessarily intended by its founding fathers of 1945 or corresponding to their original wishes, this in accord with rapidly changing conditions in the world community and in response to an ever widening and ever more representative (in ethnic-cultural and ideological terms) membership. Still, all through the first decade of its history, in that period of easy and automatic political dominance by the United States and its allies, with the comfortable, pro-Western majority voting coalition in the General Assembly, and thereafter with the first flood of admission of "new," newly decolonized states, before the Third World voting bloc had yet become cohesive and disciplined in its approach to political power in international organization, the Soviet Union and the United States, with only rare exceptions like the Korean crisis of mid-1950, never substantially departed from the interbloc ground rules—or mutual, tacit understanding and reciprocal tolerances—developed on an experiential basis and often painfully, by trial and error, through the difficult Cold War years. In particular, there was no real attempt to use or misuse the special parliamentary machinery of the United Nations to harass the other side beyond the point where the basic postwar settlement drawn up at Yalta and Potsdam would be challenged or threatened. To a sufficient extent the two rival bloc leaders observed the "rules of the game" in their mutual interbloc dealings and relations throughout the Cold War period; and the passage to the more tranquil period of East-West coexistence and then détente was thereby immensely facilitated and accelerated.

The passage from the era of East-West, Big Power coexistence and détente, its surface rivalries and name calling and its more frequent pragmatic compromises and political give-and-take, to the current era of transition is one of change from a tidy and predictable condition of Big Power condominium, where only two major players needed to be considered or even consulted, to a largely uncertain and frequently hazardous condition of polypolarity (multipolarity). This is characterized by a plurality of different and frequently conflicting value systems, involving both goal values themselves and also basic processual-institutional method and choice of problem-solving arenas and techniques. All this reflects the plurality of new players who have emerged in the world community since the political-legal consummation of decolonization and national self-determination throughout the late 1950s, the decade of the 1960s, and the early 1970s. The process of transfer of effective power in the world community has been assisted, during that time, by a certain manifest crisis of confidence on the part of each of the erstwhile bloc leaders, the product in considerable part of purely internal, domestic factors unrelated to international conditions, like the Watergate crisis, which supervened in the United States just at the apogee of East-West détente in the Nixon-Brezhnev Moscow summit accords of May 1972, and which seriously weakened that element of strong executive leadership and direction in each of the two blocs on which Big Power equilibrium or balance of power, and hence coexistence and détente had always been predicated. Parallel to the crisis of internal leadership in the United States, the Soviet Union revealed an aging, increasingly timorous and unimaginative and conservative direction at the top, unable effectively to respond to, or at times even to comprehend, the winds of change within the Soviet Union and Soviet bloc and in the world community at large. The interruption, in the early and mid-1970s, of that disciplined, ongoing process of détente that had seen a plethora of concrete and substantial East-West accords in nuclear and general disarmament and on security of territorial frontiers and related questions, meant not merely a failure to complete that resolution or synthesis of East-West contradictions that had been the main political task and intellectual challenge of the postwar era, but an embarking upon a new and uncertain course in international relations without the advantages of an orderly, tidy, disciplined transition presided over and actively patronized and assisted by the Big Powers. In fact the reversion, in the late 1970s and early 1980s, to some of the ideological name calling and polemical debate that had marred the early Cold War period, and a certain willful refusal at the higher executive levels on both sides to apply the pragmatic, empirical, problem-oriented, step-by-step approach that had highlighted the successful road to détente throughout the 1960s and the early 1970s, has complicated the quest for a new, politically viable world public order system to tide us over the remaining years of the twentieth century.

A polypolar world community with a plurality of significant players, representing in their turn a plurality of different ethnic-cultural and ideological systems, each with its own distinctive legal values and methodologies of legal problem solving, which will sometimes be the same or complementary and sometimes dissonant or in direct competition with each other, means a congeries of different legal relationships in any given problem situation. Thus, some aspects of a given problem may involve vestigial East-West, bipolar clusters of legal rules and principles; some others, by now already anachronistic European imperial-colonial clusters; still others, Latin American, intra-hemispheric "regional" rules and principles, or, for that matter, "new" North-South development law norms. Characterization of the problem is the key to successful legal problem solving, in that it permits determination of the substantive legal values to be applied and the legal techniques and processes best suited for implementing those values. And yet different players today will characterize the same problem in different ways, involving different legal value choices and different legal procedures. At the processual-institutional level, the problem is compounded when particular institutions—Security Council, General Assembly, International Court, for example—and also different problem-solving methods—diplomatic negotiation, third-party arbitration, judicial decision making, for example—are identified with particular time periods in the history of the world community and with the particular social and economic forces or ethnic-cultural groupings that then were dominant. In terms of substantive value choice, the resolution of the axiological problem implies a particular *Weltanschauung* or conception of world history that is ultimately related to one's prediction of the movement and direction of societal change in the world community today. The alternative developmental constructs or projections of such long-range historical trends become vital to the exercise of an informed policy choice in international legal decision making.

It is easier, in an era of transition, to identify time past—the old legal values and institutions of yesterday or the day before yesterday—than to try with any real confidence to postulate the legal values and institutions of the world community of, say, the few years ahead now to the year 2000. Historical determinists with optimistic conceptions of a continuing unfolding or development of human powers and human civilization are forced to admit, like J. Kohler, the possibility of "retrogressive civilizations," even if they cannot always identify them in advance. Both Western and Marxist legal theorists had no difficulty in agreeing, each group with its own distinctive legal value systems, that the postrevolutionary, fundamentalist Islamic religious regime in Iran was historically retrogressive; and both systems, Western and Marxist, either directly opposed the Ayatollah Khomeini's administration or else rendered little more than grudging deference and respect for the Iranian people's right to self-determination. The legal appraisal or characterization in each case, however, was historically relativist, reflecting the particular a priori ideological preconceptions of particular postindustrial societies, Western and Soviet, at particular stages of their own social and economic development. Neither system, Western or Soviet, has any claims to a monopoly on legal truth, which presumably, in the case of Iran, will be determined dialectically by the rise and fall of the contending political and social forces there. Truth, as William James, the founder of American pragmatism and an intellectual precursor of North American sociological jurisprudence, remarked, is not an abstract quality inherent in an idea, but something that happens to it, experientially, in action. What we can do is to try to project time past, in terms of legal values and institutions and processes, through time present—both of these capable of empirical observation and verification—and arrive at a more or less scientific extension into time future and the values, institutions, and processes of tomorrow. If this tends to mean the reign of scientific relativism—sociological jurisprudence, and the criterion of the goodness in law as its ability to reflect the dominant interests and demands in society at any time—a necessary corrective can be, and is being, applied by the increasing transcultural, intersystemic consensus manifest as to a certain minimum number of fundamental legal principles and rules—general principles of law common to all systems, to paraphrase the words of the listing of formal "sources" of law in Article 38 of the International Court of Justice statute. An era of transition in the world community, such as the one we live in today, can thus produce its own world "living law," *jus gentium,* natural law–style corpus of principles and rules. Some of these—very many, in fact—are clearly drawn from the "old" classical, Western or Eurocentric international law; some from comparative law, through comparative scientific-legal method and analysis and induction (common law and civil law; European and non-European; Communist and Western [liberal democratic, or social democratic] as the case may be); and some directly from that "new" international law emerging in the postwar period. If political decolonization and national self-determination have clearly attained, by now, a degree of general, if not indeed universal, recognition as fundamental principles of modern international law, recognition of national sovereignty over national economic and natural resources, and acceptance of human rights (political, social, and economic) are increasingly recognized today as the proper concerns of any mature legal system, international or national.

1. Historical Relativism and the *Spatial* Dimension of International Law: Competing "Regional" Systems

The *spatial* dimension of international law denotes the problem of the claims to legitimacy and universality of application today of legal principles and rules manifestly developed by one or more dominant ethnic-cultural groupings in the world community, and not by others. The *spatial* dimension and the *temporal* dimension constitute the twin aspects of historical relativism in international law. Sometimes the spatial and temporal aspects will be conjoined as the determining causal factors in the one problem situation, as with the survival into the late twentieth century of that special "colonialist" cluster of legal categories having to do with acquisitions of territories and the subjecting of aboriginal peoples overseas, which were developed essentially in the mercantilist, trading time era of the world community, when its dominant political-military forces were Western European. The spatial and temporal limitations to the "colonialist" cluster of legal categories and to their claims to continuing validity are clear enough and beyond contest today. More often, perhaps, the spatial and temporal elements in a problem situation are not of equal weight, and they can conveniently be separated for purposes of analysis. Thus the principal criticism today of "classical" international law seems to be less of its datedness, obvious enough as that is in certain areas, than of a postulated intellectual narrowness and unrepresentativeness in its ethnic-cultural base—that it has a too limited, Eurocentric quality that impairs any claims to universality in the plural world community of today that far transcends an original "European family compact" era in international relations.

Special Systems of International Law: Latin American Regional International Law

Even within the ethnically and culturally limited, European or received-European, special legal community, the claims to general application of classical international law had been historically challenged by the notion of special regional variations or exceptions. Some of these regional variations are sufficiently coherent in the thrust of their philosophical principles, and also systematic enough in the organization of their rules, to qualify as autonomous "systems" of international law. Thus, Latin American international law, the product intellectually of the general continental European civil law tradition and also of the particular Spanish and Portuguese imperial legal inheritance, may amount to a separate system of international law in its own right, with its direct challenge to classical international law in some of its more important areas. Latin American international law carries certain doctrines with a specifically Hispanic-American connotation, as with the *Uti possidetis* doctrine regulating territorial frontiers as between the "succession states" to imperial Spain, on a basis of the original Spanish imperial, internal administrative or regional boundaries. The doctrine seems to have been raised, elliptically and perhaps only half seriously, in the spring of 1982, by Argentina in the course of its dispute with Great Britain over the Falkland (Malvinas) questions. There is absolutely no reason, of course, why doctrines like *Uti possidetis* should be thought of as closed legal categories that jelled once and for all at the time of their early nineteenth-century origins, or why they should not be capable of generic extension today, at least to the point of denying European latter-day imperial claims to a colony itself appropriated by *force majeure* in the early nineteenth century. Other special Latin American doctrines[1]—such as the so-called Calvo Clause and the Drago Doctrine—were more specifically directed outward from Central and South America to European imperial powers or to the United States, either to deny the validity or, more modestly, to compel the renegotiation, on some more nearly equitable basis between the parties, of commercial concessions and licenses or financial contracts wrested from Latin American states, in their postindependence period of political weakness, by foreign powers and the rapacious private corporations that they happily sponsored, politically and where necessary militarily, in their claimed legal capacity as *parens patriae*. Such obviously one-sided, usurious commercial concessions could very easily, in doctrinal terms today, be generalized into some larger international legal category authorizing their unilateral repudiation or at least rewriting at the instance of the debtor state or the one bearing the burden of the onerous economic obligation. The special Soviet-bloc—and by now also Chinese Communist—doctrine of "unequal treaties" comes readily to mind; and though in its origins it is a category limited to the legal denunciation of inter*state* obligations only, as a matter of interpretation it should be broad enough to cover also concessions or contracts between a state on the one hand and large corporations or multinational corporations actively promoted or sponsored by parent governments. Insofar as Latin American international law, in its economic manifestation, reflects the protest by developing countries (albeit "received-European" developing countries) against Western European or North American economic imperialist practice, it has struck a responsive chord in the hearts of the numerically far larger group of Afro-Asian and Caribbean developing countries, to the point where its principles, actively adopted on a selective, piecemeal basis by the contemporary Third World bloc, now amount to an important part of the new body of international development law that would severely limit the legal rights and powers of the Western European and North American creditor and investor states.[2]

Regional Systems of International Law: Marxist-Leninist International Law, Chinese-Style; International Law of Development

The reference earlier to unequal treaties and to Chinese Communist positions raises the question of the existence today of a special body of Chinese Communist "regional" international law. The People's Republic of China is, of course, directly associated with the Pancha Shila Agreement of 1954, which it concluded with postcolonial republican India: the Pancha Shila both established a highly pragmatic live-and-let-live principle for two emerging major powers having, however, radically different ethnic-cultural and also ideological bases, and also, so far as it tried to enunciate some few ground rules to govern relations between them, provided a leitmotiv for the later Soviet and Soviet-bloc campaign in behalf of a generalized Soviet-Western coexistence. The People's Republic of China, however, in part because of its close political partnership, until 1959, with the Soviet Union, and its consequent participation in and borrowing from the more general Marxist doctrinal thinking on international law, and in part because after 1959 it seemed preoccupied with its own internal ideological quarrels, has failed to develop as yet any body of systematized international legal thought of a Marxist or even distinctively "Chinese" character. In public arenas like the United Nations General Assembly, the People's Republic, since the belated seating of its delegation in October 1971 in replacement of the group from Nationalist China (Taiwan), has participated with flair and enthusiasm in the activities of the

Third World bloc and has sometimes seemed—perhaps because of its relative freedom from encumbering, Big Power–inherited political-military obligations—to be more active than its erstwhile Soviet ideological partner in deferring, in terms, to abstract Marxist legal theory. In more concrete problem situations, distinctively Chinese legal contributions with a Marxist or revolutionary coloring seem limited to legal categories like the "unequal treaties" already referred to, themselves a derivation from Soviet (Great October Socialist Revolution–era) international law, which always cited as its most notorious examples the so-called "territorial concessions" in the coastal cities of mainland China, whereby imperial and republican China had, under manifest duress, surrendered administration and also extraterritorial legal rights to the imperial powers—Britain, France, Portugal, the United States, Japan (and, briefly, before World War I, imperial Germany).[3] To British Prime Minister Margaret Thatcher's insistence, in September 1982, in the aftermath of the successful British military defense of that other latter-day remnant of the imperial past, the Falklands (Malvinas), that the United Kingdom could still assert today a full and valid legal title to Hong Kong, the Kowloon Peninsula, and the adjacent New Territories, based on the treaties made with imperial China in the nineteenth century, the present-day People's Republic of China's administration replied—how could it do otherwise?—that the treaties signed between the British government and the Qing Dynasty were unequal treaties which had never been accepted by the Chinese people; that Hong Kong was part of Chinese territory; and that the whole Hong Kong area would be recovered when conditions were ripe. The implication of the People's Republic of China's démarche was clear enough: the British government should sensibly try to do what it had failed to do in the case of the Falklands (Malvinas) through seventeen long years of Argentine-British bilateral talks—that is, renegotiate the status of the Hong Kong area and recognize Chinese sovereignty while the situation was still timely and before it had become pathological and politically out of hand.

Soviet, Socialist International Law

The major regional systems of international law existing today separately and distinctly from classical international law are the still embryonic Third World–based international development law and, of course, Soviet international law, sometimes designated as socialist international law so as to make it include also the Soviet-bloc countries of Eastern Europe and non-European allies like Cuba. Soviet international law has the enormous advantage of a considerable body of doctrinal literature and theoretical debate on its basic premises, from 1917 onward. It also reveals, more markedly perhaps than the classical international law, the continuing antinomy between the law-in-books and the law-in-action—the theoretical constructs developed by the Soviet academicians by a process of logical deduction from a priori Marxist principles, and the actual record of concrete practice and de facto positions taken by Soviet leaders in the political give-and-take of East-West negotiations. At the level of law-in-action, Soviet international law tends to reveal an interesting blend of deference to a priori theoretical principles and the Soviet national interest as viewed in the context of the particular problem situations to be decided. The actual process of legal decision making may not be too different, in this regard, from that which occurs in Western foreign ministries, except that, in the case of the Soviet Union, perhaps because of the greater momentum of old bureaucratic ideas and perhaps because it is not so directly responsive to waves of public opinion, there is a greater tendency to vindicate the national interest on a basis of long-range consistency over a range of cases, rather than looking to advantage in the immediate case. The legal principle that you assert today, because it happens to help in the instant case, is the same one that you may have to live with tomorrow when others invoke it as a precedent in their own cases. The special Soviet international law positions as to sources of law and as to processes and arenas for international law making are canvassed more fully in succeeding chapters. For immediate purposes, the historical debate within the Soviet Union itself as to the basic definition of law—its nature and purposes—demonstrates very fully both the antinomy between law-in-books and law-in-action in Soviet international law (just as in other regional systems of international law, Western included) and also the differences, even conflicts, in intellectual attitudes toward law as between Soviet legal academicians disengaged, by virtue of their university or institute employment, from the exigent here-and-now of Soviet foreign policy, and those Soviet jurists directly charged, as officials or advisers in the Foreign Ministry, with the active utilization and implementation of legal principles and rules in pursuit of Soviet government policy objectives. It is not so much a question of Georges Scelle's principle of *dédoublement fonctionnel*—of Soviet official jurists (not less than Western official jurists) tending to shape their interpretations of legal doctrine and jurisprudence so as to suit their clients' special needs in the instant case—as of the opening to the practical world of realpolitik bringing with it a certain refreshing degree of candor and an understanding of the affirmative role of law as an instrument for resolving conflicts and striking new balances between competing social interests in the world community at any time. Dr. Gregory Tunkin, in a speech to Soviet academic jurists on the condition of Soviet legal science, used language oddly reminiscent of the American legal realists in castigating a general situation of

> weakness and incompleteness in juridical argumentation and a tendency to slip into the easier path of ready-made political argumentation reinforced by quotations . . . [producing an] isolation from actual reality, from the foreign policy of the U.S.S.R. as it is practised. . . . The writers restrict themselves to the cognitive aspects of the problem and do not aim at formulating proposals that can be employed in the practice of Soviet foreign policy. . . . The majority of works on international law appear *post factum,* after the international conferences and meetings to which they pertain and after a particular problem has been discussed in the U.N. or elsewhere.[4]

While Dr. Tunkin's accompanying strictures upon "dogmatism," "the use of citations instead of creative thought," and "the isolation from actual reality" can be readily related to the official de-Stalinization campaign led by Premier Khrushchev, with whose policies Tunkin was closely associated as principal legal adviser in the Foreign Ministry, there can surely be no doubt of the universality of application of his postulated goal for the Soviet science of international law: "The aim must not only be knowledge of what exists in international law but active participation in changing it."[5]

Tunkin's great American contemporary, Myres McDougal, had similarly excoriated American jurists of his era for their failure, as he saw it, to "achieve comprehensive description of the techniques of policy formulation and application in the World Power Process," and for their concomitant—"over-emphasis on technical rules, unrelated to policies, as factors in guiding and shaping decisions."[6]

No world power like the Soviet Union or the United States, faced with the awesome responsibilities of leadership within its respective bloc and of finding mutual accommodation where interests collided, could afford a purely passive, contemplative approach to international law that ignored all its affirmative possibilities for promoting pragmatic compromises. It is not surprising that each system should produce essentially identical legal-realist doctrinal formulations at one and the same time, and this seemingly without any direct exchange or contact between the rival jurists concerned.

The Antinomy of Marxist-Leninist Legal Principles and Socialist International Law

In Soviet internal legal discourse, Tunkin made it his main task, in the time period of the late 1950s and early 1960s, when de-Stalinization was under way within the Soviet Union itself and beginning to be projected abroad in the incipient Soviet foreign policy campaign on behalf of peaceful coexistence, to challenge more traditional, or orthodox, Soviet Marxist-Leninist legal thinkers. Thus, in his 1958 Hague Academy lectures,

Tunkin sharply criticized Professor Eugene Korovin of the University of Moscow Law Faculty for developing the thesis that each social system had its own peculiar set of international principles and norms, and that hence there could be no general international law common to both main competing world politicial systems, Communist and Western.[7] Korovin had, of course, based his general theory of international law upon the Marxist-Leninist basic premise of legal superstructure developing from, and reflecting, economic infrastructure: since law is a product of the marketplace, each economic system will thus get the body of law appropriate to its particular stage of economic development. The main theoretical or philosophical dilemma of international law in the bipolar world community of the immediate post–World War II era thus stood starkly revealed: how might two different economic systems—Communist and capitalist—yield identical bodies of international law doctrine?[8] Or, to put the question even more precisely, in orthodox Marxist-Leninist terminology, if international law, like national law, belongs to the superstructure and is determined uniquely by the base of productive relationships, how can two radically different bases yield the same superstructure of international law?[9]

A legal realist (Soviet or Western), examining the dilemma on a strictly scientific-empirical basis and without too many ideological preconceptions, might be tempted to conclude today that the Soviet and Western worlds, as postindustrial societies, have economic-industrial bases that increasingly approximate each other, and that the foreign policy imperatives of the two, in consequence, are not too different and, in fact, increasingly conservative. The legal contradiction as to the nature and character of international law had, however, to be resolved in the Soviet Union—as it also tended to be debated in the West in the Cold War years—in exclusively theoretical, nonempirical terms.

The greatest of the Soviet legal theorists, E.B. Pashukanis, who was to disappear shortly afterward in the Stalinist purges of the late 1930s and to be posthumously rehabilitated only very many years later, had tried to resolve the dilemma in 1935 by profiting from the recognized Marxist-Leninist legal distinction between *form* and *content:* although the *forms* of international law might be identical for all states, opposing social systems could avail themselves of these *forms* for their own ends. Each system could thus pour its own distinctive wine into the one set of bottles. Pashukanis thus repudiated any notion of international law as the expression of a common ideology between states, and accepted it instead as an instrument to be used by Soviet policymakers in the class struggle against capitalist states. Pashukanis for this reason concluded that it was purely scholastic, and of no help in the practical conduct of Soviet foreign policy, to attempt to define the "nature" of international law; and he considered the prior Soviet discussions of the subject the result of the continuing influence in Soviet legal circles and legal thinking of bourgeois-liberal legal methodology, itself resting on an error of association of law with substance developing in accordance with its own internal principles.[10]

After Pashukanis's political downfall in 1937, the great debate continued among Soviet international lawyers, with the dominant theory seeming to be one that presented the legal relations between the Soviet Union and the West as a combination of competition and cooperation, with existing international law as a mix of three groups of norms, each group distinguished by its particular social origin: *first,* traditional international law (with bourgeois-liberal origins), containing institutions and practices (for example, the between-the-two-World-Wars institution of the League of Nations, which the Soviet Union had then only recently joined) acceptable to, and accepted by, the Soviet Union; *second,* specifically "imperialist" institutions (for example, the League of Nations' mandates system and the "extraterritorial rights" that had been wrested by the Western powers from China) rejected by the Soviet Union; and *finally,* new elements of international law introduced by Soviet practice (for example, Soviet state trading practices).[11]

After the Second World War, the most ambitious attempts, in Soviet legal theory, at philosophical rationalization of the phenomenon of an international law that could simultaneously serve both Communist and capitalist states, were those of Professor Korovin, to which reference has already been made.[12] In Dr. Tunkin's words, in his 1958 lectures to The Hague Academy of International Law:

> Korovin developed the idea that to the States of one "social structure" are inherent certain "international law principles and norms," whereas to the States of another "social structure" are inherent other international law principles and norms; and universally recognised principles and norms of international law are "identical norms of various legal super-structures."[13]

Tunkin cited Korovin in this context only to reject his views and at the same time to reject the charge leveled against Soviet legal science by some Western jurists during the Cold War period, that it did not recognize the existence of general international law regulating relations among all states and binding upon them. Such a thesis as to the impossibility of the existence of general international law, in Tunkin's view, led objectively to justification of a "position of strength" policy and the Cold War,[14] the partisans of such realpolitik attempting to buttress their political argument by the allegation that agreements between capitalist and socialist (Communist) countries were impossible, or that such agreements were of little value, and that nowadays only the language of force was of any use in international relations.[15] With all these Cold War–period contentions Tunkin joined issue:

> Difference of ideologies has always existed. True, this difference at present is profound. But when States agree on recognition of this or that norm as a

> norm of international law they do not agree on problems of ideology. They do not try to agree on such problems, for instance, as what is international law, what is its social foundation, its sources, what are the main characteristics of a norm of this law, etc. They do agree on rules of conduct. . . . For thousands of years jurists have not been able to agree on what is law. And still throughout all this time law existed. So States may profoundly disagree as to the nature of norms of international law, but this disagreement does not create an insurmountable obstacle to reaching an agreement relating to accepting specific rules as norms of international law.[16]

The collective work on international law—first published in 1957 and intended for use in Soviet law schools, and under the general editorship of F. I. Kozhevnikov (with the collaboration of Professor Korovin; another one-time Soviet judge on the World Court, S. B. Krylov; and several others)—contains a definition of international law that, Janus-like, seems to face two ways at the same time:

> International Law can be defined as the aggregate of rules governing relations between States in the process of their conflict and cooperation, designed to safeguard their peaceful coexistence, expressing the will of the ruling classes of these States and defended in case of need by coercion applied by States individually or collectively.[17]

The emphasis on law as command comes close to the highly positivistic Soviet definition of internal, municipal law reflected in the Stalin Constitution of 1936 and in Vyshinsky's well-known textbook on Soviet internal, municipal law.[18] It also bears comparison with English common law, Austinian (command theory of law) approaches to the definition of international law;[19] and it conveniently supplies an Austinian-style sanction with the express reference to individual or collective state coercion where needed to secure enforcement. On the other hand, the reference to an "aggregate of rules governing relations between States in the process of their conflict and cooperation" is more frankly experiential or operational; and the approach to definition of international law is, for the first time, tied in, in terms, to the concept of peaceful coexistence which was to become the leitmotiv of Soviet foreign policy—and of Soviet international law in support of such Soviet foreign policy—from the late 1950s onward through the whole decade of the 1960s.

The Accommodaton (Synthesis) of Soviet, Socialist International Law and Classical, Western-based International Law: Peaceful Coexistence

While "peaceful coexistence," as a legal term of art, might seem sensibly to denote that long-range, objective, factual, existential condition of effective political-military equilibrium or balance of power on which any viable system of world public order (Western-conceived or Soviet-conceived) must rest in a plural world community, it has come, as a result of the historical accidents of its timing and sponsorship, to acquire a special legal connotation associated with the intensive Soviet diplomatic campaign, in the twilight years of the Cold War, on behalf of an immediate general act of codification of postulated international law principles of peaceful coexistence. Soviet jurists, in support of that campaign in their sustained doctrinal writings of the next few years, dropped retrospective historical footnote references to Lenin, and also (more obviously and immediately) to the Pancha Shila (or "Agreement between the People's Republic of China and India on Trade and Intercourse between the Tibetan Region of China"), made on April 29, 1954, and to the joint statement accompanying that agreement, issued by the Soviet Union's then close ideological ally, Prime Minister Chou En-lai of China, and Prime Minister Nehru, on June 28, 1954. There were, as Krylov had pointed out in his own Hague Academy lectures in 1947,[20] references to ideological coexistence to be found in the works of Lenin, Stalin, Molotov, and assorted other political leaders from the 1920s onwards. But in its main, latter-day development, peaceful coexistence was the foreign-policy brainchild of Stalin's successors and principally of Premier Khrushchev; and it was the manifestation in the foreign-policy field of the official program of de-Stalinization that had been inaugurated within the Communist party of the Soviet Union and Soviet administration itself only a few years after Stalin's death. In its specifically international law elaboration and projection, peaceful coexistence should be attributed most of all to Dr. Tunkin, speaking and writing then in his official capacity as principal legal adviser to the Soviet Foreign Ministry (before his move to the University of Moscow after Khrushchev's removal from office in 1964 and after Korovin's retirement from his law school chair). Although the Soviet proposals for an immediate general act of codification of the international law principles of peaceful coexistence, such as they might be, were initially denigrated by Western political leaders as a Trojan horse device for lulling the West into a false security while the Soviet bloc prepared quietly, in Khrushchev's own colorful phrase, to "bury the West" militarily, the concept of East-West political and military coexistence was introduced by Soviet-bloc spokesmen in a number of private, professional, and scientific arenas[21] at the same time as it was being advanced in the United Nations and in East-West bilateral diplomatic negotiations, and it acquired thereby a certain general intellectual validity and respectability. The timing of the peaceful coexistence campaign was also happy, for it coincided at the end of the 1950s with a certain weariness in both East and West with all the long years of the Cold War crisis that had lasted since the end of the Second World War in Europe. Some of the widespread impatience with bipolarity and the too rigid system of twin political-military blocs facing each other across the Iron Curtain, which physically divided Europe and imposed a barrier to East-West intercourse in any form, was manifested in the diplomatic breakthrough of the Antarctic Treaty of 1959, when the principle of joint East-West cooperation, across the ideological frontiers, in matters of common scientific concern and urgency, was established in response in considerable measure to the pressures from the intellectual-scientific establishments within each of the two blocs. The example, once established, proved contagious. Western legal spokesmen soon began a tactical switch, in their response to the Soviet coexistence campaign, from their initial blanket rejection of the principle of a general act of legal codification, to a subtler and more nuanced approach, involving a pragmatic, empirical, problem-oriented, step-by-step approach to resolution of fundamental East-West conflicts. This joinder of issue on legal methodology implied a change in emphasis from the purely abstract, high-level, and general to the more specific, low-level, and concrete. It was the apparent quiet de facto Soviet acceptance of this Western-favored problem-solving orientation in East-West relations that really opened the way for the first time to a whole series of tension-reducing measures throughout the decade of the 1960s, beginning with the Moscow Partial Test Ban Treaty of 1963 and ripening, through repetition and extension in further and continuing East-West practical accommodations on a basis of mutuality and reciprocity of interest between the two blocs, into that larger historical process known as détente, with its own special corpus of East-West treaties and legal accords. It was, however, the legal "laymen"—Western legal practitioners and university professors, outside the national foreign ministries and the ranks of their supporting, salaried legal advisers—who can be given much of the credit for the eventual breakthrough in East-West relations; for, impatient with all the surviving Cold War barriers, they refused to be constrained by official positions and insisted, in continuing international and national scientific-legal conferences and debates, that success was possible only by eschewing the bitter and largely futile debate over political ideology and concentrating instead on current tension issues in Soviet-Western relations and on their immediate range of practical solutions. If war was too important a matter to leave to the generals, finally ending the Cold War could not be entrusted solely to the national foreign ministries. It was necessary first to de-ideologize the problem of peace and war in order to approach its solution.

The original Soviet proposal for legal codification had listed five primary principles: mutual respect for territorial integrity and sovereignty; nonaggression; nonintervention and noninterference in internal affairs; equality and mutual advantage; and peaceful coexistence itself. Support within the United Nations from those "new" countries that had only recently been decolonized from their Western European "parent" imperial countries and which, at the opening of the 1960s, effectively exercised the political balance of power within the General Assembly of the United Nations, was joined to all the pressures of the Soviet-bloc countries. This led to the creation in 1963 of a special committee of the General Assembly, charged with the "progressive development and codification" of the principles of coexistence, henceforth (in response to Western objections to the term "peaceful coexistence" as a specifically Soviet or Communist invention) styled euphemistically as "Friendly Relations and Cooperation among States in Accordance with the Charter of the United Nations."[22] The special committee came up, seven years later, with a formal declaration, later embodied in a General Assembly resolution under that same name, that does not depart too substantially from the original Pancha Shila listing of principles.[23] These principles are formulated only at a very high level of generality and abstraction. They are primary principles, and, unaccompanied by more detailed and low-level secondary principles, they do not give much guidance or help as to actual problem solving. It might also be suggested that, as formulated, they do not in themselves represent too much of an advance upon existing "classical" international law.[24] The breakthrough in international law developed under the rubric of coexistence,[25] in this view, occurred experientially in the series of concrete East-West accords of the 1960s on nuclear and general disarmament and peace keeping as a whole, initiated by the two bloc leaders, usually in summit meetings, and then presented to the world community at large for signature and ratification in more general multilateral treaties.[26]

The Dialectical Development of International Law: Historical Critique of Peaceful Coexistence (Friendly Relations)

Peaceful coexistence as a theoretical legal concept was, by reason of the happy accident of its timing, historically important in the opening up of a genuine East-West legal dialogue at a moment when continuance of the Cold War had become intellectually oppressive and politically unprofitable for both the Soviet bloc and the West. Its long-range historical significance lay more in the psychological thrust that it gave to the *process* of East-West conflict resolution than in any new body of substantive legal ideas for which it might claim to stand. It was this *process,* now more generally identified as détente, that constituted the permanent or continuing element in international relations (where the Cold War and similar tension eras, with their denial of negotiation and exchange between rival systems, would represent abnormal, pathological conditions). In empirical terms, however, coexistence could properly be identified with particular substantive legal agreements stemming from its process—in addition to the nuclear and general disarmament treaties and the cultural and scientific cooperation accords already referred to,[27] certainly the territorial frontier settlements and related arrangements in Central and Eastern Europe of the late 1960s and early 1970s, now known as the *Ostpolitik* treaties.[28] In and of itself, peaceful coexistence seems to have been a fundamentally conservative concept—a rationalization, stabilization, and legitimation of Big Power interbloc relations and of the territorial and related power dispositions, including "spheres of influence" and mutual nonintervention in the internal affairs of each bloc, already long since agreed upon and politically sanctified by the wartime allies against fascism, at Yalta in 1944 and Potsdam in 1945. The *process* of coexistence manifestly worked best with relatively stable and predictable and conservative regimes in control in both blocs, Soviet and Western. Administrations like those of Kennedy and Johnson, and most of all perhaps Nixon, in the United States, and of Khrushchev and to a somewat lesser extent Brezhnev in the Soviet Union, could move confidently from mutually acknowledged positions of strength and recognize a common interest in the political-military status quo, without any need for gratuitous moralizing or ideological name-calling on an interbloc basis. As such, of course, peaceful coexistence perhaps turned out to be more nearly part of the old or "classical" system and process of international law, and certainly neither an opening to nor a vehicle for making the so-called "new" international law.

2. Historical Relativism and the *Temporal* Dimension of International Law: The "Old" and the "New" International Law

The *temporal* dimension of international law denotes the problem of the claims to legitimacy and continued application today of legal principles and rules manifestly developed in an era now past. The antinomy between an "old" and a postulated "new" international law has its historical roots in the Soviet-Western legal "great debate" occurring at the end of the 1950s and the beginning of the 1960s at a time when, with all the benefits of retrospective wisdom, we can now recognize that the Cold War was ending and a new era of Big Power coexistence and détente was succeeding it. The term "new" international law was used, innocently enough, by the then principal legal adviser to the Soviet Foreign Ministry, Gregory Tunkin, in a context in which he seemed to call in question the adequacy, in contemporary terms and having regard to the vast changes in the membership of the world community since World War II and the new range of societal interests emerging as a result, of the whole corpus of classical international law principles and rules.[1] To Western jurists, who immediately joined issue on the basis of a perceived threat to Western political, economic, and military interests which any challenge to classical international law would represent, Dr. Tunkin replied elegantly that he was advocating "new international law" only, and that he had certainly called "neither for 'a new international law' nor for a 'revolution' in international law"; and that he had "no intention of overthrowing the international law now in force."[2]

That answer, allowing for the debater's skill with which it was formulated, says something—as any empirical examination of Soviet practice over the years will surely confirm—for the long-range continuity, even conservatism, of Soviet international law and its interest in essentially incremental change rather than any fundamental act of novation. The gap between abstract legal doctrine—what Ehrlich called the law-in-books—and law-in-action or actual legal practice in concrete cases is as marked in regard to Soviet international law as in the case of any other "regional" system of international law, Western or other. Soviet international law doctrine is the heir to a revolutionary past, and the principles of the Great October Socialist Revolution of 1917 certainly operate, by way of what Harold D. Lasswell called legal folklore, to influence and shape the formulation of many current policy options; but the actual choice between those different options—legal decision making—will tend to operate in Soviet society, not less than in Western society, on a rational calculation of the national interest, short-range as well as long-range, in any problem situation.

The dynamic element in the intellectual campaign on behalf of a "new" international law comes a little later than the Soviet-Western legal "great debate" that inaugurated détente; and when it comes it is with other actors, newly or recently admitted as legal members of the world community and with interests in the world public order system that quite transcend the essentially bipolar, Soviet-Western issue of détente. The movement for a "new" international law, challenging the "old" or "classical," putatively Western or Eurocentric international law, is essentially a Third World–led movement. It draws some direct inspiration, to be sure, from the ideological inheritance of the Great October Socialist Revolution of 1917, and it would be rather surprising if it did not. Classical international law in its heyday was certainly enriched by the French Revolutionary and Napoleonic inheritance; and the great principles of nationalism, independence, and liberalism that stemmed from it were certainly reinforced and extended, in their turn, by the principles of the Great October Socialist Revolution. There is, in fact, a direct linear development to be seen, from the French Revolution through the October Revolution to the declaratory resolutions of the United Nations General Assembly, from the 1950s onwards, of the international law principles of national self-determination, decolonization, and independence.

The principal reason, however, for the contemporary Third World–based challenge to classical international law is that it is viewed, rightly or wrongly, as an instrument for preserving a world political and economic order in whose creation the Third World did not participate and which is still oriented to the interests of those dominant postindustrial societies of today (Communist and Western) that so largely made it. The challenge to classical international law as an "old" law, reflecting an "old" world public order system now under challenge and in process of disappearing, is also helped by the new legal teachings, strongly influenced as these are by theories of historical relativism and by the application of rigorously empirical methods to the study of the origins of legal principles and rules. The new teachings demonstrate clearly enough that, so far from being a body of timeless absolutes, good for all seasons and all places, and postulated a priori in advance of actual problem situations, the main principles and rules of classical international law were developed ad hoc and experientially, in response to concrete international conflicts and the need for accommodation of the rival parties and the diverse interests that they represented. Most classical international law is, in fact, of comparatively recent historical origin. If there are strictly doctrinal borrowings, extensive enough in certain areas (notably as to territorial title), from the Roman law, classical international law is still, by and large, the creation of the foreign ministers and supporting jurists of the host of small Western European succession states to the old dyarchy of Holy Roman Empire and church, whose claims to universal temporal and spiritual authority had received their legal quietus with the ending of the Thirty Years' War. The Treaty of Westphalia in 1648 had confirmed the claims to legal sovereignty of those new European societies, founded on the rise of commerce, which looked for their political and economic self-aggrandizement in trading relationships with other countries and in the assertion, by military power where necessary, of claims to territorial title and political sovereignty over newly discovered lands overseas and their aboriginal peoples. Grotius's celebrated *mare liberum* doctrine, which declared the high seas open to the ships and the commerce of all countries and incapable, therefore, of national appropriation, was to become the foundation of the "classical" Law of the Sea and to endure for more than three hundred years until our contemporary era. But it was, in fact, in its origins a particularist response, by an early seventeenth-century jurist, to the particular legal needs of the then new state, Holland, which had retained him as a jurisconsult against the historically older *mare clausum* doctrines developed by Spanish and Portuguese jurists in direct response to the legal needs of the two original European colonial empires, whose political condominium overseas had been given spiritual, if not legal, sanction by Alexander VI's celebrated papal bull dividing the New World territories between Spain and Portugal. The immediate political success of the Grotian doctrine of the Law of the Sea at the time of its formulation undoubtedly owed much to the political and military power of those states that actively sponsored or espoused it. Its extension and acceptance as *lex lata* on a well-nigh universal scale thereafter stemmed from its innate reasonableness and common sense, corresponding to the political self-interest of all the dominant actors involved in the smaller, "European" world community of that era; just as the challenge to the doctrine's legal authority in the 1970s and the 1980s resulted from the emergence of new, economic interests not present or perceived at the time of creation, and the emergence also of new, non-"European" actors in the latter-day world community.

The implications of historical relativism and recognition of the particular space-time dimension in which particular principles and rules of classical international law emerged have not yet been realized in any comprehensive reordering or rewriting of those principles and rules so as to accord with new societal conditions or needs in the world community today. Classical international law did, however, recognize and accept—albeit very late in the day and in embryonic form only—a special doctrinal category seeking to incorporate the time element into international law—namely, intertemporal law.

INTERTEMPORAL LAW: THE CLASSICAL FORMULATION, *ISLAND OF PALMAS* (1928)

In a celebrated ruling more than half a century ago, in the *Island of Palmas* case, the arbitrator, Swiss jurist Max Huber, noted that "manifestations of territorial sovereignty assume . . . different forms, according to conditions of time and place." He identified as the "so-called intertemporal law" the question "which of different legal systems prevailing at successive periods is to be applied in a particular case?"[3]

Arbitrator Huber's actual, concrete application of the concept of intertemporal law in this case was a modest one. The dispute itself was wholly polite—between two Western, European or European-derived imperial states, the Netherlands and the United States (the latter as recent legal successor to imperial Spain under the treaty of peace that ended the Spanish-American War of 1898). The limited, European "family compact" aspect of classical international law and of the rules that it specially developed or extended for those Western European commercial, trading societies that had sought their main political expansion in the establishment of colonial empires overseas, is amply reflected in the arbitrator's passing comments as to the legal rights of discovery and acquisition of "uninhabited regions or regions inhabited by savages or semi-civilised peoples." For the arbitrator, distinguished jurist as he was, this latter phrase denoted all those peoples not of European stock or culture. The step made by classical international law, over the several and more centuries preceding Arbitrator Huber's ruling, of legally equating territories inhabited by such peoples with uninhabited regions and regions therefore open to effective acquisition by the first European visitor, was perhaps logically inevitable, granted the basic Eurocentrism of those in a position to make the legally authoritative and binding decisions concerned. The cultural particularity or relativism of the special international law categories as to acquisition and retention of territorial title developed in that earlier "colonial" period of world history is obvious enough, just as is the case for their imaginative rewriting or reordering today, now that the main legal imperatives of the post–World War II era, of decolonization, independence, and national self-determination have been so largely achieved in the main political arenas of the contemporary world community.

The Institut de Droit International: The Search for a Modern Restatement

The Institut de Droit International, responding to all the pressures for fundamental legal change in a world community clearly in an era of transition from an "old," classical, Western-based public order system to a "new" one, whose exact contours and directions are not always clear, established a special research commission to report on the "problem of intertemporal law" in time for its centennial session, held in Rome in 1973. In the report,[4] and in the formal resolution adopted by the Institut at the Wiesbaden session in 1975,[5] the problematic is identified modestly as *intertemporal problems,* the Institut thereby eschewing the invitation from some of its more adventurous spirits to proceed to the development of general rules of *intertemporal law*.

Judge Manfred Lachs, as a member of the Institut's research commission, had warned against any approach to the role of time in relation to law that was too strictly confined to the study of positive law alone. In rejecting the suggested dichotomy between the time dimension "from the philosophical viewpoint" and the time dimension in its effects "in the field of positive law," he rightly reminded other members of the commissiion that, even in the natural sciences, erstwhile purely static conceptions of the time component had been sundered in modern times by the development of the theory of relativity and the more sophisticated latter-day comprehension of the whole space-time continuum.[6]

The explanation for any juridical conservatism inherent in the Institut commission's approach to one of the key legal problems of an era of transition such as our own—how to adjust, creatively and in timely fashion, the legal order of yesterday to the new societal conditions and demands of today and the emerging tomorrow—surely is not to be found in intellectual timidity on the part of its members, for it was a very strong commission with an innovatory and forward-looking *rapporteur,* the late Max Sørensen. The existing positive law base, the point of departure for any venture in the progressive development of international law, was, quite simply, too narrow in its original formulation, since it was developed at the apogee of classical Western international law, in a purely intra-Western dispute, with deliberately narrowed-down issues determined by, and corresponding to, the self-interest of the two, then only notionally adversary, colonial powers, the Netherlands and the United States, actually involved in the dispute that they had agreed to submit to arbitration. The problem of creative restatement, half a century later, of the culturally relativist and intellectually deliberately narrow and restricted positive law principles therein laid down was compounded by the asymmetrical character of the legal-doctrinal categories involved; as Judge Pescatore pointed out, such conflicts in a contemporary context would often concern treaty and custom, or bilateral and multilateral treaty, the default in parity between the categories of legal norms for which one must determine the field of temporal applications thus adding to the complexity of the problem.[7]

The Institut's attempt to define the problem, contained in its final resolution as adopted in Wiesbaden in 1975, expressly recognizes the central antinomy of international law of our times, between the status quo and the forces of change. In its preamble, it states that "any solution of an intertemporal problem in the international field must take account of the dual requirement of development and stability."[8]

It completes the purely definitional exercise by declaring that "the general intertemporal problem . . . relates to the delimitation of the temporal sphere of application of norms"; and that the problem "arises whenever a rule refers to a concept the scope or significance of which has changed in the course of time."[9]

The prescriptive part of the Institut's resolution seems to adhere rather closely to Arbitrator Huber's original formulation:

> 1. Unless otherwise indicated, the temporal sphere of application of any norm of public international law shall be determined in accordance with the general principle of law by which any fact, action or situation must be assessed in the light of the rules of law that are contemporaneous with it.[10]

The openings of the future, however, are contained in Article 3 of the Institut resolution, which, while expressly reserving to "States and other subjects of international law . . . the power to determine by common consent the temporal sphere of application of norms," makes such liberty of contract nevertheless "subject to any imperative norm of international law which might restrict that power."[11] Such "imperative norms" are, on the precedent of the Vienna Convention on Treaties, in no way defined, and will therefore in the future remain open to creative interpretation of historical evolution of norms. The attempted hedging in of this *jus cogens* limitation on the parties' liberty to contract out of the intertemporal law dating (or updating, as the case may be) of their mutual, treaty-based obligations, by the provision, in paragraph 2 of the same Article 3, that it is all to be "without prejudice to obligations which may ensue for contracting parties from previous treaties to which they are parties and from the provisions of which they cannot depart even by common consent,"[12] seems otiose and legally irrelevant and ineffectual, since, *ex hypothesi,* an "imperative norm" of international law *(jus cogens)* must be hierarchically superior to and legally prevail over any contrary rule or obligation, whether flowing from customary international law or from the parties' own self-legislation in treaty form.

Creative Judicial Legislation: The World Court

Namibia (1971)[13]

The *Namibia* advisory opinion, rendered by the International Court of Justice in 1971, represented one of those very rare instances of a second chance accorded to an international institution to correct political damage resulting to it from an earlier decision. In this case, the decision was the narrow 8–7 judgment (determined on the second, tie-breaking vote of the court's president) in 1966 in *South West Africa, Second Phase,*[14] which many liberal-minded Western jurists, likening it to the United States Supreme Court decision more than a century earlier in the *Dred Scott* case, which was thought to have hastened the onset of the American Civil War, characterized as one of the court's "great, self-inflicted wounds." In *South West Africa, Second Phase,* in 1966, the court majority finely limited its earlier, 1962 ruling in *South West Africa, Preliminary Objections,*[15] in which it had held that the complainant states, Ethiopia and Liberia, had *locus standi* to raise the issue of the legality of the white minority-ruled Republic of South Africa's continued control over South West Africa, by now holding that they did not have legal standing to receive judgment, a legal distinction that would certainly have baffled the ingenuity of the medieval schoolmen. In the angry political criticism that followed its 1966 ruling, the court was denounced in the United Nations General Assembly as a "white man's tribunal." The opportunity for political atonement by the court came when the United Nations Security Council voted to refer to the court the general issue of the *Legal Consequences for States of the Continued Presence of South Africa in Namibia (South West Africa),* this in the light of a series of United Nations-based measures following the 1966 court decision, of which the most striking perhaps was General Assembly Resolution 2145 (XXI) of 1966, declaring the Republic of South Africa mandate over Namibia (South West Africa) to be forthwith "terminated." In a judicial volte-face startling in both number and extent after no more than five years, the court in 1971, by 13–2 and 11–4 votes on the substantive issues, agreed that the mandate was effectively terminated and the Republic of South Africa's presence in Namibia was in consequence illegal, these two decisions being opposable to all states in the sense of barring *erga omnes* the legality of a situation maintained in violation of international law. The ruling of the court is a multi-opinion one, with no less than seven different, separate (majority) opinions filed, in addition to the official opinion of the court. The court majority's conclusions rest on a number of separate grounds, of which, in the present context, the issue of the time dimension in legal interpretation is of special interest to us. The Republic of South Africa's claimed legal title to Namibia derived from its original League of Nations Class "C" category mandate, conferred in 1919. The Republic of South Africa's legal argumentation before the court in the *Namibia* hearing covered, as the opinion of the court noted, "a wide field of history, going back to the origin and functioning of the Mandate," and designed to demonstrate that such mandates were "in their practical effect not far removed from annexation."[16] While cynical opinion at the time of the creation of the League of Nations mandates system no doubt viewed the mandates concept as a polite euphemism or legal fiction to veil the postwar division of defeated imperial Germany's colonies on a "to the victor the spoils" principle, a now contemporary World Court, deciding the issue in a contemporary context, flatly rejected any such assimilation of the post–World War I mandates to classical international law's colonies because that would be "tantamount to admitting that the relevant provisions of the [League of Nations] Covenant were of a purely nominal character and that the rights they enshrined were of their very nature imperfect and unenforceable."[17] Borrowing from its own earlier advisory opinion of 1950 on the *International Status of South West Africa,* the court reiterated that

> in the setting up of the mandates system "two principles were considered to be of paramount importance: the principle of non-annexation and the principle that the well-being and development of such peoples form 'a sacred trust of civilisation.' "[18]

It is here that the World Court reaches out and embraces the concept of intertemporal law. The relevant international law to apply today is not a closed body of principles, conceived and applied as in time past, the actual time of entry into force of the League of Nations' mandates system back in 1919; but something rather more dynamic, lending itself to progressive, generic interpretation and reformulation over the years since that time, in accord with the changing conditions and expectations of a world community that is today vastly more representative and pluralistic in character than that narrower, "European," special legal community that imposed its Carthaginian "victors' peace" at Versailles in 1919 and set up the League of Nations as an integral element of the postwar world public order system that it sought to use to maintain the spoils of that victory against defeated imperial Germany and its erstwhile allies in World War I.

> . . . The Court is bound to take into account the fact that the concepts embodied in Article 22 of the Covenant . . . were not static, but were by definition evolutionary, as also, therefore, was the concept of the "sacred trust." The parties to the Covenant must consequently be deemed to have accepted them as such. That is why, viewing the institutions of 1919, the Court must take into consideration the changes which have occurred in the supervening half-century, and its interpretation cannot remain unaffected by the subsequent development of law, through the Charter of the United Nations and by way of customary law. Moreover, an international instrument has to be interpreted and applied within the framework of the entire legal system prevailing at the time of the interpretation. In the domain to which the present proceedings relate, the last fifty years, as indicated above, have brought important developments. These developments leave little doubt that the ultimate objective of the sacred trust was the self-determination and independence of the peoples concerned. In this domain, as elsewhere, the *corpus iuris gentium* has been considerably enriched, and this the Court, if it is faithfully to discharge its functions, may not ignore.[19]

Western Sahara, (1975)[20]

The *Western Sahara* problem came to the World Court on reference from the United Nations General Assembly. Like *Namibia* (1971), it was at root a "colonial" issue—the attempt by the new Third World majority in the main parliamentary organs of the United Nations to compel a "parent" European, imperial power to recognize the winds of change in the world community and to concede national self-determination, independence, and decolonization to an original, indigenous, aboriginal people. Spain, through failure to decentralize and devolve its colonial administration in timely fashion, had lost almost all of its first, Latin American colonial empire within the first few decades of the nineteenth century, and had then turned, painfully and awkwardly, to build a much more modest second empire out of the morsels of Africa that had by that time been left over, forgotten, or rejected as worthless by far more rapacious or ruthless imperial powers. When the historical moment finally could not be postponed for disposing of its second, African empire, Spain seemed to have learned nothing and forgotten nothing from its earlier historical experience. For it accepted the "new" international law principles of decolonization, independence, and national self-determination for subject colonial peoples only tardily, and then seemingly most reluctantly and because there was no politically viable alternative available. On Spain's behalf it can be noted that there were certainly other imperial powers which had also decolonized either very, very late in the day and with no particular goodwill, or else on a highly partial and selective basis with only the, by then, politically and militarily indefensible colonies being yielded up in timely fashion. By comparison with these other old imperial countries, Spain had a stagnant national economy and was arguably incapable of easily and quickly recovering from the extra financial blow of loss of the revenues from the rich phosphate deposits in its Western Sahara colonies. In this context, Spain now proposed that it should go ahead and hold its own referendum in the contested West African colonial territory, a political stratagem that was viewed, perhaps correctly, by the United Nations General Assembly majority as a device for further delaying and frustrating the original people's approach to independent nationhood. Hence the Third World activism for a General Assembly reference to the court for advisory opinion, as a method of triggering or speeding up Spanish decolonization. The key question posed to the court in the General Assembly's reference directly implicated the classical Western European–derived international law rules as to acquisition of territorial sovereignty by an imperial state in relation to colonial territories and aboriginal peoples overseas: "Was Western Sahara (Rio Oro and Sakiet el Hamra) at the time of colonisation by Spain a territory belonging to no one *(terra nullius)*?"

The court, in the *Western Sahara* advisory opinion in 1975, divided 13–3 on this question, and the court's ruling, once again, sees the official opinion of the court accompanied by a plethora of separate (majority) opinions or declarations—no less than nine of these, in fact. It is thus a multiground majority ruling with, in common-law terms, no clear *ratio decidendi* or majority ground of decision apparent in the official record. Nevertheless, the issue of intertemporal law and its application in a contemporary problem situation is a core element in the court holding, and one on which a clear line of intellectual demarcation or differentiation is apparent between the more orthodox, conservative, "classical" majority within the overall court majority and what might be categorized, without any hidden value judgment being intended, as the court's more avant-garde or front-running members, with their deliberate openings to the "new" international law.

Thus the official opinion of the court decided that, for purposes of responding to the *res nullius* question, the critical time period was that beginning in 1884, when Spain proclaimed a proctectorate over the Rio de Oro.[21] While Spain had indeed mentioned certain earlier acts of alleged display of its sovereignty in the fifteenth and sixteenth centuries, it had done so, the official opinion of the court suggested, only to enlighten the court as to the remote antecedents of the Spanish presence on the West African coast and not with the design of proving any continuity between those acts and the Spanish proclamation of a protectorate in 1884. The period beginning in 1884 thus constituted the temporal context within which the two substantive questions addressed to the court by the General Assembly should be answered. It was on this basis that the official opinion of the court reasoned that the question whether or not Western Sahara was *terra nullius* at the time of colonization by Spain was to be interpreted by reference to the law in force at that period, 1884. But a determination that Western Sahara was *terra nullius* in that case would be possible only if it were established that at that time the territory belonged to no one. On the specific facts, the court found that, at the time of colonization by Spain, Western Sahara was inhabited by people who, if nomadic, were socially and politically organized in tribes and under chiefs competent to represent them. Indeed, in colonizing Western Sahara, Spain itself purported to base itself legally on various agreements entered into between the king of Spain and the chiefs of local tribes. The court was thus able to respond fairly easily and quickly to the main question posed to it by the General Assembly and to conclude that at the time of Spanish colonization Western Sahara was not a "territory belonging to no one *(terra nullius)*."[22]

A second question referred to the court by the General Assembly asked the court to state what were the "legal ties" between Western Sahara and "the Kingdom of Morocco and the Mauritanian entity." This second question, the court majority opined, would also have to be decided in the temporal context of the actual act of colonization by Spain—that is, 1884. At the time of such colonization, the court found, Western Sahara, as an area of desert with low and spasmodic rainfall, was being developed almost exclusively by nomads, who traversed very wide areas of the desert, not confined to Western Sahara, the links between the different nomadic communities being essentially tribal rather than territorial ties or ties of allegiance or vassalage. Morocco had argued, on a basis of the old Permanent Court's ruling in *Legal Status of Eastern Greenland,*[23] that a series of events stretching back to the seventh century A.D. and the Arab conquest of North Africa, even though having a "far-flung, spasmodic and often transitory character," were sufficient, in relation to a territory geographically contiguous to itself and desert in character, to establish a claim to title based "upon continued display of authority."[24] The legally novel aspect of the Moroccan case, however, was posited upon asserted common ethnological, cultural, and religious ties between Western Sahara and Morocco, the argument being that the common religious bond of Islam existing among the peoples concerned could form legal ties of sovereignty where the essentially Western, ethnocentrist notion of territory might not. While seemingly not accepting these arguments as such, the court did conclude that the available evidence provided indications that a legal tie of allegiance had existed at the relevant period between the Sultan of Morocco and some, but only some, of the nomadic peoples of the Western Sahara territory.

As for the legal ties, at the time of Spanish colonization, between Western Sahara and the "Mauritanian entity" (the latter, concededly, something that did not exist as a state at that particular point in historical time), the then contemporary state of Mauritania laid emphasis on the special characteristics of the Saharan area and the nomadic existence of many of the tribes, each of which had its own well-defined migration area with well-defined migration routes determined by the location of water holes, burial grounds, cultivated areas, and pastures. As the Mauritanian government contended, "the colonial Powers, . . . in drawing frontiers took no account of these human factors and in particular of the tribal territories and migration routes, which were, as a result, bisected and even trisected by these artificial frontiers."[25]

The Spanish government, in reply, rejected any notion of a "nation" or "people" in the Western Sahara "formed of tribes, confederations and emirates jointly exercising co-sovereignty," characterizing the Mauritanian government's case as resting on "the mere sociological facts of nomadic life."[26] This was a position that the court seemed eventually to embrace in ruling that there was no "tie of sovereignty, or of allegiance of tribes, or of 'simple inclusion' in the same legal entity."[27]

The official opinion of the court in *Western Sahara,* as we have suggested, is conservative or cautious in regard to a rather novel fact situation that seemed to invite legal innovation, since it provided unusual opportunities for the judges to move toward a progressive development of old international law categories to meet the new political and societal facts of life of the post–World War II world community. Not so the separate (specially concurring) opinions, which, while filed in support of the official opinion of the court, make, in several instances at least, such determined openings to the "new" international law as to amount almost to veiled dissents from the opinion of the court in the range and quality of the substantive law critique that they advance. The strongest and most sustained of the special opinions is that of Vice-President Ammoun, which adopts, with approval, remarks contained in the written pleadings before the court by the Zairian jurist Bayona-Ba-Meya. Such pleadings served in Vice-President Ammoun's words, to

> dismiss the materialistic concept of *terra nullius,* which led to this dismemberment of Africa following the Berlin Conference of 1885. Mr. Bayona-Ba-Meya substitutes for this a spiritual notion: the ancestral tie between the

land, or "mother nature," and the man who was born therefrom, remains attached thereto, and must one day return thither to be united with his ancestors. This link is the basis of the ownership of the soil, or better, of sovereignty. This amounts to a denial of the very concept of *terra nullius* in the sense of a land which is capable of being appropriated by someone who is not born therefrom. It is a condemnation of the modern concept, as defined by Pasquale Fiore, which regards as *terra nullius* territories inhabited by populations whose civilisation, in the sense of the public law of Europe, is backward and whose political organisation is not conceived according to Western norms. . . . This is the reply which may be given to the participants in the Berlin Conference of 1885. . . .[28]

Judge Ammoun then adopted with approval the reasoning of the Algerian jurist Mohammed Bedjaoui, who in his written pleading before the court had identified three distinct epochs in the development and evolution of the "classical" international law as to acquisition of title to territory:

- *Roman antiquity,* when any territory which was not Roman was characterised, legally, as being *nullius*;
- the epoch of the great *Western European* "discoveries" of the sixteenth and seventeenth centuries, during which any territory not belonging to a Western European *Christian* sovereign was characterised, legally, as *nullius*;
- the nineteenth century, during which any territory which did not belong to a so-called *civilised* state was characterised, legally, as *nullius*.[29]

Judge Ammoun concluded:

. . . the concept of *terra nullius,* employed at all periods to the brink of the twentieth century, to justify conquest and colonisation, stands condemned. It is well known that in the sixteenth century Francisco de Vittoria protested against the application to the American Indians, in order to deprive them of their lands, of the concept of *res nullius*.[30]

Judge Ammoun was joined, in his discussion of the spatially and temporally limited "Western" or "classical" international law character of the concept of *terra nullius,* by Judge Forster, who in a separate opinion indicated his own disagreement with the opinion of the court insofar as it had concluded against ties of territorial sovereignty between Western Sahara and the Kingdom of Morocco and the Mauritanian entity. Judge Forster thought that the opinion of the court had gone too far in

minimising the exceptional importance of the geographical, social and temporal contexts of the problem. . . . It is Africa of former times which is in question, as to which it cannot arbitrarily be required that its institutions should be a carbon copy of European institutions, for on that basis almost the entire African continent would have to be declared *terra nullius*.[31]

This was a theme recurred to by ad hoc Judge Boni, who, in a separate opinion, also reproached the authors of the majority opinion of the court for their essentially static conception of the "classical" international law cluster of legal concepts as to acquisition of territorial title.[32] The intellectual joinder of issue was thus made clearly and coherently and interestingly, in *Western Sahara,* between the "old," essentially Western, Eurocentrist international law rules in this area, and the "new," with their openings to the much more inclusive and richly pluralist world community of today. The relativism, in space-time terms, of the "old" or "classical" rules, with their origins in that limited, family-compact era of those European societies founded on the rise of commerce and consequently in search of territorial conquests and colonies overseas, thus stands sharply demonstrated, as is also the case for the imaginative restatement and rewriting of these "old" rules, so that they may better accord with contemporary societal needs.

Continental Shelf (Tunisia/Libyan Arab Jamahiriya), (1982)[33]

Continental Shelf (Tunisia/Libyan Arab Jamahiriya) is one of those rare instances in World Court jurisprudence—of the "old" Permanent Court of the between-the-two-wars era and of the "new" International Court of the post-World War II era—of a dispute between two states from outside that limited Western European, family-compact group of states that had so largely written "classical" international law and its detailed rules. In this case, it was two recently decolonized Third World countries, Tunisia (a former French colony) and Libya (a former Italian colony), that were directly involved. The conflicts between the "old" and the "new" international law that we have seen in earlier cases that produced the opportunities for progressive development of international law, symbolized in the conflict of the actual parties—usually a parent European or European-derived imperial state and its former colonial territories—are not so clear-cut and obvious. Nevertheless, the range of opinions filed in the case, from the official opinion of the court to the three separate opinions and the three dissenting opinions (Judges Gros, Oda, and ad hoc Judge Evensen), reveal clearly enough that the essentially static conservative approach to restatement of the "old" or "classical" law tended to favor one of the two parties rather than the other. By comparison, a more imaginative judicial opening to the "new" international law would be needed for that other party to succeed. The historical contradictions inherent in a court process and a court judgment rendered in an era of transition and rapid change in the world community are plentiful and obvious. We may note in passing the fact that counsel for the two parties were overwhelmingly drawn from the "old," Western European countries, notwithstanding that the client states were both newly decolonized Third World countries.

The "European" character of the handling and presentation of the case before the court seemed to carry over into the judgment and judicial opinions rendered, giving it at times a jejune quality redolent of an earlier historical era in the world community; as if the two original, parent colonial states, Italy and France, were carrying on, by some quirk of the time machine and through the proxies of their erstwhile colonies, Libya and Tunisia, their old imperial rivalries and battles of yesterday.

Our present interest in the case lies in those aspects of the judgment (concerning the delimitation of the continental shelf between the two adjacent states) that involve recourse to "new trends" in international law, as exemplified in the then still continuing Third United Nations Conference on the Law of the Sea and its project for a draft convention (particularly Articles 76 and 83), and that involve application of equitable principles with a view to achieving an equitable solution (particularly proportionality).

These deliberate judicial openings to the "new" international law as a viable alternative option to the simple restatement of the "old" or "classical" law, such as it might be, are perhaps best reflected in the dissenting opinion of the Japanese jurist Judge Oda.[34] Judge Oda noted that while the basic legal concept of the continental shelf had been strongly confirmed by the 1958 Convention on the Continental Shelf and further endorsed by the court's own judgment in 1969, in *North Sea Continental Shelf*,[35] as being established under customary international law, the actual extent of the legal continental shelf had been

> left indeterminate, because of the introduction of the equivocal notion of exploitability which suggested that the area could eventually expand under virtually the whole of the high seas. This trend was halted by the rise of the new concept of the international sea-bed area late in the 1960s. The realisation that the concept of exploitability could be interpreted to mean that all sea-bed areas of the world would eventually be divided among separate States led Malta to take the initiative by introducing the concept of the common heritage of mankind, to be applied in the area beyond a redefined continental shelf.[36]

If this, then, was the dominant *new* trend in the concept of the continental shelf, confirmed in United Nations General Assembly Resolution 2340 (XXII) of December 18, 1967, establishing the United Nations Sea-Bed Committee, the legal definition of the outer limits of the continental shelf for purposes of national appropriation was subject to fluctuating criteria, with many landlocked and shelf-locked countries, acting as a group, taking a position in 1972 opposing the idea of wider continental-shelf and/or narrower international sea-bed areas. The background to Article 69 of the so-called Informal Composite Negotiating Text of the ensuing Third United Nations Conference on the Law of the Sea was the "fact of geography that the formation of the continental shelf can be extremely inequitable for some coastal States."[37]

In the result, we find the compromise proposal that the continental shelf would be

> divided into two areas, the first being the area within 200 miles from the coast, where the exclusive interests of the coastal state would be established, and the other, the area beyond that, where a portion of the profits would be dedicated to the international community, in particular the developing nations. This parallelism is retained, with some modifications, in the draft convention as Article 82. It cannot be over-emphasised that this formula never founded part of the traditional concept of the continental shelf.[38]

Judge Oda went on to conclude, from this, that parallel with the change in the outer limit of the continental shelf—the clear trend in the evolution of international law since the 1958 convention—the

> notion of natural prolongation by which the concept of the continental shelf was embellished in the [Court's] 1969 Judgment has greatly lost its significance, particularly with the introduction of the criterion of the 200-mile distance under the strong influence of the concept of the exclusive economic zone . . . , not to mention the parallelism between that zone and a possible inner-continental shelf of 200 miles, coupled with the possibility of a different *régime* applying to the continental margin beyond that distance. . . . The concept of the continental shelf cannot have escaped change as a result of the fading-away of the geomorphological notion of natural prolongation. This notion may be said to have remained in the case where the (geomorphological) continental shelf or slope extends farther than 200 miles, yet it must be said that the concept of the continental shelf, which had been sustained by scholarly views and the imperious necessities of the 1950s, has, early in the 1980s, changed.[39]

Judge Oda's dissenting opinion represents an intellectual tour de force by a jurist who, on his sustained experience as adviser and member of his own country's national delegation to the various international conclaves on the Law of the Sea from 1958 onward, might fairly be described as a founding father of the modern Law of Sea. The extensive and detailed survey of all the *travaux préparatoires* undertaken by Judge Oda might, in and of itself, be enough, on strictly historical grounds, to dispose of the Libyan Arab Jamahiriya's case as to a "natural prolongation" of its continental shelf accepted by the court majority.

Judge Oda's excursus, in his dissenting opinion, on the role of equitable principles in contemporary international law was also interesting in the present context, insofar as he refused to regard equity as a closed juridical category incapable of further growth through time.

The court in its 1969 judgment in *North Sea Continental Shelf* had refused to accept the concept of "a just and equitable share,"[40] preferring to restrict itself to the "delimitation and not to the apportionment of the areas concerned, or their division into converging sectors."

While prepared to accept that "the sea-bed area is not meant to be parcelled out like so many fiefs," Judge Oda was at pains to distinguish and limit the 1969 court holding where it refused to embrace the idea of equitable apportionment. This part of the earlier 1969 holding, in Judge Oda's view,[41] was now

> overtaken by events. There was thus insufficient reason for the present Court, in 1982, to be inhibited from realising that the present delimitation was simply a question of equitably dividing, or apportioning, between the Parties, by means of a justifiable line of demarcation, those submarine areas which either could potentially have claimed.[42]

The opening up of the time dimension in international law was thus explicit, even if in the end Judge Oda would draw back from any court-based formulation of a "geographical equity"[43] involving "global resource policies"[44] or even "world social justice."[45] This part of Judge Oda's discussion goes, however, beyond our present concern with the operation of the time factor in international law, and will be canvased more fully in the analysis of the role of equity today among the formal sources of law.

Conclusions

The contemporary acceptance of the relevance of the time dimension in international law stems from the increasing recognition of the historical relativism of so many of the rules of "classical" international law. These rules arose, of course, in particular eras in world history, in response to particular societal conditions, needs, and expectations, as perceived and recorded by the dominant political forces of those times. It is on this basis that so much of "classical" international law—both old treaties and old rules of customary international law—is now rejected or questioned by the "new" countries of the Third World as "Western" or "Eurocentric" in character and hence as no longer authoritative and binding in the new, more richly pluralistic and inclusive world community of today, which has transcended its original, narrowly Western political base with the successful legal achievement of national self-determination, decolonization, and independence on a by now nearly universal scale. The normative quality, in legal terms today, of the old international law rules is increasingly subjected to the test of reason: those rules are to be critically reexamined in the context of the historically limited space-time dimension of their origins, and then tested in terms of their claims, such as they may be, to continuing relevance and reasonableness in the larger world community of our time. What is less clear is the exact doctrinal-legal basis on which those old substantive legal rules can be, according to the contemporary test of reason, either accepted in their original sense and meaning, or else restated and updated in symbiotic relationship with a changed (and much expanded) international society, or, finally, rejected altogether as historically anachronistic and incompatible with the evolving juridical conscience of mankind.

Karl Doehring, a jurist of the Federal Republic of Germany,[46] correctly identifies a certain ambiguity in the concept of the time factor in international law and suggests that it first be broken down into its various elements for the purpose of separate analysis and calculation of the juridical consequences.

One such element is clearly the "classical" formulation of intertemporal law represented by Arbitrator Max Huber's ruling in *Island of Palmas* in 1928. The emphasis here is clearly on the time at which the particular rule in question first arose. Since the actual conflict was between two Western powers, the arbitrator's emphasis on time of origin is not loaded in ethnic-cultural terms with regard to its consequences when applied; nor is there any particular cause for reproach of the arbitrator for his focus on time past to the exclusion of time present or even the emerging time future. Objective certainty as to the content of the claimed rule at its time of origin was the value sought by the parties, the Netherlands and the United States, both then, in Weberian terms, at the apogee of their own particular economic and legal development; and this is what the arbitrator rendered to them. It would be itself anachronistic to apply to arbitrator Huber's seminal ruling of more than half a century ago the legal standards and values of the present world community, which is in transition and fundamental conflict.

Less certain, however, is the case for the relatively traditional or conservative restatement adopted by the authoritative Institut de Droit International in 1975 in its Wiesbaden resolution.[47] Allowing for the fact that the Institut operates essentially by consensus and that its resolutions are the product of compromises within its specialized commissions and very often acquire thereby a watered-down or lowest-common-denominator character in which the status quo ante tends to prevail, the political and legal challenge to "classical" international law and the transition from the "old" postwar world public order system were already apparent at that time. The distinguished *rapporteur,* Judge Sørensen, was fully aware of the problem, as is manifest from the thoughtful argumentation he developed in his provisional and final reports. But the final resolution, while identifying the basic antinomy between stability and change in contemporary international law, offers no particular help in its solution to concrete cases. It gives, indeed, a prime emphasis to the voluntarist approach and the power of the parties to "determine by common consent the temporal sphere of application of norms," subject only to "any imperative norm of international law which might restrict that power."[48] The resolution does not provide any criteria for identifying such imperative norms[49] that would restrict the law-making power of the original parties as to the time factor. It might be suggested, of course, that the resolution's voluntarist emphasis, which makes the will of the original contracting parties determinative of the time factor, is not an adequate response to the interest in change in the stability–change legal antinomy postulated in the resolution's preamble; for it will normally be a latter-day third party, extrinsic to the original contractual obligation, who will be making the case, in contemporary terms, for imaginative rewriting and updating of the old rules and their novation in legal terms today. On legal interpretation, the Institut resolution suggests that it is "appropriate to have recourse to the usual methods of interpretation,"[50] without, however, defining these or even listing them by way of example; and it remains unclear whether the Institut envisaged these as including progressive, generic interpretation, along the lines of the International Court of Justice's advisory opinion in *Namibia* 1971.

Apart from intertemporal law *stricto sensu,* as defined by Arbitrator Huber and the Institut's Wiesbaden resolution, there are other examples of the relevance of the time factor as recognized and applied in international law doctrine and jurisprudence. Doehring, in his imaginative study published in 1964, points to Jellinek's concept, *Die normative Kraft des Faktischen,* first developed in 1922,[51] and its potential to create concrete legal consequences in problem situations of that time, such as the post–World War II territorial frontiers in Central and Eastern Europe.[52] These particular problems may now have been finally resolved, in legal terms, by the supervening *Ostpolitik* mini-accords between the Federal Republic of Germany on the one hand and the Soviet Union and Eastern European countries.[53] But the general philosophical problem of the duality of the *Sein* and the *Sollen* remains, for the final attribution of normative legal consequences to the factual, existential condition amounts to a form of international legal determinism.[54] It is no doubt on purely pragmatic considerations that the International Law Commission would confer such sanctity on treaties establishing a territorial boundary, exempting them from the ordinary rules as to fundamental change of circumstances, even though so many such treaties have been imposed under duress, at the conclusion of a war or in a European "colonial" context.[55] Granted this newly created gap in its application today, *clausula rebus sic stantibus*[56] remains one of the more potentially interesting and creative legal-doctrinal bases for adjusting old legal rules—here, treaty-made rules—to meet new societal conditions and also new values in the plural world community of today.

By and large, however, the best opportunities for imaginative application of the time factor in the progressive development of international law would seem to lie in the ordinary processes of legal interpretation, especially as applied by the International Court. As the Institut de Droit International special *rapporteur,* Judge Sørensen, expressly noted in his provisional report,[57] Verdross[58] and before him Baade[59] had accepted a qualitative difference, for purposes of legal interpretation, between limited, normally bilateral, treaties—which ought, it was suggested, normally to be referred to the law in force at the moment when the treaty entered into force—and the larger, usually multilateral "normative" conventions—which, it was suggested, lent themselves to "evolutionary notions" by which the contracting parties had "wanted to keep the door open to the development of international law";[60] such a larger, "normative" convention "acquired its own life, independent of the will of the parties at the moment of its conclusion."[61] Beyond that, the International Court of Justice has shown the way—albeit more usually in dissenting opinions like Judge Jessup's in *South West Africa, Second Phase* in 1966, but sometimes in the majority opinion of the court itself, as in *Namibia,* 1971—to "progressive, generic interpretation which, as an instrument of judicial activism, quite as properly belongs among the traditional or "classical" techniques of judicial construction[62] as that strict or literal, positivist interpretation manifested by the court majority in the opinion of the court in the politically unfortunate and much criticized one-vote-majority *South West Africa, Second Phase* opinion. What may be needed to continue to spark such creative judicial interpretation in the future is a more imaginative and dynamic approach to history on the part of counsel appearing before the court and preparing the legal *factum,* much as counsel Bayona-Ba-Meya and Mohammed Bedjaoui, appearing in argument in *Western Sahara* in 1975,[63] refused to accept past history as exercising a dead-hand control today and insisted instead, in Jean Jaurès' phase, in "taking from the altars of the past the fires, not the ashes." It is a concept well known to common lawyers, and summed up in Mr. Justice Oliver Wendell Holmes's maxim that "the life of the law has not been logic, but experience." The concept of intertemporal law, imaginatively updated and applied today, seems comprehensive enough, as a doctrinal-legal category, to encompass modern, evolutionary approaches to the interpretation of past history and their application, through the judicial process, to the novation of old legal categories through the techniques of progressive, generic interpretation.

Intertemporal law, viewed now as a formal juridical category, is, it is submitted, still inchoate but fully capable of further organic growth and development. The requirement, in analytical jurisprudential terms, is to conceptualize it into a larger, more comprehensive category encompassing at once intemporal law *stricto sensu,* at least as restated by the Institut de Droit International in its Wiesbaden resolution in 1975; that special juridical process whereby the factual or existential becomes normative, through and with the passage of time *(Die normative Kraft des Faktischen)*; and the authoritative manifestations of the "progressive development of international law" effectuated in the judgments and assorted opinions of the International Court of Justice and in the law-making decisions of other legally competent United Nations organs (declaratory resolutions of the United Nations General Assembly, agreed texts of international codifying conferences, and the like).

3. The International Law-Making Process: Sources of International Law

Closed Categories of Formal Sources

The concept of a list—a more or less closed list—of categories of formal sources of international law is the product essentially of nineteenth-century Western analytical positivism, with its emphasis on juridical formalism. Max Weber viewed logically formal rationality as the key characteristic of Western law at the apogee of Western civilization, distinguishing it from other, non-Western systems. Those distinctive legal ways of thought, more generally termed "jurisprudence of concepts" *(Begriffsjurisprudenz),* with their emphasis on identifying and clarifying claimed legal principles and rules, rather than on evaluating or testing them in ethical or even sociological terms, are amply reflected in Article 38 of the Statute of the International Court of Justice, establishing an official, authoritative list of categories of legal rules to be applied by the court in deciding disputes submitted to it.

> *Article 38:*
> 1. The Court, whose function is to decide in accordance with international law such disputes as are submitted to it, shall apply:
> a. international conventions, whether general or particular, establishing rules expressly recognised by the contesting states;
> b. international custom, as evidence of a general practice accepted as law;
> c. the general principles of law recognised by civilised nations;
> d. subject to the provisions of Article 59, judicial decisions and the teachings of the most highly qualified publicists of the various nations, as subsidiary means for the determination of rules of law.

2. This provision shall not prejudice the power of the Court to decide a case *ex aequo et bono,* if the parties agree thereto.

Article 59 of the court statute stipulates that the decision of the court in any case "has no binding force except between the parties and in respect of that particular case," thereby excluding any possibility of a common law–style doctrine of *stare decisis* or binding authority of the court's own prior decisions in subsequent cases.

Classical international law was perhaps excessively preoccupied with the quest for an ultimate, approved source for each legal rule. The notion of a legal community, it was argued, presupposed the existence of a legal sovereign, or at least sovereign authority; with legal rules being general commands issuing from the sovereign authority to the members of that community. Every claimed legal rule, therefore, to deserve the name of law, must fit into at least one of the predetermined a priori categories of such commands—into one of the sources. If not, it was not a valid legal rule.

The argument is, of course, a circular one; if the claimed proposition fits into one of the recognized sources, it must be a legal rule; and if it is a legal rule it must fit into one of the preordained sources.

By contrast, the legal-realist approach to the definition of law and to the establishing of whether or not a claimed proposition deserves the accolade of legal rule is to put emphasis on the facts rather than on the a priori legal categories. If all the interested parties accept a claimed rule as being law, it must be so without need for too much speculation as to whether or not the claimed rule fits into the preordained categories; or, for that matter, without any occasion for concern if it should turn out that the claimed rule does not. The legal principle prohibiting the orbiting of nuclear weapons in space vehicles was affirmed by the Soviet Union and the United States in joint declarations issued in 1963. The principle was subsequently written in as one of the specific provisions of the Space Treaty of 1967. What, then, was the international legal status of the principle in the four years between its solemn affirmation by the only two parties with the necessary technological capacity to do anything about it, and its formal enshrinement in one of the recognized categories of sources of international law, as proclaimed in Article 38 of the World Court statute? It is hardly possible, on the facts, to deny that the two main political protagonists, the Soviet Union and the United States, during that four-year time gap before the principle was officially enshrined in one of the formal sources of international law, treated it as fully binding on them in international law. On any law-as-fact approach, the principle had already become law in 1963, and its rendering in treaty form in 1967 was legally redundant or unnecessary—an act of legal supererogation.[1] What does that do to the tidy "classical" theory of international law that would confine the accolade of "law" to those principles and rules falling within its closed list of formal categories or sources?

The emphasis on a law-as-fact approach, with a corresponding de-emphasis of juridical formalism and of the quest for an a priori category of legal sources into which a claimed legal rule can somehow or other be consigned, is part of the new legal-realist conception of the international law-making process. In this view, the Federal Republic of Germany could be considered as legally bound by the stipulations of the Geneva Convention of 1958, even though it did not ratify the convention. This is what Judge Lachs suggested in his interesting and innovatory dissenting opinion in *North Sea Continental Shelf Judgment* in 1969, pointing to

> evidence of a practice widespread enough to satisfy the criteria for a general rule of law.
>
> For to become binding, a rule or principle of international law need not pass the test of universal acceptance. . . . The evidence should be sought in the behavior of a great number of States, possibly the majority of States, in any case the great majority of the interested States.
>
> Thus this test cannot be, nor is it, one endowed with any absolute character: it is of its very nature relative. Criteria of frequency, continuity and uniformity are involved.[2]

In the same vein, the court majority, in *Nuclear Tests (Australia v. France), Judgment of 20 December 1974,*[3] in the official opinion of the court had no difficulty in treating as a legal fact the French government's indication of its intention not to resume high-altitude nuclear testing in the South Pácific, and in holding France as legally bound by such unilateral declaration of intention, even though such declaration neither was concretized in treaty form nor came within the existing customary international law category of estoppel. When ordinary common sense and the will of the parties coincide, why should the court stand in the way of recognition and acceptance of that fact in legal terms, by doctrinaire judicial insistence on continued deference to abstract legal formalism and the legal positivists' closed categories of formal sources of principles and rules of international law?[4]

Hierarchical Ranking of Sources

Classical international law usually looked to its two main constituent legal elements—the Anglo-Saxon common law and the continental European civil law—for any guidance as to primacy, in terms of their respective juridical origins or sources, as between two different, competing legal rules. Except for the greater weight given by the common law internal, municipal law systems to judicial decisions as such, flowing from common-law doctrines of *stare decisis* and the binding authority of a legal decision, and for the civil law respect for *doctrines* (including, of course, the opinions of text writers and judicial decisions [*jurisprudence*] under this rubric), common law and civil law–derived notions of the relative ranking of the different formal sources of international law are not widely different, the practical synthesis of the two being reflected in Article 38 of the World Court statute.

While recognizing of necessity that statute (here treaty) law breaks customary law to the extent that there is any inconsistency or contradiction between the two, classical international law, as applied by the West, has as a matter of history always given a dominant place to customary international law, particularly long-established customary rules.

In international legal arenas like the United Nations and its specialized agencies and its specialized legal conferences, Western jurists have frequently been forced into a defensive position vis-à-vis the role of old custom, and have taken a correspondingly restrictive view of international legal codification conventions that purport to restate the old law, where these conventions are adopted by something less than unanimity. There has also been a denial of the normative, law-making quality of United Nations General Assembly resolutions except insofar as these are simply declarations of, and reflect already existing, customary law. By contrast, Western attitudes to the World Court and to its law-making role have tended to be tied, since World War II, to the American-inspired "World Rule of Law" campaign for extending, among other things, the court's compulsory jurisdiction; but these essentially positive conceptions of the court's position can no doubt be expected to be modified as the emerging new political majority among the judges of the court, reflecting the Third World's interest in the court and in the processes of election of its judges, shows a disposition to utilize the court's quite considerable law-making potential in the service of creation of the "new" international law.

In comparison with the West, the Soviet Union and the Eastern European countries have given prime emphasis to treaties in the international law-making process,[5] with a special exception designed to repudiate the so-called "unequal treaties,"[6] which are narrowly defined by Soviet jurists so as to apply, essentially, only to treaties made by the Soviet Union in the era of political-military weakness immediately after the Great October Socialist Revolution and to analogous "imperialist" treaties. Customary international law, and here especially old custom, may not be automatically binding on "new" countries that have come into existence after the customary rule has emerged.[7] As for resolutions of the United Nations General Assembly, recommendations of specialized international organizations, and decisions of the International Court of Justice and of international arbitral tribunals, these are relegated to the status of "subsidiary" sources only; and, particularly in the case of United Nations General Assembly resolutions, may be dependent for their legal efficacy upon the comprehensiveness, and also intersystemic representativeness,[8] of the voting majorities actually composing them.

The Third World has not merely continued the emphasis suggested by Soviet publicists on new custom at the expense of old, in whose creation the Third World countries, if they have participated at all, have participated only notionally as members of erstwhile colonial empires; but Third World countries have initiated a search for new arenas and new processes for international law making in which the Third World numerical voting powers can be exercised to the full. This involves not merely the full use of the international codifying or general legal conference directed to the elaboration of multilateral conventions involving the restatement and, in the process, reformulation or rewriting altogether of older, custom-based rules of international law, but the vigorous and imaginative recourse to law making in the newer international arenas like the United Nations General Assembly and its committees and specialized agencies. The General Assembly resolution begins to take on a declaratory, hortatory quality under the impetus of Third World drafting and direction; and in spite of the denials by Western jurists and publicists of any present law-making character, such resolutions to an increasing extent in recent years come to acquire a sense of prophecy and of law-in-the-making. In strictly juridical terms, the General Assembly resolutions on such key subjects as decolonization and independence, on national ownership and control over natural resources, and on a New International Economic Order may not be, in their immediate origins, "hard" law; but as "soft" law they have a habit of turning out to be the international law-in-action of today and the "hard" law of tomorrow or the day after tomorrow.[9] The General Assembly majorities that adopted those resolutions have, in this sense, been demonstrated in time to have a keener sense of the winds of change in the world community and the general movement and direction of world history than those established states that either opposed or abstained in the actual votes on the resolutions, or else went along with them reluctantly in final vote.

Contemporary Trends in the Sources of International Law

As H. Strebel, a jurist from the Federal Republic of Germany, has noted,[10] *sources* of international law must be recognized today as a comprehensive term veiling three different conceptions: a *creative process* (how a rule emerges as law); the *creative factors* (the instruments and machinery of international law making); and the *end product* of those creative factors operating through the creative process (that is, the substantive legal rule itself).[11]

If one puts aside any consideration of the actual substantive rules emerging in this way, some major philosophical problems exist as to each of the conventionally accepted categories of sources of international law, and the resulting legal contradictions—both between competing legal systems and also between different time epochs—will now be considered in relation to those sources.

International Custom

As to custom—the reference here is to "old" custom—what is the exact role of the consent of states, and particularly of "new" states that were not in existence in independent, autonomous form prior to the emergence of a claimed rule of customary international law? If one speaks of an implied consent in the case of such new states, as, on pragmatic grounds, we no doubt should, in spite of the legal fictional elements present in such a characterization, how is such an implied consent to be negated by a new state, and negated by how many states, for such a claimed customary rule to lose its legal quality, both vis-à-vis the individual recusing state or states and also generally? Dr. Tunkin's argument in this context, that a "new" state should not be bound by "old" rules of customary international law except insofar as it might subsequently expressly consent thereto, accords with the spirit, at least, of the late nineteenth-century (Western) voluntarist approach to law, law making, and the creation and acceptance of legal obligations. So far as it might, for example, be limited as a legal proposition to the special case of newly decolonized "new" states, in relation to the special legal burdens vis-à-vis their former "parent" European imperial states, flowing from the erstwhile colonial subordination, the requirement of the present consent of the newly decolonized state to the continued validity of those old customary law rules would seem eminently reasonable and in full accord with all the historical trends in international law doctrine since 1945. As against that, and as a political fact of life, postdecolonization "new" states have often demonstrated themselves as in no great hurry to cast off the corpus of "old," classical international law customary rules; for as the legal succession states to their former imperial masters they inherit the frequently very substantial benefits, as well as the burdens, of the old customary rules (particularly those having an economic character and concerning territorial title, territorial sea and continental shelf, and the like). Dr. Tunkin, in his learned excursus on the subject, seems to reflect this potentially dualist character of old customary rules—looking both forward and backward—for he hedges in his requirement of a supervening consent of "new" states as a condition of the continuing legal validity of those old customary rules, with the addition of the convenient legal fiction of presumption of implied consent by "new" states to such rules. The best answer would seem to be to approach the problem pragmatically, on a case-by-case basis, as to particular areas of law and legal obligations, and even as to particular states; the key to the resolution of the problem in such cases will tend to be provided by general legal notions having to do with long-range historical trends in law and the evolution of legal doctrine, including specific principles like equity and the "general principles of law" referred to in Article 38(1)(c) of the court statute.

A second problem relating to custom has to do with the time dimension inherent, as a constituent legal element, in the formation of a rule of customary international law. Just how much passage of time is actually requisite, legally? It has been pointed out correctly that in certain of the newer areas of international law the technological base of the problem is such that time has a habit of galloping. Hence one can speak only half satirically of a sort of "instant" customary international law in the law of outer space. The space-time dimension, in combination, acquires a peculiar importance in regard to the formation of rules of customary international law, for we are involved not merely with time, as with the application of the concept of *occupatio* in eastern Greenland or in the Spanish Sahara, but also with spatial notions, as, for example, the relevance, in determining the legal connotation today of *occupatio,* of Western-based, Roman law–derived conceptions of an essentially static territorial possession, in the case of Islamic, nomadic peoples such as were to be found in the Western Sahara at the time of the Spanish arrival. It is hardly possible, however, to view the concern with the space-time dimension in the formation of rules of customary international law as something limited peculiarly to "new" Third World states. Those Western societies that so largely participated in the formation of the corpus of classical international law customary rules in time past have analogous categories to custom present in their municipal, constitutional law: under the general rubric of constitutional convention, they have developed sophisticated legal doctrines as to the processes of rule formation through the development of governmental practices, and as to effective modification or desuetude of such rules through lapse or passage of time.

But the practice of states remains the key constituent element in the emergence of any new rule of customary international law. One of the more interesting applications of state practice in the contemporary era lies in the area of unilateral, initially nonlicit actions that are not effectively protested by other states and even by other states directly affected by them. Examples are, perhaps, the United States "quarantine" action in the Cuban missile crisis of October 1962, which, though the United States sought to justify it under other legal categories, undoubtedly also amounted (insofar as it was effectively protested neither by the Soviet Union nor by other countries having maritime connections with Cuba) to an extension of the existing international Law of Pacific Blockade. Further examples are to be found in the various unilateral national proclamations of a twelve-mile territorial sea and a two-hundred mile exclusive economic zone, or in the conclusion of a plethora of bilateral treaties between different countries with recitations to the same effect. Presumably, pending the completion and then the ratification and legal entry into force of the new, broadly based, multilateral convention on the Law of the Sea, which, in its final text as signed in December 1982, both extended the boundaries of the existing, custom-based territorial sea and also defined the extent of the new exclusive economic zone, the effect, in juridical terms, was to create a new general custom, or at least a new gloss on the old custom, through a series of interlocking unilateral national declarations or bilateral arrangements. This innovatory, individual, or bilateral initiative-based mode of approach to the creation of new general norms of international law may be aided by an emerging trend in the World Court jurisprudence, as evidenced in several recent judgments, to favor the granting of legal effect to unilateral declarations of state intention, even if these were not necessarily designed to have legal effect at the time they were originally made, or not directed to the purposes of present conflicts.

International Conventions (General and Particular)

The period since 1945 has been one involving large-scale exercise in treaty making, both the bilateral or limited-in-numbers–style accord, which is usually limited in space-time terms to solution of a specific problem situation inter partes, and also the larger, multilateral convention, which increasingly aspires to universality as to its members and signatories and usually has, in consequence, a global legislative or legal codification mandate. A good deal of the political debate over the continued legal validity of old customary rules of international law thus becomes more and more academic in nature and content, as old custom is reduced to codified, statutory treaty law and, in the actual process of treaty making and the political give-and-take and compromises between the different parties, revised and rewritten and modernized so as more nearly to reflect contemporary societal interests and forces.

A vestigial survival from the "old" classical international law in the area of treaty law, however, is constituted by the so-called unequal treaties. As a formal law category, "unequal treaties" are part of the legal heritage of the Great October Socialist Revolution in 1917, the doctrinal creation of that special regional system of Soviet (socialist) international law.[12] Early Soviet doctrinal writers cited as examples the agreements imposed by the Western imperial powers on imperial China from the middle of the nineteenth century onward into the twentieth century, particularly those involving the cession of Chinese ports and surrounding territories to those Western powers, and also those conceding the so-called extraterritorial status to Western nationals in China and thereby exempting them from the legal jurisdiction of Chinese courts, Chinese law, and the Chinese police power.[13] Though British Prime Minister Margaret Thatcher, on a state visit to China in September 1982, bravely asserted that the nineteenth-century accords between imperial Britain and China, which surrendered Hong Kong and the adjacent New Territories to Britain, were "valid under international law," that the United Kingdom "stood by its treaties," and that the accords in question could "not be changed unilaterally if international order is desired," there is no doubt that the accords were at the time of their conclusion infamously one-sided in law and imposed by force of arms on the crumbling Manchu Dynasty at the time of China's greatest political weakness and military humiliation. If that was their condition *ab initio,* there is absolutely nothing in the passage of time since to correct those accords' patent inequality and the fact that they were imposed and maintained thereafter by force or threat of force. If ever there were conditions under which both the Anglo-Saxon common law and the continental European civil law would regard a contract as void or voidable at option, they would be found in the British-Chinese accords as to Hong Kong and the New Territories. The doctrine of "unequal treaties," if it has any legal meaning and force, must apply here. Nor is the situation rendered more palatable by the fact that the other Western imperial powers of the nineteenth century soon joined with imperial Britain in a "gentlemen's agreement" to carve up China by mutual agreement: France took over Vietnam; Britain, Burma; Russia, Manchuria; and the United States and imperial Germany moved into their own treaty ports. Even post-Meiji Japan, as a modernizing, Westernizing nation in its own right, entered the act by seizing Korea and Formosa after the Sino-Japanese war of 1894–1895, specially launched for that purpose. The winds of change in world history have by now swept away most of these imperial enclaves on mainland Chinese territory, and the British crown colony of Hong Kong and the dependent New Territories remain today as vestigial survivals in Asia of a British imperial era that has long since disappeared elsewhere.

The modernizing, liberating potential of the doctrine of "unequal treaties" is clear, but it has to be noted that if the doctrine be rejected today by the United Kingdom, it also remains essentially inchoate even in that special regional Soviet (socialist) system of international law that first conceived it. In Soviet legal literature, indeed, it seems to be viewed as a closed historical-legal category with its own largely dated list of past examples. Apart from the special Chinese "unequal treaties" already referred to, Soviet legal science seems unprepared to sanction any generic extension of the category. Indeed, it is insisted that it does not apply to those old Siberian territorial frontiers treaties concluded in the mid- and late nineteenth century between imperial Russia and imperial China. Soviet legal science argues that any Russian-Chinese "unequal treaties" of the past imperial epoch have long since been renegotiated on a basis of full equality between the two original contracting parties, and several examples of such latter-day novation of old frontiers treaties, which rectify the original terms in favor of post-imperial China, are cited.[14] These examples go back to that relatively brief period, surviving until 1959, of Soviet Communist and Chinese Communist friendship and fraternal association, and do not involve the major Siberian territorial cessions of the nineteenth century, whose legal validity is today still bitterly contested by the People's Republic of China.

There are aspects of the special Soviet international law doctrine of "unequal treaties" that shade off into the larger Western, continental European civil law, contract law–inspired doctrine of *clausula rebus sic stantibus,* which authorizes the novation and readjustment of the terms of treaties in the event of supervening change in the fundamental circumstances under which the agreements were concluded.[15] In analytical jurisprudence terms, the task would be to evolve a larger, more comprehensive legal concept, embracing the more specific historical categories of "unequal treaties" and *clausula rebus sic stantibus,* and going beyond both. These latter categories are sufficiently accepted, and the functional utility is obvious enough to make the intellectual exercise worthwhile.

The differences in the general doctrinal-legal approach to treaties and treaty making on the part of the different regional systems of international law are to be seen in the debate over the role and purpose of legal codification as achieved through a multilateral convention to be enacted by an international codification conference or even series of conferences, as with the Law of the Sea. Is the legal codification treaty to be limited to a "restatement" of the old or preexisting international customary law,[16] with or without those comparatively modest incremental extensions normally licensed through analogical extension of the old rules—grammatical or logical interpretation, according to civil law canons; or is it to take the preexisting law simply as a point of departure for purposes of some sort of radical recasting or novation of law? Third World countries, quite understandably, tend to press for a creative, legislative function for the international codifying treaty; while the postindustrial societies, both Western and Soviet, opt more generally for a more restricted "restatement."

The increase in actual numbers of participants in international conferences consequent upon the expansion of the world community and the increase in United Nations membership in the wake of the massive decolonization and independence of the 1950s and 1960s, has had certain observable practical consequences and effects for such international conferences, which are not necessarily related to their subject matter. One such effect is the general attrition factor noticeable with so many international meetings called for the purpose of drafting multilateral conventions: the gap between the number of states officially represented at a diplomatic conference and the number actually signing the draft convention resulting from it; the further gap between the number of states signing the draft convention and the number then going on to take the further step of formally ratifying it; and, finally, the gap between formal signature and formal ratification on the one hand and the concrete legislative and administrative implementation of the treaty on the other.[17] The attrition factor is, of course, most marked in areas where the subject matter of the treaty involves a high ideological content, but where there are at the same time strong group pressures exercised on states to take part in the treaty-making project itself. An example that comes readily to mind involves the three projects for multilateral conventions directed to the reduction and control of aerial piracy—the Tokyo Convention of 1963, The Hague Convention of 1970, and the Montreal Convention of 1971.[18] The world community interest put forward to justify the treaty projects was clear—the societal interest in the freedom of the air and freedom of communications generally, something in which mutuality and reciprocity of interest of all states was inherent. On the other hand, the immediate causal factors of the rash of hijackings of military and civilian aircraft in the late 1950s and throughout the 1960s were also clear: apart from those few cases falling within the "lunatic fringe" group, the main actors usually had strong political and ideological motivations. These sometimes stemmed from Soviet-Western residual Cold War–era conflicts, but more usually derived from the Arab-Israeli political-military conflicts of the 1950s and the 1960s and the efforts of various Palestine liberation movements to use this particular form of terrorist direct action to publicize a cause (Palestinian self-determination) for which the normal arenas and processes for political expression were, in their view, effectively clogged. Deference to the postulated world community societal interest in the freedom of the air implied participation in the actual treaty-making conferences on aerial piracy;

deference to considerations of ethnic-cultural solidarity in certain cases, to covert political sympathy for the political-ideological cause (Palestinian self-determination) in other cases, pointed to a prudent dragging of feet as to the actual signature of the eventual draft treaty and, even more, as to its subsequent ratification or eventual implementation in concrete municipal law, statutory form. The pragmatic, if not necessarily very noble compromise made by so many states taking part in the treaty-making conference that adopted the draft Tokyo Convention in 1963 is revealed by the time lag between completion of the final text in 1963 and its coming into legal force qua treaty by the fact of its ratification (according to its own terms) by at least twelve states. It was not until six years later, in 1969, that the necessary twelfth state (the United States, in fact) finally ratified the treaty, though, as a law-making treaty, it is something of a legal pleonasm and hardly breaks new ground in relation to existing customary international law. The states that in practice have usually provided political havens to the politically and ideologically motivated hijackers, and refused either to extradite them for trial elsewhere or to punish them under their own national laws, have signally failed to sign, ratify, or legislatively implement the three aerial piracy conventions.

Another striking example of the attrition factor at work in the international treaty-making process, where what is involved is a project with a high political and ideological content whose basic characterization will tend to vary between different ethnocultural systems or different regional systems of law, concerns current United Nations projects for a convention outlawing international terrorism in general. These United Nations projects will be studied in some detail later. Suffice it for present purposes to say that the conflict of basic values represented by the project for so many key participants has been too fundamental to be successfully veiled as yet by elaborate legal formulas employing all the traditional language and drafting skills of diplomatic evasion. The general world community interest in a solution to the problem of international terrorism—at least in its incidence on innocent third parties, extrinsic to the main competing political parties—is accepted; but there is no sufficient consensus as yet on substantive solutions to the concrete political conflicts underlying the terrorist acts involved. And so resort is made once again to the attrition process, and to still more rounds of general diplomatic conferences, without so much an expectation of actual problem resolution as of preventing the legal joinder of issue from becoming pathological and politically out of hand. At least keep the diplomatic discussion going as a preliminary first step to eventual substantive problem solving.

A further major question in regard to multilateral conventions is how nearly universal their participants must be if a general law-making effect, going beyond the states actually signing and ratifying them, is to be achieved. At a certain point do multilateral treaties become binding even on the nonsigners and nonratifiers? In the International Court of Justice, there are, as already noted, judicial dicta, in *North Sea Continental Shelf* in 1969,[19] in support of the proposition that the Federal Republic of Germany is bound by the provisions of the Geneva Convention of 1958, even though it did not ratify that convention; the legal argument finds support on other grounds than an obligation qua convention, however. Apart from that particular proposition, would, for example, France, which was not a part to the Moscow Test Ban Treaty of 1963, be bound by that treaty's principles? According to the argument, by virtue of the overwhelming number and intersystemic representativeness of the state adhesions to the Moscow Test Ban Treaty, that treaty's legal principles may be said to have entered into general international law. The issue was present in the *French Nuclear Tests* cases, but without any necessity to be disposed of in view of the essentially procedural, adjectival law-based nature of the final decision by the International Court.[20]

When we turn to bilateral treaties, the personalities of the state participants in those treaties become all-important. The juridical equality of states is a key principle in the "new" international law, adumbrated as such in the Soviet-inspired principles of peaceful coexistence and in the corresponding United Nations Declaration of Principles of Friendly Relations and Cooperation among States in accordance with the United Nations Charter. But some states are clearly more important (or "more equal") than others in the political influence or style of leadership that they give to their own national treaty-making ventures. Viewed in terms of the international law-making process and the instruments of international law making, thc Soviet-American bilateral treaty, or else the Soviet-American jointly elaborated treaty draft which other states were free to adopt but not to alter in any significant way, had come to be decisive in the elaboration and refinement of the international law of the era of détente. The Moscow Test Ban Treaty of August 1963 represents the archetype of this process of law making on key international tension issues—through joint initiative, usually expressed through summit meeting diplomacy—of the two erstwhile bloc leaders. The Test Ban Treaty was conceived and drafted by the Soviet Union and the United States (with the largely nominal participation of the United Kingdom) through summit meetings, and was then signed by these three states, and, only subsequently to their signatures, opened to other states for their official acceptance, without those other states having participated in the process of elaboration of the treaty's terms or having the power to modify them. In the same vein, though perhaps more tactful at least in its superficial deference to the sensibilities of the other, lesser or supporting powers, was the operational methodology applied for further developing détente through the successive treaty-based measures directed toward nuclear disarmament and arms control, and to the security of territorial frontiers in Europe and the post–World War II political-military settlement in general.[21] The public arena for these later international law-making ventures was the general international conference, rather than the summit meeting *à deux;* and the chosen instrument was the multilateral treaty, and not the limited or bilateral treaty as the immediate step to the more general accord, as had been the case, for tactical reasons, with the Moscow Test Ban Treaty. Yet the close working collaboration established between the Soviet and American delegations to such general international conferences, the continuing exchange of drafts between their two delegations, and the eventual approximation of their respective projects, were indispensable to the overall political progress in pursuit of détente maintained at these conferences, and to the concrete success actually achieved with particular initiatives like the Space Treaty of 1967, the Nuclear Nonproliferation Treaty of 1968, the Treaty forbidding the emplacement of Nuclear Arms on the Sea-bed of 1971, the Treaty on the Manufacture and Stockpiling of Bacteriological Weapons of 1972, and the eventual Helsinki Accord of 1975. These were all part of the highly successful problem-oriented, step-by-step approach to East-West détente; in both its origins and its successful implementation it was undoubtedly assisted by the Western acceptance, de facto, of the Soviet preference for treaties as the prime source of international law today, and of the Soviet preference in treaty making for bilateral negotiation—if possible, through secret diplomacy at summit meetings—as the indispensable prior step in the whole negotiating process.

Outside the more general détente framework, for which, once achieved, some more general world community approval or ratification ex post facto was later considered desirable (and, eventually, more or less recorded in the Helsinki Final Act of 1975), there was still a considerable area for Soviet-American joint initiatives pursued at this time on a bilateral basis only: the Moscow summit meeting of May 1972, and the so-called SALT I accord and ABM Treaty emerging from it; and the Vladivostok summit meeting of November 1974, and the resultant SALT II document, were simply the last and most striking examples in what had been a continuing process, over a decade and a half, of détente.

International Legislation: Resolutions of the United Nations General Assembly

United Nations General Assembly resolutions are not, of course, listed among the formal sources of law established under Article 38 of the World Court statute, whose adoption had long preceded the formation of the United Nations. This in itself would not be any barrier to acceptance of their law-making authority, in spite of the tendency in Western legal doctrine to regard the list of sources in Article 38 as closed and incapable of further extension. The problem lies, rather, in the political controversy, reflected in the subsequent legal rationalizations put forward by the contending parties, over the constitutional role and potentiality of the United Nations and its main institutions.[22] Both Western doctrine and Soviet doctrine combine in denying any parliamentary character to the General Assembly, and, a fortiori, any general legislative capacity to its votes on the analogy of the statutes adopted by municipal, national legislatures. It is the "new" countries of the Third World who more and more, as their expanded numbers have given them an effective voting majority within the General Assembly, have viewed the General Assembly in symbolic terms as the "parliament of mankind" and endowed its decisions with full parliamentary-style law-making powers as a logical consequence. The Western powers, with predominant political-military and economic power in the world community until very recently, and with effective voting control over the General Assembly (through coalition-building arrangements with the then Western-leaning bloc of Central and South American states) until at least 1956, when the first major expansion of United Nations membership occurred, were hardly preoccupied with the constitutional theory of international organization and of the United Nations in particular. The Soviet Union and Soviet bloc, by contrast, finding themselves in a minority voting position in the United Nations and its main organs right from the outset in 1945, maintained an essentially politically defensive, holding operation within the United Nations, and developed special legal theories to balance that position: that the United Nations Charter, so far from being a constitution, was a mere treaty concluded between states and, insofar as it might, in terms, seem to derogate from or limit state sovereignty, it should be interpreted restrictively and against the claimed power of the United Nations. So far as General Assembly resolutions were concerned, the Soviet attitude was deliberately conservative: these were at best mere *subsidiary* sources of international law. Soviet doctrine here differentiates itself from Soviet-bloc doctrine, which revealed a tendency to concede a legally normative quality to General Assembly resolutions where these were adopted unanimously or had at least intersystemic, tri-bloc (Soviet, Western, and Third World) voting support in the General Assembly.[23]

Western political leaders had, in the first few years of the United Nations, become increasingly irritated by the Soviet veto in the Security Council, which constituted a full legal impediment to Western-favored political action in many spheres. In the Korean War crisis of 1950, the Western majority in the Security Council had been able to act owing to the fortuitous absence of the Soviet representative, who had earlier walked out on another issue (the issue of "Chinese" representation, whether Nationalist or Communist China) and not returned at the time of the first crucial Security Council votes. When the Soviet representative finally returned and the Soviet veto power threatened to paralyze any future Security Council action, Western foreign ministries and their supporting jurists worked out an "all power to the General Assembly" stratagem as a means of legally bypassing the Security Council and any future Soviet veto. With the celebrated Uniting for Peace resolution adopted by the General Assembly on November 3, 1950, under Western sponsorship, Western political leaders and Western legal publicists postulated a legal right, indeed a legal duty, on the part of the General Assembly to move affirmatively to "fill the gaps" in the United Nations Charter whenever necessary because of Security Council inaction, and this in support of the United Nations' general peace-keeping responsibilities. The Uniting for Peace resolution was adopted by an overwhelming majority (52–5, with 2 abstentions) in the then Western-dominated General Assembly. It was a decisive breakthrough in terms of United Nations practice and the general constitutional law of international organization, and a clear precedent for the future—with the full potentiality for invocation by Third World countries in the future to overcome any veto by recalcitrant Western powers in the Security Council, and not simply any Soviet veto.

It is a maxim of common law jurisprudence to be careful about the precedents you create: the new precedent that you successfully argue for today, because it helps you in your own case, may be the one you have to live with tomorrow, when it works the other way. The triumphant Western coalition that sponsored the Uniting for Peace resolution in 1950, to overcome the legal obstacle of the veto in the Security Council, suddenly began to lose its enthusiasm for General Assembly–based constitutional-legal activism as the automatic pro-Western voting majority of the first decade of the United Nations began to be swamped in the flood of new Afro-Asian states admitted to United Nations membership in the wake of large-scale decolonization and independence from the late 1950s onward. With the disappearance of the Korean War era Western enthusiasm for a claimed plenary legislative power of the General Assembly, came a reversion to the traditionally more reserved Western view that such resolutions have legal efficacy only when declaratory of preexisting law.

With the triumphant new anticolonialist, anti-imperialist voting coalition installed in political control of the General Assembly, the General Assembly resolution has become the prime instrument for the remaking of the old international law in the image of the new Third World majority. There are some limitations to all this, of course: the Third World majority is not homogeneous for all purposes, and on a number of key issues, such as the energy crisis and even the concrete implementation of the New International Economic Order, there is no longer a complete congruence of interests between, for example, the economically well-to-do oil-producing and -exporting countries and those Third World countries without major natural resources or raw materials within their territorial limits. The other limitations go to as yet unresolved doctrinal issues of just how, in analytical jurisprudential terms, to classify or categorize such resolutions, assuming that they are law in the first place. What is clear, however, is that the largely hortatory propositions of yesterday contained in such resolutions as those on decolonization, national ownership of natural resources, and the like have really represented law-in-the-making in their execution and development, and now number among the accepted principles of the "new" international law—part of the substantive principles of the as yet largely undefined *jus cogens*.

Judicial Decisions: The International Court of Justice

The older, classical, "European" special legal community of the era of the League of Nations and its judicial organ, the old Permanent Court of International Justice, greatly favored judicial settlement as a mode of international problem solving. This special legal position seems to have resulted from the confluence of two different forces: first, ingrained ethnic-cultural factors reflected in the sociological state of the world community of that era, dominated as it was by Western liberal states which had achieved, in Weber's terms, logically formal rationality in their own municipal, internal legal systems; which understood the purpose of law, in ultrapositivistic terms, as the pursuit of logical symmetry and order in the process of application of old legal principles and rules, and little more; and which, in accepting a judge-centeredness in their own internal legal systems, found it perfectly natural to project that condition into international institutions and international law-making processes generally. A second factor, which undoubtedly reinforced the play of these objective societal influences favoring international adjudication as a means of international problem solving in the between-the-two-world-wars era, was the fact that, the League of Nations itself being dominated by the Western European "victors of Versailles" group of powers, the same essential identity of basic attitudes and political expectations could normally be expected as to the judges on the court. If judicial decision making would normally reduce to a process of logical exegesis of past decisions, then those essentially Western European states actually having recourse to the court had nothing really to fear by way of judicial legislation, even limited, purely "interstitial" judicial legislation—nothing to fear as to any judicial leap into the unknown in terms of the elaboration of new international law doctrine in the process of decision making. As a "European" court functioning for the needs of a largely Western European family of states, the old Permanent Court was, in fact, a "lawyers' court," characterized by standards of technical excellence in the logical interpretation of old rules, and by an impressive intellectual objectivity and political neutrality as between the actual litigating parties; but not going beyond that essentially narrow, technical conception of its own function, and, perhaps in part for that reason, never attracting recourse to its jurisdiction for settlement of those great political-legal causes célèbres (such as rectification by peaceful means of the worst inequities of the Versailles Treaty's territorial frontiers and related settlements within Europe) that, left unattended and unresolved, were to bring the downfall of the prevailing world public order system in yet another world war.

The change from the League of Nations to the United Nations as the institutional base of world public order, in 1945, corresponded to and reflected the change in the politically dominant forces in the world community from a Western European special legal community to an ethnically/culturally broader and far more representative grouping of states; and this process was accentuated and accelerated with the achievement of decolonization and independence on a nearly worldwide scale in the 1950s and the 1960s. Changes in the character and internal composition of the court from the old Permanent Court of International Justice to the new International Court of Justice were, however, much slower in coming and hardly paralleled the marked political changes in other United Nations organs, and especially the General Assembly, over the same time period. The time lag in responding to the societal change in the world community seems due, in the case of the court, in part to the staggered, indirect system of election and the complications created by the double-majority (General Assembly *plus* Security Council) voting rule.[24] Many states, particularly "new" states, seemed unaware that the Big Power veto did not and could not legally apply to court decisions;[25] and so election of the judicial candidates presented by the permanent members of the Security Council (though not the People's Republic of China) has been accorded over the years a virtually automatic, "as of right" character that is warranted by neither the charter nor the statute of the court. Complaints as to the degree of conservatism, and commitment to the political and economic status quo and its consecration in legal form, of past and present judges of the court, can be corrected for the future through the electoral processes for the court and through attention—not less in the case of judicial candidates sponsored by the permanent members of the Security Council than of other candidates—to the degree of intellectual openness to change and modernization of international law demonstrated by their national foreign ministries. Referring to the voting system for election of judges to the court and the relative conservatism and continuity with which the actual choices have been made over the years, in spite of the vast political changes in at least one of the two electoral colleges, the General Assembly, draws attention to another important factor—the relative lack of political sophistication and political awareness on the part of the new Third World forces in the General Assembly from the 1960s onwards, as to the enormous law-making potential of the International Court of Justice and its affirmative possibilities for updating and rewriting international law in the processes of judicial interpretation, granted only the presence of judges with the intellectual commitment to fundamental legal change in response to fundamental societal change. The political watershed event for the court was undoubtedly its *South West Africa, Second Phase* 8–7 majority decision of 1966,[26] when it refused on procedural grounds to intervene against the Republic of South Africa's apartheid (racial segregation) policies; for this for the first time brought widespread Third World attention to the role of the court and bitter criticism of that decision as one rendered by a "white man's tribunal." With the staggered system of elections to the court, and only a third of its membership being renewed or replaced at each of its triennial elections, it has taken some time for the new General Assembly interest in the court to be reflected in corresponding changes in the dominant philosophy of law within the court—from the old, positivistic, jurisprudence-of-concepts approach to a new, "legislative," and more nearly functional or sociological approach. The partial election of April 1982, however, when the choice of a replacement for the recently deceased Egyptian judge, El-Erian, narrowed down to a choice between two Third World candidates, both drawn from the same essential "region" in legal terms (North Africa, Muslim, civil law), saw the election of the distinguished Algerian jurist Mohammed Bedjaoui, known (both from his impressive scientific-legal writings and also his work in the United Nations General Assembly's Sixth Legal Committee and as counsel pleading before the court in the *Western Sahara* case) as committed to a frankly legislative, policy-making, "modernizing" approach to international law, over a more traditional or legally conservative candidate who had been publicly supported by the United States and other major Western powers (though not France).

If Dr. Bedjaoui's election presaged a new political awareness in the actual electoral processes for the court and, as the long-range consequence, a new judicial activism in the court along the lines of the United States Supreme Court in modern times, and a new judicial impatience with the mere restatement of "old," classical international law, then we may reasonably expect some role reversals among erstwhile supporters and opponents of international adjudication as a prime method of international problem solving. Presumably, as Third World support for a judicial activist court seen to be challenging classical international law could be expected to grow, so past Western support for judicial settlement as a solution for international problems might be expected to decline; just as Western enthusiasm for the idea of an activist General Assembly "filling the gaps" in the United Nations Charter caused by Security Council inaction fell off sharply from the euphoria of the Uniting for Peace resolution period, as the automatic Western coalition voting majority in the General Assembly began to disappear from the late 1950s on. Only the Soviet Union seems to remain consistent in terms of long-range institutional attitudes and expectations; and the restrictive Soviet approach that has characterized the postwar period, stemming from past Soviet empirical experience, which has consistently denied any place for judicial legislation by the court, can be expected to continue to prevail with Soviet policy makers.

Article 59 of the Statute of the International Court of Justice stipulates that the decision of the court, in any case, has "no binding force except between the parties and in respect of that particular case."

This reflects the civil law attitude to past judicial decisions, not the common law approach. Unlike the rule in common law municipal, internal legal systems, there is to be no formal doctrine of judicial precedent at the international level. We know from comparative legal science that the distinction between common law and civil law in the attitude to past judicial decisions has been more notional than real: the common law, in modern times, has formally broken the fetters of *stare decisis,* even apart from its developed skills in "distinguishing," and hence limiting, unwanted or politically awkward rulings from the past; while the civil law, under the rubric of *doctrines* (rather than *jurisprudence*), accords great deference to prior court decisions. The formal stipulation in Article 59 of the court statute is therefore hardly controlling or influential in determining current court or General Assembly attitudes to court *jurisprudence* from earlier eras of court history: its legal authority will tend, in law-as-fact terms, to reflect the moral authority that it can still continue to command, as a contemporary response to contemporary societal conditions and needs. However, reflecting the perceptible transition within the court, in the political reaction after *South West Africa, Second Phase* in 1966,[27] from an essentially positivistic to a more consciously legislative, policy-oriented tribunal, the decisions of the court after 1966 are characterized by multiple opinion writing—both dissenting and also special concurring opinions; with the doctrinal divisions among the individual judges (as befits an institution in transition) often so great that it is very difficult to extract any common ground of decision—what the common law calls the principle, or *ratio decidendi* of a case—even in matters decided by near unanimity in actual voting terms.

4. The International Law-Making Process: Imperative Principles of International Law

Categories of Imperative Principles

The General Principles of Law Recognized by Nations

If treaties and custom (at least "new" or "renewed" custom) represent, together with parliamentary legislation (General Assembly resolutions) and judicial decisions, the quantitatively largest sources of contemporary international law, this has not prevented the emergence of entirely new sources hardly contemplated at the time of the adoption of the World Court statute in 1920 during the heyday of classical international law, or else inchoate and unfulfilled at that time. Article 38 of the court statute mentions, as its third category of sources, "the general principles of law recognized by civilised nations." It is an example in itself of the relevance of the time dimension in international law, and the effect of the passage of time upon the meaning of a concept assumed, without discussion, to be politically and ideologically neutral at the time of its origin and certainly free from any racist connotation. The particular verbal formulation has been criticized in recent times by Third World spokesmen in the General Assembly—rightly so, it may be suggested, in temporal terms, in the light of the evolving juridical conscience within the United Nations. Beyond that, however, the "general principles" remain today, as they were at the time of their first formulation, a largely inchoate juridical category, with an important potential for the future but little or no supporting evidentiary international practice and application.

The general principles could have been—and in analytical jurisprudential terms should have been—developed on a comparative law basis by process of induction from existing and emerging national systems of internal, municipal law. In this context, the juridical category of crimes against humanity—the most universal of all the counts in the Nuremberg War Crimes Tribunal prosecution and conviction of the Nazi German leaders in 1946, and the only count completely free from the taint of subjectivity attaching to charges involving breaches of the peace, making of aggressive war, and breaches of the law of war, when these are applied by a court composed of representatives of the victor countries only against the defeated enemy only—could certainly be characterized as a general principle of law recognized by all nations, insofar as every legal system prohibits and punishes murder and, *a fortiori,* mass murder repeated many, many times. The strong appeal of the crimes against humanity count, which has survived any latter-day critical reexamination of the essential onesidedness, as judicial process, of Nuremberg and the other postwar attempts at retributive justice against the German and Japanese war leaders, can no doubt be attributed much more to its natural law–style quality, in 1945 as now, just as in the classical Roman law the new *jus naturale,* borrowed by Roman jurists from the Greek thinkers, lent moral prestige and ultimately legal authority to that new *jus gentium* that was being induced, on a pragmatic and empirical basis, from foreign law systems by the *praetor peregrinus* as a means of softening the rigidities and reducing the overly servile deference to form at the expense of substance present in the old *jus civile.*

Natural law in municipal, national legal systems is always strongest in its appeal in a period of transition or revolution, when old legal values and institutions and processes are increasingly subjected to the cool test of reason and found wanting. In some cases, what natural law dictates in positive law terms will be clear and beyond contest; in other cases, simply because in an era of change the challenge to the old will often be made by mutually competing value systems, no firm majority consensus may have emerged as yet, and the postulated imperative principles of law remain then as legal claims for the future, to be tested experientially through time, and thereby either accepted as universal or falling by the wayside.

Equity

Although equity was always included in the list of topics referred to in classical international law textbooks on sources of law, the scholarly treatment of it was usually very modest, as if the text writer had concluded that academic propriety demanded a pious genuflection toward equity, but that there was no need for anything more than that, having regard to the record of international practice. In truth, the precedents or authorities that might be relied upon to give evidence of or to confirm the existence of equity as an operational principle of international law are relatively few and far between. There is, of course, the *Cayuga Indians (Great Britain* v. *United States)* Arbitration[1] of 1926, in which the arbitral tribunal referred to "elementary principles of justice that require us to look at the substance and not stick in the bark of the legal form" in ruling in favor of the existence of an equitable claim by the Canadian Cayuga Indians to share in an annuity covenanted by the State of New York to be paid in perpetuity to the "Cayuga Nation." There is also the individual opinion of the American judge, Manley Hudson, in the Permanent Court of International Justice's decision in the dispute between Belgium and the Netherlands on *The Diversion of Water from the River Meuse,* in 1937.[2] In his opinion in the *River Meuse* case, Judge Hudson seemed to go out of his way, in a celebrated tour de force, to conclude that although Article 38 of the court statute does not expressly authorize the court to apply equity as distinguished from law, nevertheless equity, insofar as it has an established part in the internal legal system or more than one nation, must be considered to be part of "the general principles of law recognized by civilized nations" and so, in terms of Article 38(1)(c), to be part of the official sources of international law. Judge Hudson, in the same opinion, distinguished "equity" from that power of the court, under Article 38(2) of the court statute, to "decide a case *ex aequo et bono,* if the parties agree thereto," a distinction also made by the arbitral tribunal in the *Cayuga Indians* case, which went on to note that "that much-criticized opinion *ex aequo et bono* is meant for cases . . . which call, not for principles of equity, but for a degree of compromise." So far, the World Court (meaning here both the original Permanent Court of International Justice [PCIJ], and also its successor after the Second World War, the International Court of Justice [ICJ]) has never given a decision *ex aequo et bono.* However, the absence of a ruling *ex aequo et bono* is perhaps not too significant, granted the extreme diffidence of the World Court and of the various international arbitral tribunals as to basing their decisions directly and in terms upon "equity" or seemingly cognate principles, and this in spite of the occasional hortatory judicial or arbitral comment, ex cathedra, that in the absence of rules of international law applicable to the facts of a case coming before it, the tribunal concerned should "fill the gap by deciding according to the principles of equity, while keeping within the spirit of international law, applied by analogy, and taking account of its evolution."[3]

In seeking scientific legal explanations for the paucity of direct influence of principles of equity in public international law today,[4] in both the older, historically inherited corpus of customary international law and also the newer, more largely treaty-based rules, it is helpful to look to the historical development of equity in internal law systems, most notably in English law and in Roman law. In English law, equity, though starting out as a body of moral principles intended to soften the rigidities of the common law and developed by the Lord Chancellor as "Keeper of the King's Conscience," derived its ultimate political weight and authority from the fact of its being successfully institutionalized in a court system separate and distinct from the common law courts and exercising in fact a coordinate or rival jurisdiction to the common law courts. So also in the case of the historical growth of Roman law, it was through the medium of the praetors and their court jurisdiction that *aequitas* was able to be translated into operational, legal rules capable of controlling and deciding the disposition of concrete social disputes.

Analysis of the historical origins of equity in particular national legal systems, within the international law domain, offers certain lessons. Judicial power and judge-made law have never been as important in the processes of law making in international legal arenas as in national ones, particularly those of Anglo-Saxon, common law legal systems. And even with regard to the international law-making processes, the role of the post–World War II International Court of Justice and of arbitral tribunals in the same time era has declined markedly in comparison to the old Permanent Court of International Justice of the between-the-two-world-wars era, and this in terms of both the incidence and also the intrinsic importance of the matters brought before the courts. In world community legal terms, judicial legislation as a solvent for social ills, or the recourse to the courts in general as a means of resolving major tension issues, has seemed historically to have had a predominantly Western European, or Western European–derived flavor. As the world community has increased its members, especially since 1945, to include more and more non-Western countries, the emphasis, in institutional-legal terms, has increasingly been on other, alternative modes of dispute settlement or problem solving, seeming to reflect more nearly, or certainly more avowedly, the basic power component in international problem situations and their range of possible solutions. The distrust on the part of the "new" Afro-Asian countries for judicially based problem solving was reflected in the extended discussions and debates of the United Nations General Assembly's Special Committee on Friendly Relations and Cooperation among States in accordance with the United Nations Charter, and in the very low rank given to judicial methods in the special committee's effective hierarchical ranking of the various modes of dispute settlement in its final report, which became the basis for the United Nations Declaration of Legal Principles of Friendly Relations, adopted by the General Assembly resolution of October 1970. Moreover, for reasons that may be in part intrinsically technical—the manifestly less enthusiastic acceptance of judicial legislation on the part of civil lawyers in comparison with common lawyers—and in part historical—the general Soviet and Soviet-bloc reaction to the bitter historical experience of the Soviet Union with international institutions in the League of Nations era—the Soviet Union has never been a champion of international judicial power as such, or of an expansionist conception of the jurisdictional role and possibilities of the World Court. In the face of the marked contemporary preference in the international arena for direct diplomatic methods and negotiation as a means of resolving or confining international conflicts, it is hardly surprising that the post–World War II International Court of Justice was not given too many opportunities to rule on concrete cases or controversies; and also that, in the limited number of cases that it did in fact receive, the court was hardly tempted to try to venture out and break new ground by seeking, for example, to invoke equity as the ground for decision in a case coming before it.

There is another area where the analogy from the historical development of equity in internal law systems may have relevance to the general situation of equity as a legal principle in contemporary international law. Sir Henry Maine, in his book *Ancient Law,* developed one of those powerful general propositions that have much influenced our thinking on the general growth of law in society. Maine spoke in terms of a historical progression, from the most primitive type of society, where legal fictions are the prime vehicle for legal change; through equity in more advanced communities; and on, finally, to legislation in mature societies. Maine's thesis has, as we know, been questioned in terms of its scientific validity as a historical-legal hypothesis claimed to apply to all societies; and as a thesis it may simply illustrate once again what Popper called the "poverty of historicism," insofar as that seems to imply the existence of inexorable steps or stages in the unfolding or evolution of society through time. Certainly Maine's sweeping historical generalization is hardly true as a description of the grand lines of international legal development in the world community up to the present era. But insofar as Maine's thesis might also imply that equity and the various other community law-making techniques cited by Maine are *alternative* modes of legal change that cannot or do not coexist, the one with the other, at the same time, it may be significant to note that the world community is in a period today where legislation is clearly the prime technique of international law making. And it is legislation as expressed in the form dear to the late-nineteenth-century neo-Kantian liberal jurists—namely, self-legislation through contractual bargaining and exchange, with the final consensus recorded in a written contract *(treaty)* drawn up by the parties. Legislation has become—certainly quantitatively, but also qualitatively—the main source of contemporary international law, being reflected in the current welter of multilateral treaties, with the intrinsically most important of these multilateral treaties usually stemming from an original bilateral (Soviet–United States) initiative, and with the resultant joint Soviet–United States consensus draft normally being opened up subsequently to the acceptance or adherence of other countries. The contemporary treaty, especially where it stems from such a prior joint Soviet-American accord, will normally be directed to a quite specific subject, with the contours of the problem being precisely defined in the treaty instrument and with the actual stipulations in the treaty expressed very clearly and without room for equivocation. The emphasis with the contemporary treaty is thus upon strict construction and interpretation—a point insisted upon by Soviet and Eastern European, as well as Western, jurists—this being a necessary political concomitant of the principle of *pacta sunt servanda,* which is also emphasized today by Soviet and Eastern European, as well as Western, jurists. There is thus little room in this contemporary Soviet- and Western-favored approach for invocation of supposedly higher moral principles of the sort that have sometimes been invoked in the past to overturn obligations flowing from more ancient treaties—the doctrine of "unequal treaties" (a special concept developed by Soviet jurists to enable them selectively to rid themselves of irksome pre-1917 treaty obligations); *clausula rebus sic stantibus*; and, a fortiori, the "new" international law category of *jus cogens*. Equity—*jus aequum*—is conventionally set in logical contraposition to *jus strictum*; the prime emphasis in contemporary treaty making (at least, in treaties between the superpowers) is clearly in the direction of *jus strictum*.

In the treaty area, new juristic voices are now being raised, claiming to be able to void treaties and similar legal accords on general equitable grounds, on the score, officially, that their obligations are counter to the principle of *jus cogens*—a concept that is mentioned in the Vienna Convention on the Law of Treaties, of 1969. The Vienna Convention declares, in its Article 53, "A treaty is void if, at the time of its conclusion, it conflicts with a peremptory norm of general international law." However, the Vienna Convention nowhere makes clear just what a "peremptory norm" of international law is. It does go on to offer, in the same Article 53, the somewhat open-ended or self-defining explanation that a "peremptory norm" is "a norm accepted and recognised by the international community of States as a whole as a norm from which no derogation is permitted and which can be modified only by a subsequent norm of general international law having the same character."

Not surprisingly, some jurists are tempted to argue that the "peremptory norms" *(jus cogens)* include all those "new" international law principles so triumphantly proclaimed in recent years in various United Nations General Assembly resolutions—most notably the celebrated resolution on decolonization and independence, but also the resolution on permanent sovereignty over natural resources of December 14, 1962, and similar (for their time of adoption) avant-garde political-legal pronouncements. All this, of course, takes us into the general debate over the status of the United Nations General Assembly resolutions as such, as a claimed official source of international law. We have already noted that the weight of Western legal opinion is against the notion of any inherent law-making capacity in United Nations General Assembly resolutions as such; and this in spite of the use made of them as "proof of the pertinent contemporary international standard" by Judge Philip Jessup in his notable dissenting opinion in the *South West Africa, Second Phase* in 1966,[5] and in spite also of the obvious fact, as pointed out by Manfred Lachs, that General Assembly resolutions may be the prime evidence of the emergence today of a new rule of customary international law. In the same way, the weight of Western legal opinion seems against the more ambitious, expansionist interpretations of *jus cogens,* designed to make it a vehicle for the injection of a sort of late-twentieth-century, natural law–style equity into classical international law. If a plural "living law" *jus gentium* does in fact appear to be emerging at the present time, it is coming not so much from "Sermons on the Mount" and similar abstract, a priori declarations as from concrete and specific international agreements arrived at through essentially pragmatic, empirical, problem-oriented, step-by-step methods, as demonstrated, in the areas of East-West accommodation and détente, by the range of agreements reached at the February 1972 Peking and the May 1972 Moscow summit meetings. If, as Professor Georg Schwarzenberger has persuasively argued, "the chief functions of *jus aequum* in its positive sense are to transform absolute rights into relative rights and thus to smooth the interplay of the rules of international law," and, if *jus aequum* also has the "wider meaning of common sense and reasonableness,"[6] then the process of practical accommodation and reconciliation of the competing interests of the Superpowers, in the era of détente—on the basis of reciprocity of interest and of mutual give-and-take and exchange between them, in place of the sterile doctrinal debates and the ideological name-calling of the earlier, Cold War era—succeeded in translating equitable principles in a most positive way into international law. But that process of incorporating or blending equity into international law took place through the special mode of international law making by *legislation* (treaty, and especially the bilateral treaty), rather than by the older and more conventional, *judicial* route, as envisaged by Maine and by those jurisprudential schools that followed him.

Judicial incorporation of equitable principles—particularly the more specific and concrete, or secondary, principles—into international law still has a place today, and it can have a much larger place in the future. A court rendered more nearly representative in "regional" terms, through the operation of the periodic elections to the court, should inspire more political confidence in a larger number of Member States of the United Nations, and thus more readiness on their part to invoke the court's jurisdiction, either directly in concrete case controversies or else by way of advisory opinion rulings. Specific equitable principles such as estoppel are amply noted in the decision of the old Permanent Court in *Eastern Greenland,*[7] and the decision of the "new" International Court of Justice in *Anglo-Norwegian Fisheries* in 1951;[8] while the principle of abuse of rights is referred to by Judges Azevedo and Alvarez in their special opinions in a number of cases in the immediate post–World War II era—Judge Alvarez inclining, however, to consider it rather as a principle *de lege ferenda* only.[9] On the other hand, any sustained process of judicial incorporation of equitable principles seems more likely today to be found in the case of regionally based supranational communities that happen to already have a substantial value homogeneity or basic political consensus, and that have certainly also a common record of governmental experience with and public acceptance of the institution of judicial review of the constitution. One thinks, in this regard, of the developing role of the High Court of Justice of the European Communities.

At the international judicial level, judicial ventures in the invocation of equitable principles in court decisions have tended to be limited to the special concurring opinions or to the dissenting opinions. In these opinions the judicial author, freed from the intellectual constraints involved in writing an official opinion of the court, which by definition must be a collective opinion representing a court majority and so take on something of a lowest-common-denominator quality, can feel free to act as a judicial front-runner and so not be afraid to innovate and break new legal ground. An example of just such an opinion is Judge Ammoun's special opinion in *North Sea Continental Shelf, Judgment* in 1969.[10] Noting that the court majority had taken the view that, failing a method of delimitation of the boundaries between adjacent states, of the North Sea continental shelf which the parties (the Federal Republic of Germany, Denmark, and the Netherlands) were bound to use, those parties should be called upon to negotiate an agreement by the application of equitable principles, Judge Ammoun used this as a point of departure for a comprehensive philosophical examination of the nature and character of equity in contemporary national and international law:

> What is just is . . . not always equitable, witness the well-known adage: *summum jus summa injuria*. And it is in order to mitigate this inconvenience of strict justice that recourse may be had to equity whose role is to moderate the rigour of law.
>
> "The truth of the matter is that the principle of equity which must be

applied is not the abstract equity . . . but that which fills a lacuna, like the principle of equity *praeter legem,* which is a subsidiary source of law.[11]

Judge Ammoun then examined the question whether there existed a

general principle of law recognised by the nations, as provided for by Article 38, paragraph (c), of the Statute of the Court, from which would follow a rule to the effect that the continental shelf could, in case of disagreement, be delimited equitably between the parties?[12]

Judge Ammoun proceeded, in passing, to castigate the particular court statute formulation of Article 38(1)(c) "general principles of law recognised by civilised nations," rejecting the qualification "civilised nations" as "an ill-advised limitation":

The discrimination between civilised nations and uncivilised nations, which was unknown to the founding fathers of international law, the protagonists of a universal law of nations, Vittoria, Suarez, Gentilis, Pufendorf, Vattel, is the legacy of the period, now passed away, of colonialism, and of the time long-past when a limited number of Powers established the rules, of custom or of treaty-law, of a European law applied in relation to the whole community of nations. Maintained and sometimes reinforced at the time of the great historical settlements—Vienna 1815, Berlin 1885, Versailles 1920, Lausanne 1923, Yalta 1945—European international law has been defended by jurists of indisputable authority in the majority of branches of international law. . . . it is centered on Europe alone and Europe's exclusive interests. However great and powerful the thinking of these renowned jurists may be, their concept of a family of European and North Atlantic nations is nonetheless beginning to be blurred by the reality of the universal community, in the thinking of the internationalists of a new age such as S. Krylov, M. Katz, W. Jenks and M. Lachs. What is more, the universalist jurists of Europe had been preceded by those of Asia and the Middle East: Sui Ichoan-Pao, Bandyopadhyoy, Rechid. . . .

Thus it is that certain nations, to whose legal systems allusion was made above, which did not form part of the limited concert of States which did the law-making, up to the first decades of the 20th century, for the whole of the international community, today participate in the determination or elaboration of the general principles of law, contrary to what is improperly stated by Article 38, paragraph 1(c), of the Court's Statute. . . . The criterion of the distinction between civilised nations and those which are allegedly not so has thus been a political criterion—power politics—and anything but an ethical or legal one. The system which it represents has not been without influence on the persistent aloofness of certain new States from the International Court of Justice.[13]

All this was by way of prelude to the specific question in *North Sea Continental Shelf, Judgment* whether there was a general principle of law recognized by the municipal law systems of the community of nations "from which would follow a rule to the effect that the continental shelf could be delimited equitably between the parties."[14]

Judge Ammoun here had strictures both for "Romano-Mediterranean legal thinking, breaking the chrysalis of outgrown formalism which encompasses it, . . . to open the door to political and social reality";[15] and for "the normative school and its pure theory of law, in rejecting the moral, social and political elements, described as meta-juridical, becom[ing] isolated from international realities and their progressive institutions."[16] Instead, Judge Ammoun saw the principle of equity manifested equally in the law of Western Europe and of Latin America, "the direct heirs of the Romano-Mediterranean *jus gentium*"; in the common law; in Muslim law; in "Chinese law, with its primacy for the moral law and the common sense of equity, in harmony with the Marxist-Leninist philosophy"; Soviet law; Hindu law; and the laws of the former colonial countries of Asia and Africa.[17] On this general basis of equity as a form of *jus gentium* common to all those "main forms of civilisation and . . . the principal legal systems of the world," mentioned in Article 9 of the World Court statute, Judge Ammoun then proceeded to reject, as not being in conformity with equity on the concrete facts of the case, any delimitation of the North Sea continental shelf in accordance with the strict equidistance system. Judge Ammoun did note at the same time his personal preference for an "equidistance–special circumstances" method,[18] even though this method had not been accepted by the court majority, since it was a rule of neither treaty law nor customary law. He would, however, reject as irrelevant to the consideration of such "special circumstances" questions of "economic objectives, such as the unity of deposits . . . submarine resources . . . the riches secreted by the bed of the sea."[19] In the judge's opinion, this should be left to voluntary agreement by the parties and did not fall within the category of a factor or rule of delimitation.

Continental Shelf (Tunisia/Libyan Arab Jamahiriya), Judgment,[20] in 1982, involved the delimitation of the continental shelf in the Mediterranean between the two adjacent former colonial states of Tunisia and Libya. The opinion of the court representing the majority judges, and also some of the special and dissenting opinions, approached the issue in the light of recent trends in the Law of the Sea, arising since *North Sea Continental Shelf,* which had been admitted at the Third United Nations Conference on the Law of the Sea and which were reflected in particular in Articles 76 and 83 of the then draft convention emerging from that conference. Judge Oda, in his dissenting opinion to that judgment,[21] offered a detailed and very well-researched excursus on the role of equitable principles in contemporary international law. Pointing out that the court in its 1969 judgment in *North Sea Continental Shelf* had refused to accept the concept of "a just and equitable share,"[22] Judge Oda noted that instead the court majority had preferred to restrict itself, in that case, to the "delimitation and not to the apportionment of the areas concerned, or their division into converging sectors."[23]

Judge Oda expressed his own agreement therein for the present case, "in the sense that the sea-bed area is not meant to be parcelled out like so many fiefs."[24] But Judge Oda proceeded then to distinguish and limit the 1969 court holding insofar as it refused to embrace the idea of equitable apportionment, viewing the early, 1969 holding as now

> overtaken by events. There was thus insufficient reason for the present Court, in 1982, to be inhibited from realising that the present delimitation was simply a question of equitably dividing, or apportioning, between the Parties, by means of a justifiable line of demarcation, those submarine areas which either could potentially have claimed.[25]

Judge Oda was not very sanguine as to the possibilities of a judicially based "geographical equity." Noting that

> various political, social and economic factors could have been suggested. . . : the size of the territories and their population, the distribution of natural resources, the degree of development of the economy and industry, etc., of the respective Parties,"[26]

he concluded nevertheless that

> such questions involve global resource policies, or basic problems of world politics which not only could not have been solved by the judicial organ of the world community but stray well beyond equity as a norm of law into the realm of social organisation. . . . In sum, the inequality of geography is a fact of the world, nature cannot be refashioned, and the Court has no competence to guess at or initiate any future policy of world social justice, going beyond the existing principles and rules of international law.[27]

After marshaling the most cogent intellectual and scientific criticisms of the court majority's doctrinally somewhat static or conservative legal reasoning and holding, as he saw it, Judge Oda's dissenting opinion might appear as something of a psychological letdown. It did not appear to offer very much of a positive character by way of new prescriptions for applying equitable principles to the updating and progressive development of international law. Passing over also the notion of proportionality as a function of geographical equity, Judge Oda came to rest finally with a quite specific and low-level application of the rule of equidistance that is deliberately tied to the facts of the case in question and thus of rather limited application for other, future problem situations. The reasons for this particular judicial denouement, it might be suggested, had to do with matters intrinsic to the judicial process, involving the conception (itself a somewhat traditional one, which may no longer be applicable or relevant to the role of the International Court today) of the limits of judicial policy making and of the special obligations of judicial self-restraint on the part of a minority dissenting judge vis-à-vis his majority colleagues and the official opinion of the court.

Jus Cogens

Something of this phenomenon of the emergence of legal principles through their validation in action—the process of law-in-the-making—can be seen in the history of the development of the "new" international law category of *jus cogens*.[28] The draft articles on the Law of Treaties, prepared by the International Law Commission and adopted in 1966, from which there eventually emerged, after amendments, the Vienna Convention on the Law of Treaties of 1969, contained a draft Article 50, entitled "Treaties conflicting with a peremptory norm of general international law *(jus cogens)*."[29] The substantive part of the draft article (Article 50) read: "A treaty is void if it conflicts with a peremptory norm of general international law from which no derogation is permitted and which can be modified only by a subsequent norm of general international law having the same character."

The draft article represented a compromise, in legal theory terms, between positivism and natural law. The legal positivists insisted that the concept of *jus cogens* either did not exist or was too vague to be given legal meaning, and that in any case the adoption of such a specific derogation from the free will of the parties to a treaty to conclude whatever agreement they wished would impair the sanctity of the written word and the principle of *pacta sunt servanda*. The natural lawyers insisted that the principle of a *jus cogens* limitation to the contractual power of the parties was one common to all legal systems, existing under various rubrics, "public policy" and the like, but amounting essentially to the same thing. In "regional" international law terms, it was the Anglo-Saxon common lawyers who were most unhappy about *jus cogens,* the United States in particular[30] opposing its incorporation in the draft treaty prepared by the International Law Commission. Continental European civil lawyers, by contrast, were more nuanced in their approach and usually supportive,[31] the idea of *jus cogens,* after all, having some classical Roman law antecedents, and certainly deriving rich support from nineteenth-century civil law pandectist teachings. The Soviet Union and the socialist countries of Eastern Europe, and some Third World countries influenced by Marxist legal thought, were quite enthusiastic as to inclusion of the *jus cogens* limitation on treaty-making power,[32] this attitude deriving in part, no doubt, from vestigial Roman law and civil law influences, but principally from consideration of the substantive content of any postulated *jus co-*

gens, the strong suggestion being advanced here that the five legal principles of peaceful coexistence should be accepted as applications of *jus cogens*.

Within the International Law Commission and in the subsequent Vienna Conference on the Law of Treaties, which brought out a final draft convention, a lengthy debate went on between those who favored spelling out the contents of *jus cogens,* perhaps by establishing a list of examples, and those who for various reasons—some because of the difficulty involved, and some because they were opposed to *jus cogens* anyway—opted for avoiding any definition altogether. Those who favored a defintion of *jus cogens* offered examples which tended—apart from the principles of peaceful coexistence already mentioned—to be narrow and also perhaps self-evident. Sir Humphrey Waldock, in his 1963 report on the Law of Treaties (Article 13), offered, as examples of violations of *jus cogens,* treaties involving the use or threat of force in contravention of the principles of the United Nations Charter; any act or omission characterized by international law as an international crime; and any act or omission in the suppression or punishment of which every state is required by international law to cooperate.[33] In the General Assembly's Sixth (Legal) Committee there were references to unjust, inequitable, or leonine treaties.[34] In spite of the objection that without examples the whole draft article on *jus cogens* would become unworkable and unreal, the commission finally adopted a formulation without any concrete examples, and this approach is followed in the final Vienna Convention on the Law of Treaties, whose text (renumbered as Article 53) does not differ too substantially from the ILC's draft article. It was, as one of the members of the British delegation at Vienna, Sir Ian Sinclair, remarked, "one of the most crucial and controversial issues" debated at the Vienna conference,[35] and the compromise solution of adopting a skeletal legal category whose content is deliberately left open both recognized the political realities and also, fortuitously, provided an opening to the future by permitting new content to be incorporated easily into the new category, in accordance with the developing juridical conscience in the world community. This is in line with Professor A. von Verdross's argument, advanced in 1966 after publication of the ILC draft articles, that *jus cogens* must denote "all rules of general international law created for a humanitarian purpose," and also the general principles adumbrated in Article 2 of the United Nations Charter.[36]

The term *jus cogens* itself is hardly mentioned in classical Roman law.[37] In the OLC drafting committee, the common lawyers had preferred the English term *peremptory* principles, rather than the French term *(impératif)*.[38] It was agreed that, to avoid misunderstanding, the Latin term *jus cogens* should be maintained in the title or heading of the article, though not used in the actual substantive text itself; and this, in fact, is what was done with the final treaty text, confirming the conclusion that a good deal of the confusion and conflict in the *jus cogens* debate, within the ILC and also at the Vienna conference, had to do with purely technical legal considerations arising from what the Polish jurist Stanislaw Nahlik described as "the particularities of the Anglo-Saxon legal system."[39] A less periphrastic way of stating the matter might be to attribute the Anglo-American intellectual resistance to *jus cogens* to the common lawyer's instinctive aversion to, and inability easily to debate and discuss, abstract general legal notions, whether "general principles of law" or any other. Such intrinsically technical-legal attitudes were reinforced, of course, by highly pragmatic considerations of the vested interest of the major Western powers in the corpus of existing treaties—old treaties, preferably restrictively and not imaginatively reinterpreted today. As the distinguished British jurist Professor Schwarzenberger suggested:

> The unilateral invocation of *jus cogens* as a justification of non-compliance with a burdensome treaty becomes a novel form of restricting the area of the rules governing the principle of consent. . . . It is more likely that the function of this draft article, like the *clausula rebus sic stantibus* before it, will be to serve as a means of undermining the sanctity of the pledged word.[40]

Professor Schwarzenberger's analogy to *clausula rebus sic stantibus* and its potentially (depending on one's particular viewpoint) destructive or liberating consequences as to the burden of old treaties may provide the key to the final position of the Soviet Union at the Vienna conference on the *jus cogens* issue. Where Soviet-bloc jurists provided the main intellectual leadership within the ILC for an opening up of the public policy limitations inherent in any international treaty making, the Soviet Union acquiesced in a final treaty text (Article 53 of the Vienna Convention) that amounts to not too much more than a legal pleonasm. While a treaty is to be void "if, at the time of its conclusion, it conflicts with a peremptory norm of general international law," the definition offered of such a "peremptory norm" in the final Vienna Convention reduces to the following:

> A peremptory norm of general international law is a norm accepted and recognised by the international community of States as a whole as a norm from which no derogation is permitted and which can be modified only by a subsequent norm of general international law having the same character.

In retrospect, it seems a pity that nothing more concrete and detailed was ventured upon in the final Vienna Convention, even if it might have meant the loss of one or more Western signatures—as the British representative in fact threatened. As against the cautious, conservative final text, the Polish jurist Dr. Nahlik points to the quite substantial coincidence of views among the various national representatives as to concrete, substantive law examples of *jus cogens*: various articles of the United Nations Charter (mainly Articles 1, 2, 33, 51, and 103); the principles as to the prohibition of the use of force, nonintervention, peaceful settlement, sovereign equality of states, respect for international obligations; specific low-level categories already recognized under general international law, like the prohibition of slavery and the prohibition of piracy; some "new" international law categories, like the prohibition of genocide and of racial discrimination; "classical" international law principles that have clearly been renewed today, like the freedom of the high seas, and also diplomatic and consular immunities (as then recently codified in the two special Vienna Conventions of 1961 and 1963.)[41] Nahlik is clearly correct, one may suggest, in inducing from this the two prime examples of *jus cogens,* viewed now in terms of substantive law rules: the principles set out in the United Nations Charter and the principles of human rights.[42] If one adds to these the Legal Principles of Friendly Relations (peaceful coexistence) sponsored by the Soviet-bloc countries as their own prime instance of *jus cogens,* which some (including, perhaps, the Soviet jurist Dr. Tunkin) would equate with the principles of the United Nations Charter; and decolonization and national self-determination, which, for Third World countries at least, would amount to the most basic and elementary of human rights in the post-World War II era, we would have a "new" international law category which, if still in many respects inchoate, is capable of infinite generic extension and application, in accordance with emerging world community expectations, in the present era of transition.

Contemporary Trends in Sources of International Law

In an era of very rapid societal change in the world community, it is inevitable that there should be corresponding pressures for rapid changes in the positive international law, to correpond to the societal change. What we have today is a plurality of sources of international law, both "old" sources and "new" ones, with the clear majority political preference in the United Nations being for the newer, "democratic" instruments of law making such as the United Nations General Assembly resolutions or the recommendations of specialized international organizations. There is a concomitant favoring, also, of newer, more informal modes of international law making, without too much regard for their conformity, or otherwise, to the old, preordained, closed formal categories of sources established in the era of dominance of legal positivist thinking on international law. In legal-realist vein, the question now is increasingly likely to be whether the parties regard themselves as being legally bound in concrete circumstances, rather than whether a claimed rule fits into one or other of the long-established legal categories. The doctrinal emphasis thus becomes one of law-as-fact, in the constant tension today between stability and change in the world community and in the positive law rules that are supported to reflect basic societal conditions and demands in the world community.

Looking, for the moment, only to those other (lesser) categories of sources listed, apart from treaties and custom and judicial decisions, in Article 38 of the World Court statute, we find, understandably enough in a world community characterized by a plurality of different social and economic systems, that "the general principles of law recognised by civilised nations" have not played very much part, to date, in concrete problem solving. Where they have emerged, it has tended to be by way of the special (concurring) or dissenting opinion of the intellectual front-runner on the World Court, or else as an isolated avant-garde comment *(obiter dictum)* offered in passing, in the official majority opinion of the court. Perhaps it would have been too much to expect any really comprehensive and systematic recourse to, and application of, the "general principles" before scientific-legal study in depth had provided the necessary comparative municipal law backup of an international *jus gentium* composed of principles and rules common to all main legal systems today, in both adjectival (processual) and substantive law terms. Without any such empirically based comparative municipal law, *jus gentium* foundation, the "general principles" (with the politically offensive—in contemporary space-time terms—suffix "recognised by civilised nations" deleted, as Judge Ammoun very properly suggested),[43] have been reduced to a priori truths of a very high level of generality and abstraction, and capable of becoming operational as international law-in-action only at those very rare moments in time when a wave of moral indignation, transcending all main social and economic systems, has compelled a natural law-style consensus.[44] This happened certainly in the aftermath of the war in Europe in 1945, when the revelations of the mass murder in Nazi Germany brought both the crimes against humanity count in the Nuremberg Tribunal indictments of the Nazi leaders and also the movement, at the world law level, to establish the new international crime of genocide. But the victors of World War II (Soviet and Western) seem to have lost their crusading vigor on behalf of such "general principles" very quickly with the onset of the Cold War years; and even with the succeeding era of détente, it would seem that new international initiatives on behalf of a new international natural law compelling changes in the existing positive law will have to come from Third World political leaders and jurists or not at all. The quest for a definition of the legal extensity of *jus cogens*—so far a legal category without very precise content—could provide just such an intellectual-legal challenge. The absence of definitional limits or any closed list of examples for *jus cogens* means that, as a legal category, it is capable of generic extension and growth, as law-in-the-making.

Teachings of the Most Qualified Publicists: "Dédoublement Fonctionnel"

The "teachings of the most qualified publicists of the various nations,"[45] once a most prestigious form of legal authority in the era of that narrower, Western or European-based world community, have been affected by the marked expansion of United Nations membership without a corresponding development of a corpus of non-European or non-European-derived *doctrines*—on a quantitatively equivalent basis, at least.[46] The classical international law *doctrines* of the late nineteenth and early twentieth centuries remain, thus, too narrow in their particular cultural roots and in their original socioeconomic base to retain their erstwhile prestige and legal authority. At the same time, the "publicists"—the law professors and legal text writers—as a legal skill group have been too generally touched by what Georges Scelle called the *dédoublement fonctionnel* involved in accepting legal briefs or acting as legal advisers to their own national governments in pursuit of national political interests; the legal publicists may therefore run the risk of being seen as being *parti pris* and of losing, in consequence, that reputation for intellectual detachment and political neutrality that characterized the writings of the great text writers in the classical nineteenth century and early twentieth century era of international legal doctrine, with the proliferating new national yearbooks or journals of international law, by the same token, declining into exercises in "regional" legal particularism and the propagation of parochial national legal interests. The publicists turned official governmental legal spokesmen or apologists will, of course, continue to contribute in important ways to the general international law-making process. The difference is that the contribution will no longer be qua publicist, with all the legal authority or prestige of the old *responsa prudentium,* but as part of the ordinary political-dialectical process of development of international law, where contending political protagonists try to maximize their contending national interests, with the final legal solution either one of political accommodation or compromise among the interests involved. Is there a place for the independent legal scholar and jurist of yesteryear?

"Soft" Law and "Hard" Law

Lastly, equity, which might once have seemed to offer hopes for the innovatory updating of old international law customary rules in response to rapidly changing societal conditions in the world community, tended, from the outset of the World Court's jurisdiction (both the old Permanent Court and the new International Court), to be regarded—as it became finally in English legal history—as a series of closed precedents, to be submitted to all the developed skills of logical exegesis without the chance of any inductive judicial leap into the future.

It was no doubt their recognition of the very limited possibilities for utilization of the traditional categories of sources for the purpose of re-making the "old" international law that persuaded the Third World effective majority in the United Nations General Assembly and its specialized agencies to innovate so dramatically where the instruments of international lawmaking were concerned. The "soft law" of the hortatory-style General Assembly resolution has a habit of ending up eventually as "hard" law,[47] in terms of concrete follow-up action both by the Third World countries and by other countries reacting defensively to the international pressures against them. The "wild" custom, originally created by unilateral state action interlocking with similar and reciprocal unilateral state action by other members of the world community over a period of time—such as the original Pacific coast Latin American states' proclamations of a two-hundred-mile fishing zone—starts as a species of particularized or localized "regional" international law gloss on the general international law. It then becomes more generalized as other countries outside the original "region" involved begin to follow suit; and it acquires in the process a revisionist finality and becomes declaratory of new law.[48] In the same way, the consensus accord of an international legal conference that might otherwise sunder if submitted too soon to the harsh test of a formal, recorded vote on a definitive treaty draft, ripens in its own time into a new-style programmatic international law for the future. These have been the practical ways—processes, procedures—in which the "new" international law has tended to emerge, as law-in-action, in response to the new forces in the world community.

5. Law-Making Arenas: Security Council, General Assembly, and International Law Commission

Examination and appraisal of the law-making record of the main international arenas and institutions take us immediately into consideration of the space-time dimension in international law. In temporal terms there is a clear difference between an original, historical, founding fathers' conception of the new United Nations Organization and its special institutions and processes at the particular time of its formation in 1945, and subsequent expectations and preferred demands of its main participants in response to rapidly evolving events in the world community in the succeeding years. In spatial terms there is a clear, observable difference, right from the outset in 1945, in the inherited baggage of national legal doctrine on international organization, of the different main participants, and in what they expect that the new organization should and should not do by way of international law making in present and future crisis situations. Such distinctive, historically received national attitudes on international organization can be expected to be modified through time by way of ad hoc, pragmatic responses to the national interest as seen in particular problem situations; but it is remarkable, nevertheless, how much long-range consistency, historical continuity and predictability remain at the end.

United Nations Membership: "Original Members," "Peace-Loving States"

It is sometimes said that the United Nations was conceived and developed as a universal organization embracing all states without regard to their distinctive ethnic-cultural character or ideology, in a convenient and open-ended neutrality with no subjective value criteria as to admission to membership. Not so. The "principle of universality" of membership is historically supervening postulate, developed by particular main players when it finally came to suit their own interests, and achieved—to the extent that it has been achieved or maintained to date—only as the result of sometimes very difficult and painful low-level political compromises, to which issues of long-range legal principle seem to have been largely irrelevant. In the earliest planning stages the United Nations was projected as a continuance into peacetime of the "wartime alliance against fascism" and an instrument for maintaining the victors' peace, based on "unconditional surrender" of the Axis powers, sketched out on a basis of sometimes cynical political give-and-take and bargaining at Yalta and at Potsdam in 1945, between the wartime Big Three. By definition, the defeated Axis powers did not participate in the new organization, and they were, further, subjected to the punitive "enemy states" clauses expressly inserted into the positive law of the Charter (in Articles 53 and 107) and constituting such extraordinary exceptions to the Charter's main peacekeeping principles and philosophy as to amount to a major "gap" in the law of the charter.

The Charter created, in its Article 3, a category of automatic "founding" membership for states parties to the wartime alliance, insofar as these were the only states invited to participate in the preparatory founding conference in San Francisco in 1945 that actually drew up the Charter, or that had previously signed the wartime Declaration by United Nations of January 1, 1942. Even so, in spite of the apparent objective certainty of this proven wartime "anti-fascist" membership criterion, there was a political flurry at San Francisco over the issue of Polish membership. Two Polish delegations—one the Soviet-sponsored Lublin government, which had been installed by the advancing Red Army, and the other the British-sponsored London government-in-exile—were contenders for the legally guaranteed and automatic Polish seat. The host powers at San Francisco, already politically divided along lines that presaged the subsequent Cold War ideological conflicts, could not agree on the Polish representation, though it was characterized as a "credentials" and not a "membership" problem, and finally resolved with the announcement of the composition of a new "all-party" Polish government on June 28, 1945—too late for the San Francisco Conference itself. Everyone else who could not qualify for entry at the San Francisco Conference would henceforward have to run the gauntlet of admission through the political processes of a double United Nations vote, as stipulated in Article 4 of the Charter—"decision of the General Assembly upon the recommendation of the Security Council." Article 4 established, at the same time, some manifestly highly subjective criteria for membership, which presumably were to govern the General Assembly and Security Council in their actual votes:

> Membership in the United Nations is open to all other peace-loving states which accept the obligations contained in the present Charter and, in the judgment of the Organisation, are able and willing to carry out these obligations.

It was very soon understood that the application of the legal criteria specified in Article 4 to govern membership questions could give rise to serious political conflicts in concrete cases, granted the legal role given to the Security Council in the application of those criteria and the always present possibility, therefore, of a veto by a permanent member of the Security Council stultifying any action. The early years of the United Nations saw the Big Power tug-of-war of the emerging Cold War period translated into direct conflicts over admission of new members. This in turn brought a search for ingenious political and legal methods for breaking the stalemate, involving very often a recourse to what the distinguished Danish jurist Alf Ross called legal "casuistry,"[1] or what the common law jurisprudence has traditionally called pious perjury. In the debates in the Ad Hoc Political Committee of the General Assembly as early as November 1948, in an attempt to circumvent the Big Power veto in the Security Council, which was then blocking action on admission of new states to the United Nations, the delegate of Argentina pointed out that, while Article 4 speaks of a "recommendation" by the Security Council as a condition precedent to General Assembly action, it nowhere states that this must be a *favorable* recommendation. According to argument, the General Assembly could act to admit a new applicant state as a member of the Organization even though the Security Council had not given a favorable recommendation; and the General Assembly should therefore proceed to act upon the International Court of Justice's advisory opinion of May 28, 1948, on Conditions of Admission of a State to Membership in the United Nations, and admit Italy, Austria, Finland, Transjordan, Portugal, and Eire to membership, ignoring the negative attitude of the Security Council, which was based on the exercise of the veto by a single permanent member.[2]

In the International Court's advisory opinion of 1948, the Soviet jurist Judge Krylov, in a dissenting opinion sometimes seemingly written tongue-in-cheek and with sly, sardonic judicial humor, highlighted the political problems inherent in the subjective criteria of membership set out in Article 4 of the Charter.[3] Judge Krylov suggested that Eire was not a "peace-loving" state as stipulated in Article 4(1) of the Charter, because it had not taken part in World War II. Judge Krylov suggested that to be peace-loving implied no mere passive state of mind, as the terms used in the French text of the Charter—*"état pacifique"*—might imply. On the contrary, the English text's "peace-loving," the Spanish text's *"amantes de la paz,"* and also the Russian and Chinese texts had a more active sense, which made "tak[ing] part in World War II alongside the democratic countries" the relevant criterion for admission to membership in the United Nations.

In its advisory opinion on March 3, 1950, on the Competence of the General Assembly for the Admission of a State to the United Nations, the International Court of Justice, in its ruling rendered by a vote of 12–2, necessarily rejected the Argentinian argument. The latter had been deliberately designed to circumvent Big Power obstructive action in the Security Council by interpreting the Security Council "recommendation" as a prerequisite to any General Assembly action so that it could mean any recommendation whatever, favorable or unfavorable.[4]

The majority holding of the International Court was that Article 4(2) "envisages a favorable recommendation of the Security Council and that only." On the other hand, the very strong dissenting opinion of the distinguished Latin American jurist, Judge Alvarez, who dissented, together with Judge Azevedo, from the court majority ruling, appealed strongly for a break from the "precepts of traditional or classic international law, which were established on an individualistic basis and have hitherto prevailed," and for decision on the basis of the "new international law, which is now emerging." With a political prescience that may seem surprising in an opinion rendered as long ago as 1950, Judge Alvarez, who qualifies through his scientific writings[5] as well as his judicial opinions as one of the founders of the "new" international law, asserted the right of the General Assembly to appraise the actual user of the veto in the Security Council, where a state seeking membership in the United Nations obtains the requisite number of votes in the Security Council but would fail for admission nevertheless because of the negative vote of a permanent member of the Security Council. Judge Alvarez suggested that the right of veto is not an unqualified one, but must be interpreted and applied within "proper limits," defined as matters concerning the maintenance of international peace and security, in which, of course, in terms of Article 24(1) of the Charter, the Security Council has "primary responsibility." Judge Alvarez concluded that the right of veto may be abused; and that it is open to the General Assembly to determine this and, if the answer is that the veto has been abused, to proceed with the admission to membership without any recommendation by the Security Council.

In his emphasis upon a teleological interpretation of the Charter derived from continental European civil law, and directed toward what he saw as the then emerging new international "regime of interdependence," Judge Alvarez paralleled in remarkable measure contemporary North American, legal-realist, instrumental or "policy-oriented" approaches to interpretations of the charter, first developed to bypass or circumvent the Big Power veto in the Security Council, which might otherwise legally inhibit the United Nations from acting in concrete problem situations—in the most notable North American–sponsored examples, the Security Council resolutions of 1950 on the Korean question, adopted during the absence of the Soviet Union; and also the Uniting for Peace resolution passed by the General Assembly.[6] While clearly it would, as Judge Alvarez himself noted, be an "absurdity" if any United Nations action under Article 4 as to admission of new members, and a fortiori any action under Article 5 as to suspension from the exercise of the rights and privileges of membership, or under Article 6 as to expulsion from the United Nations, could be frustrated altogether by a Big Power veto, any political corrective action against such a situation would seem to call for the prior political support and authority of a further World Court opinion, addressed to the same general issues as contained in the court's advisory opinion of March 3, 1950, but this time directed particularly to Articles 5 and 6 of the Charter (suspension of rights and privileges of membership; expulsion).[7]

United Nations Charter: Limited Treaty or Constitution?

The intellectual legal debate—in the General Assembly and also within the ranks of the International Court—over the membership issue and the proper juridical approach to be applied both to the interpretation of the criterion of "peace-loving" established in Article 4, and also to the issue of whether the Security Council, in making its "recommendation" as stipulated in Article 4, could and should be required to act legally and strictly in accordance with that criterion, or whether it could ignore the criterion altogether and act arbitrarily on purely political grounds, bespeaks a larger doctrinal-legal conflict over the nature and character of the Charter itself. Is it a limited wartime treaty, under which its state signatories, for certain specific purposes, accepted certain specific limitations to their national sovereignty but no more than that? Or is it something else—as some American jurists, in the first post-1945 flush of idealistic euphoria for a new venture in international organization, argued—a constitution intended to endure for the ages and consequently to be interpreted and applied, in the tradition of the great early Chief Justice John Marshall of the United States Supreme Court, in a broad, liberal, creative spirit, with the constitutional Charter expanding in the process beyond the literal text established by its founding fathers or their original historical intentions, so as to enable it to meet new community demands and expectations hardly envisaged at the actual time of creation of the Charter? The difference is crucial, of course, in terms of the philosophy and also the actual rules of construction and legal interpretation that it implies in concrete cases, and summed up in the antinomy, well known to both civil law and common law jurists and under somewhat similar terminology, between, on the one hand, strict and literal (grammatical or logical) interpretation, and on the other hand, instrumental or policy-oriented (teleological) interpretation.

Not surprisingly, the Soviet Union, which, both at the San Francisco Conference in 1945 (which drafted the Charter) and in the early years of the new international organization with its then very limited (pre-decolonization period) members, faced the prospect of an invariably pro-Western majority voting coalition in the General Assembly and the other main United Nations institutions (including the International Court), took a very limited and restricted, and conservative in doctrinal-legal terms, approach to the nature and character of the Charter. The fact that the Soviet Union, in the between-the-two-world-wars era of international relations, had conceived the then embryonic world organization, the League of Nations, as a prime instrument of the main Western European powers for maintaining the spoils of their military victory in World War I (and one, in any case, loaded against the Soviet Union, which, admitted to membership belatedly, had been expelled only a few years later in 1940, in the last political act of the League of Nations before it disappeared into the maelstrom of World War II) established doctrinal-legal continuity and historical precedents for post–World War II Soviet action. It is another example of that bureaucratic momentum of old ideas in Soviet foreign policy which tends to give it a long-range consistency and predictability as to future decisions and actions that is hardly present, for example, in United States foreign policy. This essentially defensive, political holding-operation approach to the United Nations, and its implications for actual interpretation of the Charter, is strikingly present in the dissenting opinions of the Soviet and Soviet-bloc jurists in the advisory opinion of the International Court of Justice of July 20, 1962, on *Certain Expenses of the United Nations,*[8] a court ruling that, in its majority holding, precipitated the politically controversial and, in the end perhaps politically unfortunate Western-sponsored action to deprive the Soviet Union and France of their votes in the United Nations General Assembly by virtue of Article 19 of the Charter. The then president of the International Court, the Polish jurist, Judge Winiarski, formulated principles of interpretation which revealed dramatically the basic doctrinal-legal differences between East and West of that time, as to the nature and character of the Charter:

> The Charter, a multilateral treaty which was the result of prolonged and laborious negotiations, carefully created organs and determined their competence and means of action.
>
> The intention of those who drafted it was clearly to abandon the possibility of useful action rather than to sacrifice the balance of carefully estab-

> lished fields of competence, as can be seen, for example, in the case of voting in the Security Council. It is only by such procedures, which were clearly defined, that the United Nations can seek to achieve its purposes. It may be that the United Nations is sometimes not in a position to undertake action which would be useful for the maintenance of international peace and security or for one or another of the purposes indicated in Article 1 of the Charter, but that is the way in which the Organization was conceived and brought into being. . . .[9]

Judge Koretsky of the Soviet Union made the same point, but even more succinctly, in his own dissenting opinion in the same case:

> I am prepared to stress the necessity of the strict observation and proper interpretation of the provisions of the Charter, its rules, without limiting itself by reference to the purposes of the Organization: otherwise one would have to come to the long ago condemned formula: "The ends justify the means."[10]

President Winiarski had some further comments in the same case on a different but related point, namely the legal argument that practice, here the detailed record of what actually happened within the General Assembly over the years as, in effect, law-in-action, could effectively create a new legal gloss upon the Charter in supplement to the bare bones of its actual text:

> Reliance has been placed upon practice as providing justification for an affirmative answer to the question submitted to the Court. The technical budgetary practice of the Organization has no bearing upon the question, which is a question of law. . . .
>
> It is . . . difficult to assert, in the case before the Court, either that practice can furnish a canon of construction warranting an affirmative answer to the question addressed to the Court, or that it may have contributed to the establishment of a legal rule particular to the Organization, created *praeter legem,* and, still less, that it can have done so *contra legem*.[11]

The countervailing intellectual legal approach to that of President Winiarski, Judge Koretsky and their colleagues in dissent was that favored by many Western jurists—particularly American jurists in the period of great intellectual energy and creativity in American law schools in the immediate post–World War II years and of great optimism about the future of the United Nations and world organization generally. It is best summed up in Chief Justice John Marshall's dictum: "Never forget that it is a constitution that we are expounding." Such special American and Western doctrinal approaches to international law correspond to the period of American and Western voting dominance in the main political and parliamentary organs of the United Nations, and especially the General Assembly. They achieve their highest flowering and expression, in positive law terms, in the famous Uniting for Peace resolution adopted by the General Assembly in 1950, though they have hardly stood the test of time and popularity in political results-oriented terms.

Security Council: The Permanent Members' Veto

In his report to the General Assembly at the opening of its thirty-seventh annual session in September 1982, the secretary-general of the United Nations, Dr. Javier Pérez de Cuéllar, commented on what he described as the

> reluctance of parties to some conflicts to resort to the Security Council or to use the machinery of the United Nations. The fact is that the Council too often finds itself on the sidelines at a time when, according to the Charter, its possibilities should be used to the maximum. Allegations of partisanship, indecisiveness or incapacity arising from divisions among Member States are sometimes invoked to justify this sidetracking of the Council. We should take such matters with the utmost seriousness and ask ourselves what justifications, if any, there are for them and what can be done to restore the Council to the position of influence it was given in the Charter.[12]

A Special Committee (appointed by the General Assembly by resolution of December 1980) on the Charter of the United Nations and on the strengthening of the role of the Organization, which submitted its report in time for debate at the thirty-sixth annual session of the General Assembly in the autumn of 1981, was even more categorical in its criticisms of the Security Council and in its concomitant call for a strengthening of the role of the General Assembly to fill the gap in decision-making power within the United Nations created by the Security Council's inability to act. Members of the Special Committee suggested variously that "the right of veto had paralysed the Security Council; reforms were needed if the Council was to function effectively."[13] It was also contended that such paralysis "touched upon the credibility of the Security Council and, since criticism of the Security Council's ineffectiveness reflected upon the United Nations, affected that Organisation's image."[14]

There is no doubt of the original historical intention of the founders of the United Nations to confer preeminent decision-making power upon the Security Council. Article 24 speaks in terms of the conferring on the Security Council by members of the United Nations of "primary responsibility for the maintenance of international peace and security," and indeed the peace-keeping sections of the Charter, Chapter VI (Articles 33–38) and Chapter VII (Articles 39–51), can only be understood in the light of such a design. In fact, the Security Council, with its built-in legal power of veto on the part of the five designated permanent members (Article 27), was the principal legal instrument for achieving and perpetuating Big Power influence and control in the new international organization to be set up for the postwar world that was just about to emerge when the San Francisco Conference was being held. The creation of the politically elitist institution of the Security Council, with its special Big Power–controlled, weighted voting system and its practical dominance, in terms of the constitution-as-drafted, over the more nearly popular or universal General Assembly, was an attempt at a constitutional reflection of the political facts of life in the world community at war's end in Europe and Asia in 1945—a wartime Big Three, subsequently expanded, with the inclusion of Nationalist China and liberated France, into a notional Big Five, coolly casting lots for the high and the low of the postwar world soon to be upon them, and without too many moral inhibitions or backward glances at the historical lessons to be learned and political errors to be avoided from past imposed nonconsensual "victors' peace treaties" officially terminating earlier international conflagrations.

But the seeds of the internal decay of the postwar world public order system were already there, even before the Charter had been brought into full working operation, as a result of the Big Powers' failure to resolve basic contradictions inherent in their constitutional blueprint for the future. For a start, the original political premise of a dominant or controlling Big Five acting as a sort of post-Congress-of-Vienna-style "concert of the world" to maintain their war's end consensus as to the desired shape of the postwar world, hardly corresponded to the real facts of power in 1945. Of the postulated postwar Big Five, the United Kingdom had been exhausted economically by her wartime efforts, and failure to mount an effective and rapid postwar economic recovery plan made the United Kingdom, in many respects and for a considerable number of years, the veritable "sick man of Europe." France, for her part, took longer than had been expected to recover from the trauma of wartime occupation and the Vichy episode, the painful path to decolonization and liquidation (sometimes by *force majeure*) of her overseas empire, and the quest for a disciplined, strong executive-based constitutional system and a stable economy. Nationalist China, finally, was soon to be plunged into a full-scale civil war, from which it had neither the military competence nor the political intelligence to extract itself successfully. In short, three of the postwar Big Five, on whom the extraordinary privilege of the legal veto in the Security Council was constitutionally conferred, were only notionally—by legal fiction, if you wish—major world powers; and the constitutional Charter thus had from the outset a certain noncorrespondence with reality. This gap between the law and power became even more potent, in regard to the right of veto of the five permanent members of the Security Council when, with the passage of time over little more than a decade, the defeated enemies of World War II, the Federal Republic of Germany and Japan, had achieved their own economic recovery miracles and also successfully reestablished constitutional government on a firm and continuing basis. It would have been sensible if the United Nations Organization could have been adjusted easily and gracefully to these new political and economic facts of life. Unfortunately, because of the Soviet-American vestigial Cold War stalemate over the "two Germanies" question and perhaps also residual psychological-legal inhibitions still stemming from the hue-and-cry "enemy states" clauses (Articles 53 and 107) of the Charter, it was not until September 1973 that the Federal Republic of Germany could be admitted as a member of the United Nations—in a package deal involving the simultaneous admission of the German Democratic Republic. By one of those extraordinary legal fictions maintained for several decades and more by an effective political combination of residual Western voting strength and also a battle over proceduralisms (the treating of the issue as an "important question" and hence as requiring a two-thirds voting majority in the General Assembly, in terms of Article 18, to change it), Nationalist China (Taiwan) had been artificially maintained with legal credentials of China's sole legal representative in the General Assembly as late as October 1971, even though Nationalist China's military position had become hopeless and it had been forced to abandon mainland China to the Communist populist forces by the end of the 1940s. The rational thing to do in internal, municipal, national constitutional law, when a patent contradiction occurs between constitutional text and political reality, is to utilize the constitutional amending machinery so as to correct the letter of the constitutional charter and bring it into line with the political facts of life. Such an obvious constitutional remedy in relation to the status and condition of the permanent members of the Security Council—by, for example, replacing several incumbents by the Federal Republic of Germany and Japan or even adding to the numbers of permanent members in Article 25—is effectively enjoined by the constitutional requirement of the consent of all existing permanent members to any proposed constitutional amendment, in terms of Articles 108 and 109 of the charter. The contradictions already referred to as to the right of veto over Security Council decisions by any or all of the five permanent members stipulated in Article 23 were certainly brought to the fore in the spring of 1982, when the United Kingdom applied a veto to Security Council initiatives designed to bring an immediate cease-fire in the British-Argentinian armed conflict over the Falklands-Malvinas dispute. Quite aside from the troubling question of the compatibility of a purported legal exercise of a power of veto with the elementary legal principle (known to both common law and civil law systems) of *nemo judex in sua causa,* the raison d'être and political justification of the veto power was always the unwisdom and impractibility of trying to restrain by legal means a major power when its vital interests and security were threatened. It is difficult to believe that either the original historical intent or the spirit of the veto power in the Charter extended to rescuing an erstwhile European imperial power from casual political embarrassment resulting from its failure to dispose in timely fashion (and before the situation had become pathological and politically out of hand) of a vestigial colonial remnant from its empire of yesterday.

The following are to be found among the proposals of the Special Committee of the General Assembly on the Charter of the United Nations and on the Strengthening of the Role of the Organization, for correcting the current malaise in the Security Council:

(i) increasing the membership of the Security Council so as to take more account of the principle of equitable geographical distribution;
(ii) extension of the veto power to one or two non-permanent members, by rotation among the different geographical regions represented on the Council;
(iii) limitation of the veto power itself by increasing the category of "procedural matters" under Article 27(2) to which, by definition, the veto does not apply;
(iv) limitation of the veto power by stipulating, in the Security Council rules of procedure, that the decision whether or not a given matter is procedural should be made by an affirmative vote of nine members of the Council;
(v) a gentleman's agreement among the permanent members of the Council that the veto should not apply to certain categories of matters, for example, the appointment of commissions of enquiry or fact-finding missions or commissions to serve humanitarian purposes;
(vi) amendment of the Council rules of procedure to the same effect;
(vii) a gentleman's agreement among the permanent members, or amendment of Council rules of procedure, to provide that the veto is not to apply in matters relating to the maintenance of international peace.[15]

The first two proposals are designed to offset the political preponderance in the Security Council of the permanent members by increasing the numbers or legal authority of the nonpermanent members. All the other proposals are designed, quite frankly and avowedly, to cut down on the occasions and range of exercise of the permanent members' right of veto under Article 27. Against the Big Power veto, it was argued that it offended against the principle of the sovereign equality of states,[16] which the General Assembly Declaration—of October 1970—of the Principles of Friendly Relations and Cooperation among States had raised to the rank of an imperative principle of contemporary international law, if not *jus cogens;* that the use of the veto by certain permanent members, in cases in which they were themselves party to the dispute, offended against the principle *nemo judex in sua causa*[17] and thereby touched upon the credibility of the Security Council itself and on the image of the United Nations as a whole. To these criticisms and proposals for change the permanent members of the Security Council replied—not altogether accurately, as we have already suggested—that the veto power of the five permanent members stipulated as such way back in 1945 "correctly reflected the international balance of power"; further, that "all proposals aimed at expanding [the Council's] membership were fraught with danger . . ."; that "the careful balance between the two major organs of the United Nations, the Security Council and the General Assembly, would be destroyed . . ."; that the approach of amendment of the rules of procedure of the council "seemed somewhat premature"; that the veto power "corresponded to the reality of the political situation existing in the world."[18] All these, of course, are essentially defensive arguments that hardly go to the merits of the case against the actual record of use of the veto power by the five permanent members over the years since the establishment of the United Nations in 1945. But the arguments of the defenders of the five permanent members' veto power do still reflect the basic political and legal fact of life that the Charter cannot be formally amended so as to cut down on the veto power without the full concurrence of each one of those permanent members—all this as stipulated by Articles 108 and 109 on amendments to the Charter. This means effectively that if the veto power, in its use and abuse, is to be attenuated for the future, this will have to be achieved either by the exercise of self-restraint on the part of individual permanent members—something that is quite unlikely on the past record of their practice—or else by those indirect processes of change common to most municipal, national constitutional systems, namely by developing constitutional custom and convention emerging as glosses upon the actual text of the Charter. This means that if, for example, the normal peace-keeping functions of the United Nations are blocked through interposition of a permanent member's veto, there is every right to turn to alternative law-making methods and processes to fill the gap otherwise created in the Charter system. The legal precedent for such corrective law-making action by other organs of the United Nations already exists and is amply recognized by now in international legal doctrine, having been tested, and then by its manifest political success confirmed, in the Korean crisis of 1950, as a result of direct American and Western political-legal initiative in the General Assembly when the practical paralysis of Security Council action seem to the Western powers to be threatened.

Filling the Gaps in the Charter: General Assembly Legal Innovation

From the outset of the United Nations the power of veto of the permanent members of the Security Council was viewed as basic to the political survival of the Organization. As the Special Committee of the General

Assembly on the Charter of the United Nations and on Strengthening of the Role of the Organisation noted in its report in 1981, it "constitut[ed] the very foundation of the Organization, since it assured the equality of the States of the two major economic systems."[19] As a matter of United Nations law-in-action, that is the key to understanding the operation of the veto in the early years of the United Nations. Viewed not in any textual, literal sense of a five-state oligarchy purporting to function as a form of collective international executive, but in the numerically narrower, East-West intersystemic sense of the postwar world public order system as resting on bipolarity and an interbloc minimum consensus between the two rival superpowers and bloc leaders, on peace keeping, recognition of spheres of influence, and other matters deemed by them to be fundamental in their mutual relations and interactions, the legal power of veto in the Security Council accurately and adequately reflected the basic political facts of life in the world community after 1945. Incorporated as it was in 1945 into the positive law of international relations, it was also a necessary part of those Cold War "rules of the game"—interbloc mutual tolerances and reciprocal understandings—which often seemed to be deferred to more scrupulously by the rival blocs and their leaders than the constitutional law of the Charter itself.

It was this tacit acceptance by both sides, even during the height of the Cold War, of the veto and the propriety of its actual exercise whenever any one of the two superpowers felt—however irrationally or unfairly—that its own special interests were threatened, that explained the anger with which Stalin and his political advisers in 1950, greeted what they regarded as a unilateral Western-promoted violation of the United Nations constitutional "rules of the game" over the Korean crisis.

On January 10, 1950, the Soviet representative in the Security Council submitted a draft resolution proposing that the Security Council should decide "not to recognize the credentials" of the representative of Nationalist China (then the Chinese government-in-exile in Taiwan after its military defeat and withdrawal from the mainland), "and to exclude him from the Security Council." After the rejection of this proposal, the Soviet representative walked out of the Security Council and did not return to it until August 1, 1950, when, under the ordinary system of rotation, the Soviet representative, Mr. Malik, became eligible to be president of the Security Council. In the meantime, however, on June 25, 1950, the Security Council took note of the invasion of South Korean territory by North Korean forces and adopted (in the absence of the Soviet representative) a resolution declaring that the North Korean action constituted a breach of the peace and calling for the withdrawal of the North Korean forces.[20] On June 27, 1950, the Security Council voted to recommend that members of the United Nations furnish assistance to the

Republic of Korea,[21] and on July 7, 1950, the Security Council proceeded to establish a unified military command led by the United States.[22]

When the Soviet representative, Ambassador Malik, returned to the Security Council in August 1950, he criticized the action taken by the Security Council in the absence of the Soviet representative in the following terms:

> Taking advantage of the absence from the Security Council of . . . two permanent members—the U.S.S.R. and China [Mr. Malik meant, here, Communist China]—and dictating its will in the Council to its military and political allies, the United States has hurriedly forced upon the Council a series of illegal and indeed scandalous resolutions, designed on the one hand to cover up United States aggression in Korea and, on the other, to promote to the furthest possible extent the plans for war in Korea and the Far East by involving other States in this war. . . . The resolutions adopted in the Security Council under the dictate of the United States delegation and in violation of the United Nations Charter have no legal force. They were motivated by the desire of the aggressor to cloak and mask his aggression and are in no way directed towards strengthening the cause of peace.[23]

Soviet diplomatic spokesman and jurists reserved even harsher criticism for the General Assembly's law-making innovation immediately thereafter, by way of the famous Uniting for Peace resolution. This resolution was adopted by the General Assembly on November 3, 1950, by a vote of 52–5, with 2 abstentions, and laid down for the first time, as United Nations parliamentary constitutional law, the legal doctrine that exercise of the veto in the Security Council by a permanent member should not, and in strictly legal terms could not, paralyze the United Nations or relieve the General Assembly of the plenitude of its powers under the Charter. According to the text of the Uniting for Peace resolution, Resolution 377 A*(V)*,

> . . . if the Security Council, because of lack of unanimity of the permanent members, fails to exercise its *primary* responsibility for maintenance of international peace and security in any case . . . then the General Assembly shall consider the matter immediately with a view to making appropriate recommendations to Members for collective measures, including in the case of a breach of the peace or act of aggression the use of armed force when necessary, to maintain or restore international peace and security.[24]

In terms of the Uniting for Peace resolution, if the General Assembly is not in session when any such threat to the peace, breach of the peace, or act of aggression occurs, then it may meet in an emergency special session within twenty-four hours of a request initiated either by the Security Council, on the vote of any seven members, or by a majority of members of the United Nations.

In the debate on the Uniting for Peace resolution in the General

Assembly, the then chief Soviet delegate, Andrei Vyshinsky, saw the resolution, correctly, as designed to circumvent the Security Council and its special voting provisions allowing for the Big Power veto. Mr. Vyshinsky interpreted the resolution (again correctly, no doubt) as an attempt to revise the Charter principles dividing legal competence between the Security Council and the General Assembly, and thereby to weaken the Security Council in its special role as a guardian of Big Power interests.[25]

As one looks back on the Korean crisis of 1950 and the legal measures taken in the United Nations to resolve that conflict in accordance with the Charter's principles, it is clear that there was a certain ad hoc quality to the Western tactical legal response. The Security Council action in the summer of 1950, taken in the absence of the Soviet Union, may have been militarily necessary to avert a North Korean takeover of South Korea. But it violated Soviet conceptions of parliamentary constitutional law, for in Soviet legislative bodies an absence is considered equivalent to a negative vote. It also disturbed some Western jurists, to judge by the debate in Western scientific-legal journals over both its legality in Charter terms and its political wisdom.[26] There is little question that the continued absence of the Soviet Union during the crucial Security Council debates and votes authorizing the United Nations military action in Korea resulted from lack of full policy coordination between the United Nations operations division of the Soviet Foreign Ministry and Soviet military planners, rather than from any Soviet conviction that the Soviet Union's absence per se would legally paralyze the Security Council. From the viewpoint of Western legal tacticians, the political-military advantages of action authorized by the Security Council in Korea would have to be weighed against the resultant damage, if any, to the constitutional "rules of the game" as they were then known and observed on both sides in the Cold War struggle.

It was, however, the Uniting for Peace resolution that was potentially more challenging to settled expectations as to the operation of the main United Nations institutions and their relations inter se. One may indeed, with all the advantages of retrospective wisdom, question the whole Western constitutional strategy, and the tactical arguments in support thereof, that led to the Western political sponsorship of the Uniting for Peace resolution. In the light of the collective Western-based military action under the official aegis of the United Nations, already authorized by the Security Council to resolve the Korean crisis, it may be doubted whether the Uniting for Peace resolution did more than serve as an additional legal argument, *ex abundante cautela,* in case the Western-based legal arguments that a Soviet absence from the Security Council did not equal a Soviet veto should fail to win approval in the court of world public opinion.

The sobering political realization that the legal precedent that one creates today to suit one's own conceived political advantage may be successfully invoked against one tomorrow, when it may work the other way, seems to have come to some of the key Western players in the Uniting for Peace resolution strategy only a few years later. In the Suez crisis of October 1956, when the British and French governments acted, (as we now know, collusively) with the Israeli government in a military attack upon Egypt, British and French vetos were immediately applied, in literal accord with Article 27, to defeat a Security Council draft resolution presented by the United States, calling for an immediate cease-fire. The vote in the Security Council was 7 in favor, with 2 Western permanent members, the United Kingdom and France, against, and 2 further Western states (Australia and Belgium) abstaining.[27] The American resolution was lost because of the British and French negative votes in their capacity as permanent members.[28] A second, Soviet draft resolution, calling for the immediate withdrawal of Israeli armed forces from Egypt to behind the established armistice lines, was also lost because of British and French vetos. Yugoslavia then moved a resolution which, taking note of the fact that the British and French vetos had prevented the Security Council from "exercising its primary responsibility for the maintenance of international peace and security," called for an emergency special session of the General Assembly, on the precedent of the Uniting for Peace resolution 377 A*(V)* of November 1950. This Yugoslav resolution was adopted with an identical vote—7 in favor, 2 against, and 2 abstaining—to that by which the original American resolution had failed. This time the negative votes of the two permanent members of the Security Council, the United Kingdom and France, could not prevent the resolution's adoption, the matter of convoking an emergency special session of the General Assembly being treated as a "procedural matter," to which the veto power, in terms of Article 27, did not apply. British and French legal arguments during the course of the Security Council debate on the Yugoslav resolution, purporting to cut down or distinguish the Uniting for Peace resolution as a legal precedent for allowing the General Assembly to act in default of any Security Council action, were summarily rejected in the Security Council, as were subsequent British and French reservations regarding the legality of the Security Council decision.[29] If the British and French governments had thus made a complete legal and institutional volte-face in the space of only six years, from November 1950 to November 1956, from their earlier enthusiastic endorsement of the principle of General Assembly law making to fill the gap in the Charter resulting from Security Council paralysis through Big Power veto, it was too late in the day to turn the legal clock back. Henceforth Western permanent members of the Security Council would have to live with the precedent they themselves had created. The only serious questions relating to the Uniting for Peace resolution as a precedent justifying affirmative peace-keeping action by the General Assembly go not to legal considerations but to purely political ones. Is it wise to invoke General Assembly powers to try to override a veto exercised by either one of the two superpowers in matters that it considers fundamental to its national security and vital interests? Such superpower issues go to the basic premises or *Grundnorm* of the United Nations and its survival as a world public order system. One of the intriguing questions in the Falklands-Malvinas affair and the resulting British-Argentinian military conflict of the spring of 1982, in fact, was the failure of Argentina and more generally Latin American and Third World states to press for a transference of the dispute from the Security Council to the General Assembly, once it became apparent that the Big Power veto, as exercised by the United Kingdom and its surrogate in the dispute, the United States, would paralyze United Nations attempts to achieve an immediate military cease-fire.[30] The explanations for the failure to initiate General Assembly action to fill the resulting gap in the Charter seem political and certainly not legal.

International Law Commission: International Legal Codification, "Progressive Development"

Article 13 of the Charter establishes an obligation of the General Assembly to "initiate studies and make recommendations for the purpose of . . . encouraging the progressive development of international law and its codification." The concept of codification—of reducing hitherto disparate clusters of legal rules and principles, emerging through custom established over the years, to one single comprehensive legal statute—is one dear to civil lawyers brought up and educated in countries that "received" or were influenced by either one of the two great Western European civil codes, the Code Napoléon of 1804 and the Bürgerliches Gesetzbuch of 1900. There is a great deal of scientific-legal writing,[31] and also legal folklore, concerning the nature and quality of the act or process of codification—when it should be attemped and when not, and how best to go about it (whether by expert commission, for example, or by some less structured or formal committee of lay persons). In comparative law terms, the great debate over legal codification centered historically on the bitter early nineteenth-century conflict over the issue of whether to codify the "received" Roman law of the politically still divided German states that remained after the Napoleonic Wars. The German codification debate was initiated in 1814 in a brilliant polemical-legal exchange between two great German legal theorists. Anton Thibaut,[32] impressed by the clarity and rationality and cohesiveness of the then recently enacted Code

Napoléon, which had been introduced into Rhineland Germany and elsewhere in the baggage trains of the Emperor Napoleon's invading armies, had argued the merits of attempting just such an act of codification for the German states, politically scattered as they were under a number of different independent princely rulers. Thibaut's case had all the intellectual attractiveness and prestige of natural law—the statement of legal principles by a rational, legislative act of the German will—and it also had the immediate political appeal of seeming to offer a step toward the eventual goal of German national unity, in municipal, civil law if not yet in international law terms. Yet Thibaut's case was countered very strongly by the legal historian F. K. von Savigny,[33] who marshaled nationalist *(Volksgeist)* legal arguments in his own way to reject the case for any act of codification, at least then and there. Von Savigny's case rested on the issues of timeliness and also expertise. As to timeliness, the contention was that some eras in history, and in this case national history, were "ripe" for codification, and other eras (perhaps the majority of eras) simply were not. One should in particular not attempt to codify while a society is still growing and has not yet reached its apogee of political, social, and economic development, lest a "premature" codification should act as a brake upon the unfolding of its history. On the issue of expertise, the contention was that, in the period of transition in which the German states and Europe as a whole were then living at the close of the Napoleonic era, there simply were not available the professional legal talent and experience and discipline required not only to master all the technical legal detail involved but also to attempt that grand philosophic-legal synthesis necessary to provide ordering principles to guide and direct codification.

The nineteenth-century German debate, limited though it was to codification of the internal civil law, has obvious lessons to offer today as to the attempt at codification of international law. Unless a sufficient societal consensus exists at any time as to the goal values and future historical trends and directions of the world community, ventures in legal codification are likely to be stillborn unless they are limited to narrowly technical questions to which issues of legal philosophy or ideological principle and preference are irrelevant or marginal only. Implicit in this, of course, is the notion that codification is not limited per se (and that it should not be) to the attempt at a mere mechanical restatement of the existing positive law, such as it may be; but that it includes, in the process of collecting, analyzing and sifting such positive law, an element of conscious selection and preference and, in the end, of active participation in changing, updating, and modernizing that law at the same time that one purports merely to record it.[34] The potentially ambivalent, two-faced aspect of legal codification—turning backward to the past and to the legal status quo of yesterday, and at the same time looking forward to the emerging legal principles and rules of tomorrow—is present in Charter Article 13 injunction which links the General Assembly's express codification mandate, in terms, to the "progressive development of international law."

The actual record of the International Law Commission, since its establishment in 1947 and the holding of its first session in 1949, in fulfillment of the General Assembly's codification mandate under Charter Article 13, has tended to be sober, cautious, conservative, and technical, and very, very slow-moving.[35] The commission's work agenda has involved topics sometimes chosen by the commission itself and sometimes referred to it by the General Assembly or the Economic and Social Council. Some of the most impressive commission work has involved the formulation of draft articles to serve as working documents for subsequent international diplomatic conferences convened by the General Assembly for purposes of adopting multilateral conventions.[36] The four United Nations Conventions on the Law of the Sea of 1958—namely, the Convention on the High Seas, the Convention on the Territorial Sea and Contiguous Zone, the Convention on Fishing and Conservation of the Living Resources of the High Seas, and the Convention on the Continental Shelf—are the product of this two-step (technical-legal draft prepared by the ILC, followed by diplomatic-legal enacting conference) approach to international law making, and its signal success contrasts sharply with the frustrations and foot-dragging delays of the subsequent Third United Nations Conference on the Law of the Sea, where the successive diplomatic-legal conferences, throughout the 1970s and up to the end of 1982, did not have the immense technical-legal asset, at the start of their Sisyphean labors, of just such an "expert" draft already prepared by the specialist, technical International Law Commission. Aside from the four Geneva Conventions on the Law of the Sea of 1958, the International Law Commission has never really been entrusted with or become actively interested in those high policy issues of international law where positive law and political ideology tend to exist in symbiotic relationship. Instead, with the International Law Commission's role as generator successively of the substantive-legal proposals that became the four Geneva Conventions on the Law of the Sea adopted in 1958, the Vienna Convention on Diplomatic Relations adopted in 1961, the Vienna Convention on Consular Relations adopted in 1963, and the Vienna Convention on the Law of Treaties adopted in 1969, there evolved what became known as the "classical" method of United Nations progressive development and codification, involving meticulous preparatory work by the International Law Commission, followed by submission to the General Assembly of proposals in the form of a final set of draft articles, and then, finally, convening of a United Nations plenipotentiary conference.[37] But in counterpoint to the undoubted technical-legal advances produced by this "classical" method came the widespread criticism within the United Nations itself that the ILC was overly preoccupied with the petit-point needlework of international law rather than with the imaginative reshaping and rewriting of international law to meet new conditions in international society;[38] and there was also, in the words of the British diplomat and lawyer Sir Ian Sinclair,

> a conviction that the International Law Commission had deliberately eschewed the more controversial and politically charged topics of international law such as the rules regulating the threat or use of force in international relations, non-intervention, self-determination and the peaceful settlement of international disputes.[39]

It was a natural impatience of the "new" countries emerging from the historic process, within the United Nations, of what by the beginning of the 1960s had jelled as the United Nations approach to progressive development and codification of international law that brought demands that the General Assembly itself take up the challenge of legislating in the "new," more policy-charged areas of international law. Specifically, the demand was made that the codification of the legal principles of peaceful coexistence—a project dear to the Soviet government of the day and also a leitmotiv of Soviet and Soviet-bloc foreign policy during the Khrushchev period—should be undertaken by the General Assembly. As it happened, at the opening of the 1960s the General Assembly's Legal Committee, the Sixth Committee, was in the intellectual doldrums, with only matters of relatively small consequence to consider; for although the Sixth Committee continued to act as the body overseeing the work of the ILC, it had made no attempt since the earliest days of the United Nations to assert an independent role in progressive development and codification. During 1960 and 1961, in the discussions within the Sixth Committee on future agenda items, the coexistence codification issue was raised, and it was a natural and inevitable progression from this to the decision by the General Assembly in 1963 to set up a special committee of twenty-seven Member States (later expanded to thirty-one) charged with drawing up a definitive report to serve as the basis for progressive development and codification of what were now renamed (in deference to Western political-semantic concerns) Principles of International Law concerning Friendly Relations and Cooperation among States.[40] The special committee began work in 1964 and submitted its report and draft declaration of principles six years later, and the Declaration was formally adopted and legislated by United Nations General Assembly resolution of October 24, 1970.[41] Whatever the qualitative criticisms that might be leveled at the substantive contents of the Declaration of Principles of Friendly Relations emerging from this General Assembly process, there is no doubt of its political success in bringing to a harmonious conclusion a legal codifying exercise that always had strong ideological undertones and that strikingly presented both the temporal antinomy in contemporary international law—the conflicts between the "old" and the "new"—and also the spatial one—the differences in legal characterizations and basic legal methodology arising as between the main competing "regional" systems of international law, Soviet and Western, of the day. That it was necessary to bypass the International Law Commission, to arrive at the successful Friendly Relations codification seems clear. Sir Ian Sinclair suggests that many states in the General Assembly's Sixth (Legal) Committee felt it undesirable to entrust the task to the ILC in view of the status of its members as "independent experts elected in their personal capacity," which status might be impugned by having a mandate with such a high political content as friendly relations (coexistence).[42] Such a state attitude to the ILC may be a little precious or artificial, given the high politicization of the quinquennial elections to the ILC and also the fact that so many Member States of the United Nations, the superpowers not least among these, have tended to choose as their candidates for the ILC posts foreign ministry legal advisers rather than politically more independent jurists.[43] Where states have reached out to the universities or to private legal practice for their nominees to the ILC, it has tended to be to professors or practitioners already enfeoffed to their own national governments by long years on government retainer and hence touched, in their quality and claims to politically disengaged independent expert status, by what Georges Scelle identified as the *dédoublement fonctionnel.* There is no reason, in principle, why this trend to politicization of the elections and hence, in turn, of the work program of the ILC cannot be accepted and lived with, as it has been in other institutions and organs of the United Nations. It means, however, that any division of the progressive development-codification work load between the ILC on the one hand and special ad hoc committees of the General Assembly or even the Sixth (Legal) Committee can hardly be justified in a priori terms on the basis of any distinction between "technical-legal" and "political-legal" questions. The distinction that has emerged de facto over the years seems due more to the bureaucratic momentum within the ILC of old work habits too painstakingly maintained today, and its institutional incompetence, in consequence, to adapt easily and gracefully to new functional demands.[44]

The ILC, as originally established in 1947, consisted of fifteen members and was able very easily, because of its limited numbers, to function collegially, in plenum or committee of the whole. Further, its original membership was dominated by university professors who, even if their counsel might often have been sought by their own governments in the past, had superb academic qualifications and thought of themselves as legal scholars rather than government spokesmen. One speaks here of J. L. Brierly (United Kingdom), J. P. A. François (the Netherlands), Manley Hudson (United States), V. M. Koretsky (Soviet Union), and Georges Scelle (France). These men imposed research and debate methods, including the making of an ally of time, perhaps more suited to what Judge Manley Hudson in another context called an "academy of jurists" than to yet another political-diplomatic legal arena.[45] The French delegate to the Sixth (Legal) Committee in the autumn of 1981, Guy de Lacharrière, pointed out that the Vienna Convention on the Law of Treaties was not finally achieved until 1969, although its study had been undertaken by the ILC as early as 1949; the Convention on State Succession was achieved in 1978, although referred to the ILC for study in 1962.[46] M. de Lacharrière raised the key question: Is it reasonable, if a problem is important and urgent, to wait such a long time to dispose of its legal solution? He also pointed to a signal contradiction in the contemporary international law-making process, namely the reversal of the roles of treaty-based and custom-based law making. Treaty-based law making, viewed in the immediate postwar years, as the "modern," expeditions approach to law making, is now yielding to custom as the favored instrument for rapid contemporary growth in law. In taking note of the emergence of what has been called euphemistically "instant customary law," M. de Lacharrière remarked that in the labyrinthine discussions and negotiations throughout the 1970s of the Third United Nations Conference on the Law of the Sea, a clear *opinio juris* had appeared and been recognized in spite of the political difficulties in agreeing on treaty texts. Thus the revolutionary notion of an economic zone of two-hundred nautical miles had emerged as customary international law even before any final treaty text, or for that matter draft text, had been adopted. The innovation, in terms of the international law-making process as such, was the institution of a form of parliamentary or legislative system of law making under the guise of the treaty-making process; a process of creation of customary law was thereby grafted onto what was officially a treaty-making process that often seemed interminable.[47]

The debate in the Sixth Committee in the autumn of 1981 concentrated on the issue of "reform" of the ILC to correct what was then identified as its general malaise. The ILC President, Doudou Thiam, noted that the "quasi-totality" of judges of the International Court of Justice were former members of the ILC;[48] and this may in itself be one of the causal factors in promoting a view of the ILC as a mere temporary staging post between participation in the Sixth (Legal) Committee and election to the court. Ambassador Bedjaoui of Algeria spoke, in passing, of the time delays in the ILC and the "transitory phase of adaptation" of international law in which it was engaged, before the dynamic interaction of changing political, economic, and social facts on international relations should bring about its own authentic juridical order reflecting those facts; and he also referred to the contemporary conception of treaty making as the more "democratic" mode of law making, in comparison to custom-based law, in whose origins not all states, and particularly the "new" states, had participated.[49] The *reductio ad absurdum* of the ILC's preoccupation with detail or matters of only marginal importance in an era of transition was seen, however, in its undertaking of a two-year study, with a special *rapporteur* and with six draft articles appearing in 1981 and elaborating specific rules, on the subject of status of the diplomatic courier and the diplomatic bag not accompanied by diplomatic courier.

Disappointingly, the proposals for reform of the ILC that surfaced at the 1981 annual session of the General Assembly focused upon further enlarging its membership, which had already gone from the original fifteen at establishment in 1947[50] to twenty-five in 1961, in stated response to the need to provide a much wider regional representation on the commission. The political problem for the thirty-sixth session of the General Assembly, in 1981, was the fact that no less than forty candidates were nominated for the twenty-five places on the commission,[51] which suggested the need for considerable prior discussion and compromise within each of the various regional and subregional voting groups and informal alliances in the General Assembly, if their voting power was to be fully mobilized and the loss of seats through costly intrabloc feuding and rival candidacies avoided. The elections for the ILC were therefore postponed for some weeks to allow such prior political compromises as to candidates to be made; and it was during this period that a proposal surfaced to increase once more the number of members of the commission, in purported response to the further increase in United Nations membership as a whole. The suggested new increased size varied between twenty-nine and thirty-one, and finally ended up, by common consent, as thirty-four, with the actual quinquennial election of members following immediately on adoption of the "reform." The increase to thirty-four involved formal amendment of the statute of the commission, and at the same time the opportunity was taken to record in positive law form detailed stipulations as to the allocation and reservation of the thirty-four seats on a "regional" basis: eight for nationals from African states; seven for Asian states; three for Eastern Europe; six for Latin America; eight for "Western European or other States"; one further seat to rotate between Africa and Eastern Europe, but to be allocated to Africa in the present elections; and one final seat to rotate between Asia and Latin America, but to be allocated to Asia in the 1981 elections.[52]

The increase in the membership of the ILC seems to have been decided upon with little or no examination of its consequences for the internal working of the commission in fulfillment of its mandate, in terms of Article 13(1)(a) of the Charter, for "the progressive development of international law and its codification." Only one (Western) state seems to have raised the issue of the effects of the proposed changes on the functional integrity of the commission. The amendment to the statute of the commission coincided with publication of a thoughtful UNITAR study which raised searching questions as to the relative decline in performance of the commission since about the time of the 1961 changes in the statute of the commission, including here a marked degree of chronic absenteeism among its ranks.[53] Would increasing the ILC membership correct these errors or simply accentuate the basic problem? The conclusion remains that an opportunity for some more fundamental reexamination of the role of the ILC and the United Nations mandate for the progressive development and codification of international law was lost in the autumn of 1981. In default of any bold and imaginative ILC initiatives in this field, the institutional machinery for the "new" international law will have to be found in alternative law-making arenas—special committees of the General Assembly created ad hoc as with the Friendly Relations (Coexistence) Committee, or existing institutions that have the intellectual inclination and civil courage to chart out a new, modernizing law-making role for themselves, as perhaps with the International Court of Justice in more recent years. The court has its own problems, of course—procedural, adjectival law ones that condition and limit the opportunities of judicial policy making, as well as the better known and debated philosophical queries as to the "legitimacy," in political terms, of judicial legislation. But there is some considerable reaction, too, as to the operational utility of treaty making, and particularly the large, multilateral convention, given the observable attrition rate between adoption of the text of a treaty in a formal diplomatic conference and actual legal ratification of the treaty text thereafter by individual state signatories, and, even more, direct implementation of the agreed treaty text in concrete national legislation.[54] The attrition rate is most marked in regard to those multilateral conventions concerning subjects with a high "political" content, on which different, competing "regional" systems of international law might well differ as to basic values and also as to means of problem solving. The treaties on control of aerial piracy—the Tokyo Convention of 1963, The Hague Convention of 1970, and the Montreal Convention of 1971—come readily to mind.[55] Many states, particularly smaller states caught in the crush of rival ideologies, seem to have found a pragmatic, compromise resolution of their resultant political embarrassment by taking part in the diplomatic conference summoned to codify the law and thus resolve the problem, and even agreeing to the final text of the treaty, but then returning home and dragging their feet interminably as to treaty ratification and treaty implementation in national legislative form. It was precisely this type of dilemma—potentially involving intersystemic, interbloc conflict, though this was much less apparent (in Soviet-Western terms, at least) in the aerial piracy law-making exercises than in some later ones like the Third United Nations Conference on the Law of the Sea—that helped persuade the ILC to keep to its low-profile, technical-legal approach and to eschew the larger, global "scope" issues of international law making.[56] Since all the pressures for change and innovation in international law are there, however, it is certain that they will be directed elsewhere, to other arenas and institutions for law making.[57]

6. Arenas and Institutions: International Court of Justice and Judicial Policy Making

COURT JURISDICTION: *INTER PARTES* AND ADVISORY OPINION

The Charter, in its Article 92, establishes the International Court of Justice as the "principal judicial organ of the United Nations," and also declares the statute of the court (based on the statute of the old, between-the-two-world-wars Permanent Court of International Justice, to which the new International Court succeeded) as "form[ing] an integral part of the present Charter." All members of the United Nations are, according to Article 93 of the Charter, ipso facto parties to the statute of the International Court; and the annual report of the court for 1981–1982, submitted to the thirty-seventh annual session of the General Assembly, noted that the total was then 157, plus Switzerland and two mini- or quasi-states. Articles 36(1) of the court statute provides that the jurisdiction of the court "comprises all cases which the parties refer to it and all matters specially provided for in the Charter of the United Nations or in treaties and conventions in force." Under Article 36(2) of the court statute, the states party to the statute may declare that they "recognise as compulsory *ipso facto* and without special agreement, in relation to any other state accepting the same obligation, the jurisdiction of the Court in all legal disputes. . . ." The annual report of the court for 1981–1982[1] noted that at that time there were forty-seven states which had opted to recognize the compulsory jurisdiction of the court in terms of Article 36(2) of the court statute, though a number of these states had attached reservations to their acceptance of such compulsory jurisdiction, particularly (as with the United States) reservations excepting from such acceptance matters within their own domestic jurisdiction as they themselves might choose to interpret that. A potentially fecund source of jurisdiction for the International Court remains the advisory opinion jurisdiction established by the Charter, Article 96:

> 1. The General Assembly or the Security Council may request the International Court of Justice to give any advisory opinion on any legal question.
> 2. Other organs of the United Nations and specialised agencies, which may at any time be so authorised by the General Assembly, may also request advisory opinions of the Court on legal questions arising within the scope of their activities.

The annual report of the court for 1981–1982 noted that, in addition to the General Assembly and Security Council, the list of United Nations organs and specialized agencies at present legally authorized to approach the court for advisory opinions included the Economic and Social Council, the Trusteeship Council, the Interim Committee of the General Assembly, the Committeee on Applications for Review of Administrative Tribunal Judgments, and specialized agencies such as the ILO, FAO, Unesco, International Bank for Reconstruction and Development, International Monetary Fund, and others.

Comparative "Regional" Attitudes to International Adjudication

The central dilemma in international adjudication in our times concerns the dwindling away of the effective working jurisdiction of the International Court of Justice since its inauguration in 1946, in comparison, certainly, with the rich years between the two world wars, when the old Permanent Court of International Justice was in operation. Part of the explanation for the latter-day crisis in the work load of the International Court—too few cases, too few client states—is indeed to be found in the comparison between the two periods of international adjudication, that of the "old" court and that of the "new" court. For the old Permanent Court was in operation in that earlier, European "family compact" era of international organization when the League of Nations, as the embryonic world government of the time, reflected the interests and aspirations of the politically dominant Western European states that had imposed the Treaty of Versailles of 1919. Judicial settlement of disputes, in this context, reflected the special cultural attitudes and intellectual outlooks of Western European society in the golden years of its political, military, and economic power; and the notion of "judicializing" international conflicts and their concrete resolution had a special appeal, therefore, in what was an essentially homogeneous, limited, special legal community, whose key members shared the same essential values. The expansion of the world community after World War II to take in—particularly as decolonization and national self-determination began to be achieved on a near worldwide basis—so very many new, non–Western European, Afro-Asian states presaged a decline in the erstwhile prestige and authority and popularity of the court-based approach to conflict resolution, even though so many of the "new" states had, for their own part, very substantial "received" European (whether Anglo-Saxon common law, or French or German civil law) legal traditions. It was not only a matter of basic legal-institutional method and process involved in the concept of judicial settlement of disputes, but also one of the substantive legal values and value choice thought likely to emerge if the fundamental political-legal conflicts of the post–World War II era were referred to the courts for arbitrament.

We have already noted the Soviet opposition to any expanded role for the International Court within the United Nations system, and *a fortiori* to any form of judicial legislation or judicial policy making for the future. Such Soviet attitudes toward the World Court, which have the merit of consistency and avoidance of any purely ad hoc response in pursuit of temporary national advantage in the instant case, stem historically from pre–World War II Soviet doctrinal positions in regard to the old Permanent Court and to the League of Nations as a whole, and reflect that defensive "holding operation" style of approach that the Soviet Union has always felt to be appropriate for itself and its political allies in their approach to international organization, in view of their more or less permanent minority voting situation in each and all of the main international organs and specialized agencies. But the Soviet special position on the International Court also reflects purely internal, municipal Soviet legal doctrinal writings on "Western" separation-of-powers concepts, denying, as "undemocratic" and as an infringement of the prerogatives of the other, "popular", elected organs of government, any asserted power of constitutional review or constitutional control on the part of the judiciary in relation to the executive and legislative branches of government. In *Certain Expenses of the United Nations* in 1962.[2] as we have noted, the two Soviet-bloc judges on the International Court, President Winiarski and Judge Koretsky, took care to insist that the United Nations Charter was not a constitution, to be interpreted and applied in any broad, creative, expansive way, but rather a multilateral treaty, in terms of which the contractual parties had given up some of their own powers for certain quite limited purposes but no more, and which was therefore to be treated and interpreted restrictively, without regard to the claimed "purposes" of the Organization or, for that matter, to supervening practice of the Organization, whatever it might be. The Soviet-bloc approach to the role—strictly, non-role—of the International Court in the international law-making process thus denies any form of judicial policy making and certainly any form of teleological interpretation—even of the style recommended by Gény at the close of the nineteenth century as a necessary, alternative approach to "grammatical" and "logical" interpretation of the Napoleonic Civil Code if the civil law were to maintain its historic quality of a "living law" in constant relation to changing societal needs. The comparisons with the analytical positivists or "black letter" lawyers of the English Common Law are clear, and it is not by accident, therefore, that Judge Winiarski could feel free to join with the court president, Sir Percy Spender, and that great classical common law jurist Sir Gerald Fitzmaurice in making the bare majority—8–7, on the second, tie-breaking vote of President Spender—in *South West Africa, Second Phase* in 1966,[3] whereby the court denied to the two complainant states legal standing to obtain a decision. The states in question—Ethiopia and Liberia—were protesting the white-minority-governed Republic of South Africa's continued apartheid administration over the former German colony and later League of Nations mandate over Namibia (South West Africa). Since the court, by an 8–7 majority, had earlier, in 1962,[4] conceded to the same two states full legal standing to bring the suit in the first place, the purported legal distinction in 1966 that their legal standing did not extend to receiving judgment would have baffled the ingenuity of the medieval schoolmen. It says a good deal for Judge Winiarski's sense of fidelity to law and consistency in the application of his legal principles that he was prepared to participate, as the logical consequence thereof, in a majority judgment that clearly ran counter to the "new" imperative principles of international law—decolonization and national self-determination—so actively sponsored by Soviet-bloc delegates in all the main political arenas of the United Nations since its founding in 1945. *South West Africa, Second Phase* in 1966 was a watershed decision for the International Court, and for many external observers of the court's work a political disaster—one of the court's "great, self-inflicted wounds," as Chief Justice Charles Evans Hughes once said of the American Supreme Court decision in the *Dred Scott* case, which hastened the onset of the American Civil War. It confirmed, in one single blow, all the suspicions and fears—however ill-founded they might be in fact or as a matter of historical record—of the "new" Afro-Asian countries in the General Assembly that international organization as a whole and the court in particular were politically loaded in favor of maintenance of the political-legal status quo. The angry denunciations in the General Assembly that the court's 1966 judgment was a "white man's" decision, rendered by a "white man's" tribunal, were only partly assuaged by political action in the General Assembly itself, whereby in October 1966 a resolution was adopted, by 114 votes to 2, with 3 abstentions, declaring the Republic of South Africa's original League of

Nations–conferred mandate to administer South West Africa to be legally "terminated," and also declaring that the territory now came under the "direct responsibility" of the United Nations. The political backlash to the court's 1966 decision also brought a Security Council vote in 1970 to request an advisory opinion from the court on the "legal consequences for States of the continued presence of South Africa in Namibia (South West Africa)," and thus a rare second chance for the court to retrieve a prestige and authority already severely compromised politically, if not indeed lost, by the 1966 decision. But the political damage had been done already, and it could not have come at a worse time for the court in terms of an opportunity lost for encouraging the wave of newly decolonized states entering the United Nations in the late 1950s and throughout the 1960s to bring their disputes and conflicts to the court for peaceful settlement. It would prove to be a long and difficult road back for the court, in spite of courageous and avant-garde law-making decisions like that rendered by the court in 1971[5] on the Security Council request of 1970 for advisory opinion on *Namibia* (South West Africa).

Election of Judges: Political-Legal Factors.

In some senses, of course, the "new" countries may have exaggerated the inbuilt quality of permanence within the court itself, as to basic conceptions of the judicial decision-making role in great political-legal causes célèbres and also of the degree of respect and deference to be accorded by the judges to the existing corpus of "old" or "classical" international law. More, perhaps, than any other final tribunal, national or international, of our times, the court can be made responsive to fundamental change in societal conditions within the world community (including that marked expansion of the membership of the United Nations that made it more nearly "representative" or universal by the end of the 1960s) through the processes of selection of its judges. The constitutional legitimacy of the International Court as a law-making institution flows from the election of its members by absolute majority vote in the General Assembly and in the Security Council, sitting separately—as stipulated in Article 10(1) of the court statute. The stipulation for the double majority, General Assembly and Security Council, gives some weighted voting advantage to the five permanent members of the Security Council insofar as, if they were ever to remain united, they would amount to a one-third voting bloc in the council. But, contrary to popular impression, the permanent members have no right of veto in Security Council elections of judges, Article 10(2) providing expressly that the Security Council vote is to be taken "without any distinction between permanent and non-permanent members of the

Security Council." There is thus absolutely no power on the part of the permanent members, acting individually or collectively, legally to block election of the candidate from any state or legal or ideological system, or a fortiori to impose the election of their own national or nationally favored candidates. World Court elections are thus subject, like any other United Nations elections, to the skills of coalition building and the political give-and-take and bargaining inherent in any composite, compromise list of agreed candidates. The fact that four of the five permanent members of the Security Council (the People's Republic of China excepted) have managed to maintain continuing national representation on the International Court since its inauguration in 1946, through political success of their candidates in the periodic elections of the judges, is due to a number of different factors. The virtually unanimous endorsement of the official Soviet and American candidates, over the years is clearly due to the acceptance by all Member States of the basic political fact of life of post–World War II international organization, namely the Soviet-American balance and the need for an effective presence of both superpowers in all main United Nations institutions and agencies. As to the two remaining permanent members of the Security Council, the United Kingdom and France, their unbroken record in maintaining their official candidates—though with sharply declining majorities in the most recent elections in the case of the United Kingdom.[6]—can no doubt be attributed to the high technical-legal qualifications of their candidates, and perhaps also to the continuing bureaucratic momentum of past General Assembly–Security Council habits of voting quasi-automatically for permanent members, irrespective of whether they were the two superpowers or simply the two other European vestigial survivals of the wartime Big Five.

The triennial elections to the court, with a third of the membership retiring at each election, have seen the emergence of complicated but politically sophisticated customs or conventions as to the division and allocation of the fifteen seats on the court on a "regional"—mixed legal-systemic, linguistic, political-ideological, and geographical—basis, with the only real contests being internal ones within each of the "regions" as to the filling of the particular regional seat involved; or, more rarely, interregional conflicts calling for marginal readjustment in the exact numbers of seats to be awarded to one region rather than another under the "gentlemen's agreement" on voting. With the belated seating in the United Nations, in 1971, of the People's Republic of China, it seems certain that the customary "Chinese" seat on the International Court will be restored whenever the People's Republic decides to present a candidate, this both because of the People's Republic's quality as a permanent member of the Security Council and also the political fact of life of China's political status today as a world power. But the seating of a

Chinese judge will mean, on a fifteen-member tribunal, loss of a seat for one of the existing "regional" groups. Should the Chinese seat be created out of the existing Asian regional group, or out of the Latin American group, or out of the Western European group (which already includes Japan)? The one thing that seems clear is that the African regional group can hardly be called on to make the sacrifice. Much behind-the-scenes political maneuvering and a good deal of political anguish can be expected when the existing "gentlemen's agreement" on voting has to be rewritten to take account at least of the Chinese fact. It is not impossible, of course, that the International Law Commission precedent of simply increasing the number of judges on the court will be resorted to, to resolve the dilemma of choice. Whatever the merits, on purely technical and institutional grounds, for reexamining the composition and internal organization of the court, including its members, it would be a pity if purely expedient considerations were to produce such a short-range political solution, without any prior consideration of its effects upon the court in terms of long-range efficiency and work capacity.

The filling of casual vacancies on the court arising from the death or retirement of an incumbent judge before the end of his regular nine-year term offers the occasion, since usually only one vacancy is involved, for ordinary "regional" considerations to be influenced or overwhelmed by larger East-West or even North-South conflicts intruding into the electoral processes. There has been a custom or convention—it is only that, and not a positive law requirement—of replacing a deceased or retired judge by another of the same nationality, to fill the unexpired judicial term still remaining. But with almost 150 Member States of the United Nations now competing at the regular triennial election for the five seats open on the fifteen-member court, a contemporary reinterpretation of that custom or convention might suggest filling the vacancy from the same "region" as the judge being replaced, but not necessarily by a judge of the same nationality. All these considerations came to the fore early in 1982, with the election to fill the vacancy on the court created by the death of Judge El-Erian of Egypt in late 1981. In "regional" terms—which sometimes offer the advantage of not being too precisely, and hence too rigidly, defined—the seat was an Arab, Islamic seat, with the extra subregional refinement of being North African and also involving a country with a French civil law, internal municipal law base. The official nominations for the election saw candidates from Egypt itself, Algeria, Libyan Arab Jamahiriya, Benin Madagascar, and Israel,[7] but most of these were purely honorific nominations, and the actual choice soon narrowed down to one between the Egyptian candidate (nominated by twenty-five countries, including, most prominently, the United States), and the Algerian candidate (nominated by thirty-five countries, predominantly Third World and headed by Brazil, Mexico, Saudi Arabia, and Yugoslavia, but also including France and the Soviet Union.[8] The behind-the-scenes lobbying was intense, and so the characterization of the contest as a North-South one, with the United States and West-backed candidate losing out to the Third World candidate, is no doubt a fair one, in spite of the obvious crosscurrents presented by the French and other politically farseeing Western states' support for the Algerian candidate, Dr. Bedjaoui. The result of the partial election of March 1982 may have served as an index of the increasing political sophistication within the United Nations ranks as to the affirmative law-making role of the International Court and, in consequence, the relevance and propriety of inquiry into a judicial candidate's legal values and his degree of commitment to the principle of the progressive development of international law. It also indicated that, in a contest for a particular seat from the one regional bloc on which compromise has not been reached by diplomatic arrangements within the bloc before the public stage of the General Assembly-Security Council vote, all things otherwise being equal, the intellectually and professionally more qualified candidate is likely to prevail. Dr. Bedjaoui of Algeria, who was elected to the court, had already won his spurs internationally—as a distinguished academic jurist and writer and as a professional legal diplomat—in the universities, and as his country's representative to Unesco and in the United Nations General Assembly's Sixth (Legal) Committee and in the ILC.

The Judges as Legal "Honoratiores"

The different "regional" attitudes to the nature and character of the International Court and of the international adjudication in general, and the impact on them of the time factor and the shifting balance of political forces within the United Nations are amply reflected in the distinctive national approaches to selection of official candidates for election to the court and to the support of candidates from other states.[9] Article 2 of the court statute speaks of a

> body of independent judges, elected regardless of their nationality from among persons of high moral character, who possess the qualifications required in their respective countries for appointment to the highest judicial offices, or are jurisconsults of recognised competence in international law.

If the principle of judicial settlement of disputes be viewed as an ethnocentrist, distinctively Western one, it is, within the Western legal family, even more American than Western European. One remembers the enthusiastic, perhaps somewhat simplistic, American-based "world rule of law" campaign for extension of the jurisdiction of the World Court, launched in the immediate postwar years, notwithstanding the basic political inconsistency that the United States government, by reason of its own self-defining "domestic jurisdiction" exception to its acceptance of the compulsory jurisdiction of the International Court under Article 36(2) and (3) of the court statute, had created a major effective legal gap in the court's jurisdiction and any hopes of establishing it, as law-in-action, on a nearly universal basis. As the pro-Western automatic voting majorities in that smaller United Nations of the late 1940s and early 1950s have disappeared into history, the deemed "politicization" of the main United Nations organs, the Security Council and General Assembly has brought about a revision, albeit in a somewhat belated way, of dominant attitudes to the court and to international adjudication. The United States and other Western countries seem to be moving more and more toward basic Soviet and Soviet-bloc positions on the court and its potentialities for radical novation of international law under the impulse of Third World-initiated legal processes decided by new and regionally more representative court majorities, in which Third World judges will increasingly predominate. This has meant more and more a Western defensive or "holding operation" conception of the court, paralleling that of the Soviet Union, and a tendency, again paralleling that in the Soviet Union, to nominate professional foreign ministry lawyers or longtime advisers, rather than the "independent judges" or "jurisconsults" perhaps too idealistically envisaged under Article 2 of the court statute. Many of these same foreign ministry professionals and advisers will, of course, be distinguished jurists in their own right, and in fact some of the intellectually most sparkling members of the court in recent years, from both East and West, fall into this category. But to have the two superpowers and their supporters apply such a frankly realistic political approach to selection of candidates for the court hastens the disappearance of the legal fiction of yesteryear that judicial adjudication is inherently neutral in substantive, philosophical terms, and that international law itself can be reduced to Rudolf von Ihering's "heaven of juridical concepts," remote from social and economic reality. The de facto operation of the international law-making processes in international diplomatic conferences, in the United Nations General Assembly, and in its specialist Sixth (Legal) Committee, as a form of resolution of competing interests pressed by contending states according to their own special political, social, and economic advantage, warrants in measure the increasing conception of the path to the court as a progression from Sixth (Legal) Committee to the ILC and then on. What Max Weber called the legal "honoratiores" will thus have changed from the academic-legal jurisconsult, more nearly intended by the court statute, to the professional-legal jurist who has refined his foreign ministry experience by some substantial direct United Nations experience. It is another unconscious historical irony that the Third World pressures for remaking the International Court into a more affirmative law-making posture, to which these changes in judicial selection criteria in the West respond, have drawn a principal intellectual inspiration from the American internal, municipal constitutional law teachings of the 1940s and 1950s on judicial activism and judicial legislation for societal change, within the United States Supreme Court.

Law and Policy: Judicial Self-Restraint and Judicial Activism

The International Court reflects, in fact, not less than the United States Supreme Court or other major final appellate tribunals of our times, the polar doctrinal positions as to the role of courts in community policy making summed up in the antinomy of judicial self-restraint and judicial activism. The distinction, under other names, is well known to both common law and civil law schools of legal interpretation—the difference, in common law terms, between strict "black-letter law," analytical, positivist approaches to legal construction, on the one hand, and purposive, policy, sociological approaches on the other; the difference, in civil law terms, between grammatical or logical interpretations which try to hew to the words of a charter, code, or statute as written, and teleological interpretations which look rather for a larger social purpose behind the original legislative formulation. In terms of the International Court and its actual practice, the differences in basic judicial approaches are better represented less as a strict dichotomy than as a philosophical-methodological continuum, with one judicial approach shading off into another and with certain intellectual cross-currents created by special procedural, adjectival law factors present in the court's jurisdiction. The International Court also started off in 1946 with a substantial backlog of analytical positivist, jurisprudence-of-concepts style of case law precedents inherited from its predecessor, the old Permanent Court, which, with a relatively stable and ideologically homogeneous group of states adhering to its jurisdiction in the limited "West European"-dominated world community of that era, could afford to limit itself to a strict and literal interpretation, in which policy elements were consciously subordinated by the judges and indeed hardly sought or welcomed by the parties invoking the court's jurisdiction in the first place.

South West Africa, Second Phase,[10] rendered in 1966 by the 8–7 majority, was, as already noted, a watershed decision for the court, looking both backward to the old and honorable analytical positivist tradition, and also forward to the newer policy imperatives of the progressive development of international law in an approaching era of fundamental political, social, and economic change in the world community. Though heralding the end of the old, the *South West Africa, Second Phase* opinion of the court is a masterly exercise in the classical self-styled neutral approach to judicial interpretation, as befits its distinguished authors, the court's president, Sir Percy Spender of Australia, and the British judge Sir Gerald Fitzmaurice, whose hand is obvious in the reasoning and drafting of the opinion. The criticisms of the opinion of the court in *South West Africa, Second Phase* go not to its intrinsic legal logic, which can hardly be faulted, but to legal logic unsparingly pursued to the bitter end, to the absolute exclusion of policy in law and indeed everything else—an exercise in logic and not in life!, as the British political theorist Harold Laski remarked in another context.

After this politically charged and controversial decision, which brought a great wave of criticism of the court in the General Assembly, the court began its difficult journey back into public political approval and confidence. The way back had been foreshadowed already in the 1966 decision itself, by the dissenting opinions, particularly that of the American Judge Philip Jessup,[11] which, fulfilling the traditional role of a judicial dissent as an appeal to the future in law, ventured unashamedly into natural law in its appeal to the "views and attitudes of the contemporary international community" and the "accumulation of expressions of condemnation of Apartheid . . . proof of the pertinent contemporary international standard," in order to reject the Republic of South Africa government's case and to strike down governmentally practiced racial discrimination. Judge Jessup, in correctly sensing winds of change in the world community, functioned in the full spirit of judicial liberal activism, while the court majority, in contrast, practiced an extreme form of judicial self-restraint in the face of a burning social issue on which the world community, through its main parliamentary organs, had made its own moral position quite clear and categorical from the early 1950s onward. But it was the dissent by Judge Jessup, rather than the more orthodox majority opinion of the court of the 1966 decision that served as the inspiration for the International Court's volte-face five years later, in *Legal Consequences for States of the Continued Presence of South Africa in Namibia (South West Africa)* (1971).[12] There, by lopsided majorities of 12–2 and 11–4 on the substantive legal issues, the court reached out for the concept of intertemporal law and the time dimension in legal interpretation to conclude that, whatever the character in 1919 of the League of Nations mandate then given to South Africa over the former German colony of South West Africa, progressive, generic interpretation dictated that such a mandate be regarded as evolutionary rather than static, particularly in respect to that "sacred trust of civilization" that mandates connoted. So far from being a closed body of principles that had become fixed once and for all in 1919, when the League of Nations system came into force, the notion of mandate was something rather more dynamic, lending itself to contemporary reformulation in accordance with changing societal conditions and expectations. Specifically, the court found that fifty years of important historical developments since 1919

> leave little doubt that the ultimate objective of the sacred trust was the self-determination and independence of the peoples concerned. In this domain, as elsewhere, the *corpus iuris gentium* has been considerably enriched, and this the Court, if it is faithfully to discharge its functions, may not ignore.[13]

If the court majority in *Namibia (South West Africa)* in 1971 thus embraces openly for the first time judicial activism and the cause of judicial law making in general, the advisory opinion majority holding is not without its own built-in antithesis—specifically a strong dissenting opinion by the British judge Sir Gerald Fitzmaurice, who quoted with approval comments by the American law professor and one-time judge on the old Permanent Court, Manley Hudson,[14] on the necessity of the court to keep "within the limits which characterise judicial action," especially when exercising the advisory opinion jurisdiction. The court, in Manley Hudson's words as adopted by Judge Fitzmaurice, must always be at pains to act "not as an 'academy of jurists' but as a responsible 'magistrature.' "[15]

Court in Transition: Contradictions and Conflicts

After *Namibia (South West Africa)* in 1971, the International Court majority seemed prepared to move boldly and chart out new legal frontiers, without too many inhibitions left over from its earlier "strict and complete legalism" approach. The practical problem, however, was that it had virtually no cases in which to expound and develop its new liberal activism. The "new" countries, still distrustful of the court after *South West Africa, Second Phase* of 1966, and slow in taking note of the political changes already brought about by the triennial election processes to the court's membership, were not yet prepared to bring their problems to the court for judicial solution; while the "old" countries, who were politically more sensitive, perhaps, to the intellectual transformation already under way on the court in terms of basic legal philosophy and legal thinking, seemed less and less inclined to venture their legal fortunes on a politically more and more uncertain and changing majority coalition within the court's ranks. The result was a few cases, widely scattered in time and often with flawed procedures—not a very happy base on which to build new experiments in judicial policy making.

Nuclear Tests (Australia v. France; New Zealand v. France),[16] which arose in the early 1970s, might have seemed to present a glorious ready-made opportunity for the court to place itself on the side of the angels and to participate, if not indeed lead, in the progressive development of the new international law for the protection of the natural environment. Newly elected Socialist administrations in Australia and New Zealand, in spite of several decades of continuingly uncritical and enthusiastic cooperation in American and British nuclear test explosions in the South Pacific region on the part of their predecessor right-of-center governments, moved in the International Court to try to halt high-altitude nuclear test explosions in the South Pacific launched by the French government. The court's approach to decision on the case was complicated procedurally by the French government's denial, in legal terms, of the court's jurisdiction and its consequent refusal to participate in the proceedings before the court or to present oral argument (though it did issue a White Paper corresponding in many respects to a written *factum*).[17] The court's approach to preliminary jurisdictional objections in the past has resulted from precedents and its own decisions, the matter not being elucidated in the court statute itself. One approach, and that invariably applied by municipal, national tribunals, both common law and civil law, has been to regard the preliminary jurisdictional objection as a prior question that must be answered in favor of jurisdiction before the court can venture on to the merits and substantive law issues—in the court's own jurisprudence, the *Mavrommatis* precedent.[18] A looser, more facultative approach has been to permit simultaneous proceedings on the prior jurisdictional issue and on the merits, on the pragmatic argument that sometimes these two questions would be inextricably intertwined and incapable of separation.[19] The intellectual dilemma for the court had seemingly been resolved in its 1972 rules—new Article 67(1) (6) and (7)—which lays down that the court must resolve the question of its jurisdiction before entering upon the merits, and that as to other (nonjurisdictional) preliminary objections going to other grounds, the court should either uphold the objection, reject it, or declare that it "does not possess, in the circumstances of the case, an exclusively preliminary character." If this latter decision is taken, the court then enters upon the merits, and the preliminary objection, now ruled to be not "exclusively preliminary," simply becomes one among the various defenses to be invoked by the respondent.

The preliminary jurisdictional question complicates the analysis of the International Court's two judgments in *Nuclear Tests*—the 1973 order granting interim measures of protection, which was decided by an 8–6 majority (with an official opinion of the court and four other, individual majority opinions, and four individual dissenting opinions); and the 1974 final judgment, which ruled that the issue had become moot (and therefore would not need to be decided on the merits), which was decided by a 9–6 majority (with an official opinion of the court and four other, individual majority opinions, and one joint dissenting opinion signed by four judges, and two other, individual dissenting opinions). The plethora of individual judicial opinions, (specially concurring opinions on the majority side and dissenting opinions on the other) present in the two judgments of 1973 and 1974, plus a complete change in the composition of the judicial majorities between the two cases, point to profound philosophical disagreements, quite apart from any incidental personality clashes, within the ranks of the court. Though the preliminary jurisdictional issue is a complicating factor in those internal court disputes, since it constitutes procedural cross-currents to the substantive law differences, it does not appear that the final judgment in 1974, which addresses itself to questions essentially of procedural, adjectival law, is limited in its implications to that issue. In a significant judicial role reversal, some of the more liberal activist-inclined members of the court combined to make the final majority in 1974, ruling the issue to have become moot and so passing up the opportunity for ruling on "new" international law substantive issues otherwise dear to them. The key judicial holding, in the final judgment in 1974, was that the issue had become moot with the unilateral declarations of intention by the French president and by French ministers, indicating the termination of any further above-the-ground nuclear tests by France in the South Pacific. This particular judicial holding was at once innovative in terms of legal doctrine and conservative, in that it applied the doctrine of judicial self-restraint and avoided ruling on substantive policy issues where lesser, procedural issues could provide a solution. The dossier in *French Nuclear Tests* was not completely satisfactory for purposes of a major policy ruling by the court. The key complainant, Australia, then seeking the court's aid in developing and applying "new" international law principles of environmental protection to strike down the French government action, did not come into court "with clean hands" in view of its past association and endorsement (albeit through a different government) of similar American and British government action. There was also a not altogether explained incident involving an unauthorized leak by the Australian prime minister of the court's interim ruling of 1973, prior to its official release by the court. The two judgments in *Nuclear Tests,* of 1973 and 1974, are better seen, it may be suggested, as examples of the trial-and-error testing inherent in ventures in judicial law making on the part of courts not as yet fully experienced or confident in that domain. The prime lesson from *Nuclear Tests,* 1973 and 1974, therefore, would be that judicial activism requires, for its effective exercise, a proper procedural, adjectival law base and a dossier uncluttered by matters extraneous to the key policy choice involved.

Both these elements—proper procedural base and uncluttered dossier—were present a year later in the *Western Sahara* case of 1975.[20]

Once again the court's judgment was accompanied by a plethora of individual judicial opinions, and this in a case where the verdict was reached by lopsided judicial majorities. However, in *Western Sahara* the openings of judicial activism were patent and unequivocal, perhaps because the occasion—a conflict between "old" international law categories invoked by a European "colonial" power, and "new" international law principles invoked by Third World "decolonized" countries—presented the opportunity for a clear-cut policy choice, while *Nuclear Tests,* as a dispute between wholly Western postindustrial "colonial" societies, did not. The issue of the legal title to former Spanish colonies in the Western Sahara (Rio de Oro and Sakiet El Hamra) provided, in fact, the opportunity for a far-reaching reexamination and updating of classical international law rules on the acquisition of territorial title by colonization, in respect to lands previously occupied by non-European indigenous or aboriginal peoples *(terra nullius).* The issue came to the court by way of a United Nations General Assembly request for an advisory opinion. The colonial power, Spain, in anticipation of United Nations action, had announced a decision to hold its own referendum within the colony; this move was viewed by the neighboring Third World countries and potential successor states—Morocco, Mauritania, and Algeria—as a clever stratagem designed to maintain Spain's political and economic influence over the Western Sahara after its by now inevitable decolonization and independence. The individual judicial opinions annexed to the court's holding in *Western Sahara* have an importance that transcends the particular issues of that case. Was the Western Sahara territory, at the time of its colonization by Spain, *terra nullius?* The court noted that Spain itself relied for its original claim to title on agreements, "documents," and "deeds of adherence" signed by the chiefs of the local communities with Spain and confirmed by the king of Spain; for these reasons alone, the argument that the Western Sahara was *terra nullius* at the time of colonization would be refuted. But three of the specially concurring judicial opinions in particular go beyond the necessities of the case to dispose of the concept of *terra nullius* itself—those of Vice-President Ammoun, Judge Forster, and ad hoc Judge Boni, all of them distinguished Third World jurists. Vice-President Ammoun in particular rejected as a purely Western, ethnocentrist conception "classical" international law's formal categories as to the legal modes of establishing sovereignty and sovereign title over territory. Thus the legal category of *terra nullius* had been effectively employed until the beginning of the twentieth century to justify European military conquest and colonization overseas. Given the time dimension in international law, these were outdated legal categories that corresponded, in historically relativist terms, to an era of Western and

European domination in the world community, now past. Six years earlier, in 1969, in his specially concurring opinion in *North Sea Continental Shelf,* a strictly intracontinental Western European dispute, Judge Ammoun had taken the opportunity to reject in passing the unconscious juridical "racialism" inherent in such well-accepted "classical" international law categories as that cited in Article 38 (1) (c) of the World Court statute—"the general principles of law recognized by civilized nations."

Judge Forster, in his specially concurring opinion in *Western Sahara,* echoed Judge Ammoun in his strictures upon the spatially and temporally limited "Western" or "classical" concept of *terra nullius*. He pointed out that "It is Africa of former times which is in question, as to which it cannot arbitrarily be required that its institutions should be a carbon copy of European institutions." Ad hoc Judge Boni went a step further in suggesting that, in determining the character of territorial sovereignty today, the modern principle of self-determination of peoples required obligatory consultation of the inhabitants of the territory concerned.

Western Sahara, 1975, not merely in its lopsided judicial majorities (16–0, 14–2, and 15–1, on the substantive issues) but in the very intellectual range and breadth of the special opinions filed in support of its rulings, provided an admirable vehicle for judicial activism in the progressive development of international law, and for the successful passage from the "old" to the "new" in terms of international law doctrine. One would have to wait until the end of the decade for a case presenting a comparable interrelation of law and politics, and opportunity, in consequence, for a judicial policy ruling. This was *United States Diplomatic and Consular Staff in Tehran,*[21] but the case was complicated, as *Nuclear Tests* had been before it, by preliminary procedural questions and the fact that the Iranian government, like France before it in *Nuclear Tests,* chose not to be represented before the court in answer to the United States' complaint (though the Iranian government did send a letter to the court). It might, of course, be suggested (and this was confirmed by the actual experience in the court decision making in *United States Diplomatic and Consular Staff in Tehran*) that absence of representation before the court may not in fact be too much of a practical disability, the judges, following precedents well observed by municipal, national courts, seeming then to be at pains to take up initiatives on behalf of the absent party; and that, in terms of fact-finding and the taking of judicial notice of political events bearing on the political issues, the absent party may turn out to be more advantaged than if he had actually been present and had to carry the burden of proof of such facts and leading evidence in his own behalf. And so, perhaps, it was in *United States Diplomatic and Consular Staff in Tehran*. This case, brought by the United States against Iran, arose from the taking over of the United States Embassy in Tehran and the forcible detention of United States diplomatic and consular personnel by Iranian demonstrators in November 1979, immediately after the United States government's decision to admit the ex-Shah of Iran to the United States for medical treatment. The Iranian government chose not to be represented before the court.

In its interim order of December 1979, the court took note of a letter received from the Iranian foreign minister, contending that the issue of the American hostages represented only

> . . . a marginal and secondary aspect of an overall problem, one such that it cannot be studied separately, and which involves, *inter alia,* more than twenty-five years of continual interference by the United States in the internal affairs of Iran.[22]

The American government's application to the court, in the Iranian foreign minister's view, could not be

> . . . divorced from its proper context, namely the whole political dossier of the relations between Iran and the United States over the last twenty-five years . . . in particular the *coup d'état* of 1953 stirred up and carried out by the C.I.A., the overthrow of the lawful national government of Dr. Mossadegh, the restoration of the Shah and of his regime which was under the control of American interests, and all the social, economic, cultural, and political consequences of the direct interventions in our internal affairs.[23]

The response of the court to these averments was, first of all, a technical one. It insisted that it was for the Iranian government to bring forward all the requisite proof and clearly establish the facts alleged, to the satisfaction of the court. This, of course, Iran had not done, since it had chosen not to present its case before the court. The court's second line of argument was that, even if the allegations of persistent American government misconduct had been established, they could not be regarded as justification for Iran's conduct and a defense against the United States' claims in the present case. This conclusion was reached on the basis that the Vienna Convention on Diplomatic Relations of 1961 and the Vienna Convention on Consular Relations of 1963 provided their own built-in remedies against abuses of diplomatic privileges and immunities by way of espionage or interference in the internal affairs of the receiving state—namely, declaring the offending diplomatic staff persona non grata and thus compelling their recall.

This last-cited remedy was well known and well used, from the Cold War era onward, by the Soviet Union and the United States. It has certainly been practiced often enough by the two bloc leaders, with almost jovial good humor, and usually on a quid pro quo basis. It may have been somewhat unrealistic for the court to suggest it as a meaningful remedy in bilateral relationships other than Big Power ones, or in situations where the same relative parity of political-military strength does not exist. Perhaps, again, the two Vienna conventions are already somewhat dated and unresponsive to the political facts of life of the post–Cold War era, when the diplomatic missions of the Big Powers are actively used as agencies of quiet diplomacy to influence events within smaller countries.

The judges of the World Court were unanimous in holding that the Iranian government must immediately end the detention of American diplomatic and consular personnel, allow them to leave Iran, and restore diplomatic premises, property, and archives to the United States. Several of them went beyond the official opinion of the court to base such an obligation on sources outside "classical" Western-based international law. Judge Lachs, in his separate opinion, expressly cited the large number of Afro-Asian states that had ratified the two Vienna conventions; and Judge Tarazi, in his dissenting opinion, referred to Islamic law on the inviolability of diplomatic envoys, to the teachings of Muhammad, and to the practice of Arab states from the seventh century. Judge Lachs felt, however, that the court majority should have applied "sound judicial economy" and not gone into the issue of Iran's obligation to make reparation, apart from the return of the diplomatic personnel, premises, and property.

Judge Tarazi, in his dissent, adverted to the court's affirmative duty of judicial fact finding. He felt that the American government's actions in Iran in 1953, on behalf of the shah, were sufficiently in the public domain to have been made a subject of judicial notice. Judge Tarazi also considered that the American government was perfectly aware that its authorization for the ex-shah to enter the United States in October 1979 "might have untoward consequences"; therefore, any responsibility on the part of the Iranian government had to be envisaged "in the context of the revolution which took place in that country and brought about, as it were, a break with a past condemned as oppressive." Judge Tarazi was finally very critical—as was Judge Morozov in his dissenting opinion—of various American government actions before and after the court was seized with jurisdiction in the case: the freezing of Iranian economic assets in the United States, and their preparing to satisfy various private American claims, and the abortive American military operation of April 1980. All of these actions were undertaken while the court was embarking on its deliberation prior to judgment, and in Judge Tarazi's view they "constituted an encroachment on the functions of the Court."

The court thus unanimously reaffirmed the inviolability of diplomatic personnel and premises. Though it could hardly do otherwise, since the two conventions concerned were very recent and quite explicit, the character of the opinion of the court and the three individual opinions is such that the principle must be considered an imperative one, ranking almost as *jus cogens*. Beyond this point, however, the individual opinions—the separate opinion of Judge Lachs and the dissenting opinions of Judge Morozov and Judge Tarazi—properly introduce additional nuances not fully present in the official opinion of the court and important to the progressive development of international law doctrine. This is just what special judicial opinions are supposed to do, and with proper balance in their exercise they are fully compatible with the court's maintaining its collegial quality while it ventures on judicial law making.

Institutional Reform within the Court: Special Chambers

Criticism of a malaise in particular institutions within the United Nations Organization usually brings a demand for institutional reform or novation, sometimes confused, as in the case of the International Law Commission in 1981, with an increase in the numbers in the institution concerned. The case for the institution of special chambers within the International Court of Justice has, however, as Judge Lachs pointed out,[24] historical roots that long precede the present court and go back to the original Permanent Court of International Justice and to the Treaty of Versailles, particularly Articles 336 and 376, and the provisions of the peace treaties dealing with questions of navigation, transit, and communications, the intention being to establish chambers of five judges to deal with these cases. There was also provision for a chamber of summary procedure composed of three judges.

These provisions, not acted upon in regard to the old Permanent Court, were taken up in the 1946 court statute, Article 26 of which authorized the formation of chambers of three or more judges for dealing with particular categories of cases, labor and also transit and communications being mentioned specifically. The court is also given a general authority under its statute to form chambers to deal with particular cases, "the number of judges to constitute such a chamber [to] be determined by the Court with the approval of the parties" (Article 26 [2]); and with cases to be heard and determined by the chambers "if the parties so request" (Article 26 [3]). It is expressly stipulated that a judgment given by any such chamber "shall be considered as rendered by the Court" (Article 27), and there is also provision for the formation annually of a chamber of five judges which, at the request of the parties, may hear and determine cases by summary procedure (Article 29).

The idea of activating special chambers of the court was taken up and reinforced in the 1972 rules of court, particularly Articles 24 to 27 of those rules, and restated in the current rules of court, adopted in 1978, particularly Articles 15 to 21 of those rules. The case for such special chambers appears to have hinged, then, upon arguments that there were very many small cases that were unworthy of being handled by the full court of fifteen judges or that hardly warranted the lengthy and costly procedure involved in such plenum hearings. The emphasis in the argument here is upon the relative importance or unimportance of a case and its financial burden.[25] There is no reference to the irritation, voiced sotto voce in a number of capitals after *North Sea Continental Shelf,* 1969,[26] that a regionally limited Western European case, between Western European parties, was being decided by a court that was numerically dominated by "strangers" to the special Western European family, who then compounded their putative offense by insisting on filling their own individual separate or dissenting opinions. Apart from any latter-day nostalgic desire to turn back the clock to an earlier "European family compact" era of international adjudication between the two world wars, such an objection draws attention to the spatial dimension of international law and its increasing regionalization today in legal-systemic, linguistic, ethnic-cultural, and ideological terms. Does it make good sense, then, today to recognize and institutionalize this regionalization of international law, in international adjudication, by conferring on states from the one regional system the ability to regionalize their dispute settlement by opting to create their own special regional chamber within the framework of the International Court? It might certainly encourage a greater readiness to have recourse to the court if the parties, sharing common regional values, could thus opt in advance to exclude the "wild" judicial votes that they might fear to be present in the larger forum of the full court. But, as against that, it might simply accentuate and exaggerate the current historical tendency to fragment international law into a plurality of different subsystems and deny its claims to universality. What would this do, in any case, to the stipulation in Article 27 of the court statute that the judgment of any such limited, regional chamber "shall be considered as rendered by the Court" and thus of equal legal authority to the full court's jurisprudence? The 1972 rules of court, in many respects, appear designed to increase the role of the parties in the selection of the members of the special panel or chamber: while Article 26 (2) of the court statute speaks merely of the "number" of judges to constitute a chamber as something to be "determined by the Court with the approval of the parties," Article 26 (1) of the 1972 rules of court requires the president of the court, far more broadly, to consult with the parties regarding the "composition of the Chamber," this in addition to the requirement in Article 26 (2) of the 1972 rules of court to determine the "number" of judges with the approval of the parties. Article 17 (2) of the present rules of court, which were adopted in 1978 to replace the 1972 revised rules, is a restatement of the requirement in Article 26 (1) of the 1972 rules, and perhaps just a little stronger verbally in the role it gives to the views of the parties in the final composition of the court. While Article 26 (1) of the 1972 revised rules requires the president of the court to "consult the agents of the parties regarding the composition of the Chamber, and [to] report to the Court accordingly," Article 17 (2) of the present, 1978 rules stipulates that "When the parties have agreed, the President shall ascertain their views regarding the composition of the Chamber, and shall report to the Court accordingly." Is the intention here, in the interests of increasing the International Court's working jurisdiction, to edge toward court acceptance of the parties' complete freedom—as in the constitution of a special arbitral tribunal—to choose their own panel of judges by mutual agreement and bargaining?[27] If so, it would be a departure from the normal conception of a court as something independent of and above the actual parties, and the necessary and useful classical institutional distinction between court of law and panel of arbitrators, with different legal values and legal processes and even different legal objectives as to dispute settlement, would tend to disappear.

Judge Lachs seems to have envisaged the utilization of the special chamber system of the court as being directed toward certain specific subject matters and thus encouraging some mobilizing of specialist expertise within an increasingly "generalist," nonspecialist tribunal.[28] The specialization by chamber would be of a *functional* character, one panel suggested by Judge Lachs to be devoted to the subject of protection of the environment, particularly as to pollution of rivers and lakes on borders between states; the other panel suggested by Judge Lachs to be devoted to the Law of the Sea.[29] One is reminded of the lesson of the Sibylline Books and of the merits of acting in timely fashion, especially as to the adoption of proposals for institutional reform. If Judge Lachs's suggestion for a specialist Law of the Sea chamber of the International Court had been acted upon even a decade earlier, it might have successfully headed off or controlled what by the end of the 1970s had become the burgeoning pressures not simply to create a plurality of special chambers within the one International Court but to duplicate that court by creating a plurality of tribunals specialized by function, with a specialist Law of the Sea tribunal heading the list. The movement for creation of such functionally specialized international tribunals has gained strength from the Third World's image of the International Court of Justice as a highly conservative, traditional tribunal mired in the legal procedures and values of the past and hence committed inevitably to the legal status quo. It is no doubt helped also by the tendency, common enough in United Nations circles, to proliferate institutions even where this means overlap or duplication, or to proliferate numbers of personnel within existing institutions, as a somewhat roundabout way of increasing opportunities for professional placement for nations of the 150-odd Member States. Judge Lachs is right to point to the disadvantages of competing jurisdiction and jurisprudence involved in the creation of such additional specialist tribunals, and the challenge to the organic unity of international law.[30] On the other hand, specialist final tribunals, just as much as special senates or chambers within the one final court, are very much part of continental European civil law experience, even if they tend to be foreign to the Anglo Saxon common law systems, and on the basis of such continental European civil law experience should be capable of being lived with if they do in fact develop.

Some of the political as well as legal problems inherent in the special chamber system, particularly as applied under the International Court of Justice's statute and rules of court, are demonstrated in the experience of the constitution of the first such chamber of the International Court, in regard to *Delimitation of the Maritime Boundary in the Gulf of Maine Area (Canada/United States of America),* as the International Court's order of January 20, 1982, *Constitution of Chamber,*[31] strikingly indicates. The two state parties had concluded a special agreement in March 1979, entering into force in November 1981, by which they agreed to submit to a chamber of the court a question as to the course of the maritime boundary dividing the continental shelf and the fisheries zones of the two parties in the Gulf of Maine area. The special agreement provided for the submission of the dispute to a five-member chamber, to be constituted in accord with Article 26 and Article 31 of the court statute. The original understanding of the two parties was that the five-member panel be constituted without any national from either party; there was a certain obvious common sense in this arrangement, as a five-member tribunal with one national judge and one (necessarily) ad hoc national judge would reduce immediately, in effective terms, to a three-member tribunal. The original understanding had been reached with the then president of the International Court, Sir Humphrey Waldock, but his sudden death before the expiration of his term, and before the court had completed formation of the special chamber, upset the whole process; and matters were further complicated when the United States government insisted that its own national judge sit on the case, which meant, of course, that an ad hoc judge must be appointed for Canada to balance the American judge. Even more complicated was the insistence by the lame-duck plenum of the International Court, one-third of whose membership would automatically be replaced on February 5, 1982 (by the five judges elected or reelected by the General Assembly and Security Council in the autumn of 1981), on deciding immediately on the composition of the special chamber—apparently with the concurrence of the two parties. This was done by the court order of January 20, 1982, rendered only two weeks before the expiration of the retiring judges' term and thus also of their eligibility to be included in the special chamber. In fact, one of the judges so selected was Judge Gros, whose membership in the International Court of Justice automatically expired two weeks later. The objection here, if objection there be, is notional only, rather than substantial. The major criticisms of the court order of January 20, 1982, would be addressed first of all to the haste with which it was rushed through in the dying hours of the particular fifteen-member plenum of the court making the decision. In a tribunal whose personnel and philosophy of law are subject to change, and properly so, through the operation of the legal processes of selection of judges at the regular triennial elections, the judges already elected and waiting to take their seats were denied the opportunity of ruling on a matter which by no stretch of the imagination could be represented as requiring an urgent, immediate decision. The remaining criticisms address the fact that it was the two parties who in fact determined the choice of the five members of the special chamber, with the full court of fifteen apparently merely rubber-stamping their choice in the court order of January 20, 1982. This would seem to go well beyond the letter of the relevant provisions of the court statute, and even, it may be suggested, beyond the spirit of the more facultative provisions of the court's revised rules of court.[32] In the result, the two parties chose a five-member tribunal which, apart from the two national judges from English-speaking North America, was wholly Western European in composition. We thus have a tribunal which, in its membership and composition, reflects that "classical" Western, Eurocentrist character which has been the Third World's main ground of complaint against the old Permanent Court's jurisprudence, and also that of the new International Court since its foundation in 1946. Add to that the fact that, by reason of the bilateral consensus required to achieve the parties' own special agreement as to the constitution of the chamber, one of them apparently objected to selection of that member of the full court with the greatest acquired expertise in the subject matter of the suit, the Law of the Sea—Judge Oda of Japan. What can and should be the status, qua court jurisprudence, of the eventual decision of the five-member special chamber, with its own special "regional" composition, granted the insistence by the Third World states and other regional groupings in the world community that the Law of the Sea today cannot be reduced to the "classical" international law conception of logical, analytical construction divorced from policy, but must be considered instead in the light of the "new" international law—equity, the general principles of law recognized by nations—and as a constituent element in the New International Economic Order? It may be, in fact, that the eventual judgment of the special chamber, because of the special political factors in the chamber's composition and organization, will come down to a decision *inter partes*—like that of the arbitral panel it was supposed to avoid—and thus not be ranked as general international law jurisprudence and part of the progressive development of international law. The declaration appended by Judge Oda[33] to the court's order of January 20, 1982, and also the two dissenting opinions of Judge Morozov[34] and Judge El-Khani[35] indicate very clearly the objections, philosophical and practical, going to the character and integrity of the special chamber qua court, attaching to the plenum of the court's apparent conceding of carte blanche to the parties as to the choice of the actual members of the chamber. Judge, later President, Jiménez de Aréchaga, in his discussion in early 1973 of the court's 1972 revised rules of court, had suggested that the main change effected thereby was to give the parties

> decisive influence in the composition of *ad hoc* Chambers. . . . Recourse to *ad hoc* Chambers would prove more attractive to potential litigants if the election of their members were to be based on a consensus between the Court and the parties.[36]

This may or may not be so, but it would hardly be a justification in itself for making a change, *praeter legem,* going beyond the clear language of the court statute, to which, of course, the rules of court are and must remain subordinate, and which requires the court to act "with the approval of the parties" only as to the "number" of judges. Judge Jiménez de Aréchaga further suggests that

> from a practical point of view, it is difficult to conceive that in normal circumstances those Members who have been suggested by the parties would not be elected. For that it would be necessary for a majority of the Members of the Court to decide to disregard the expressed wishes of the parties. This would be highly unlikely since it would simply result in compelling the parties to resort to an outside arbitral tribunal or even to abandon their intention to seek a judicial settlement of the dispute.[37]

To all of which it might be asked, should that matter? If the parties wish to have the extra political prestige and legal authority of a court judgment, as provided in Article 27 of the court statute, then they would seem morally obligated to accept, in good faith and with good cheer, the normal principle that they practice in their own internal, municipal, national law of the independence of the judiciary and the legal incapability of the parties to dictate or control the composition of a court qua court. From the court's own viewpoint it would seem at the least undignified—even if the court is indeed short of cases for its roster—to surrender on such a fundamental point of the integrity of courts and the judicial process simply to attract or retain otherwise unwilling parties.

Judge Oda, in his declaration attached to the court order of January 20, 1982, on *Gulf of Maine Area,* contented himself with the tart comment:

> While I voted in favour of the Order, it should in my view have been made known that the Court, for reasons best known to itself, has approved the composition of the Chamber entirely in accordance with the latest wishes of the parties as ascertained pursuant to Article 26, paragraph 2, of the Statute and Article 17, paragraph 2, of the Rules of Court.[38]

Judge Morozov, in his dissenting opinion, was more caustic. Not merely did he consider that the full court's choice of the special chamber's members should have been postponed for the two weeks necessary to enable the full court *as newly reconstituted after the autumn 1981 judicial elections* to make the choices involved, but he also castigated the majority order as taking as

> point of departure the erroneous presumption that, contrary to Article 26, paragraph 2, of the Statute, the Parties . . . may not merely choose what should be the number of the members of the Chamber, but also formally decide and propose the names of the judges who should be elected by secret ballot, and even present these proposals to the Court in the form of some kind of "ultimatum."[39]

In rejecting the "incorrect presumption of the Parties that they may dictate to the Court who should be elected," Judge Morozov insisted on the "sovereign right of the Court to carry out the election independently of the wishes of the Parties, by secret ballot in accordance with the provisions of the Statute and Rules of Court."[40]

Judge El-Khani, in his dissenting opinion, was equally hostile to the court majority's acceptance of the parties' dictate as to the composition and membership of the special chamber:

> I find that the imposition of an unduly close time-limit for the Chamber's formation and of a particular composition renders the Court no longer master of its own acts, deprives it of its freedom of choice and is an obstacle to the proper administration of justice. Furthermore it diminishes the prestige of the Court and is harmful to its dignity as the principal judicial organ of the United Nations. It results in its regionalisation by depriving it of its basic and essential characteristic of universality. . . . On these grounds I find that this ought not to constitute a precedent, as it would be a dangerous course to follow in the future.[41]

The Future of Judicial Settlement

If the special chamber system within the court, at least as interpreted by the court majority in *Gulf of Maine Area* in 1982, as involving the court's acceptance of the dictate of the parties as to membership of the chamber, appears very much like a reform *manqué* and, in any case, one ventured on too late and only *after* the political pressures for creation of specialist tribunals functionally specialized by subject matter and separate and distinct from the International Court had gathered strength, there still remains reason for optimism as to the future of judicial settlement. notwithstanding all the bitter political criticisms of the International Court following on its *South West Africa, Second Phase* decision of 1966. *First,* the new political sophistication in the General Assembly–Security Council processes of election of judges to the International Court, and the possibilities thereby of creating—with only some modest patience in view of the staggered triennial system of election of judges—a liberal-activist majority on the court genuinely committed to the progressive development of international law, should do a great deal to remove the earlier marked suspicion and distrust of Third World countries in regard to the court, and their reluctance to see their great political-legal causes célèbres transferred before it. As early as 1971, one of the politically most dispassionate and intellectually open Western students of the court, Leo Gross, was able to suggest persuasively that even by that time the "new" countries might be considered as having achieved "equitable representation" on the court, and this perhaps at the cost of full "equitable representation" on the part of the "traditional clients of the Court."[42] If it be too much to expect the "new" countries—after the negative example of the United States' own self-defining "domestic jurisdiction" exception to its acceptance of the court's compulsory jurisdiction,[43]—themselves to opt for unreserved acceptance of the court's compulsory jurisdiction, at least in regard to conflicts between themselves and the West, or for that matter the Soviet bloc, there is absolutely no reason why they should not resort to the court in purely "regional" intra–Third World conflicts, as, for example, the Tunisian-Libyan dispute over their respective continental shelves.[44]

The major hope, however, for fruitful extension of the court's work load and its role, in consequence, in international law making in an era of transition, would appear to be in the advisory opinion jurisdiction. The charter provisions as to recourse to such jurisdiction are broadly framed and are facultative in outlook. In terms of Charter Article 96, not merely the General Assembly and the Security Council may each request an advisory opinion from the court, but also other United Nations organs and specialized agencies at any time so authorized by the General Assembly may make a similar request, and the list of such additional institutions and agencies is already extensive and not closed to future names.[45] Some of the International Court's most impressive and intellectually imaginative and courageous work has, in fact, been achieved in the form of advisory opinions: Judge Lachs cites[46] as examples *Reparations for Injuries Suffered in the Service of the United Nations* of 1949;[47] and *Namibia (South West Africa)* of 1971, which, following on earlier General Assembly action in the immediate aftermath of the judgment in *South*

West Africa (Second Phase) of 1966, and designed to "correct" that judgment by declaring the Republic of South Africa's old League of Nations mandate over South West Africa to be terminated forthwith, set in motion a train of political events toward national self-determination and independence for Namibia. We should certainly add to that list *Western Sahara,* 1975, with its openings to the "new" international law as to sovereignty and title to territory. The surprise, indeed, is that the General Assembly has not been tempted to approach the court more often and more systematically, as a supplement to its own action, as in *Namibia,* 1971; or as an alternative thereto when its own internal political processes become clogged or bogged down in proceduralisms, or when its coordinate parliamentary organ, the Security Council, finds its actions legally frustrated by a permanent member's veto. To fill the gaps in the United Nations effective peace-keeping powers in the case of such Big Power veto arbitrarily applied in the Security Council, the legal remedies are not only General Assembly action on the precedent of the Uniting for Peace Resolution of 1950, but also recourse to the court for advisory opinion, or a prudent and staged combination of both.

Suggestion that there exists a malaise within the court that can be cured only by increase in its membership or by more special chambers should be looked at coolly. There is no firm evidence as yet that an increase in members would increase the court's efficiency, and it hardly seems necessary as yet to correct its "representativeness," for which other, political-electoral remedies are available under the Charter. As for the special chamber system, the evidence suggests that the reform of 1972 was not fully thought through, and that it would be sensible to reinforce or restore the court's own sovereignty and absolute control over choice of members of such panels; within this premise, there is scope for adoption of Judge Lachs's suggestion of functionally specialized chambers having jurisdiction over such matters as environmental protection and the Law of the Sea. The main challenge to the International Court today, however, would appear to be to use, and to use to the full, the very ample facilities and processes already existing under the Charter, the court statute, and the revised rules of court.[48] The court itself could help, even without any change in its existing rules of court, by moving to "demystify" its own internal processes, particularly those concerning the preparation of the written brief or memorial, and the character and conduct of oral argument. A notion exists that somehow or other the preparation and presentation of a case before the court is an esoteric art, with its own elaborate folkways enjoined by the judges, ending up suspiciously like the forms of appellate advocacy (particularly oral advocacy) practiced and applied in one or two Western countries only. So far from these being ideal types or models for all the rest of the world community, comparative legal science today teaches us that there are very many different roads to Rome in terms of legal argumentation and advocacy addressed to a court, and that no one system, common law or civil law, Western or non-Western, has any monopoly on truth in this regard. The court, taking note of the potentially intimidatory (and no doubt designedly intimidatory) effect upon litigant states from the poorer areas of the Third World created by the batteries of expensive, and often quite unnecessary, counsel maintained by the wealthier states who regularly appear before the court, has already done something to allow itself to limit and control any such excesses.[49] Beyond that, however, the court could recognize that form should sensibly yield to substance, even in the realm of procedure. The court could both clamp down on unnecessarily prolonged or gratuitously mannered oral argumentation and also liberate the parties from any special obligation of deference to past stereotypes of written pleadings.[50] Such a liberating intellectual-legal approach on the part of the judges might allow a break-out from the small "club" of predominantly Western lawyers who seem to monpolize the court's practice today, and also encourage more and more non-Western states to approach the court with their own national teams of jurists.

7. International Law-in-the-Making: United Nations Charter Reform, The Manila Declaration on Peaceful Settlement

Notwithstanding the debate of the earlier years of the United Nations—highlighted in the joinders of issue by individual judges of the International Court in *Certain Expenses of the United Nations* in 1962[1]—over whether the Charter should be viewed as a constitution or as a mere limited treaty between states, it is no longer possible to deny that the Charter has taken on, increasingly over the years, many of the characteristics of a constitutional instrument in its inherent capacity to expand and adapt creatively to rapidly changing circumstances and needs of the world community. This has occurred in a number of ways, both formal and informal; and, as has been the case, as a matter of comparative legal science, with other constitutional charters that are genuinely operational as law-in-action, it has been the informal modes of constitutional change that have tended to predominate and in the end to be the most pervasive.

Direct Amendment of the Charter

Like all good constitutional instruments, the Charter includes, in written terms, its own amending machinery. Article 108 allows for the direct amendment of the Charter by vote of two-thirds of the members of the General Assembly, followed by "ratifi[cation] in accordance with their respective constitutional processes by two-thirds of the Members of the United Nations, including all the permanent members of the Security Council."

An alternative constitutional amending machinery is provided by way of a constitutional assembly, as stipulated in Article 109 of the Charter:

> A General Conference of the Members of the United Nations for the purpose of reviewing the present Charter . . . at a date and place to be fixed by a two-thirds vote of the members of the General Assembly and by vote of any nine members of the Security Council. Each Member of the United Nations shall have one vote in the conference.

As with the amending machinery under Article 108, however, any proposals for alteration of the charter made by a general conference under Article 109 must be recommended by a two-thirds vote of the conference and then "ratified in accordance with their respective constitutional processes by two-thirds of the Members of the United Nations including all the permanent members of the Security Council."

The Chapter XVIII (Articles 108, 109) provisions of the Charter seem to have been influenced in considerable measure by the machinery for amending the United States Constitution, with the alternative legislature-based and special constitutional-assembly-based approaches to direct constitutional change. But, as with many other genuinely operational *national* constitutional instruments, it has proved very, very difficult to mobilize the necessary political consensus and momentum to effect changes by the direct route, the requirements of special weighted voting majorities at critical stages of the process seeming to create insurmountable psychological and practical political barriers to this exercise of direct constituent power. The prime obstacle to the route to constitutional change in Chapter XVIII of the Charter, has been the legal requirement, built in to both Articles 108 and 109, of the concurrence of all the permanent members of the Security Council in any proposed amendment. It is not surprising that, going well beyond the various *national* constitutional amending systems already referred to, the constitutional amending machinery expressly established in the Charter has not worked, except for changes considered to be innocuous by the permanent members of the Security Council and not especially harmful to their interests—the increase in the size of the Security Council from eleven to fifteen members in Article 23, and the corresponding changes in Article 27, without touching the permanent members' veto power. As with the changes to the statute of the International Law Commission in the autumn of 1981, which saw the enlargement, for a third time, of the commission's membership as a method of satisfying the claims of more and more states, but with little or no prior thought as to the effects of such increase in numbers on the functional integrity and efficacy of the organization concerned, it may be doubted that the change involved amounted to a "reform" so much as to a constitutional step backwards. Might it not have been a useful intellectual exercise at least to have considered, as an alternative constitutional option, maintaining the Security Council at its original eleven-member strength but improving its representativeness, in response to the general expansion of United Nations membership, by eliminating some of the original permanent member seats—the historical raison d'être, in at least some of the cases, (like the Big Five at the war's end in 1945), having by that time disappeared? While clearly doomed to failure as long as the permanent members concerned were not excluded as "interested parties" from attempting legally to veto proposals for Security Council reform involving their own demise, such reform proposals would have helped focus attention on the widening gap between the charter as originally written in response to the 1945 political facts of life and more contemporary political realities of the new historical forces in the world community. Substantive changes being effectively barred by the front-door method of direct constitutional amendment, the search inevitably began within the United Nations system, as in so many national constitutional systems, for alternative, more informal modes of constitutional change. Such informal modes of change, developing through practice normally not involving direct conflict with the text of the constitutional charter, and subjected to the test of constitutional reasonableness as interpreted and applied in continuing community consensus, are the life's blood of any living constitutional system. Variously styled in comparative legal science as "conventional" change through developing constitutional custom, or changes by way of "glosses" on the constitutional charter emerging through authoritative interpretation or application through time, they have been a necessary and inevitable part of the growth of United Nations constitutionalism over the years and its creative renewal or updating in response to rapidly changing societal conditions.

The Special Committee on the Charter of the United Nations and on the Strengthening of the Role of the Organization

The Special Committee established by General Assembly Resolution 3499 (XXX) of December 15, 1975, submitted its report to the thirty-sixth session of the General Assembly in the autumn of 1981,[2] and then a very detailed supplemental report for the thirty-seventh session in the autumn of 1982.[3] The 1981 report focused upon the principal contemporary political problem of the United Nations: the erosion of its credibility through nonimplementation of its resolutions[4]—a problem which the report attributed directly to the Security Council and its all too frequent paralysis by veto, or threat of veto, by any single permanent member.[5] The solution to the problem, as so defined, implied some form of redefinition of the legal relations between the General Assembly and the Security Council and an increase in the powers and competence of the General Assembly in the case of practical breakdown in the Security Council.[6]

The 1981 report of the special committee contained an "informal compilation" of charter reform proposals submitted to it.[7] Among these, Proposal 17 recommended an increase in the membership of the Security Council—"taking into account the principle of equitable geographical distribution."[8] This particular proposal was opposed, as surely could have been expected, by the permanent members of the Security Council on the argument, surely made tongue in cheek, that the Security Council was "very carefully balanced and, in its present form, correctly reflected the international balance of power" and that the permanent members' right of veto was "not a right or a privilege, but a heavy and serious responsibility, constituting the very foundation of the organisation, since it assured the equality of states of the two major economic systems."[9] The basic defect of Proposal 17, however, would seem to have been that it did not address itself to the real problem—namely, threat of paralysis of Security Council powers through any one permanent member's veto at any time. Mere increase in Security Council membership, without at the same time cutting down or qualifying the permanent members' veto power, would hardly touch the problem, save in respect of those very limited and politically marginal "procedural" matters to which, in terms of Article 27 (2) of the Charter, the veto power did not legally apply. Increase in the numbers of nonpermanent members of the Security Council beyond the present ten could certainly offset somewhat the voting weight on "procedural" matters of the five permanent members—assuming these latter should ever vote as a bloc in opposition to the nonpermanent members on "procedural" matters. But that was hardly a practical problem!

The more substantial reform proposals in the 1981 report of the special committee did indeed address themselves to the permanent members' veto in the Security Council. Proposals 23 to 32 in the informal compilation[10] suggested variously the attenuation of the veto by increase in the category of "procedural" matters, to which, of course, under Article 27(2), the permanent members' veto could not be applied, with amendment also of the Security Council rules of procedure to ensure that the decision of whether a given matter was "procedural" or not should be decided by an affirmative vote of nine members (without any right of veto thereover). In addition, it was proposed that the veto should not apply to such matters as the appointment of commissions of inquiry or fact-finding missions or commissions to serve humanitarian purposes;[11] that, on the principle common to most legal systems of *nemo iudex in sua causa,* the permanent members should abstain whenever they were parties to a dispute[12] (though in fact Article 27(3) already, in terms, enjoins this in decisions under Chapter VI of the Charter [Pacific Settlement of Disputes, Articles 33–38], and under Article 52[3] [regional arrangements]). More modest, and no doubt politically more palatable suggestions, so far as the permanent members of the Security Council were concerned, endeavored to achieve the same desired result of cutting back on the veto by appealing for "self-restraint" on the part of the permanent members and a "gentlemen's agreement" that they would not try to apply the veto in cases of armed conflict.[13] In somewhat contradictory vein, another reform proposal would accept the political fact of the right of veto but in effect "share the wealth" by extending it on a more equitable basis to "one or two non-permanent representatives, by rotation, from each geographical region represented on the Security Council."[14]

The supplemental report, presented by the special committee to the General Assembly for its thirty-seventh session in the autumn of 1982,[15] represented twelve months of mature reflection on the proposals raised in the 1981 report. In particular, the draft recommendation presented by Egypt on behalf of the Non-Aligned Countries[16] is a balanced and pragmatic document which always keeps in mind the art of the politically possible, having regard to the fact that any direct amendment of the Charter touching on the prerogatives of the permanent members would require their own assent thereto. The thrust of the Non-Aligned Countries' recommendation concerns the examination of areas in which the permanent members' veto power "should be limited." By way of example, the Non-Aligned Countries' draft recommendation lists the following:

(a) ascertaining facts by the Security Council and dispatching of United Nations observers with the consent of the host country to observe and report to the Council;
(b) entrusting the Secretary-General with functions in dispute settlements in accordance with Article 98 of the Charter and rule 23 of the provisional rules of procedure of the Security Council;
(c) the examination of other matters under Chapter VI [Pacific Settlement of Disputes, Articles 33–38];
(d) ensuring full adherence to Article 27(3)—stipulating that "in decisions under Chapter VI, and under paragraph 3 of Article 52 [regional arrangements], a party to a dispute shall abstain from voting"—which did not provide a distinction between permanent members and non-permanent members;
(e) adoption of resolutions calling for cease-fire, separation of armed forces and withdrawal behind respective borders in cases of armed conflict;
(f) admission of new Member States.[17]

The 1982 supplemental report reflects the Non-Aligned Countries' realism as to the origins of the veto—"from the historical standpoint, the balance of power following the Second World War"—and also their disillusionment as to actual practice thereafter:

> If, as provided in Article 24 of the Charter, the permanent members exercised their veto power with a sense of duty in strict accord with the purposes and principles of the Charter and with a sense of their responsibility towards all Member States, their international peace and security would be effectively guaranteed, but that such was not the case, so that the Security Council was often unable to play its role. Experience so far had shown that the whole matter was a question of attitudes. Attitudes which were incompatible with the provisions of the Charter on questions of international peace and security were to be blamed for the sufferings of the last 35 years and not the Charter of the United Nations.[18]

The Non-Aligned Countries' draft recommendation stressed that it did not call for direct amendments to the Charter, and that it certainly did not seek to replace the Security Council, but to increase its effectiveness and flexibility within the existing framework.[19] What was implied was not amendment of the Charter but perhaps a place in the provisional rules of procedure of the Security Council.[20] If the goal, therefore, was not so much removal of the rule of unanimity but its limitation, the question arose as to the method of limitation. Three methods, in fact, were constitutionally possible: *first,* direct amendment of the Charter; *second,* change by way of "interpretive decisions" of the Security Council, or the United Nations, purporting to interpret the provisions of Article 27(2) ("procedural matters") in relation to certain categories of decisions; *third,* an understanding ("gentlemen's agreement") among the permanent members of the Security Council that, in their voting practice, they would refrain from casting a negative vote in certain matters or in certain circumstances.[21]

Within the special committee as a whole a good deal of attention was given in debate to paragraph (b) of the Non-Aligned Countries' draft recommendation, concerning the role of the Secretary-General of the United Nations.[22] It was suggested—correctly, it is submitted—that the Secretary-General's functions in dispute settlement under Article 98 of the Charter, which are quite separate from his power under Article 99 to "bring to the attention of the Security Council any matter which in his opinion may threaten the maintenance of international peace and security," were not subject to permanent-member veto in the Security Council.[23] And there was also very strong support voiced in the special committee for the proposal in paragraph (e) of the Non-Aligned Countries' draft recommendation that the Security Council should have the capacity, unhindered by the veto process, to prevent conflicts from spreading by the adoption of resolutions calling for cease-fire, separation of armed forces, and their withdrawal behind their respective borders.[24]

As a result of the debate in the special committee, Egypt introduced a final document on behalf of the Non-Aligned Countries,[25] which essentially reproduced the recommendations contained in their earlier draft recommendation, plus a new category (g)—"establishment of subsidiary organs as referred to in Article 29 of the Charter," to which the permanent members' veto in the Security Council should not apply.[26]

Lest it be thought that the special committee was as one in the thrust of its reform proposals to limit the powers of the Security Council and its permanent members, one of the permanent members, France, launched its own counterattack[27] referring to the historical limitation of permanent members' prerogatives in the Security Council already long since established, as a matter of constitutional conventional (customary) law and by law of legal "gloss" on the Charter, in the famous Uniting for Peace resolution of November 1950. In a proposal coming perhaps strangely from a state that had itself participated, enthusiastically and without any backward glances, in the successful Western political maneuver in 1950 that confirmed the constitutional-legal right of the General Assembly to move affirmatively to fill the gap in effective peace-keeping powers created by paralysis of the Security Council through Big Power veto, France proposed to amend Rules 8, 9 , and 19 of the rules of procedure of the General Assembly so as to delete all express references therein to General Assembly Resolution 377A(V) (the Uniting for Peace resolution) as the legal authority for summoning emergency special sessions of the General Assembly.[28] The express references to Resolution 377A(V) had been inserted into Rules 8, 9, and 19 at the fifth annual session of the General Assembly in 1950.

Just what France intended by this is not completely clear, insofar as, though proposing deletion of the express references to Resolution 377A(V), it would substitute for those references new language that would leave the substantive meaning and effect of Rules 8, 9, and 19 unchanged. The French move did, however (and perhaps that was its design and intention), excite a good deal of critical reexamination within the special committee of the historical circumstances under which the first real challenge had emerged, in the United Nations internal practice, to the permanent members' veto in the Security Council. This resulted in a veritable tour de force on United Nations actions in the Korean crisis of 1950. The Uniting for Peace resolution, adopted by the General Assembly in November 1950, was now cited variously as

> [a] discredited document . . . an illegal document dictated by one side during the Cold War; . . . attempts . . . to systematically undermine the United Nations, its basic provisions and the well-established balance between the principal organs, . . . attempts . . . proven futile; . . . adopted during the Cold War . . . that controversial resolution was today an anachronism.[29]

Such ventures in instant or retroactive legal history in regard to the United Nations and its developed practice seemed quite often to be arch and contrived and exercises in political and legal special pleading. Sober voices within the special committee commented by way of rejoinder that it was

> not appropriate to characterise past General Assembly resolutions as "illegal," even though with hindsight experience might have shown they were ill-advised. The point was to try to search for ways to make the Organisation more effective and to improve its capabilities, not to condemn past actions.[30]

Again, it was suggested that it simply was

> not positive to cast aspersions on those who had desired to protect and codify the residual role of the General Assembly in the maintenance of international peace and security. Even though decisions such as resolution 377A (V) were taken more than thirty years ago, their important contribution to the functioning of the Organisation could not be denied.[31]

This may have been a bridge-building gesture by the French, who had supported the Uniting for Peace resolution in 1950, toward the Soviet Union and Soviet bloc, which had always opposed it. It was perhaps designed to secure and protect the permanent members' veto in the Security Council, in which France shared no less than the Soviet Union. However, the French move in the special committee appeared to be self-defeating in its immediate objective. In long-range terms it nevertheless served as a convenient rallying point for an unholy alliance of the Soviet Union and the Western members of the Security Council, now united (for no doubt different ideological reasons) in a determined defense of the legal prerogatives of all the permanent members of the Security Council. A legally quite avant-garde draft resolution submitted by a group of Third World states (Benin, Iran, Libyan Arab Jamahiriya, Mali, and Mauritania)[32] was defeated in the Sixth (Legal) Committee on a proceduralism. It had called for finding an effective alternative to the veto; took affirmative note of the report of the Secretary-General and its proposals for developing the United Nations' capacity for the maintenance of international peace and security; and then asked the special committee to examine eliminating adverse effects of abuse of the veto. Specifically, it had proposed that the veto not be resorted to in matters relating to the "inalienable rights of peoples struggling for self-determination, against colonialism, apartheid, foreign domination, intervention, aggression and occupation"; that the special committee elaborate its proposals for strengthening the role of the General Assembly according to Article 11(2) of the Charter (maintenance of international peace and security); that the possibility be studied that resolutions of the General Assembly relating to the maintenance of international peace and security be considered binding and to be implemented.[33]

This draft resolution having been disposed of procedurally, the way was thereby opened for the Sixth (Legal) Committee, and thereafter the General Assembly, to adopt a somewhat blander resolution continuing the work of the special committee to the next, thirty-eight session of the General Assembly in the autumn of 1983, and asking it to accord priority in its work to the question of the maintenance of international peace and security, to the revised draft recommendation already presented by Egypt on behalf of the Non-Aligned Countries, and to other proposals, "including those relating to the functioning of the Security Council."[34]

The Manila Declaration on the Peaceful Settlement of International Disputes

The Manila Declaration,[35] adopted by the General Assembly on November 15, 1982, by consensus,[36] represented the fruits of three years of diplomatic negotiations within the United Nations and its Special Committee on the Charter of the United Nations.[37] The Manila Declaration's adoption was hailed by the Secretary-General as "an important landmark in the history of the United Nations"; and the Secretary-General welcomed in particular the call in the declaration that he himself make full use of the powers entrusted to him by the charter and the implicit argument for a stronger, more activist secretary-general role in international law making for the future.[38] The Manila Declaration, however, in its language and also in the modes of its political achievement, represents an excellent case study of the international law-making processes within the United Nations—both the political give-and-take and exchanges in actual negotiations, and also the cumulative process, through frequent reiteration, by which international law is developed and extended by way of glosses on the Charter. Thus the General Assembly's declaration of October 1970, on Principles of International Law Concerning Friendly Relations and Cooperation among States in Accordance with the Charter of the United Nations, forms a key element in the new Manila Declaration on the Peaceful Settlement of International Disputes, being not only cited separately and in its own right[39] but also expressly mentioned in the context of two other postulated principles—equal rights and self-determination of peoples, and the "need for all States to desist from any forcible action which deprives peoples, particularly peoples under colonial and racist regimes or other forms of alien domination, of their inalienable right to self-determination, freedom and independence."[40] These are included as preambular policy declarations, and they continue and extend the legitimation and political sanctification of the friendly relations principles occurring over the years since their adoption in the General Assembly declaration of October 24, 1970. When first legally adopted by a General Assembly resolution, the declaration had seemed to come almost as a political-legal anticlimax, after the excitement of the peaceful coexistence debate at the opening of the decade of the 1960s. Fundamental East-West, or specifically Soviet-American, accommodation and détente had already been achieved and legally concretized in other arenas, and the friendly relations operation had long since been abandoned by the superpowers to lesser, supporting actors, among whom India, Sweden, Mexico, and Yugoslavia played major roles. But the declaration of principles of friendly relations has begun to acquire, through time, a legal life and authority of its own, independently of any original superpower sponsorship. As one of the United Nations General Assembly's jurisconsults—the last of an original young group of founding jurists of the United Nations' early years, Shabtai Rosenne—remarked at a retirement function at the thirty-seventh annual session in the autumn of 1982, many of the "new" countries that were not present at the creation in San Francisco in 1945 and that only latterly were admitted as members of the United Nations seemed to feel something of a latter-day, second-wave, founding-fathers relation to the friendly relations declaration, and to accord it, in consequence, a special pride of authorship and their active political-legal support thereafter. There is political and psychological importance, of course, in allowing all members of the United Nations to participate fully in its legal renewal or updating from time to time; and the act of renewal itself acquires in the process a certain fundamental legal quality like the redefinition of a legal *Grundnorm*. As a "gloss" upon the Charter achieved by the legislative act of General Assembly resolution (though not formal amendment of the Charter), the friendly relations principles may thus be seen as advancing toward the status of imperative principles of international law, or *jus cogens*. Some of the same sense of participatory democracy and direct involvement in the renewal or extension of United Nations—international law can be seen in the long-continuing process, from the opening of the 1970s, of the Third United Nations Conference on the Law of the Sea, which culminated in the December 1982 formal signing of the final treaty text. Would its principles rank as imperative principles to the point of binding nonsignatories also?[41]

The Manila Declaration on Peaceful Settlement, in its substantive parts, offers what is considered by some a new legal term of art, "*contemporary* international law,"[42] emerging in recent Soviet doctrinal writings. In and of itself it is a value-neutral, purely descriptive term denoting international law such as it exists today in both *doctrines* and practice. Many Western jurists (including the present writer) have used it in this context. But as a new legal term of art it has much to recommend it. The "new" international law, emerging in the postwar era in opposition to the "old" classical international law that was then being too unimaginatively or conservatively interpreted and applied, has tended, with the passage of time and its political acceptance and success, to solidify somewhat, acquiring its own special legal connotation linked to the legal principles of decolonization and independence, national self-determination, national control over economic resources, and international development law. *Contemporary* international law would represent, by this token, a larger "postcolonial" legal category, embracing all of the "new" international law norms but not limited to them, and capable indeed of expansion beyond them in the new postcolonial phase of international law-making. It is a point to remember when, as a matter of the purely internal business and organization of the General Assembly, the Fourth Committee, whose principal charge and mandate has always been decolonization and colonial questions generally, is manifestly short of business and facing the public embarassment, for a committee that was once one of the mainstays of the United Nations annual sessions, of running out of an agenda and thus terminating its annual activities well in advance of the other committees of the General Assembly.

In its substantive provisions, the Manila Declaration covers a good deal of ground, particularly the reiteration of imperative principles of international law and the "new" international law, already familiar through the friendly relations declaration and similar earlier law-making acts. What is new, perhaps, is the stress also upon institutions, arenas, and processes of law making, in a refreshingly mature and pragmatic recognition that principles can hardly exist in the air and that they need to be rendered operational as international law-in-action. In the peaceful settlement of disputes, above all, principles and process need to be thought of together. In its institutional and processual emphasis, the Manila Declaration shades off into the substantive proposals as to charter revision contained in the report of the Special Committee on the Charter of the United Nations already referred to, and so it is not surprising that that special committee devoted so much of its intellectual energies, and also so much of its actual report of 1981 and the supplemental report of 1982, to canvasing the institutional implications of the Manila Declaration.

In this context, we see in the same breath as the statement that states should "strengthen the primary role of the Security Council so that it may more fully and effectively discharge its responsibilities,"[43] a stress upon the "important role conferred on the General Assembly by the Charter of the United Nations in the field of peaceful settlement of disputes,"[44] and a recital of the General Assembly's own independent powers to discuss any situation, regardless of origin, which it deems likely to impair the general welfare or friendly relations among nations and (subject only to Article 12 of the Charter—no General Assembly recommendation, except at the request of the Security Council, when the Security Council itself is acting on a dispute) to recommend measures for peaceful adjustment of a dispute. There is also specific mention of the inherent powers of the Secretary-General, under the Charter, as to dispute settlement, and an express recital of his independent power of initiative to bring before the Security Council any matters which in his opinion may threaten the maintenance of international peace and security. There is also an important and timely reminder of the regional security arrangements under the Charter (Ch. VIII, Articles 52–54),[45] and the stipulation that the members of any such regional groups should attempt to use such regional security arrangements for peaceful settlements *before* approaching the Security Council.[46] Finally, and as evidence of the political give-and-take inherent in any collective law-making venture based in the United Nations, the Manila Declaration accords special mention to the role of the International Court of Justice as the "principal judicial organ of the United Nations," with the additional injunction that "legal disputes should as a general rule be referred by the parties to the International Court of Justice."[47] This is backed up by further recommendations for, variously, the inserting in treaties of clauses providing for the submission to the International Court of disputes arising from the interpretation or application of such treaties; that states should opt to accept the compulsory jurisdiction of the court in terms of Article 36 of the court statute; and also for greater recourse to the advisory opinion jurisdiction of the court on the part of the main United Nations organs and specialized agencies.[48] The acceptance on the part of the Soviet Union and its Soviet-bloc allies of the strong case made for judicial settlement as an instrument for peaceful settlement represents a very considerable departure from more traditional Soviet international legal doctrine as expressed over the years, and must be regarded as one of the major political and legal breakthroughs achieved in the Manila Declaration.

8. International Law Makers

In Weberian sociology of law, the direction and pace of legal development in any society at any time are determined in very large measure by the particular type of specialized legal skill group that dominates or controls its legal system—the judges and other priestly castes, the law professors and similar rather precious intellectual-legal elites, the more rudely pragmatic and empirical practitioners of law. Weber gave such classes of authoritative interpreters of law the name of legal "honoratiores," or dignitaries of the law. Within the United Nations Organization itself there is a certain shifting balance of forces and interplay at any time between the professional bureaucracy headed by the politically elected and doubly (through Security Council and General Assembly vote) mandated Secretary-General and his personal cabinet and legal secretariat; the state-appointed political assembly of the Sixth (Legal) Committee of the General Assembly; and the General Assembly–elected, and postulated scientific-legal International Law Commission.

The Secretary-General: Legal Competence and Powers

The Charter, as originally drafted, refers to the office of Secretary-General only briefly, and in fairly general terms (Chs. XV, Articles 97–101). According to Article 97, the Secretary-General is to be appointed by the General Assembly upon the recommendation of the Security Council, and he is to be the "chief administrative officer" of the United Nations. The powers of the office and its limits are not explicitly defined, apart from the power of initiative, already referred to, under Article 99 to inform the Security Council of "any matter which in [the Secretary-General's] opinion may threaten the maintenance of international peace and security."

The principle of the double mandate—vote of the General Assembly upon the recommendation of the Security Council—as a legal condition of election of a Secretary-General has been compounded by the developed practice, right from the beginning, of treating the prior Security Council recommendation as a nonprocedural matter and therefore (in terms of Article 27 (3) of the Charter) as requiring the concurring votes of the permanent members of the Security Council. The practical necessity of a Big Power consensus on any viable candidacy for the post suggests a quest for a bland or neutral figure, or at least one who would treat the office and its powers narrowly and restrictively—something that would correspond exactly with the Soviet doctrinal-legal position on the United Nations and its main institutions and offices, including the Secretary-Generalship. The difficulty is that, once elected, the Secretary-General is to all intents irremovable during his term; and unless, therefore, he wishes to run for reelection, he is on his own and may seek to give his own personal dimension to an office that is, after all, defined in very general terms, without limiting detail. The first two Secretaries-General, Messrs Lie and Hammarskjöld, construed their office broadly and ventured upon an activist role and interpretation of their own legal competence, particularly in dispute settlement. Since their activism happened or was seen to correspond, in its concrete application and end results, with the political interests of the then dominant pro-Western voting majority within the General Assembly, it meant a collision course with the Soviet Union and an end to any hopes of electoral renewal in a fresh term of office as secretary-general. It was a reaction, in particular, to the strong, crusading Secretary-General image that Dag Hammarskjöld sought to bring to the office and his conscious choice of sides in the United Nations peacekeeping operation in the Congo in 1960 and 1961 that spawned the Soviet "troika" campaign for, in effect, converting the office into a (Soviet-Western–Third World) triumvirate, under which a tri-bloc consensus would be a legal prerequisite to any action. This Soviet campaign, which was only forestalled by Secretary-General Hammarskjöld's untimely death, would have effectively emasculated the office. Hammarskjöld's successor, U Thant, was not merely from the Third World himself but, both by temperament and by pragmatic experience in observation of his predecessor's political difficulties, he was not inclined to assume an activist role and contented himself with an ideologically consciously neutralist approach and an eschewing of direct personal interventions or initiatives in Big Power conflicts. U Thant's successor, Kurt Waldheim, followed in the same footsteps, less from conviction and philosophy, seemingly, than from a temperament addicted to the political trimmer's arts and back-room diplomacy and deals. But the times, in the decade of the 1970s, of Dr. Waldheim's two terms as Secretary-General were different from those of U Thant. The apparent breakdown of Big Power détente, and the growing world crisis manifested in a renewed superpower nuclear armaments race and the collapse of the world monetary and trading systems, called for affirmative leadership and direction, which, in the absence of constructive initiatives from the Soviet Union and the United States, must come from elsewhere. Why not from the United Nations? But Dr. Waldheim seemed to be unwilling to risk treading on the toes of either one or both of the superpowers, and a vacuum therefore developed in the peace-keeping field, with leadership coming from neither the Soviet Union nor the United States nor, finally, the United Nations. Though the acknowledged "establishment" candidate of the postindustrial societies, European Communist and Western capitalist, in the North-South equation, Dr. Waldheim ran into a Chinese veto in the Security Council and determined Third World opposition and finally gave up his bid for reelection. A genuine Third World candidate not unacceptable to either of the superpowers, Dr. Pérez de Cuéllar, emerged as the acceptable compromise and was quickly confirmed. Would he, however, respond to the feeling now manifest within the United Nations of a dangerous drift in international relations and the need for someone outside the two contending blocs, the Warsaw Pact and NATO, to try to produce new, affirmative policies for a world community in transition? An answer seemed offered by the Report of the Secretary-General on the Work of the Organization, presented by the new Secretary-General to the thirty-seventh session of the General Assembly in September 1982.[1] Speaking with, in his own words, "the utmost frankness," Dr. Pérez de Cuéllar identified the key problem of the contemporary international organization as

> the reluctance of parties to some conflicts to resort to the Security Council or to use the machinery of the United Nations. The fact is that the Council too often finds itself on the sidelines at a time when, according to the Charter, its possibilities should be used to the maximum. Allegations of partisanship, indecisiveness or incapacity arising from divisions among Member States are sometimes invoked to justify this side-tracking of the Council. We should take such matters with the utmost seriousness and ask ourselves what justifications, if any, there are for them and what can be done to restore the Council to the position of influence it was given in the Charter.[2]

The atrophy of institutions created for specific functions but unable effectively to discharge them in practice is a common enough phenomenon of comparative constitutional legal science. It would be normal and sensible to allow the peace-keeping and dispute-settlement competence of the Security Council (and perhaps, if necessary, even the Security Council itself) to lapse into constitutional desuetude, as a matter of constitutional law-in-action, so that other constitutional institutions could fill the gap and exercise the constitutional functions of the Security Council in its place. There are enough objections, in contemporary international law terms, to the composition and ground rules of the Security Council as established in the Charter to justify limitation of its competence by the "conventional," customary law route of supervening practice. Among these contemporary international law objections are the anachronistic character today of the particular (1945) temporal identification of the Big Five in world politics, to whom "permanent member" status and veto power would be accorded under Article 27 (3), and its inherently undemocratic character insofar as, by establishing two categories of states—the one specially legally privileged and the other not so privileged—it runs counter to the fundamental principle of equality of states, which the friendly relations declaration of October 24, 1970, and other post-1945 constitutional acts of the United Nations have sought to raise to the rank of imperative principles of international law. The analogy to the municipal, national constitutional law notion of "*unconstitutional* constitutional norms"—norms established in the constitutional Charter itself but which, through the passage of time and the evolving community juridical conscience, take on a character contrary to the Charter's overall principles—seems proximate in the case of the Security Council permanent members' status and veto power. In a contemporary United Nations context, the case is not so much for the veto power's formal abolition—politically impossible, in any case, given the special constitutional amending machinery established under the Charter and the fact that the permanent members' veto would itself presumably apply to any attempt to remove or reduce the veto power. (One says "presumably," though it is not beyond legal doubt, since the permanent members would themselves be interested parties who should, in terms of Article 27 (3), abstain from voting on such a project for amendment.) Rather the case would be for minimizing possible adverse effects of arbitrary and capricious use of the permanent members' veto power by, as a matter of interpretation and application of the Charter, maximizing the utility of alternative problem-solving arenas and techniques.

In his report of September 1982 the Secretary-General stopped short of identifying the causal factors in the contemporary malaise of the Security Council and the atrophy of its "primary responsibility for the maintenance of international peace and security"[3] granted by the Charter in Article 24(1). Instead, the report concentrated on affirmative possibilities, within existing charter-based institutions and processes, for

> reconstruct[ing] the Charter concept of collective action for peace and security so as to render the United Nations more capable of carrying out its primary function. . . . Governments in fact need more than ever a workable system of collective security in which they can have real confidence.[4]

Turning to his own office, in the postulated objective "to avoid the Security Council becoming involved too late in critical situations," the Secretary-General commented:

> It may well be that the Secretary-General should play a more forthright role in bringing potentially dangerous situations to the attention of the Council within the general framework of Article 99 of the Charter. My predecessors have done this on a number of occasions, but I wonder if the time has not come for a more systematic approach. Most potential conflict areas are well known. The Secretary-General has traditionally, if informally, tried to keep watch for problems likely to result in conflict and to do what he can to preempt them by quiet diplomacy. The Secretary-General's diplomatic means are, however, in themselves quite limited. In order to carry out effectively the preventive role foreseen for the Secretary-General under Article 99, I intend to develop a wider and more systematic capacity for fact-finding in potential conflict areas. Such efforts would naturally be undertaken in close coordination with the Council.[5]

The Secretary-General's reference to quiet diplomacy and to his own inherent powers under Chapter XV (Articles 97–101) of the Charter veils the fact that in a number of instances already, in his first year in office, he had tested the creative possibilities of executive-based "quiet diplomacy," using the legal doctrine of implied powers: in the Venezuela-Guyana border dispute; in the Iran-Iraq War, where the initiative of a peace force intermediary was accepted by one side but not the other; and in the United Kingdom–Argentine conflict on the Falklands-Malvinas question, where the Secretary-General's efforts, complicated as they were in the early stages by the gratuitous interventions of a third-party superpower, may be considered for the historical record as "almost successful" (accepted by both parties within the United Nations negotiating context, but not ratified afterwards by one of the party's home government). These Secretary-General initiatives, and also the suggestions made in the September 1982 report for new constitutional competences, seem constitutionally sound under the Charter and fully supportable in doctrinal-legal terms. Their further development as a matter of constitutional law-in-action would be dependent upon pragmatic considerations concerning the choice of favorable timing and problem situations. The announcement in late December 1982 that the Secretary-General would, notwithstanding protests from the Polish government, begin an inquiry into human rights in Poland, through the medium of an investigation headed by an Argentinian lawyer-diplomat and sometime United Nations official,[6] might be just such an occasion, provided that the Secretary-General could succeed in balancing it, in East-West regional terms, by a similar high-level inquiry into human rights in any one of several parallel conflict situations in Western-leaning or Western-allied states. The inquiry into human rights in Poland had been requested in March 1982 by a vote in the United Nations Commission Human Rights by 19–13 with vestigial East-West Cold War undertones, the 19 states in favor being predominantly Western or Western-leaning, and those against being Soviet-bloc or Soviet-leaning states. Not surprisingly, the Polish delegate to the United Nations Commission on Human Rights, Adam Lopatka, characterized the commission majority resolution as "unlawful, null and void, politically harmful and morally two-faced." The General Assembly of the United Nations, in one of the closing acts of its thirty-seventh session, on December 18, 1982, adopted, 81–38, with 20 abstentions, a motion urging all states to cooperate with investigations by the Commission on Human Rights, thus strengthening the Secretary-General's hand.

Auxiliary Legal Offices: United Nations Legal Counsel, Codification Division (Office of Legal Affairs)

In November 1982, near the end of his first year in office, Secretary-General Pérez de Cuéllar announced the appointment of a new United Nations Undersecretary-General for Legal Affairs and Legal Counsel, Carl-August Fleischhauer of the Federal Republic of Germany,[7] in succession to Erik Suy of Belgium, who was transferred, in a lateral move, to be Director-General of the United Nations office at Geneva. The new appointment as Legal Counsel, the highest legal post within the Secretariat, was widely viewed as Dr. Pérez de Cuéllar's attempt to build his own executive team or cabinet within the Secretariat in his bid to chart out a new personal course for the office of Secretary-General. The retiring legal counsel, Erik Suy, was well respected as an intellectually robust scholar who was not afraid to express his legal opinions frankly: in an opinion on December 3, 1982, for example, he told the Special Political Committee of the General Assembly that a draft resolution calling on the Secretary-General to ensure the protection of Palestinian refugees in Israeli-occupied territories ran counter to the provisions of the 1949 Geneva Conventions providing that responsibility for ensuring human and other rights within such occupied territories attached to the occupying power. Dr. Suy suggested that any attempt by another authority or by an international organization to assume part of that responsibility would seem to weaken or at least obscure this duty of the occupying power, and that it was difficult to see how the Secretary-General could ensure the safety of the Palestinians without in effect exercising certain sovereign powers, including police powers, or else exerting authority or control over the occupying power itself.[8] These are sober words, of course, and on reexamination they perhaps appear less designed to erect another legal barrier against United Nations aid to the Palestinian refugees than an attempt to suggest that any such United Nations-based activism should be undertaken with full awareness of the practical legal challenges involved. Nevertheless, there was a generalized impression within the United Nations that the specialized legal talents of the Secretariat had been used, during the Waldheim secretary-generalship in the decade of the 1970s and until Dr. Waldheim's departure at the end of 1981, as an instrument for delaying and frustrating United Nations actions rather than as a facilitating or liberating agency designed to promote the progressive development of international law. Too much deference to the political sensitiveness of the superpowers on the part of Dr. Waldheim had permeated downward to all sectors of the secretariat, producing in the legal division in particular a juridical conservatism that was frequently out of touch with the aspirations of a majority of members of the General Assembly. The political pressures that the two superpowers are still capable of exercising on the office of the Secretary-General are considerable, of course, because of their relative contributions, under the budget quota system, to the United Nations annual finances. If one joins to the Soviet Union's historical and doctrinally based restrictive, limiting approach to the United Nations and international organization generally, and to the office of Secretary-General in particular, the United States' attempt in the early 1980s to translate domestic "Reaganomics" and budget paring to the international arena and its increasing conservatism and timorousness in the face of the robust Third World majority in the General Assembly, one has an unholy alliance of formidable dimensions. On November 18, 1982, the ambassadors of the Soviet Union and the United States, accompanied by the British ambassador, called upon the Secretary-General in a joint meeting that was reported officially as "an exploratory conversation on measures to improve the efficiency of the United Nations"[9]—widely interpreted as a euphemism for an attempted exercise by these three permanent members of the Security Council of financial pressures on the Secretary-General as a way of expressing their inability to cope with the new political trends and consensus emerging within the United Nations as a whole.

Within the United Nations secretariat's legal division, there has always been the built-in contradiction of a two-headed, bipolar, balancing conception of legal policy making. The legal counsel has always been from a Western-bloc country, while the director of the Codification Division of the Office of Legal Affairs has always been from the Soviet Union. At a purely personal level, this bicephalic organizational approach does not seem to have been obtrusive or to have created too many practical difficulties. But objectively it has been a factor helping induce a static approach to new legal issues, reinforcing the other pressures toward juridical conservatism coming from the external political organs of the United

Nations through the two superpowers and their satellites or supporters, and from the office of the Secretary-General itself during the Waldheim incumbency.

The trend within the United Nations and United Nations law-making process to bypass the specialized Sixth (Legal) Committee in favor of other, frequently ad hoc or similar special committees with their own special legal staffs has undoubtedly been assisted by an image of the Sixth Committee and its supporting regular Secretariat staff as too conservative and too slow-moving in regard to the new challenges to classical international law and the positive law of the Charter. A Third World request for a detailed, empirically based study of the actual practice over the years as to Big Power permanent member veto in the Security Council—a vital aid to the rational approach to reform of that section of the Charter (Article 27) dealing with the problem—was killed in the Codification Division of the Office of Legal Affairs, apparently by the legal counsel in response to pressures from above, which themselves stemmed from fear of an adverse reaction from the two superpowers. Have the superpowers reason to be afraid of a study of the facts of past practice? Similarly, a proposal that the Codification Division study the limits of the Charter Article 51 on the right of self-defense (including necessarily the so-called anticipatory or preventive self-defense), was mysteriously allowed to die within that division; it would have been especially relevant to a number of crisis situations current in 1982—the Israeli armed incursion into Lebanon and bombardment and subsequent military occupation of its capital, Beirut; the Argentinian original takeover of the Falklands-Malvinas and the legally permissible limits and duration of the subsequent British riposte. Was there discreet superpower pressure once more, or anticipatory self-restraint by the Secretary-General to avoid a hostile reaction by the superpowers? A third example, the handing over of the detailed researches and documentation for the projected debate at the thirty-seventh annual session of the General Assembly in the autumn of 1982 on the New International Economic Order, from the Codification Division to the United Nations Institute for Training and Research (UNITAR), seems to have stemmed from a failure to respect the Codification Division's own rigorous scientific-legal standards in the definition of the scope and the modalities of the research involved. The fact that UNITAR, working under extreme pressures of time[10] and with a largely part-time staff hastily organized, produced within the year's deadline only half the desired report, and one in any case that many states in the Sixth (Legal) Committee debate—Canada[11] and Italy in particular—were to characterize as quite inadequate from the scientific-legal viewpoint, tends to confirm the wisdom of the Secretariat's permanent legal division's prior reservations. But, in default, the legal research burden was passed on to UNITAR. By and large, the Codification Division, with a specialist legal staff that is very small in numbers, has performed very well indeed and with a refreshing nonpartisan quality to its work. It could benefit, however, from an increase in personnel; from more autonomy as to the development of a systematic and comprehensive approach to legal research, corresponding to the United Nations' own overarching responsibilities in many areas; and from more effective immunization from the political pressures of permanent members of the Security Council operating upon the office of the Secretary-General and transmitted downward to the Legal Counsel and then to the Office of Legal Affairs. The Secretary-General in the *Proposed Medium-Term Plan for the Period 1984–1989,* filed at the thirty-seventh annual session of the General Assembly in the autumn of 1982, made proposals for a significant expansion of the facilities and services of the secretariat on legal and what he characterized as "important legal-political" questions.[12]

The Sixth (Legal) Committee

The Sixth Committee, because it is a specialist legal committee and so many national delegates to the General Assembly are lawyers themselves, has tended to be a stellar committee. Also, almost all great political, social, and economic conflicts have important legal aspects, and so very many of them end up, or are touched on in various ways, in the Sixth Committee. For a combination of reasons, then, there are strong attractions in serving on the Sixth Committee; and in time a sort of temporal progression, in successive stages, has emerged—from membership in the Sixth Committee to candidacy and election to the International Law Commission and then candidacy and election to the International Court of Justice. It has not been without a certain price, however—already noted in regard to the International Law Commission—in the work performance of the Sixth Committee. Some of the members of the Sixth Committee, being stars, have many and varied responsibilities and interests and may not always be able to be present for all or even most of the regular annual autumn session of the General Assembly. This particular problem is compounded when Sixth Committee membership is combined, at the same time, with membership in the ILC. Though it will often mean a constructive interplay between both bodies, based on the superior knowledge gained from working in both, there may also be questions of a separation-of-powers character concerning the desirability of maintaining a full independence and autonomy as between the two bodies.

Being a body with a very large membership today, coterminous with that of the greatly expanded United Nations of today, the Sixth Committee is rather large and unwieldy and suffers from a rapid turnover of personnel from year to year, with new arrivals each year having to learn the internal processes and group dynamics in order to operate effectively and make their influence felt. Further, the offices of chairman and vice-chairmen, which are perhaps unwarrantedly prized, are sought after and must therefore rotate from year to year, so that there is difficulty in maintaining a corpus of acquired experience and direction at the top and in planning the annual three-month autumn agenda on a systematic, long-term basis with due regard to a period of years. A strong, interventionist Secretariat could help, but the permanent professional officers of the United Nations, from the legal counsel to the director of the Codification Division, have tended to feel—correctly, no doubt—that control of the agenda and establishment of a disciplined hierarchy of subjects, arranged and allocated time according to their relative political importance, involved political value choices properly beyond their own special competence.[13] Each year, therefore, the Sixth Committee's work program bears evidence of a largely ad hoc organization resulting from the inability to plan it on a long-term basis over a period of years.[14] In the early and middle years of the United Nations, when membership was smaller and when there was much greater continuity in the diplomatic personnel returning each year, the Sixth Committee acquired something of a club spirit, with a continuing oral tradition of precedents and practice passed on from year to year. One need only mention legal stars of the decade of the 1960s like Bailey of Australia, Bartos of Yugoslavia, Hambro of Norway, Krishna Rao of India, Lachs of Poland, and Rosenne of Israel. By the early 1980s, they were largely gone or had moved on to higher posts, for example on the International Court, without a later, equivalent generation of jurisconsults having emerged to take their place. With the rare exceptions of long-serving lawyer-diplomats like Rosenstock (USA) and Rosenne, there was no one there to recall past experience, and so a certain trial-and-error process of learning anew was evident, with the inevitable loss of time. For a combination of reasons relating to its assumed conservatism and intellectual timidity or disdain in the face of new legal issues, its unwieldiness resulting from its sheer size, and its lack of continuity from year to year, the Sixth Committee has seen itself bypassed more and more in terms of "new" international law making, with these categories of subjects taken over increasingly by special or ad hoc committees or commissions created for the purpose. Thus coexistence (friendly relations) and codification of its legal principles went to an ad hoc special committee of the General Assembly; outer space and the legal principles as to direct broadcasting from satellites, to the Special Political Committee of the General Assembly; the codification of the "new" international law and the "new" international economic law, as to the sea and the conservation and development of its natural and economic resources, to a special continuing commission created ad hoc for the purpose—the Third United Nations Conference on the Law of the Sea—with its own special and separate Secretariat recruited from the Sixth Committee and the regular United Nations Secretariat. There is some justification for saying that the successful flight of these subjects from the Sixth Committee's natural jurisdiction was assisted by the personal ambitions of key political delegates within the General Assembly, who reasoned, correctly as it turned out, that they could advance their own cause better by operating autonomously and independently of the regular Sixth Committee. These same people were able to assist their case for jurisdictional autonomy by pointing to the Sixth Committee's record and reputation for long delays and, in the end, a somewhat static, traditional approach to "new" international law making. That if you want change in law it is better to start afresh with a new organization became almost a maxim; but it has been at a certain cost to the functional integrity of the United Nations and to a comprehensive, overarching approach to the progressive development of international law into which all the separate, disparate elements can be integrated.

The Reformed International Law Commission

The debate in the Sixth Committee at the thirty-seventh session of the General Assembly, in the autumn of 1982, on the report of the International Law Commission on the work of its thirty-fourth session (held in the summer of 1982), was the first Sixth Committee examination of the ILC since the purported reform effected twelve months before, when the commission's membership had been expanded from twenty-five to thirty-four to take account of the flood of new candidates at the quinquennial elections of 1981. Although certain delegates to the Sixth Committee bravely hailed the expansion of numbers of the commission as having given it "a more authentic international character by reflecting a wider representation of legal systems," there was as yet no empirical evidence to suggest that the commission had managed, in the intervening year since the 1981 amendment to its statute, to master the basic problem, as defined by Ambassador Rosenne, of "how the Commission in its restructured state is to continue to carry out its duties under a Statute which was drafted under entirely different conditions in 1947, thirty-five years ago."[15]

Ambassador Rosenne pointed out that even when the commission was much smaller—it had only fifteen members from the first elections in 1948 until 1956, twenty-one from 1956 until 1961, and twenty-five from 1961 to 1981—he had not been in favor of a system of work based upon the division of the commission into subcommissions, and that the commission had never in fact set up subcommissions to do substantial work on draft articles. The jump in 1981 from twenty-five to thirty-four members would evidently make it impossible for the commission to function as a plenum in a single annual session of ten or twelve weeks without radical recasting of its work methods. If it were to attempt to resolve the problems of numbers in what had by now been transformed from a small committee suitable for group drafting exercises to a reasonably sized debating chamber, by operating through delegation to smaller subcommissions, it would be essential that each such subcommission, in Ambassador Rosenne's words,

> should consist of approximately fifty percent of the membership of the Commission (excluding the President), and that the general representation of the principal legal systems of the world in the Commission itself should be accurately reflected in the subcommissions.[16]

Otherwise, one would run the risk of having to debate the work of each subcommission over again when it should eventually come back to the plenum of the commission. Again in Ambassador Rosenne's words, "the final report and commentaries must be adopted, and I stress the word 'adopted,' by the full Commission. Otherwise the final phase simply will not succeed, and the credibility of the Commission will be impaired."[17]

The commission itself noted, in paragraph 272 of its report, that "without prior notice the practice followed since 1949 of listing in each summary record of a Commission meeting the names of Commission members present at that meeting was discontinued."[18] The commission expressed its own regret at the deletion in this way of the attendance record at each meeting; apparently the decision was made by the General Services Division of the United Nations office at Geneva. Ambassador Rosenne noted that, even more startling than the dropping of the detailed attendance records for individual meetings of the commission, was the omission from Chapter I of the commission report of the "customary sentence regarding the attendance of its members at the session. I know this may sometimes be a delicate matter, but there is no reason why this well established practice should be dropped."[19] One has the uncomfortable feeling that, sorely embarrassed by the revelations and trenchant criticisms made in the UNITAR study of the International Law Commission in 1981, as to chronic absenteeism or nonattendance among the members even of the then much smaller, twenty-five-member commission,[20] the Secretariat had thought it prudent to try to draw a veil over the whole matter. But it is obvious that with any expert working group functioning on a collegial basis, not everyone is of equal intellectual capacity, and it is very important, therefore, for the intellectual weight and authority of the final product, that one should know just who was present and who was not present at any meeting of the commission.

In paragraph 259 of its report, the commission recited the subjects commended to it by the General Assembly by its resolution of December 10, 1981:

> question of treaties concluded between states and international organizations or between two or more international organizations; state responsibility; international liability for injurious consequences arising out of acts not prohibited by international law; the law of the non-navigational uses of international watercourses; jurisdictional immunities of states and their property; status of the diplomatic courier and the diplomatic bag not accompanied by diplomatic courier; and relations between states and international organizations (second part of the topic).[21]

In addition, the General Assembly had invited the commission to resume its work with a view to elaborating the draft code of offenses against the peace and security of mankind.[22]

It is apparent, from the General Assembly's projected list of subjects for the commission's work agenda from 1981 through 1986, that the commission would be leaning very heavily on the codification side of its dual, progressive development/codification of international law mandate—and codification as restrictively and conservatively defined. There is nothing here, really, to meet the basic political criticism advanced all along against the ILC and its own interpretation of its mandate, that it has passed up the great tension issues of international law of the day and chosen to restrict itself to subjects of no great urgency and of only secondary importance at best. Such a self-denying ordinance might be appropriate for a select academy of university lawyers, removed from the exigent here-and-now of contemporary ideological conflicts, but it comes rather strangely from a special legal group that is in fact very strongly identified with the respective national foreign ministries and that has emerged from what has become in recent years a very highly politicized system of elections. For it is, of course, with few exceptions in recent times, the "foreign office lawyers" who have dominated the ILC, not the supposedly (though not always) politically detached representatives of the universities and scientific academies.

A justification for part of the ILC's self-denying ordinance as to "new" international law making is sought by some on the basis of a postulated dichotomy—between "politics" and "law"—which contemporary Western law schools teach as being untrue. Still others would justify a policy of conscious inaction in relation to the burning legal issues of the day with the statement that such subjects simply are not "ripe" for codification. Iterated and reiterated without any further demonstration, that particular statement takes on the quality almost of a cliché—a convenient mask for a lack of intellectual imagination or of civil courage in law making on the part of those who enunciate it. It involves, in any case, a misunderstanding of von Savigny's original historical thesis on the dangers of "premature" codification before the necessary *Volksgeist* should have emerged. Von Savigny's strictures were directed against generalized, universal acts of legal codification and were never intended to prevent or impede specific legislative acts directed toward specific and immediate social tension issues for which legal solutions could not safely be postponed. Otherwise, all the lessons of historicism would be reduced to dead-hand control from the past and a recipe for community inaction in regard to affirmative law making for the future. As A. V. Dicey was to remind his Anglo Saxon Common Law legal audiences, law and society exist in symbiotic relationship and mutually interact. Society may operate to limit or divert legal remedies and prescriptions, but positive law, in its turn, when consciously and rationally conceived and applied, can significantly shape and control and form societal attitudes. There is a necessary methodological distinction to be made, therefore, between abstract, a priori universal codification, and empirically based, step-by-step acts of individual codification; and there is absolutely nothing to inhibit the ILC from venturing on the "difficult" subjects within this latter category. In default of ILC initiatives, legal codification will still occur, but it will be done elsewhere, in other, special arenas, as with the friendly relations (coexistence) great codification exercise of the decade of the 1960s, and the Law of the Sea codification exercise of the decade of the 1970s and the beginning of the 1980s, which emerged under the rubric of the Third United Nations Conference on the Law of the Sea.

The distinguished French scholar and jurist and current president of the International Law Commission, Paul Reuter, in his formal declaration to the Sixth Committee in the autumn of 1982, on the report of the ILC,[23] put the best face possible on the enlargement of the commission and the effect upon its work habits and work capacity. The commission had already, at drafting committee stage, four of the subjects proposed in the General Assembly resolution of December 10, 1981, as the work program for the 1981–1986 term: treaties concluded between states and international organizations (now completed in its drafting); state responsibility; jurisdictional immunities of states and their property; the status of the diplomatic courier and the diplomatic bag not accompanied by diplomatic courier. Beyond these four subjects, the commission had proceeded to prepare its future work program, taking note again of the detailed recommendations of the General Assembly in its resolution of December 10, 1981. Among these, the project for a draft code of offenses against the peace and security of mankind had already been initiated with the designation of a special *rapporteur*, and the same action had been taken on the subject of the nonnavigational uses of international watercourses. It was hoped to make progress with the subject of international liability for injurious consequences arising out of acts not prohibited by international law, and at least to proceed to the study of the second part of the subject of relations between states and international organizations.

It was, however, in his closing statement to the Sixth Committee, on November 16, 1982,[24] toward the end of the committee's debate on the report of the ILC, and by way of response to the intervening debate, that Professor Reuter chose to answer directly some of the strong criticisms of the commission and its work methods and methodological approach to international law making, voiced in the committee debate and also in the corridors of the General Assembly. He insisted that the commission, as an independent commission, had always demanded a certain liberty in regard to the organization of its work. This, seemingly, was in response to the debate within the Sixth Committee and a certain "regional" East-West division appearing therein, with the Soviet Union insisting that it is precisely the General Assembly that defines the mandate of the ILC and sets its priorities of work (which would make the ILC the servant of the General Assembly), and the Western bloc countering that it is only for the General Assembly and the Sixth Committee to indicate their preferences as to priorities and emphasis in a list of subjects, with the ILC then deciding at its full discretion (which would, of course, free the General Assembly and Sixth Committee from responsibility or blame if the ILC dragged its feet or appeared too timid in its approach to and selection of subjects). It was, of course, an issue that had been present from the beginning of the commission and was unlikely ever to be resolved in absolute terms, the earlier seemingly much more independent stance in relation to choice and control of its own agenda and work program undoubtedly reflecting the far greater relative scientific-legal prestige and standing and "authority" of that earlier commission membership.

President Reuter did, however, contend that the commission has only a very limited margin of choice, its action being defined by a very precise statute which defines its object and its procedures:

> We are neither a university institution nor a club of fine spirits consecrating their leisure time to international law, but an instrument at the service of the General Assembly.
>
> It is true, and several delegations have singled out this aspect, that the General Assembly has chosen to orient our work by wishes, recommendations, consultations, and supple directives rather than by imperative resolutions. But it little matters what juridical form the General Assembly has chosen to let us know its desires, for the weight of the indications given by the General Assembly is, for us, the same: our work has value only in the reception that is given to it by governments within the General Assembly.[25]

To the criticisms directed at the membership of the commission, and the election in more recent times of the "men of affairs" who are so often absentees, Professor Reuter offered the rejoinder:

> The General Assembly, by the choice of members of the ILC, has wanted it to remain open to every experience brought by the effective exercise of international functions: the Commission is therefore formed, in principle, of persons who have heavy obligations, sometimes at a very high level, outside the Commission. In a certain measure the Commission must take account of that.
>
> The organization of the Commission's work must thus be marked by a great flexibility.[26]

In facing up very frankly (and perhaps sadly) to the present-day realities of the ILC, Professor Reuter also took note of the principle of the formal legal equality of its members, which, among other things, necessarily limited the possibility of accelerating work completion through multiplication of subcommissions, each member of the ILC having the legal right to participate in all decisions and there being no right of substituting an alternate for an absent member. He also defended the commission against the charge of dragging of feet, pointing out that since 1966 the commission had drafted eight conventions, which he considered a very satisfying average.[27]

The central paradox still remained, after President Reuter's closing intervention and the customary rather bland resolution in the Sixth Committee thanking the ILC for its achievements over the past year and expressing the hope that it would continue its work in the future.[28] How could such a body, whose membership was so fiercely contested in the quinquennial elections and with such a degree of attention to "regional" factors, and which as a result was now stocked with "foreign office lawyers" sophisticated in United Nations internal politics and lobbying, be content to remain at the periphery of the great events of contemporary international law making, and to be bypassed or excluded when great new issues of the progressive development of international law should arise? The answer seems to have been present from the beginning in a certain innate pessimism on the part of the first, "founding" generation of commission members, in the era of its great jurisconsults: the belief that in an era of ideological conflict and rapid political, socioeconomic, and technological change it was futile to venture upon ambitious projects of legal codifications.[29] Later generations of lawyers within the General Assembly, perhaps legally less well formed and disciplined than the great jurisconsults of the earlier postwar years, felt no such psychological inhibitions. Fearing that, if it were to be left to the ILC, the old "precolonial" legal regime would still predominate in any "new" international law making, since the work would be done or effectively controlled by the lawyers of the Big Powers,[30] they did not hesitate to form their own legal power base, with their own special staff, outside the ILC and indeed (and if necessary) outside the Sixth Committee with its traditional ties of consanguinity to the ILC.[31] "New" international law thus continued to be made, in spite of the Big Powers and their large pools of lawyers; but insofar as it was made outside the ILC, it was made without the benefit of the developed expertise and knowledge of past precedents and how and when to liberate oneself from them, supposedly reposing in the ILC as the United Nations Organization's specialized body for the progressive development of international law and its codification.

9. Ideological Pluralism and Contemporary International Law Values: Self-Determination of Peoples, Economic Sovereignty

The values of international law at any time in its historical development are reflected in the authoritative decisions made in all main arenas and through all main processes of world community law making. In the contemporary era, the values are to be found in the resolutions of the General Assembly; decisions of the Security Council and of the principal United Nations specialized agencies; the judgments and advisory opinions of the International Court of Justice; the self-legislation involved in international treaty making (multilateral, but also limited, bilateral treaties), and in state acts (including unilateral declarations of state intention) and sometimes the decision to refrain from state action, which may operate by way of estoppel.

Jural Postulates of a Civilization Area and Civilization Period

The American jurist of the first half of the present century, Roscoe Pound, who conceived of law as a process of reconciliation of competing community interests (public, social, individual), saw the need for identifying key ordering principles of law if the process of balancing interests in resolution of conflicts was to be rendered rational and placed on a predictable, objectively verifiable basis. Such ordering principles of law, in Pound's view, would be extrapolated from the authoritative decisions of a given society by a process of induction, and then rationalization and generalization, from the mass of competing interests present in the particular societal problem situations being decided in the society and from the particular community choices made among those competing interests in the final resolution of conflicts. The ordering principles of law that were thus induced were named by Pound as the jural postulates of a civilization area and civilization period.[1] Pound's approach to identification and choice of the jural postulates was thus thoroughly empirical and as a result necessarily relativist, reflecting the values officially applied in a given society, through its official law-making arenas and processes, at a given time, but not more than that; and certainly not new or inchoate values still in process of emergence and acquiring public recognition and acceptance through the ordinary community dialectical processes. The jural postulates, once identified, would perform a clarifying and ordering function in the general community law-making processes, unifying otherwise disparate details; and for a stable society, with a certain cultural homogeneity and an already existing consensus on political, social, and economic basic questions, this might well be the prime objective in legal development. For nonhomogeneous, nonstable societies that were still in full evolution in their attitudes to fundamental issues of political, social, and economic choice, however, the jural postulates, insofar as they would reflect the value choices of official decision makers taken at a particular point in time only, would be likely to operate conservatively, as a brake on societal development or an instrument for maintaining the status quo.

The way out of this dilemma clearly lay in developmental theories of law and society, involving, in the end, historical determinism and conceptions of the long-range trends and direction of society. The German liberal democratic legal theorist of the Wilhelminian era, J. Kohler,[2] made his own essay at solving the dilemma through the neo-Hegelian notion of the unfolding of civilization in law, with the official decision maker's legal mandate and role thereby becoming one of actively assisting and furthering this process of historical development. This still left the question, present not less with historically deterministic theories of law than with simple legal relativism, of what to do in the case of a "retrogressive" civilization, and how indeed to recognize it as such at the moment of decision. Should the official decision maker be emancipated in such cases from his legal mandate and duty to apply the jural postulates of the civilization, and, if so, on what basis should he finally decide?

The question became especially acute in Kohler's own national society, Germany, a generation or more after he developed his theories. For some jurists the ideal personal solution of the dilemma of value choice would be one of escape into von Ihering's "heaven of juristic concepts" (Begriffs-Himmel) and of the deliberate immunization of oneself from problems of value choice and value application in law. For others with more civil courage, however, the *moral* dilemma of legal value choice was to prove not so difficult to resolve in actual, concrete cases, the answer being provided by a recognition of the existence of some at least minimum principles of humanity and decency basic to any civilized legal system. If then, in extreme or pathological situations the problem of ultimate value choice is likely to be more notional than real, there will still remain the issue of how to identify and select among competing values in a society that is plural in ethnic-cultural terms; that is clearly in transition as to its basic social and economic organization; and that has not yet achieved a full ideological synthesis of opposing views as to the movement of history and as to its own long-range direction and objectives. There are many such societies, of course, at the municipal, national level; but it is to the contemporary world community that we must now address ourselves in particular.

Values and Value Choice

The contemporary world community, viewed as a particular civilization area at a particular moment in history or civilization era, manifests a number of main dilemmas as to identification and choice of jural postulates or goal values.[3]

Value Identification

The contemporary issue here is what are or should be the main ordering principles or goal values of an ideologically and ethnic-culturally plural world community, not merely in transition in its basic social and economic organization but with different regions or groupings of states at markedly different levels of social and economic development and co-existing of necessity together. Modern constitution-making ventures for municipal, national societies usually attempt to resolve the problem of the goal values of society by postulating them in the constitutional charter itself as an authoritative guide to official decision makers at all levels and, more generally, as an attempt to inform and educate the public about the main aspirations of the society. The drafters of the Spanish Republican Constitution of 1931 established a constitutional innovation, since borrowed in the Irish Republican Constitution of 1937 and the postdecolonization Indian Republican Constitution of 1950, of listing directive principles of state (or social) policy[4]—concerning the main issues of community choice in cultural, social, and economic matters—in a special chapter included in the constitutional charter itself. Other, contemporary constitution makers may seek to achieve the same result by incorporating such social and economic postulates into a constitutional bill of rights, particularly where such a bill of rights seeks to go beyond the somewhat skeletal Anglo-Saxon Common Law, essentially laissez-faire, constitutional model that is normally limited to the "open society" style of political and civil rights, and to enter directly upon the key issues of social and economic choice of today. Most of the constitutional charters adopted, or proposed after World War II illustrate this new trend in constitutional drafting; it is most pronounced in the case of non-Western societies, but some of the better "renewed" Western constitutional charters of recent years show the same positive openings to social and economic issues. Still other constitution makers may use the preamble to the constitutional charter for the enunciation of high-level philosophical principles as to law and society; such charters acquire, in consequence, a hortatory, pedagogical quality, and will need institutional and processual follow-up if the necessarily abstract general norms of the preamble are effectively to be translated into constitutional law-in-action in the future. But at least the official state intents as to the goals and directions of the society for the future are conveniently collected in the one place and presented clearly and unequivocally.

The United Nations Charter, as the basic constitutional instrument of international society, must constitute the principal legal source of the jural postulates or legal goal values of its own particular civilization area and civilization era, the contemporary world community. It is, in comparative constitutional terms, a modern document, enacted as recently as 1945. But, as noted in other areas of international law, time has a habit of galloping today, and so the Charter's postulates, such as they are, may need supplementing and updating and, in some cases, renewal or redefinition. In the actual drafting of the Charter there were, as we have noted, historical differences among its founding fathers as to just what the Charter was intended to do and as to just what its legal characterization should be—a limited treaty between sovereign states, on the more restrictive, Soviet approach, or something more, as many Western countries seemed to imply. In the result, and in what concerns postulation of goal values or philosophical objectives, the Charter comes closer to the rather skeletal Anglo-Saxon Common Law constitutional charter model than to the philosophically much richer and more detailed paradigms developed in continental European civil law constitutionalism (both Western and Eastern Europe) and in related non-European systems of the postwar period. The Charter is very strong and usually very explicit in its enunciation of institutions and procedures and decision-making processes, but correspondingly much lighter in its approach to definition of goal values, ordering principles, and even legal standards; and there is no attempt to organize these and collect them in a disciplined fashion in any one place—for example, in a special charter-based chapter or bill of rights. While the Charter preamble is richly poetic in language, it tends to be abstract and general and unconcrete in dealing with the purposes of the Charter and of the new international order that it set up. There are references in the preamble to the "scourge of war"; "fundamental human rights"; "the dignity and worth of the human person"; "the equal rights of men and women and of nations large and small"; "justice and respect for the obligations arising from treaties and other sources of international law"; to promoting "social progress and better standards of life in larger freedom" and to promoting also the "economic and social advancement of all peoples." The immediately ensuing Chapter I ("Purposes and Principles") (Articles 1 and 2) attempts to offer somewhat more low-level and concrete secondary legal principles in application of the preambular high-level formulations; and these do indeed establish an emphasis, befitting a world public order system established at the end of a great military conflict, upon peace keeping, on peaceful settlement of disputes, and on refraining from the "threat or use of force against the territorial integrity or political independence of any state" (Article 2 [4]). Chapter I of the Charter also postulates the "sovereign equality" of all members of the United Nations (Article 2 [1]); though, as with the original definition of constitutional "equal protection" under the United States Constitution's post–Civil War Fourteenth Amendment, it is, in terms, a formal, juridical equality only.[5] There is explicit mention of the principle of "equal rights and self-determination of peoples" (Article 1 [2]), and the affirmation of the need for "international cooperation in solving international problems of an economic, social, cultural, or humanitarian character, and in promoting and encouraging respect for human rights and for fundamental freedoms for all without distinction as to race, sex, language, or religion" (Article 1 [3]). Beyond the preamble and Chapter I ("Purposes and Principles"), there are, scattered through the detailed machinery sections of the Charter, the type of "standards" provisions to be found in every national legal system, that call out for evaluation in any given case and development on a case-by-case basis; for example, the reference in Chapter II ("Membership") (Articles 3–6), to the fact of membership being open to "*peace-loving* states, which accept the obligations contained in the present Charter and, in the judgement of the Organization, are able and willing to carry out these obligations." References, such as that already referred to above, to the mandate of the General Assembly under Article 13 (1)(a) to promote and encourage the "*progressive* development of international law and its codification" may, in strictly juridical terms, authorize an activist approach to international law making for the future, if the decision makers concerned have the civil courage and the necessary political consensus behind them to want to attempt that.

In sum, except for peace and peace keeping, self-determination, and equality of states, the Charter itself does not provide too much help as to the jural postulates or goal values to guide the updating and future development of international organization and international law generally. Fortunately, however, like the earlier Anglo-Saxon common law laissez-faire constitutional models which appear to have influenced its drafting, the Charter is relatively open-ended and neutral in philosophical terms, once one goes beyond the several ordering principles already referred to. There is therefore absolutely nothing to prevent the Charter—in the fashion of other living constitutional instruments before it—from being built upon and added to by other, subsequent constitutional acts or customary law "glosses" not in conflict with its original text. This process of creative novation, on an incremental, sometimes case-by-case basis over the years since 1945, through developing United Nations practice as expressed in the formal legislation of declarations based on General Assembly resolutions or similar fundamental acts, judicial decisions, executive-administrative acts, and the like, has been the lifeblood of international organization in the postwar era. Rendered necessary, in terms of the instruments and processes of constitutional change, through the complicated machinery for formal amendment of the Charter established under Chapter XVIII ("Amendments") (Articles 108–109), which establishes virtually insurmountable barriers to direct change to the Charter except on trivial issues not touching on the Big Powers' prerogatives, this system of indirect change presents all the advantages of continuing, organic development on a pragmatic, empirical, step-by-step basis. There has indeed been a dialectical development of United Nations law and practice since 1945, with historical unfolding from year to year in accordance with the continually evolving consensus within the General Assembly over that time period. Teleological or purposive interpretation, in accord with that continuing consensus, has guided the historical evolution and adaptation of the Charter and charter law, as it has done with all viable national constitutional systems. The important point is that whatever the Charter may lack in terms of postulated a priori constitutional ordering principles or values, on a thoroughly empirical approach there has been little difficulty in identifying the key jural postulates or goal values of contemporary United Nations law-in-action, and little difficulty in maintaining the necessary political consensus and support for their practical implementation—in supplement to the very few such postulates that are indeed formally identified, a priori, in the preamble and the opening two sections of the Charter. Current dilemmas as to the goal values of contemporary international law tend to concern questions other than their identification as such, and relate rather to their factual application in concrete cases or their ranking inter se when they happen to conflict in action.

Value Ranking

The problem here is that most legal problem situations are polycentric and will involve two or more goal values present in one fact complex. Sometimes those goal values will be in direct competition, leading to quite different end results, depending on which one is invoked by the rival parties and by the authoritative decision makers concerned. To take an example, in the original charter formulation the peace imperative, involving among other things the legal interdiction of the threat or use of force, is clear, just as is the principle of self-determination of peoples. Is a subject people entitled to have recourse to the use of force, with or without the direct military aid of its ideological allies or associates outside the country, when the dominant (imperial or colonial, and in any case foreign) power imposes clogs upon the orderly, constitutional realization of the political self-determination principle? The resolution of the value dilemma in this context would require, in the abstract, the establishment of some sort of hierarchy or ranking of values, establishing authoritatively and on an a priori basis, in advance of all actual problem situations, which of the competing values is the most important and deserving of preference by decision makers. In the concrete, and as a matter of United Nations developing historical practice (in the absence of any advance, a priori, authoritative ranking of values), there have not been too many problems. The developing juridical conscience of the world community, as expressed through General Assembly resolutions and other official acts, has supplied reasonably clear guidelines for harmonizing and rendering compatible the invocation and application of the values in concrete cases.

Value Concretization

The jural postulates or goal values, to the extent that they are indicated in the preamble and the opening sections of the Charter and also in legal-doctrinal writings, are formulated only at a very high level of generality and abstraction. To be made operational, they need to be rendered into much more low-level and concrete secondary or even tertiary principles capable of immediate application to actual problem situations. Once one moves from the abstract and general *primary* principles to the more specific and practical secondary or tertiary principles, one finds that the tidy intersystemic consensus as to the goal values of United Nations and contemporary international law begins to become strained. For not merely do the various political-ideological systems have frequently differing conceptions of the meaning or connotation of those goal values, but they may also disagree as to their factual application in concrete cases or even as to whether they apply at all in the specific fact contexts. Thus it is clear, for example, in the area of human rights, to which, as an abstract principle or goal value, all major political ideological systems have pledged their allegiance, that for reasons of particular historical background and development and also the basic socioeconomic infrastructure, the three main blocs or groupings of states within the United Nations—Western, Socialist, and Third World—differ as to the range and extent of the concept itself. Such interbloc, intersystemic ideological differences influence the purported application of the concept of human rights so as to include the "new" social and economic rights as well as the "old" or "classical" political and civil rights, and also the degree of practical deference to be accorded to each; and the relevance of the "new" concept of collective or group rights in contradistinction to the "old" personal or individual rights.[6] It is an area in which the charge of Eurocentrism and of a morally self-righteous and self-serving ignoring of the socioeconomic infrastructure underlying all legal right-duty relationships is most often raised against the Western-bloc countries. The historical contradictions here between the rival political-ideological systems have not yet been fully and finally resolved within the United Nations' own internal dialectical processes. But significant advances have been made, and the lines of possible eventual reconciliation or synthesis of the distinctive attitudes and approaches of the rival systems are appearing. One needs to make an ally of time for purposes of an eventual resolution of the problem.

Other problems will arise, however, in the factual application to specific problem situations of goal values already agreed upon, at the level of the abstract and general *primary* principles, by all main legal systems. Everyone accepts—in public, at least—the principle of the self-determination of peoples. But there may be disagreement in terms of its more concrete and immediate application. For example, is the principle of self-determination of peoples limited only to classical colonial situations involving a European "parent," imperial country holding subject the indigenous native population of an overseas colony—a legal category now approaching the point of being exhausted as a result of the General Assembly's successful political drives in the 1950s, 1960s, and 1970s to liberate the remaining remnants of the old European colonial empires of yesteryear? Or does the principle apply also to new, *post*-decolonization, or even noncolonial, situations? There are also problems of factual characterization when, in a noncolonial situation raising self-determination claims, a "parent" European imperial country may insist that the matter is, in terms of Article 2 (7) of the Charter, one "essentially within the domestic jurisdiction" of itself, and hence, by definition, not raising international law self-determination issues and therefore not licit in legal terms. Once again, United Nations practice over the years reveals that questions such as these, while raising political difficulties, are not legally intractable; and the evolving juridical consensus within the United Nations has come through, in time, to provide an agreed interpretation and solution that have been perforce accepted by, if not altogether satisfying, all main blocs—Western, Socialist, and Third World.

Contemporary International Law Values: Self-Determination of Peoples, the Decolonization Imperative

On all the empirical evidence of United Nations practice, we would have to consider self-determination of peoples—in its narrower original historical, pre-Charter formulation as *political* self-determination—as the motor principle in the progressive development and unfolding of United Nations and general international law since 1945. More than any other legal principle, political self-determination has been the catalyst for United Nations legal activism, stimulating fundamental change to the basic fabric of the world community—a veritable political and social revolution, effectuated peacefully in disciplined and systematic fashion, in the interstices of legal reform measures, here a series of General Assembly resolutions and executive-administrative and judicial acts building upon the original Charter-based principle. The Charter enunciation finds its most concrete and explicit formulation in problem-oriented secondary principles in the Declaration on the Granting of Independence to Colonial Countries and Peoples, adopted by General Assembly Resolution 1514 (XV) of December 14, 1960. The vote on the General Assembly resolution was an overwhelming 89–0, but there were nine abstentions (Australia, Belgium, Dominican Republic, France, Portugal, Spain, Union of South Africa, United Kingdom, United States), the abstaining states (which had not cared to vote no!) being for the most part the still remaining European imperial powers that had not yet liberated their colonial territories overseas. If it was the declaration of 1960 that so largely erected self-determination, decolonization, and independence into imperative principles of international law, or *jus cogens,* the drive for political self-determination was given practical realization, in a highly pragmatic fashion, in a host of executive-administrative and judicial actions in other United Nations arenas. Small independent African states like Ethiopia (which had briefly and fleetingly been twice exposed to Italian "colonization") and Liberia (a free settlement in Africa made in the nineteenth century by the erstwhile victims of the European slave trade and their descendants, newly liberated in the United States) began a veritable guerrilla war of litigation before the International Court of Justice, designed to liberate southern Africa from the white minority rule of the Union of South Africa, itself a latter-day survival of Dutch, and then British, imperial colonial development. The immediate object before the International Court was the termination of the old League of Nations mandate over South West Africa (Namibia), the former German colony, which the victors of Versailles had conferred upon the Union of South Africa in their peace treaty of 1919 dictated to defeated imperial Germany, and which the Union of South Africa had then proceeded to assimilate to full legal ownership and control. After a series of procedural, adjectival law-based rebuffs for the moving Third World countries,[7] the International Court of Justice, following on fierce General Assembly criticisms of the substantive consequences of its earlier decisions, finally in 1971[8] declared the Union of South Africa's mandate to be legally terminated. The prologue to the court's effective volte-face, in its 1971 advisory opinion was effectively coordinated political action within the General Assembly and Security Council, producing the formal request to the court for ruling on the issue of the continued validity, then, of the original mandate, given the evolution of international law in the intervening half-century and the preeminent role accorded in contemporary international law to political self-determination. The actual legal follow-up to the court's 1971 ruling ran into a number of political roadblocks in the General Assembly and elsewhere, but the end of the road seemed clear and inescapable: final decolonization, independence, and self-government for Namibia and, after that, full majority government for South Africa, as the legal culmination of the drive for political self-determination for southern Africa initiated with the General Assembly's first inquiries, at the opening of the 1950s, into the "racial situation" in South Africa.

Discussion of the Namibia question directs attention to the fact that it required a certain intellectual-legal jump for authoritative international decision makers to accept applicability of the Declaration on the Granting of Independence to Colonial Countries and Peoples not merely to "colonies" as conventionally understood to be the overseas territories, inhabited by indigenous non-European peoples, of the European imperial powers, but to what was in abstract, formal legal terms not a "colony" as such but a League of Nations mandate. But once the International Court of Justice had summoned up the civil courage and intellectual-legal imagination to break through the artificial procedural, adjectival law barriers that it had itself created in its earlier rulings on South West Africa, that substantive law jump proved not too difficult or intellectually demanding to make. More serious questions today have to do with whether the legal imperative of political self-determination denotes not merely what we might now almost call "classical" *first phase* decolonization situations—those involving liberation of aboriginal (non-European) peoples from their original European imperial masters—but also *second phase* decolonization situations, where no substantial aboriginal population is involved in the European colonial territory, and, much more important, *non*-colonial situations where no European colonial power is any longer involved and what we are dealing with is a contest for political power within one state between two or more "succession" (postimperial) indigenous, aboriginal peoples, without the complication of a significant expatriate European presence.

The first of these problems is clearly the easier one to answer, for there are so few of them remaining. They are the accidental remnants of European colonial empires—isolated lumps of rock or uninhabited islands seized, by *force majeure* where necessary, to guard the long sea routes to some distant inhabited colonial territory, now lost, or to serve as a refueling station or a botanical or scientific observation post. Granted ordinary common sense, an imperial power that had already lost the inhabited colonial territories that these scattered colonial outposts once served as naval stations would have made its own cost-benefit analysis in reasonably timely fashion and proceeded to liquidate its remaining colonial investment as expeditiously and painlessly as possible. That erstwhile imperial powers do not always do so can be attributed, no doubt, to a number of factors: simple oversight or absent-mindedness; the hope, against all hope and rational scientific verification, that there may be oil or something else of value in those bleak remaining outposts and the desire for a quick (if temporary) economic gain at the expense of some political embarrassment. Over and beyond all these, however, there seems to be a special nostalgia or madness that besets former imperial powers looking back in anger from an often economically dismal present to the conceived romantic splendors of the imperial past. It seems to be psychologically very, very difficult for ancient imperial proconsuls and their attendant lawyers and scribes to give up, so strong is the bureaucratic momentum today of old imperial ideas. The Canadian government discovered, to its surprise and its own ill-concealed irritation, in the period 1980–1982 that diehard back-bench members of the British Parliament still insisted that (somehow or other in legal terms) those back-benchers remained "legal guardians" of the Canadian Constitution, invested with "legal trustee" powers to supervise the practical functioning of the Canadian federal system. The Canadian government insisted successfully that since Canada had obtained her full juridical independence from the United Kingdom a full half-century before, such British Parliament back-benchers' legal pretensions were, in fact, legal nonsense and legally unacceptable—a Canadian government legal position in which British Prime Minister Thatcher acquiesced. But if members of the British Parliament could as late as 1982 tilt at legal windmills in support of a fanciful claim still to exercise some form of legal hegemony over independent Canada—long since, in effect, decolonized on an amicable, fully consensual basis in the so-called Statute of Westminster of 1931—how much more difficult would they find it to acquiesce sensibly and gracefully in the liquidation in the same year, 1982, of the largely abandoned naval refueling base in the far South Atlantic originally taken, a century and a half before, by *force majeure* from the Argentinians,—the Falklands (Malvinas).[9] Seventeen years of British-Argentinian bilateral negotiations had apparently seen the British government ready on two occasions to withdraw from the Falklands (Malvinas), but the matter was never considered of high priority and was allowed to drift, the British-Canadian bilateral negotiations of 1980–1982 over final "patriation" of the Canadian Constitution having further delayed action on the file in the British Foreign Office. We shall refer in another context to the rash action of the Argentinian government in resorting to direct military action before bilateral diplomatic negotiations had been broken off or political-diplomatic possibilities within the United Nations had been fully explored and exhausted. Suffice it to say here that the Falklands (Malvinas) do not fall into the "classical" decolonization category, there being no indigenous, aboriginal people already in place on the islands, before whose claims the European imperial power must yield. Argentina's legal claims rested, in fact, on other still quite substantial legal grounds: an original Spanish imperial territorial title maintained by Argentina under the rules of state succession and through the special Latin American regional international law doctrine of *uti possidetis;* an original Argentinian effective occupation of the islands that had been terminated only illegally and by *force majeure* by the British imperial power; and, finally, "new" international law doctrines of geographical contiguity as the basis of legal title, in the absence of other countervailing claims of a recognized legal character. Cumulatively, the Argentinian claims were sufficient and impressive. By contrast, the British claims rested on no more than an original, patently illegal act of seizure of the islands, followed by long-term occupation. The latter-day claim, advanced in 1982 after the opening of military hostilities between the United Kingdom and Argentina, that the British subjects settled on the islands by Great Britain, and their descendants—in fact, a scant 1,800 people today—had a legal right of national self-determination, to be exercised by remaining as a British imperial colony, hardly deserved to be taken seriously in the context of United Nations history and practice over the years since 1945. *De minimis non curat lex,* as a legal *maxim,* applies as much to national self-determination as to other areas of law. The United Nations had, on a legally principled basis, refused to countenance political partition of Cyprus into two independent units so as to give separate political self-determination to 120,000 Turks and to 480,000 Greeks, as a solution for that island's problems, even though the two national communities concerned occupied essentially distinct and different geographical regions; and the United Nations was hardly likely to concede to the 1,800 on the Falklands (Malvinas), as a basis for rejecting Argentina's legal claims, what it had declined to concede to very much larger population units elsewhere. The British argument as to the privileges and interests of the 1,800 British-descended inhabitants of the Falklands (Malvinas) would seem better realized legally in a claim for some degree of regional autonomy and local self-government within the framework of an eventual political settlement returning the islands to Argentina, and for some degree of financial subsidy or compensation to those inhabitants desiring to emigrate from the islands after such eventual political settlement. These were policies, after all, which the United Kingdom had been advancing in the approach to political settlement of her own long-standing Ulster problem—the British-held territorial enclave remaining in the northeast corner of the Republic of Ireland after its political independence and separation from the United Kingdom. Within that British enclave the British government had so far resisted, on a *de minimis* basis, the arguments of the Roman Catholic minority (forming nearly half the population), who wanted to join with the predominantly Roman Catholic Republic of Ireland.

Discussion of the Falklands (Malvinas) problem directs attention to the fact that, with the major exception of South Africa and the exception also of the remaining vestigial remnants of the old British colonial empire (Gibraltar, Hong Kong, and the so-called New Territories), the book has been virtually closed on decolonization questions proper. A glance at the agenda of the General Assembly's Fourth Committee, which is specially charged with decolonization questions, in search of other items, reveals largely picayune questions, apart from some strictly *post*-decolonization, "succession state" problems arising after the departure of the European imperial power concerned. Of these only the Western Sahara problem,[10] involving final determination of the identity of the successor state or states to imperial Spain, now departed, appears of major importance or as having in it the seeds of future international, intraregional conflict. So much so, indeed, that the Fourth Committee was able to complete its agenda and terminate its work for the thirty-seventh session of the General Assembly on November 19, 1982, a full month before the other specialized committees. (One should add, perhaps, that the Antarctica question is potentially important, insofar as the 1959 Antarctic Treaty dedicating the region to scientific research and cooperation simply froze existing territorial claims, such as they were, without purporting to confirm or deny them. Insofar as the original territorial claimants, signatories to the 1959 treaty, were in very large part former imperial powers or their dependents, who had taken part in the original imperial "rush for spoils" in colonial territories overseas, there seems no reason for extending special credence or legal deference to their territorial claims, in terms of contemporary international law in its postcolonial evolution and development.)[11]

The real, and burning issues as to political self-determination today are likely to be, then, *post*-decolonization and even *non*-colonial in character. Almost all the "succession states" to the old European colonial empires in Africa and even Asia have been multinational states in ethnic-cultural and linguistic terms, whose ethnic composition and political frontiers were so often arbitrarily or casually determined, either by imperial fiat or by intra-European international agreement like the Congress of Berlin of 1885. European statesmen then drew up territorial borders for regions hardly known to the Europeans concerned, often cutting up existing tribal communities, and in any case defining static geographical boundaries for what were in some cases purely nomadic communities that did not recognize such territorially based fixed divisions. The "division of the spoils" in Africa was, as recognized in the International Court of Justice's 1975 advisory opinion in *Western Sahara,*[12] not merely European in its political motivations but Eurocentrist in its conceptualizations and legal configurations; and this is what was passed on to the postdecolonization "succession states." Does political self-determination apply, as an imperative principle of law today, to rectify the frequently arbitrary, capricious, and irrational territorial dispositions made by the European imperial powers among themselves in that purely European "rush for the spoils"? In terms of United Nations received opinion and practice, the answer today is No!; or, at least, Not Yet! It is pointed out that the "made-in-Europe" territorial dispositions concerned were for the most part made three-quarters of a century, or even much more, before the decolonization of the 1950s and 1960s; and that, for better or worse, the historical accident of particular European colonization had given a degree of second (European) language and also legal and administrative cohesiveness and unity that supplied an element of integration and common collective purpose that was sorely needed to overcome the invariable postdecolonization economic difficulties. Attempting to turn the clock back in history and to redress today, on a purportedly ethnic-cultural or tribal basis, the received imperial colonial frontiers would create much confusion and impede realization of the postdecolonization planning imperatives. History, here imperial-colonial history, creates its own political and social facts of life, and it may sometimes be easier to start with those facts and try to correct them in the future on a consensual basis, through the ordinary constitutional process in the postcolonial societies concerned. Beyond that, however, lies the far more important principle of stability and continuity—legitimacy, if you wish—in the vastly troubled postdecolonization "succession state." A distinguished Arab diplomat whose own state, by a happy accident of history, has no very significant ethnic-cultural or national minority problems commented, in relation to the Ethiopian-Somali border conflicts and to Somalian irridentist claims against the Ogaden region, that the new Third World "succession states" that had succeeded in the postwar era to the old European colonial empires in Africa and Asia had too many problems of their own and could hardly afford the luxury of a European-style, post–Treaty of Westphalia of 1648 century or two of territorial wars between rival states to "rectify" frontiers problems. For these purposes, even at the price of some "regional" hardships or injustices, political stability in the face of grave external and internal challenges, economic and other, dictated that the principle of state sovereignty (including sanctity of existing frontiers, such as they might be) should prevail over the principle of political self-determination. It is an axiological or interests-balancing approach well understood and accepted as such within the United Nations family, and it is recognized de facto in the settled United Nations practice as to post-decolonization territorial and frontiers questions of "succession states." In another, different if parallel situation, the then chancellor of the Federal Republic of West Germany, Willy Brandt, accepted the political facts of the war's-end territorial settlements imposed by the Yalta and Potsdam Conferences in Central and Eastern Europe, and the two-Germanies solution, as the price to be paid for East-West, interbloc peace and security in Europe. This was, in essence, the political and legal trade-off involved in the so-called *Ostpolitik* series of bilateral treaties effected between the Federal Republic of Germany and its neighbors in Eastern Europe at the end of the 1960s and in the early 1970s, which both legitimated the de facto political-military divisions of 1945 and also promised cooperation in political and economic relations across the existing ideological Iron Curtain.[13] In purely noncolonial situations, existing unitary states like France and the United Kingdom which have been rediscovering particularist ethnically-culturally or linguistically based minorities that were thought to have been long ago assimilated or absorbed, are now experimenting with regional autonomy and territorial decentralization of decision-making power. Constitutional-institutional pluralism is, of course, another and perfectly acceptable approach to political self-determination within an existing state that does not choose to bifurcate or otherwise to fragment itself. Perhaps the postdecolonization "succession states," insisting on state sovereignty and security of existing frontiers as the lesser of two legal evils today, could experiment with federalism and pluralism as a means of allowing political self-determination *within* the state, until such time as they might feel confident enough to allow a completely free choice of other options involving territorial redistribution or reallocation across existing state frontiers.

Problems like the Western Sahara, since the removal of the imperial Spanish element, seem more readily assimilable to "classical" decolonization exercises, and therefore more open to application of classical modes of exercise of the right of self-determination—for example, popular consultation by way of referendum or similar tried and tested popular consultation. The Palestine issue, including both the West Bank and the Occupied Territories, is far more complex because of the superpower interest and involvement on both sides, and should be examined in that context; though it can be said here that it is also strictly a *post*-decolonization affair, the original act of decolonization having occurred with the termination—in part by *force majeure* and the pressure of direct action from an original Israeli national self-determination movement—of the British League of Nations–derived mandate in 1948, and the division of the mandated territory and creation, inter alia, of the new "succession state" of Israel.

Contemporary International Law Values: The Economic Sovereignty Imperative, New International Economic Order

Economic sovereignty or economic self-determination may in contemporary international law terms, be viewed as simply one part of the larger concept of self-determination of peoples, which, in its early nineteenth-century origins in Western laissez-faire liberal thinking on international law and relations, was concentrated on its *political* outlet and expression only. Economic affairs, according to laissez-faire scholars, were beyond the domain of the state and organized political society as a whole. Contemporary scientific thinking on international law and relations, both Soviet and Western, would acknowledge, with varying degrees of emphasis and enthusiasm, a necessary and inevitable interrelation between political ideas and economic ideas. It is not simply the Marxian notion of law as being a mere superstructure of rules and principles erected on an underlying base of the social and economic organization of society. In Western legal thinking at the apogée of laissez-faire influence, at the close of the nineteenth century and early in the twentieth century, a conservative "old Court" majority on the United States Supreme Court could indeed rule, over the strong dissents of Justices Holmes and Brandeis, that legislation on minimum wage and maximum hours of work deprived a worker of his "liberty of contract" and should therefore be struck down as unconstitutional. However, in more contemporary eras, Western courts and Western political decision makers have been legally sophisticated enough to distinguish between liberty of contract in the abstract and liberty of contract in the concrete, and to recognize the state's right to intervene by legislation to correct economic imbalances in society and to equalize economic opportunities. The increasing political impact of social democratic ideas in Western society in modern times has brought recognition of the close ties between political and economic facts, and the acknowledgment that economic development is a prerequisite to full political expression.

Nevertheless, economic sovereignty or economic self-determination as an imperative principle of contemporary international law, as a matter of history, developed separately and independently of the United Nations Charter and of United Nations practice generally. Woodrow Wilson's Fourteen Points, which provide an intellectual bridge between the nineteenth-century Western liberal postulate of national self-determination and the Charter principles, were silent, to the point of being politically naive or anachronistic, about the basic economic facts of life in international relations. The historical application of Wilsonian idealism in political self-determination in Central Europe broke up the one stable economic and trading unit then existing and created in its place a myriad of small "succession states" that were quite incapable of existing as viable economic units in their own right. In part because of the inherited intellectual tradition of exclusively *political* emphasis in the principle of self-determination—in part, no doubt, also because of the prime emphasis on the political-military element in the peace settlement imposed by the ideologically disparate members of the World War II victors' alliance (lest attention to social and economic issues should threaten their already, by war's end, fragile victors' consensus)—the United Nations Charter, as drafted in 1945, largely skirts or avoids economic issues. The emergence of those economic issues thereafter is part of the historical, dialectical process of development of United Nations law through subsequent legislative acts of the General Assembly and specialized agencies and committees, and through developing custom and practice by way of "conventional" glosses on the Charter. The new economic orientation and objective of the principle of self-determination—a development that is fully compatible with the original Charter preambular formulation—is achieved by a process of development separate from and parallel to the recognition and expansion of political self-determination in United Nations law. The starting point may be taken as General Assembly Resolution 626 (VII) of December 21, 1952, which recognizes the right of peoples freely to use and exploit their natural wealth and resources, as inherent in their sovereignty; and this principle emerged within the United Nations in direct political response to the Anglo-Iranian oil crisis of 1951, when Iran's premier, Muhammad Mossadegh, nationalized the foreign (British)–owned assets of a British-based multinational oil company then exercising an economic monopoly stranglehold on the production, exporting, and pricing of Iran's oil resources. This emerging new principle of economic self-determination was continued and extended through General Assembly Resolution 1515 (XV) of December 15, 1960, on the sovereign right of states to dispose of their wealth and natural resources, and General Assembly Resolution 1803 (XVII) of December 14, 1962, on permanent sovereignty over natural resources. These two major legislative acts, enacted by General Assembly resolution, were the products of the special Commission on Permanent Sovereignty over Natural Resources, itself established by the United Nations General Assembly Resolution 1314 (XIII) of December 12, 1958, and of the continuing debates in the United Nations Economic and Social Council. The rapidly evolving consensus within the Economic and Social Council and in the General Assembly concerning the economic base of international law and relations and international development logically and inevitably led to the three great economic law-making ventures of the early 1970s, which formulated by General Asembly resolutions the Declaration[14] and the Programme of Action[15] for a New International Economic Order, and the Charter of Economic Rights and Duties of States.[16] The New International Economic Order (NIEO) becomes a political and legal term of art, denoting the drive within the United Nations itself—the leitmotiv of General Assembly international law making for the balance of the 1970s and the early 1980s[17]—to redress the North-South political imbalance in the contemporary world community by economic means, through United Nations "affirmative action" (or "reverse discrimination," to use some current, Western common law, constitutional terminology) on behalf of economically depressed Third World countries.

The trilogy of law-making acts on the New International Economic Order was the product of a working coalition of forces within the General Assembly among a number of groups, some informal and loosely organized and some well-disciplined and cohesive, and in any case overlapping in their membership. Coalition building, which is best achieved through membership and participation in as many as possible of the General Assembly's plurality of alliances and associations, with their assorted political-ideological, cultural-linguistic, economic and trading, regional and geographical criteria, was the key, then as now, to successful law-making ventures within the United Nations. The de facto alliance on behalf of the New International Economic Order involved the so-called

Non-Aligned Countries, originally developed as an Afro-Asian neutralist group trying to establish political disengagement from the two rival political-military blocs, Soviet and Western, of the Cold War era; and the so-called Group of Seventy-Seven, which developed later, had a strong Latin American component, and was concerned primarily with economic questions, especially the renegotiation of original economic ties and contracts with Western industrial countries concerning development and exploitation of primary products and raw materials. With the expansion of membership in the Group of Seventy-Seven to well over a hundred (the original name was, however, retained), there came an extension of the influence of the Arab-Asian central core of the Non-Aligned Countries' group, as a result of the substantial overlapping of ranks between the two groups. When there are added to these two groups the OPEC countries, Communist China, and the Soviet Union and Soviet bloc, a very powerful and cohesive voting alliance emerges with members who in certain cases are associated with more than one of the different components of the alliance.

On the other hand, the major Western countries, not having membership in any of these various "regional" groupings making up the NIEO alliance, were left isolated, as reluctant participants in a law-making process that they seemed incapable of either defeating or influencing constructively. The declaration and the program of action were adopted, without vote, at the General Assembly's sixth special session in May 1974. The Charter of Economic Rights and Duties of States was adopted by the General Assembly at its twenty-ninth regular annual session in January 1975, by a vote of 120–6, with 10 abstentions. The six negative votes were all cast by Western-bloc countries: Belgium, Denmark, the Federal Republic of Germany, Luxembourg, the United Kingdom, the United States. The ten abstentions were by Western countries, plus two Western-associated countries, Israel and Japan.

The decisions on the three NIEO acts clearly represented a major political defeat for the Western bloc, though part of the Western voting embarrassment can be attributed to a confusion over the "consensus rule" as applied at the sixth special session of the General Assembly in May 1974.[18] The Third World countries were certainly annoyed at the decision of major Western countries to accompany their silent acquiescence, in the consensus adoption and enactment of the declaration and the program of action, by the filing of express "reservations" to those documents.[19] And so the Third World countries were not disposed to compromise in regard to the subsequent Charter of Economic Rights and Duties of States, and their resulting intransigence over that text meant the loss of the votes of the main (Western) countries whose support and cooperation would be sorely needed in the practical implementation of the programmatic approach to a new economic base for international relations. It would hardly be possible to adopt a new economic framework as a basis for a world public order and render it operational as international law-in-action, by legislative fiat alone.

The Charter of Economic Rights and Duties of States, as the product of a coalition of forces within the General Assembly, bears the evidence in a number of places of drafting compromises or exchanges that militate against its overall conception and styling.[20] On the one hand, it follows what may be called the cornucopia approach to legal drafting: when in doubt, put everything in and leave it to subsequent historians to work out why. It also embraces what historically is known as the Weimar Constitution drafting principle: if faced with latent or even patent contradictions in demands pressed in the drafting stage, include them all and hope that the passage of time will resolve the antinomy by disposing of one or the other alternative. Thus the Charter proclaims state sovereignty in unrestrained form in its opening articles:

> Article 1. Every State has the sovereign and inalienable right to choose its economic system as well as its political, social and cultural systems in accordance with the will of its people, without outside interference, coercion or threat in any form whatsoever.
>
> Article 2. (1) Every State has and shall freely exercise full permanent sovereignty, including possession, use and disposal, over all its wealth, natural resources and economic activities.
>
> (2) Each State has the right:
>
> (a) To regulate and exercise authority over foreign investment within its national jurisdiction in accordance with its laws and regulations and in conformity with its national objectives and priorities. . . .
>
> (b) To regulate and supervise the activities of transnational corporations within its national jurisdiction and take measures to ensure that such activities comply with its laws, rules and regulations and conform with its economic and social policies. . . .
>
> (c) To nationalize, expropriate or transfer ownership of foreign property, in which case appropriate compensation should be paid by the State adopting such measures, taking into account its relevant laws and regulations and all circumstances that the State considers pertinent. . . .

But the Charter also goes on to apply stern injunctions against any one state's attempt to influence or coerce another state through economic measures.

> Article 16. (2) No State has the right to promote or encourage investments that may constitute an obstacle to the liberation of a territory occupied by force. . . .
>
> Article 18. . . . In the conduct of international economic relations the developed countries should endeavour to avoid measures having a negative effect on the development of the national economies of the developing

countries, as promoted by generalized tariff preferences and other generally agreed differential measures in their favour. . . .
Article 32. No State may use or encourage the use of economic, political or any other type of measures to coerce another State in order to obtain from it the subordination of the exercise of its sovereign rights.

Some parts of the Charter are essentially rhetorical proclamations, as with the pronouncement on the elimination of apartheid (Article 16 [1]). Other parts of the Charter are the new "socialist" international law of the late 1950s and the early 1960s, with a postulated duty of the advanced industrial states to make restitution and compensation to other states (Article 16 [1]). There are also specific articles on the Law of the Sea (Article 29) and on international environmental policy (Article 30). The range is very wide, and so the coverage tends to be somewhat diffuse, leaving the impression that the new Charter may be largely hortatory and perhaps intended as such. How, then, is it to be rendered operational, and thus influential or controlling in economic relations between the developed and developing countries, for the future? The problem, as stated, is polycentric, and so must be the answer.[21]

One aspect of making the New International Economic Order operational, as proclaimed in the new Charter, lies in its moral example in providing clear signals to the governments of the main capital-exporting countries, which those governments will then communicate to their own major national corporations (and also multinational corporations effectively controlled by them) as economic guidelines to investment in natural resources discovery and exploitation in Third World countries. The effect of publication of such economic rules of reason in international law documents like the new Charter may be to discourage or drive away national corporations or multinationals from foreign investments in certain cases, and in that sense might be viewed as counterproductive in terms of the long-term aspirations of the ad hoc voting coalitions that produced the enactments in the General Assembly in the first place. On the other hand, more pragmatic business leaders in postindustrial societies may well discover, on examination, that they can adjust quite easily and live with the stipulations in the new Charter, which amount in the end to rules of prudence or economic good citizenship for investors and traders operating in international arenas. This in fact, it may be suggested, is proving—with the aid of calmer counsel from the main Western foreign and trade ministries concerned—to be the case.

A second aspect of the campaign to make the programmatic New International Economic Order genuinely operational lies in the forms of economic direct action that had been initiated even before the NIEO's formal enactment in General Assembly resolutions in 1974. This involves cartel-like action by Third World countries that may happen to control large percentages of the world's assets, in particular, scarce natural resources. The pressures successfully applied by the OPEC cartel after October 1973, for massive increases in world market prices of crude oil, demonstrated the first real solidarity among Third World countries in the use of their control of raw materials as an economic weapon. They may also have given developing countries a real sense of political power in the world community for the first time. Yet, paradoxically, the oil price increases also exaggerated differences between Third World countries because of those countries' extremely divergent growth rates. No such moves could occur without innocent victims, and the victims—those most affected by the oil price increases—were very poor already. The Western industrial countries might have provided some help, for instance through the oil facility of the IMF, but they clearly preferred to favor their own group within the OECD. The OPEC countries did come to the aid of the poorer countries,[22] but they applied their own system of preferred grading, according to special cultural links, and Arab and Muslim countries seemed to come out ahead in this. What the OPEC cartel-style action has served to indicate, however, is the practical limits to such collective economic pressure-group activity. Operating for the best part of a decade throughout the 1970s, under the most favorable circumstances, with the seemingly most indispensable of all natural resources, oil, the OPEC countries were eventually beset by drastically falling prices, themselves the product of the drives (which their own cartel-like activities had stimulated) for development of alternative energy sources (including nuclear energy and the revival of the use of technologically outmoded energy sources like coal), for discovery of new oil supplies not controlled by OPEC countries, and for reductions in unnecessary national consumption of energy. So effective were these responses to the OPEC actions that member countries of OPEC began themselves, covertly or otherwise, to violate OPEC directives as to production quotas and pricing, accelerating the decline in oil prices themselves. If such problems could arise with a world oil cartel, how much more difficult would it be to organize and maintain similar collective Third World economic pressure-group activity on other less essential or less scarce natural resources—mineral or commodity foodstuffs? The conclusion is, and must be, that such primary products cartels, if organized, can be at best only a limited, ancillary or subsidiary weapon for attaining a New International Economic Order.[23]

A politically more promising approach, long-range, might be the extension of the same generic methods successfully employed in achieving the legislative acts on the NIEO in the General Assembly to other United Nations specialized committees or commissions or conferences endowed with a special economic mandate or opportunity.[24] Such an occasion was provided, throughout the decade of the 1970s until the formal signature of its resulting final act or treaty, in December 1982 by the so-called Third United Nations Conference on the Law of the Sea.[25] This started out as what seemed to be a normal legal codification exercise, but one deliberately kept away from the International Law Commission and even the General Assembly's specialist Sixth (Legal) Committee out of fear that those forums would be dominated by the lawyers of the Big Powers and produce only a conservative restatement of the "old" or classical international Law of the Sea with its presumed inbuilt bias in favor of the Western states that had been politically dominant in the classical Law of the Sea's origins and development. The Third United Nations Conference on the Law of the Sea, however, soon showed itself to be an important arena for developing and extending the New International Economic Order in application to marine and submarine resources, both fishing and mineral. While more traditional legal issues still received attention, the biggest battles throughout the decade of detailed political and legal negotiations concerned such economic resources and their disposition and control and profit for the future. What was striking, in fact, was the number and range of states ready to abandon over three centuries of *mare liberum* doctrine in favor of a new species of *mare clausum,* in which more and more areas of the sea, its fishing and marine life stocks, and its submarine mineral resources were blocked off and appropriated by individual states. Only certain types of states continued to maintain the classical international law concept of the sea: the two superpowers, with large military submarine fleets and interests in maintaining a right of overflight for their military aircraft over as much of the sea as possible; states with large merchant marine fleets and therefore a clear and immediate economic interest in preserving existing rights of passage at sea; and states with either no coastal fishing resources of their own or no continental shelf and hence no offshore mineral and related resources to exploit. The traditional three-mile territorial sea of "classical" international law gave way to a "patrimonial sea" that often extended as far as two hundred miles out from the low-water line along the coast and was recognized and enforced by means of interlocking, usually bilateral accords concluded between states sharing the same special economic interests. Even more dramatic in their impact were the claims advanced for control over the continental shelf, the seabed, and the ocean floor and their resources. Here a clear conflict emerged. The advanced industrial states alone had the scientific-technological capacity to exploit the oil, mineral, and other resources involved and therefore favored a laissez-faire approach, which in theory meant that these resources would be open to all states, but which in practice meant that they would be reserved for the advanced postindustrial states themselves. On the other hand, the industrially underdeveloped countries, and also the landlocked or coastal states with no continental shelf and thus no offshore mineral resources of their own to exploit, favored "internationalizing," in a special ad hoc UN control authority, the ownership of the resources concerned, the direction and planning of their mining, and the sharing of financial profits on some generally equitable basis. These rival claims were in a certain real sense unbridgeable, except by the sort of exercises in reciprocal give-and-take to which the two superpowers had become accustomed in working out détente. Here, however, the two superpowers were not the two opposing key players, for their interests were often complementary, and the number of players was very much greater. This, and the fact that the differences were much more North-South than East-West in the conventional post–Cold War sense, explained the delay throughout the 1970s in reaching substantial consensus on the content of a new Law of the Sea.

The final United Nations Convention of the Law of the Sea, which emerged from the more than a decade of work of the Third United Nations Conference on the Law of the Sea, was signed in Jamaica in December 1982.[26] It extended classical international law's territorial sea to twelve marine miles; established an exclusive economic zone for every coastal state, extending two hundred miles beyond its shores, in which it would have exclusive rights to fish and other marine life; and declared the exclusive right of the coastal state to exploit the oil, gas, and other resources in its continental shelf up to 350 miles from its coast. The most crucial and politically divisive sections, however, concerned seabed and ocean floor mining beyond these limits. The mineral resources concerned were, in effect, declared—in the words originally employed by Malta's Ambassador Pardo in the General Assembly a number of years before, when the campaign for the new treaty was started—to be "the common heritage of mankind," with a special international seabed authority to administer them, to allocate licenses to mine and to establish mining quotas, and ultimately to determine allocation of profits, and with a special international tribunal to resolve disputes arising under the new convention. Although 119 states signed the treaty on December 10, 1982, the first day it was open for signature,[27] the United States was conspicuous by its nonsignature. In fact, twenty-two countries attended the signing ceremony but did not sign the treaty—among these, as already indicated, the United States, and also the United Kingdom, the Federal Republic of Germany, Italy, Belgium, Japan, the Republic of Korea, and Israel. Twenty-four other countries, which had been invited to attend, did not. As the United Nations legal counsel, Erik Suy, pointed out, however, the 119 signatures constituted a record, in United Nations terms, for the first day that a treaty had been open for signature.[28] What would the nonsignatories do? There were some suggestions that the United States and its predominantly Western or Western-associated cohorts would sign their own "mini-treaty" (in opposition to the official, "maxi-treaty" signed by the 119 states in Jamaica on December 10, 1982), purporting to allow them to carve up the seabed and its mineral resources among themselves;[29] that the United States and others might choose to apply the Jamaica treaty selectively, treating only those parts that suited their own special interests (right of innocent passage through the territorial sea and free passage for military and nonmilitary ships and planes beyond) as normative in legal terms, but choosing to ignore altogether those treaty rules (particularly those as to seabed mining) that they disliked. The latter approach would have some doctrinal-legal base, of course, insofar as large parts of the Jamaica treaty purported merely to restate classical, customary rules of international law, and these would, of course, be binding in the absence of the treaty and binding on nonsignatories too. But such a selective approach was scornfully rejected by signatories to the Jamaica treaty; in the words of a Soviet minister, Mr. Guzhenko, the United States could not pick from a basket of fruits only what it liked.[30] As for the suggestion that the United States and its Western cohorts would sign their own "mini-treaty" as a purported legal base and authority for acting in defiance of the Jamaica treaty, the president of the conference, Ambassador Tommy Koh of Singapore, indicated politely but firmly that any such action would be promptly challenged before the International Court of Justice.[31] What was striking at the Jamaica signing ceremonies in December 1982 was the new attitude of quiet confidence on the part of the Third World leaders. The realization that they might have committed a major political blunder and isolated themselves by not rallying to the 119 state signatories on the opening day seems to have come belatedly to some of the Western nonsignatories; some indicated discreetly that since the treaty would remain open for signing for two years, there would be time for possible changes or revisions in the convention text before they would need to make a final decision.[32]

A mere codification exercise was transformed over a decade of diplomatic negotiations, into something more—a case study in the elaboration and application, in one major area of world community activity, of the new economic development law. Moreover, the Third United Nations Conference on the Law of the Sea's international law-making process was complemented and extended by another important legal venture. This was supplementing the essentially high-level abstract, general, *primary* principles of international law as to the New International Economic Order, contained in the General Assembly declaration, program of action, and Charter of 1974–1975, by some more concrete and immediate and secondary or tertiary legal rules and norms. A project to "operationalize" the international law of the New International Economic Order was launched by several successive General Assembly resolutions. Resolution 166, adopted at the thirty-fifth annual session in the autumn of 1980, requested the United Nations Institute for Training and Research (UNITAR), to "prepare a list of the existing and evolving principles and norms of international law" in this area; to "prepare an analytical study, on the basis of the list referred to"; and to complete it in time for the next, thirty-sixth annual session in the fall of 1981. The study was continued from the 1981 session by Resolution 107, with a direction to complete the work in time for debate at the thirty-seventh annual session in the autumn of 1982. In fact, UNITAR could make only a partial fulfillment of that mandate by the indicated deadline, the failure being readily attributable to lack of a permanent, qualified research staff and the necessity, in consequence, of organizing work on an ad hoc basis. The preliminary UNITAR report,[33] subtitled "Analytical Papers and Analysis of Texts of Relevant Instruments," limited itself to *four* postulated principles of international law concerning the NIEO:

(i) preferential treatment for developing countries;
(ii) stabilization of export earnings of developing countries;
(iii) permanent sovereignty over natural resources;
(iv) right of every state to benefit from science and technology.[34]

It was indicated that the remaining principles of the NIEO, still to be researched, would be the following:

(v) entitlement of developing countries to development assistance;
(vi) participatory equality of developing countries in international economic relations;
(vii) common heritage of mankind.[35]

Although the UNITAR research project had extensive recourse to such source materials as resolutions of the General Assembly, bilateral and multilateral agreements, international tribunal decisions, and international arbitral awards, from which to induce its legal rules and norms concerning the NIEO, it was criticized in the debate in the General Assembly's Sixth Committee for a certain apparent superficiality and selectiveness or partiality in its approach to its work.[36] These more obvious deficiencies might be remedied by reaching out to other, more empirically based sources for the follow-up report[37]—for example, as UNITAR itself indicated, *national* court decisions and teachings of the most highly qualified publicists of the various nations, agreements between states and transnational corporations, and national legislation.[38] A list of "eminent persons representative of all geographical regions," stated to have been consulted by UNITAR in its work, revealed itself on examination to be somewhat heavily Eurocentric in character (particularly weighted toward United States professors),[39] though perhaps this had been done deliberately by UNITAR in order to forestall any criticisms of Third World bias by overcompensating with a patent Eurocentric (here, American) emphasis in the formation of the expert advisory panel. However, there was nothing to suggest that these and other intellectual problems with the research project's planning and development could not be corrected in the future. For the ordinary United Nations historical-dialectical process of elaboration and concretization of principles, through the give-and-take of debate and discussion and compromise in the Sixth Committee and the General Assembly, would undoubtedly follow in the usual way.

10. Ideological Pluralism and Contemporary International Law Values: Peace, "One World," Enlightenment, Human Dignity

The Peace Imperative: Outlawing the Use of Force.

Peace and peace keeping stand out in the Charter—in its preamble and in its opening chapter (Chapter I, "Purposes and Principles," Articles 1–2)—as the first among the imperative principles of international law and of the world public order system then being established. This is understandable enough for a constitutional instrument for international organization devised at the end of a great military conflict and worked out and elaborated on the basis of political compromise and give-and-take among the key members of the soon-to-be-victorious wartime coalition of ideologically disparate forces. As a compromise document, the Charter is no doubt realistic in political power terms, and it certainly shows evidence of the skills of accommodation between the rival systems. But as a matter of history there was nothing to suggest that it was necessarily wiser or more magnanimous or that it had a longer historical vision than earlier victors' peace treaties and postwar order systems like the badly flawed and one-sided imposed Carthaginian peace Treaty of Versailles of 1919. The Soviet Union, which had carried the main weight of the Axis powers' invasion and military occupation and systematic political repression and economic depredations for more than three years of World War II, was understandably preoccupied with its own postwar military security and economic recovery and with punishment of the defeated Axis leaders.

The Western powers, with very much lighter political and material losses, succumbed no doubt too easily to purely Manichaean conceptions of historical causation, placed all the moral and material blame for the still recent military conflagration on the defeated enemy, and, in consequence, felt immunized from any need to seek for a substantively more just and equitable system of world order for the future. In historical terms, the Charter cannot be divorced from those great wartime diplomatic acts concluded between the major Allied leaders, especially the Yalta and Potsdam agreements of 1945, which constitute the political basic premise or *Grundnorm* of the immediate post-1945 world public order system. For the Yalta and Potsdam agreements shaped, determined, and ratified, on a basis of political exchange and barter between the two main players, the Soviet Union and the United States, the basic postwar political-military settlement—in Central and Eastern Europe in particular, but also more generally. This basic political-military settlement of 1945 has persisted ever since. A rereading of the terms of those 1945 arrangements, the one made on the eve of the German defeat and the other on the conclusion of military hostilities in Europe, confirms a high degree of cynicism present among the two main players and their diplomatic teams, which they sought to justify by the rapid pressure of unfolding political and military events and the urgent necessity to forestall postwar conflicts among the wartime victors over the territorial domains, satellite states, spheres of influence and politically neutral no-man's-land states. The effect on the San Francisco negotiations for the United Nations Charter, and on the Charter itself, of these concurrent great political-military dispositions for the postwar era is clear enough. The Charter, in its overall purposes and philosophy, stresses maintaining the peace and, in doing so, the basic political, social, and economic order then existing, and the underlying territorial and state arrangements supporting it. Peace, in an era of nuclear weapons and nuclear warfare, must be the prime imperative as the condition of survival; but, in the absence of effective institutional machinery for peaceful change, how do you redress major imbalances or inequities in access to, or distribution of, the world community's territories and resources, without recourse to war or armed force as in the past? In that sense, with its prime emphasis on peace keeping without a correlative emphasis on peaceful change of a fundamental character, the Charter, like the Covenant of the League of Nations before it, appears linked to the status quo of yesterday—in this case the political-military settlement dictated by the two superpowers at Yalta and Potsdam in 1945. This is not an argument against the Charter or its prime peace imperative so much as a case for accepting also the other prime imperative—international law making, under the Charter and through its main institutions and processes, designed positively to redress the extreme political and economic inequities as between states established or confirmed by the diplomatic acts of 1945 that accompanied the Charter's adoption.

Within the Yalta and Potsdam framework of political-military facts, the Charter, viewed as a peace-keeping instrument, is subject to some embarrassing exceptions, the so-called "gaps" in the Charter. Among these, the "enemy state" exceptions (Articles 53 and 107) seem in retrospect to have been quite unnecessary in 1945 terms and thus purely vindictive and motivated by a spirit of revenge inconsonant with the Charter as a whole—an application of that subjective moralizing, Manichaean spirit that is common enough among military victors, ancient and modern. Articles 53 and 107 of the charter have long since fallen into desuetude and, for the sake of the overall integrity of the Charter, should, it may now be suggested, finally be deleted.

Another major gap in the Charter is its expressly licensed "inherent right of individual or collective self-defense" pending Security Council "measures to maintain international peace and security" (Article 51 of the charter). This Charter-based right of self-defense is complicated by several factors. First, resisting Soviet legal-doctrinal pressures to establish as the sole test (and one certainly capable of easy objective verification) of "aggression" the question of who *first* crosses a frontier,[1] Western jurists have advanced the legally interesting notion of a right of anticipatory self-defense.[2] In an era of nuclear weapons, it may, of course, be courting national disaster to wait until a potential aggressor has actually armed his missiles with nuclear warheads before taking preventive action, but such an extra degree of legal license in self-defense simply enlarges the "gap" self-defense already constitutes in the Charter's peace-keeping system and arrangements. Second, the conditioning of the legal termination of such right of self-defense upon the Security Council's taking of action means an institutional limitation that is itself predicated on action or inaction by the Big Powers. The permanent members' right of veto in the Security Council is enough legally to inhibit political action within the United Nations to produce, for example, a military cease-fire in operations where one of the parties invokes the right of self-defense. Although, according to the text of the Charter (Article 27 [3]), a permanent member of the Security Council that is itself a party to a dispute cannot legally invoke the veto in such cases, this did not stop the United Kingdom from applying the veto in the course of its Falklands (Malvinas) dispute with Argentina, when the Security Council, on June 4, 1982, by a clear majority voted 9–2 (United Kingdom, United States), with 4 abstentions, in favor of an immediate cease fire.[3] Of course there is absolutely nothing to stop a Big Power from applying the veto to block Security Council peace-keeping action directed against one of its allies or associates (including a Big Power party to a dispute), as in fact the United States did on behalf of the United Kingdom in the same Security Council vote of June 4, 1982.[4] The issue of the precise legal ambit and legal limits of such a right of self-defense—in spatial and also temporal terms—became legally relevant in the Falklands (Malvinas) when, for example, a British submarine sank the Argentinian cruiser *General Belgrano,* with heavy loss of life,[5] well outside the military control zone decreed by the United Kingdom itself,[6] and also when hostilities continued indefinitely and with disproportionate loss of life on the Argentinian side. It is a major "gap" in the Charter, in such cases, if peace-keeping action is prevented by Security Council veto; and the pressures in such cases for alternative legal action in other arenas—particularly General Assembly action, on the Uniting for Peace resolution precedent of 1950—becoming as compelling politically as they are persuasive in international law terms.

Another aspect of the legal limits, under the Charter, of recourse to the use of force arises with regard to political direct action in the absence of affirmative United Nations measures. India, after decolonization from the United Kingdom, seized the Portuguese colonial enclave of Goa when Portuguese procrastination impeded its peaceful return to India, the principle of self-determination of peoples being invoked by India as the justifying imperative legal principle; and Indonesia moved finally, in 1976, against another vestigial Portuguese colonial territory, the East Timor enclave within Indonesian territorial boundaries after Indonesia's decolonization from the Netherlands. Argentina, frustrated by seventeen years of delays in the bilateral Argentine-British negotiations over the Falklands (Malvinas), chose direct action in 1982—unsuccessfully, as it turned out, in immediate United Nations terms. As a legal element in these comparatively rare or isolated cases, which are rapidly receding into history as the decolonization imperative becomes finally consummated, there exists the principle, postulated by some jurists within the General Assembly, of a legally based right of recourse to direct military action in pursuit of the principle of self-determination, in the case of a "war of national liberation" directed by a national liberation movement against a "parent" European imperial state in a "colonial" situation.[7] Not merely does use of armed force against the imperial state become legally licit and fully in accord with the Charter under such circumstances, it is contended, but other states may have a right and even a duty to rally to the aid of the national liberation movement concerned—an application of the notion of "hue and cry," and ultimately of the Grotian notion of the "just war," in affirmative support of Charter principles.

United Nations practice—while still evolving in an area of international law concerning decolonization, independence, and self-determination, whose very success in political terms may make the issue academic—seems to go a certain way toward accepting the right of direct action and use of armed force in furtherance of other Charter imperatives, where the ordinary United Nations political-legal arenas and processes for achievement of such imperatives are clogged or rendered inoperable, whether by Big Power veto or otherwise. A certain ambivalence within the United Nations—so many Third World leaders and current General Assembly delegates are themselves graduates of successful national liberation movements in their own former colonial countries—is reflected in the General Assembly's well-known Resolution 147 (XXXII) of December 16, 1977, on the need to combat international terrorism, a subject on which there exists a widespread intersystemic consensus within the United Nations, at least as to the need to control terrorism's effects on innocent third parties not directly involved in the particular political disputes that are at its roots. The title of the General Assembly resolution itself indicates the doubts and contradictions as to the axiological, value-choice questions:

> Measures to prevent international terrorism which endangers or takes innocent human lives or jeopardises fundamental freedoms, and study of the underlying causes of those forms of terrorism and acts of violence which lie in misery, frustration, grievance and despair and which cause some people to sacrifice human lives, including their own, in an attempt to effect radical changes.[8]

It is not surprising that, because of the deep feelings on the substantive ends of such direct action movements, organized responses in the United Nations to international terrorism have proved difficult and slow to negotiate.[9] The most successful such United Nations–based measures—the three conventions of Tokyo (1963), The Hague (1970), and Montreal (1971), on aerial piracy and the illegal diversion of aircraft—have chosen an essentially technical, low-level approach directed to removing or reducing the injurious consequences of terrorist actions for international commerce and intercourse,[10] rather than addressing themselves to the substantive issues of ideological choice involved in the terrorist acts themselves.[11]

The Peace Imperative: Nuclear and General Disarmament

Disarmament must be, in actual quantitative terms, the source of the largest number of resolutions at each annual session of the General Assembly from the end of the 1970s onward. This reflects a certain fear, and growing anger, on the part of Third World countries outside the two main blocs, Soviet and Western, at the slowdown, perhaps a breakdown, in

East-West interbloc negotiation and discussion over nuclear and general disarmament, manifest from the United States Senate's failure to act on and therefore to ratify the SALT II treaty, in the mid-1970s, onward. Prior to that time there had been more than a decade of richly productive Soviet-American direct bilateral negotiation for nuclear and general disarmament, producing an impressive and effective special methodological approach: the pragmatic, empirical, problem-oriented, step-by-step approach. As one of the key elements in Soviet-American and general East-West détente, and as part of a large détente process, this special methodological approach produced a whole series of precise legal accords directed to ending the Cold War rivalry and tensions, beginning with the Memorandum of Understanding of June 1963, on the establishment of a direct communications link between the United States and the Soviet Union (the so-called hot-line agreement), and continuing through the Moscow Partial Test Ban Treaty of August 1963, banning nuclear tests in the atmosphere, in outer space, and under water; the Space Treaty of 1967, *inter alia* banning the orbiting of nuclear weapons in space vehicles (itself a confirmation of an earlier informal Soviet-American understanding to the same effect in the autumn of 1963, recorded in General Assembly Resolution 1884 ([XVIII] of October 17, 1963); the Treaty on the Nonproliferation of Nuclear Weapons of 1968; and other measures. The apogee of the Soviet-American joint *process* of détente as manifested in disarmament was the detailed Strategic Arms Limitation agreements (SALT I) negotiated between President Nixon of the United States and Secretary Brezhnev of the Soviet Union and signed in Moscow in May 1972, as part of the more general agreements on Soviet-American cooperation, known as the Moscow Accords. The further, follow-up agreements, worked out between President Nixon and Secretary Brezhnev and signed in Washington in June 1973, the so-called Washington Accords, were intended to culminate, as the next and final step soon to be reached, in definitive arrangements as to nuclear disarmament and nuclear weapon control between the superpowers—SALT II. Unfortunately, domestic, internal American political events—the so-called Watergate episode and the resignation of President Nixon in mid-1974—interrupted the Soviet-American détente process by suddenly breaking the personal relationship of confidence and trust between the two leaders, which had been the key to its successful implementation over the immediately preceding years. With the best will in the world and with much the same State Department advisory and negotiating team, President Nixon's successor, President Ford, was not able to reestablish the rhythm or momentum of the movement to East-West consensually based nuclear disarmament and general détente. The actual measures discussed at the first Soviet-American summit meeting, in November 1974, in the new American presidential term—the SALT II framework of agreement, arrived at between President Ford and Secretary Brezhnev at Vladivostok—could not effectively be followed up with the American Congress by President Ford after his return home from Vladivostok. East-West relations seemed to worsen, after President Ford's defeat in the elections of November 1976, with the new Carter presidency. A new "moralizing" approach in American foreign policy emerged that seemed to heighten the intensity of Soviet-American invective without any concrete advances in the step-by-step diplomacy on disarmament under the earlier Kennedy, Johnson, and Nixon administrations or positive gains to show in terms of concrete Soviet-American tension-reducing agreements. A dangerous drift set in, in the general armaments race, without real guidance or leadership by either one of the superpowers, even though, as an issue of fact, the terms of the SALT I accords and the later, inchoate SALT II agreements were essentially observed and respected by the two superpowers. *Faute de mieux,* positive initiatives toward nuclear and more general disarmament would have to come in other international law-making arenas. Why not the General Assembly? Why not, indeed?—and this explains the flurry of activity by way of special resolutions of the General Assembly at the regular annual sessions in the late 1970s and early 1980s, and also the convening of special sessions of the General Assembly on disarmament, like the first special session in 1978 and the second special session in 1982. These could and did demonstrably exercise a certain psychological pressure on the two superpowers by way of trying to "shame" them into stopping the armaments race; but in the end the multilateral approach through the General Assembly would have to yield to the basic political fact of life that nuclear disarmament, by its intrinsic character, was an affair primarily of the superpowers and dependent on the reestablishment of their mutual confidence and trust to become operational again as a process.[11]

The "One World" Imperative: Common Heritage of Mankind

During the debates in the General Assembly when the idea of the Third United Nations Conference on the Law of the Sea—which led on to the remarkably innovative United Nations Convention of the Law of the Sea, concluded in December 1982—was being born, the delegate from Malta, Ambassador Pardo, launched the phrase "common heritage of mankind" to describe the ocean bed and the sea floor outside national jurisdiction. Ambassador Pardo's desire was to preserve these regions and their potentially enormously rich natural resources from a latter-day predatory neocolonial style of exploitation by the highly developed postindustrial societies, and to share the wealth from their mining among all the peoples of the world community. In a large sense, we can apply the phrase "common heritage of mankind" to the earth as a whole and all its natural resources today.

Concern with the protection of the natural environment, and with the conservation and more prudent utilization (trusteeship) of the earth and its diminishing supplies of natural resources, is a relatively recent development in the Western postindustrial societies. These had, almost as a way of life, achieved their own industrial revolutions by ruthless plundering of natural resources—their own indigenous natural resources and those they had acquired, or were in the the process of acquiring, with their imperial expansion in overseas colonies.

The environmental protection movement in the West is a political phenomenon of the late 1960s and later, a middle- or upper-middle-class movement that is very articulate but low in numbers and therefore doomed to playing a marginal, at best "nuisance" or balance-of-power role in national politics. Its influence is not inconsequential, however, and the various ecological pressure groups in North America and the so-called Green movements in the Federal Republic of Germany and elsewhere, seem able to influence other majority parties or coalitions to adopt at least some of their ideas in policy programs. For many Third World countries, however, the contemporary ecological movements often appear as latter-day affectations of wealthy Westerners who have long since cut down their own forests and wildlife preserves and polluted their own rivers and streams, on the way to industrial riches, and who now wish to deprive non-Western states of the fruits of economic development by delaying those non-Western states' industrialization. There is, without doubt, a certain amount of truth in this charge of Eurocentrism in current Western-based drives, in the General Assembly and in special codifying conferences, for environmental protection. On the other hand, among many non-Western peoples, for example the original, native Indian inhabitants of North America, who long preceded the first European settlers and colonizers, we find the concept of homeland and the special historical relationship of the Indian peoples to the earth and its resources clearly present. Is not the concept of the earth as the common heritage of mankind one common to all systems, part of a general, *jus gentium*–based natural law, and therefore capable of transcending the particularist Western origins of current General Assembly drives on behalf of ecology?

The pragmatic response to the Eurocentrism charges would be for the Western countries to volunteer to assume the financial burden of the effective costs of preserving the environment, if it is at the expense of Third World industrialization in concrete cases. This would be a practical way of fulfilling the general mandate of the 1972 United Nations Conference on the Human Environment, held at Stockholm to inaugurate a decade of consciousness about world environmental issues. In fact, the achievements flowing from the Stockholm conference are already considerable: the United Nations Environment Program (UNEP), stemming directly from the Stockholm conference; the global environmental monitoring system; the regional seas program, designed to control land-based chemical and general industrial pollutants and sewage in a number of regional seas, including the Mediterranean, the Red Sea, the Caribbean, and the East Asian seas; the desertification program, addressed in particular to the Sahel region of Africa with its increasing problems caused by droughts, overgrazing, and deforestation; and cooperation among states sharing common natural resources.[13] In addition, specific treaties like the Convention on the Conservation of Antarctic Marine Living Resources, concluded in 1980, are endowed with an overall conservation motivation and purpose, building on some earlier concerns expressed in the original Antarctic Treaty of 1959.[14] In the cognate problem area of outer space, the agreement governing the activities of states on the moon and other celestial bodies—the so-called Moon Treaty of 1979—reflects a similar ideal.

On the whole, we can say that there is a sufficient degree of regional interbloc, intersystemic consensus as to this value, its exact meaning and implications, and also the degree of priority to be accorded to it in concrete cases when it is in competition with other values, to make it operational in United Nations terms as an imperative principle of contemporary international law. It is, of course, not such a big jump from the principle of protecting and conserving scarce natural resources—whether the land and the sea and their living resources or mineral resources—to a corollary principle of sharing those resources on some more nearly equitable basis among all states. This latter principle would have major implications for state sovereignty, of course, and classical international law's precepts as to absolute state ownership and title to territory and resources acquired through the accidents of past conquest, inheritance, or long-time occupation. Is that the international law of tomorrow, in an increasingly overcrowded world with rapidly diminishing food and other resources?

The Enlightenment Imperative: New World Information and Communications Order

The enlightenment imperative—the right to knowledge, as some have called it—is a necessary correlative of every other international law value today, since access to information uncolored by particularist ethnic-cultural or ideological assumptions at its source and origins is a prerequisite to rational decision making and choice in every area of contemporary international law. However, the campaign on behalf of what has been called variously the New International Information Order and the New World Information and Communications Order has developed separately and in its own right and gathered an independent political momentum of its own, so as to constitute a case study or model of United Nations–based international law making. The reasons for the separate and autonomous political development have to do in part with the plurality of different arenas for law making within the United Nations (including specialized agencies like Unesco), and the accidents of intellectual imagination, personal style, and civil courage among the various national delegations and the permanent civil servants located in them; and also the suspicion (which may often be unfounded, but which we have already noted in other instances) that the official United Nations committee, commission, or agency to whose jurisdiction the matter would normally be charged is too conservative, or too timid, or too narrowly traditional and limited (Eurocentric) in its international law outlook to be able to approach "new" international law making with energy and enthusiasm. In fact, the legal activity on behalf of a New World Information and Communications Order is yet another illustration of the thesis that there are indeed many roads to Rome and that there is no reason why international law making should not proceed by several different routes at the same time. The quest for the New World Information Order has proceeded simultaneously, though at different levels of activity and concentration, in Unesco, in the United Nations Committee on Information, and in the ITU (the International Telecommunication Union, the United Nations' own specialized agency for communications).

Soon after the successful law-making acts on behalf of a New International Economic Order—the Declaration, Program of Action, and Charter of Economic Rights and Duties of States—adopted by the General Assembly in 1974–1975, the quest for a New World Information Order was argued by Third World leaders, in Unesco and also in the General Assembly, as being linked generically to the quest for a new economic base for international relations, then already partly achieved.[15] The Third World leaders' thesis was that access to ideas and information on a free and balanced basis, without the overarching control of Western-owned and -dominated news agencies which, it was contended, effectively monopolized the world's flow of news, was a necessary element in economic development and economic decolonization. Intellectual self-determination, on this argument, was the legal correlative of economic self-determination, then being successfully enacted within the United Nations.

The project for a New World Information Order has predictably encountered strong opposition from some Western countries, particularly those actually controlling the major private news agencies. A report,

"Public Perceptions of the United Nations System," prepared by the United Nations Secretariat and submitted to the United Nations Administrative Committee on Coordination at the thirty-seventh session of the General Assembly, in November 1982, strongly criticized Western news media for their perceptions of the United Nations and their alleged negative reporting of its main activities, which carried over, by the fact of Western control of news dissemination, to negative reporting on the United Nations in Third World countries. The report was strongly attacked by the United States delegation to the General Assembly,[16] and Secretary-General Pérez de Cuéllar then publicly dissociated himself from certain paragraphs in the report that made unfavorable comparisons between Western and Soviet press coverage of the United Nations.[17]

The project for a New World Information and Communications Order had been legitimated and sanctioned as a priority concern in international law making by General Assembly Resolution 115 (XXXIII), adopted in 1978. The General Assembly resolution followed upon and was clearly the intellectual product of a major Unesco initiative of 1976, the formation of a special International Commission for the Study of Communication Problems, composed of representatives of the Western and Soviet blocs and the Third World, and known (after its chairman) as the MacBride Commission. The mandate of the commission was to review "all the problems of communication in contemporary society seen against the background of technological progress and recent developments in international relations with due regard to their complexity and magnitude." It was, in fact, a very representative commission in regional (ideological and legal-systemic) terms, and all the main political actors in international communications debates—the United States, Soviet Union, France, India, Japan, Nigeria, Canada—were included. The commission report, *Many Voices, One World: Communication and Society Today and Tomorrow,* published in 1980,[18] supported wholeheartedly the establishment of a New World Information Order, but ran into problems immediately with its identification of means for achieving that goal, such as the licensing of journalists and the monitoring of news and wire services so as to achieve balance and avoid possible distortion.[19] This brought strong criticism from the United States, and the suggestion that a Unesco-based attempt to formulate press rules and to regulate news content would violate international press freedom and produce, so far as it purported to be applied to the American media, a direct collision with the United States Constitution's First Amendment (freedom of speech and of the press) guarantees.

Soviet reactions to the commission report were also negative, though for somewhat different reasons. The main Soviet objection centered on the notional right to a "free flow of information" at the international level, with its implications as to a right to transborder news communication, which, in the Soviet view, had absolutely no recognition in interbloc, intersystemic legal terms. There was also the Soviet suggestion that the report pulled punches as to the allegedly damaging impact of the Western mass media on Third World indigenous national cultures.

The rallying of criticism from the two rival superpowers at the same time says something for the report's balance and neutrality in interbloc, legal-systemic terms; though it is also an indication, once again, of the significant number of problem areas in which the two superpowers may find themselves with a common interest, different from or in direct opposition to the Third World countries. As it stands, the MacBride Commission report provides a significant degree of identification and synthesis of the conflicting interests present in international communications today, even if some of the main antinomies are left unresolved. Perhaps the answer lies in the meaning of freedom today, when it is used in such concepts as the free flow of information and ideas across state frontiers, with the distinction between liberty-in-the-abstract and liberty-in-the-concrete, well known to Western constitutional lawyers from their historical experience in their own municipal, national legal systems, deserving of some more empirically based examination.

The International Law of Communications, unlike the Law of the Sea, now conveniently reduced to one great legislative act with the successful completion of the United Nations Convention on the Law of the Sea of December 1982, lacks its own comprehensive, overarching body of legal principles rationalized and unified by way of treaty or other law-making instrument. As it is, the general principles of the International Law of Communications have to be obtained by way of induction from a number of separate, disparate sources recording a number of separate and disparate problem situations with, very often, quite different legal players because of the different legal arenas involves—Unesco, the United Nations General Assembly, and the ITU.

In the United Nations General Assembly the year 1983 was designated by General Assembly Resolution 40 (XXXVI) of 1981 as World Communications Year, with special attention to development of communications infrastructures, and with the ITU and the United Nations Economic and Social Council having special responsibility.

Unesco's second Medium-term Plan was adopted by the General Conference at its fourth extraordinary session, held in Paris from November 23 to December 3, 1982. Major Program III is entitled "Communication in the Service of Man" and is a basic guide to Unesco activities in the communications field for the balance of the decade of the 1980s.[20] In the debate, the Third World countries regretted the West's virtual monopoly over the gathering and dissemination of information around the world and held the Western information media responsible for using their power in the information and communications field to perpetuate the Western countries' economic, social, and cultural dominance over the rest of the world. The Third World argument was that it was Unesco's responsibility to take positive measures to correct the imbalance. Further, it was suggested that the extraordinarily rapid development in the communications industry in recent years—the evolution of electronic information systems, the advances in space and computer technology—had served simply to accentuate the problem by still further widening the gap in the information and communications field between developed and developing countries. To Western arguments on behalf of the "free flow of news," without international or national institutional or other legal constraints, the Third World leaders replied, that if one descended from abstract theory to the level of facts, one would find that nowhere in the world was the flow of information absolutely free, given the influence and control of lobbies and special interests and similar pressure groups in the West and of governments elsewhere. To illustrate the stranglehold on Third World communications exercised by the West, it was pointed out that developing countries in Africa and elsewhere still in many cases lacked the telex and telephone equipment to contact neighboring countries, so that such calls still had to be routed through the former European parent, imperial countries from which they had been decolonized.[21] The Unesco medium-term plan for the 1980s, as finally approved, reflected the pragmatic efforts of the Director-General, Amadou-Mahtar M'Bow of Senegal, to conciliate the opposing viewpoints. The commitment to the achievement of a New World Information Order was maintained, but some of the sterner strictures against the Western-controlled news and information agencies were modified, and there was a commitment on the Western side to providing training and fellowship for news reporters and editors from Third World countries and also technology for Third World periodicals. Unesco's concrete efforts toward the same objective of developing skills and technology in Third World countries will be channeled through a new agency, the International Programme for the Development of Communication (IPDC), formed in 1980 and already seeking financial backing for a number of quite specific multistate projects—the development of a pan-African news agency and an Asia-Pacific news network.[22]

In another United Nations specialized body, the United Nations Commission on Transnational Corporations, the impact of new technology for the news and information industry was being canvased in its application to transborder data flow and the inevitable issues of confidentiality and privacy and national sovereignty. It is obviously an area of intense interest to economic entrepreneurial groups, in view of the high financial profits involved, and so, understandably, it has been the subject of research and discussion by private foundations as well as the United Nations. Of these foundations, the Intergovernmental Bureau for Informatics (IBI) in Rome is preoccupied with the coordination and harmonizing of the various national laws and national systems of control over the international transmission of facts, economic and other, posing these problems in the context of the larger question: Is there an international *right* to information, and if so, what measures should be adopted to guarantee the legitimacy, and also the security, of the actual user of such data?

In the General Assembly's Special Political Committee, at the thirty-seventh annual session of the General Assembly in the autumn of 1982, a coalition of Third World countries, joined by the Soviet bloc, was able to secure the adoption by overwhelming majority vote of a resolution establishing a code of principles governing the use by states of artificial earth satellites for direct television broadcasting.[23] In plenary session of the General Assembly, the resolution containing the code of principles was adopted by a vote of 107–13, with 13 abstentions, over the objections of the United States.[24] The thirteen negative votes were cast, apart from the United States, by Belgium, Denmark, the Federal Republic of Germany, Iceland, Israel, Italy, Japan, Luxembourg, the Netherlands, Norway, Spain, and the United Kingdom. The resolution took note in its preamble of a full decade of work in the United Nations on problems flowing from international direct television broadcasting, such a United Nations study having been initiated by General Assembly Resolution 2916 (XXVII) of November 9, 1972, and having spilled over into the Committee on the Peaceful Uses of Outer Space. The resolution's preamble also referred to the "significant international political, economic, social and cultural implications" of direct broadcasting from satellites—a recognition of the fact that by the end of the 1980s the new and inexpensive technique of relaying satellite television broadcasts directly to home receivers without the necessity of passing through a ground receiving station would ensure direct mass audiences around the world for such broadcasts. The code of principles, as adopted in the General Assembly resolution, starts with an enunciation of "purposes and objectives" of international direct television broadcasting from satellites, and stipulates that any such activities must be

> carried out in a manner compatible with the sovereign rights of States, including the principle of non-intervention as well as with the right of everyone to seek, receive and impart information and ideas as enshrined in the relevant United Nations instruments; . . . with due respect to the political and cultural integrity of States; . . . with the development of mutual understanding and the strengthening of friendly relations and cooperation among all States and peoples in the interest of maintaining international peace and security.

In its substantive parts, the code of principles sets out a notion of *state responsibility*: "States should bear international responsibility for activities . . . carried out by them or under their jurisdiction and for the conformity of any such activities with the principles set forth in this document."

It also stipulates that any state intending to establish or authorize such activities should "without delay notify the proposed receiving State or States of such intention and shall promptly enter into consultation with any of those States which so requests"; and that any service shall only be established after these conditions have been met and "on the basis of agreements and/or arrangements in conformity with the relevant instruments of the International Telecommunication Union and in accordance with these principles."

It was these particular parts of the code of principles that were criticized by the United States and various other Western states—that is, the definition of purposes and objectives of international direct television broadcasting, the statement of state responsibility, and the emphasis on a consensual approach through consultations and agreements between states. It is difficult to see why. The definition of purposes and objectives is a particularly good example of the pragmatic approach to international legal drafting now well developed as a compromise approach in the main United Nations arenas: the main opposing points of view are all included together in the one formulation, without any attempt to resolve the legal antinomies at this time but leaving it to future development on a case-by-case basis. The statement as to state responsibility is no more than a legal pleonasm, restating the already existing general international law in the present more specific context. As for the emphasis on proceeding by consultations and agreements between states, surely it does little more than reflect the traditional (Western-favored) approach of developing international law consensually or by agreement? Charges, in any case, like those advanced by a United States spokesman during the course of the General Assembly debate, that the code of principles would "afford every other state, including totalitarian states, an unconditional veto over this form of broadcasting"[25] seem very much exaggerated and, in their very absolutism, to have been an impediment to the obtaining of further pragmatic adjustment in favor of Western positions in the final drafting formulation.[26]

This is, of course, a peculiarly complex area of international law, which, more perhaps than others, seems to require a blending, in the negotiating team, of advanced technical-scientific expertise in the particular subject matter and also a grasp of emerging general principles of international law. Ideally, a negotiating team would include both the specialist technicians and the generalists, and the eventual national position in negotiation would represent a working synthesis of the two. In the negotiations and debate over international direct television broadcasting from satellites, within the United Nations, the last-ditch unsuccessful Western fight to prevent adoption of the new code of principles seems to have been dominated by the specialist technicians, who disliked *general* principles that represented very little advance upon already existing United Nations–based international law.

After the General Assembly's enactment of the new principles for international direct television broadcasting, the movement toward a New World Information and Communications Order will, of course, continue. There are still difficult issues to resolve that do not lend themselves easily to categorization and hence to decision making in historically received and understood "regional" (interbloc, intersystemic, East-West or North-South) terms. Among these is the issue of whether the geostationary orbit along the equator, which is the most favored location for direct television broadcasting satellites and communications satellites generally, should be characterized legally as a scarce natural resource, subject as such to the jurisdiction of the states lying beneath it; or whether it should be treated instead as part of the "common heritage of mankind," on the contemporary Law of the Sea analogy; or whether, finally, it should be treated, as it has effectively been treated in the immediate past, as a sort of no-man's-land, open to the first comers who are technologically capable of exploiting it. Obviously, on some of the claims advanced, it has to be considered not only in the context of the legal antinomies of the emerging New World Information Order, but also, and more immediately, as an element, in its own right, of the development and application of the New International Economic Order. The likelihood is, in any case, that the International Law of Communications, including the New World Information Order, will be made in a plurality of different arenas—the General Assembly and its Special Political Committee, the specialist Sixth (Legal) Committee, and the technically sophisticated Committee on the Peaceful Uses of Outer Space, which, because of the happy accidents of personality, gave such imaginative and decisive leadership to the movement, from the early 1960s on, toward progressive development of an International Law of Outer Space; Unesco, with its overall cultural commitment and a certain inbuilt institutional preference therefore for maximizing access by all states to news and information sources and for establishing general rules of conduct that ensure proper respect for the cultural integrity of all states; and the more technically based and functionally oriented ITU.

In terms of law-making process, the new international law will sometimes be achieved through the postulation of necessarily rather abstract codes of general legal principles and sometimes through more specific and concrete, functionally based arrangements; in substantive law terms, sometimes through stipulations applying to all modes of communication and sometimes through arrangements limited to perhaps one medium only—telegraphic communications, newspapers and other printed forms, radio broadcasting, satellite television. We do not seem as yet to be at that particular point in time where—as with the contemporary Law of the Sea at the opening of the 1970s—one could launch the idea of a single comprehensive, overarching law-making act with some prospect of success in reasonably timely fashion. The progressive development of international law in this area will thus perforce continue through the same pragmatic, empirical, problem-oriented, step-by-step methods, using a plurality of different United Nations legal arenas and a plurality of actors (the legal technicians and the legal generalists included).

THE HUMAN DIGNITY IMPERATIVE: CONTEMPORARY ANTINOMIES

"Specialists" and "Generalists" in International Legal Negotiations

Human dignity and the raising of standards of living and well-being are the postulated objectives of every main municipal, national constitutional system, and the announced goals of all the main ideological systems in the contemporary world community. Yet no area of contemporary international law has been more marked by fierce partisan conflicts. The specialized United Nations arenas having jurisdiction over such matters have been characterized by pejorative, name-calling debates recalling the intellectually most sterile years of the old Soviet-Western Cold War era, and by Manichaean black-and-white characterizations in which opposing viewpoints are viewed as wholly evil and one's own opinions as totally free from sin. Such simplistic legal approaches render no service to the progressive development of international law! A good deal of the fault must be attributed to the patterns of selection of national delegates to the specialized United Nations arenas normally dealing with such questions. Just as in technologically highly sophisticated areas of contemporary international law making that also require high policy choices—direct television broadcasting from satellites, as an example—the interplay and interaction of the strictly technical and the philosophical, policy elements require unusual skills in problem solving, involving a prudent combination of the "specialists" and the "generalists" on the negotiating team—so human rights, as a prime area of United Nations responsibility from 1948, the year of the Universal Declaration, onward would seem to call for extra qualities of intellectual eclecticism, freedom from a narrow national parochialism, and skills of pragmatism and compromise, if the abstract norms or law-in-books of United Nations codes and declarations are ever to be made operational as international law-in-action of the contemporary world community. Unfortunately, many states do not always seem to take the same care in forming a prudent and balanced national negotiating team in this area as they do for other specialized arenas of United Nations activity. It is too easy to make up a delegation with single-issue, pressure-group spokesmen addressing their highly political messages to their own national constituencies at home rather than being concerned with the often necessarily patient and unpublicized negotiation behind closed doors that is at the core of international problem solving in concrete cases. Politically more detached national delegations that are (happily, in their own view) not too tightly embraced by either one of the two super-powers have complained of the atmosphere of a criminal courtroom, with each side intent on pillorying the other,[27] that has pervaded the periodic Conferences on Security and Cooperation in Europe established in the aftermath of the Helsinki conference of 1975 as what was hoped would be a continuing and accelerating "Helsinki process" of removal of legal and other barriers to trade, commerce, and intercourse between Eastern Europe and Western Europe across the old de facto political-military frontiers of 1945. Not merely has the "Helsinki process" not worked as was once hoped, but the actual empirical, statistical record of East-West cooperation and exchanges (including reunification of families and even visits) shows a regression in relation to what has already been achieved on a Eastern European–Western European limited bilateral basis[28] up to the time of the Helsinki Act and in the larger multilateral or "universal" approach that it had presaged.[29] Clearly something had gone wrong! Would it be better to drop for the time being the "universal" approach to East-West cooperation in Europe under the aegis of the Helsinki review process, and to revert to the pre-Helsinki intra-European "regional" approach through limited ad hoc, problem-oriented agreements between the European countries directly concerned? That larger East-West cooperation, transcending European special concerns and interests, could always be continued in other, more nearly "universal" arenas, including general United Nations arenas, which would normally be liberated from the excess ideological baggage accumulated under the Helsinki review process by the late 1970s and the early 1980s, and which would normally also be staffed by national delegates with a larger, more comprehensive view of the United Nations and its international law-making processes.

United Nations Charter-based Principles and Processes

The United Nations Charter as drafted and adopted in 1945, unlike most modern constitutional instruments, including those drafted about the same time as the Charter or in the postwar period generally, does not have its own autonomous, self-contained chapter or constitutional bill of rights. The historical reasons for this are clear and have already been referred to:

the desire of the key members of the wartime alliance against fascism, who dominated the Charter drafting process, to maintain their consensus from their wartime alliance of convenience sufficiently to establish their own preferred model of a postwar world public order system safeguarding their own conceived vital interests. Peace and security interests are thus preeminent in the Charter as drafted in 1945. When linked to the special Soviet conception of the Charter itself, this tended to militate against rhetorical flourishes, such as a constitutional bill of rights, on which in any case it would have been difficult and time-consuming to obtain any common interbloc ideological consensus. The Charter does, however, contain a number of references to human rights, most of these, admittedly, at a very high level of generality and abstraction, and consequently somewhat open-ended in legal terms. Thus the preamble of the Charter refers variously to "faith in fundamental rights, in the dignity and worth of the human person, in the equal rights of men and women"; "social progress and better standards of life in larger freedom"; "economic and social advancement of all peoples." The nearest thing to a constitutional chapter on rights is Chapter IX, "International Economic and Social Cooperation" (Articles 55–60); but only Article 55 among these addresses itself specifically to substantive rights, and here again it is in very general terms:

> . . . The United Nations shall promote:
> a) higher standards of living, full employment, and conditions of economic and social progress and development;
> b) solutions of international economic, social, health, and related problems; and international cultural and educational cooperation; and
> c) universal respect for, and observance of, human rights and fundamental freedoms for all without distinction as to race, sex, language, or religion.

Chapter X (Articles 61–72), establishing the Economic and Social Council of the United Nation, gives a skeletal institutional and processual support for constitutional rights by authorizing the new council to make "recommendations" as to "human rights and fundamental freedoms for all" (Article 62), and to set up commissions "for the promotion of human rights" (Article 68). Other areas of the Charter endowed with other objectives—for example, Chapter XII, "International Trusteeship System" (Articles 75–85)—may attach, also, human-rights criteria to their more specific mandate: Article 76, in defining the "basic objectives of the trusteeship system," lists, inter alia, the encouraging of "respect for human rights and for fundamental freedoms for all without distinction as to race, sex, language, or religion" (Article 76 [c]), and the ensuring of "equal treatment in social, economic, and commercial matters for all Members of the United Nations and their nationals, and also equal treatment for the latter in the administration of justice" (Article 76 [d]).

It is from these relatively modest and (quantitatively) limited and scattered constitutional sources that the quite ambitious United Nations law-making ventures on human rights have stemmed; and the correlative United Nations–based institutional developments are legally related to those same sources. The first United Nations law-making act, the Universal Declaration of Human Rights, was adopted by General Assembly Resolution 217 (III) of December 10, 1948. The Universal Declaration was the carry-over of the American wartime and immediate postwar idealism, in relation to international organization in general, into the United Nations General Assembly, in which, of course, at that time the United States, with its allies and supporters, was able to command an effective majority voting coalition. The General Assembly vote, in the smaller United Nations of 1948, was 48–0 in favor of the Universal Declaration, with 8 abstentions. These latter abstentions reflected the political climate of the times: apart from the Union of South Africa and Saudi Arabia, the Soviet Union and its two constituent republics and three other Soviet-bloc countries abstained. The Universal Declaration of 1948 was followed up by three further United Nations law-making acts in the same general intellectual spirit: the International Covenant on Economic, Social and Cultural Rights; the International Covenant on Civil and Political Rights; and the Optional Protocol to the International Covenant on Civil and Political Rights. These three instruments were all adopted by General Assembly Resolution 2200A (XXI) of December 16, 1966.

The practical implementation of these various human rights acts is based institutionally in a number of United Nations specialized bodies and arenas, most notably perhaps the Commission on Human Rights, which meets annually in Geneva, and its Sub-Commission on Prevention of Discrimination and Protection of Minorities. The Economic and Social Council, established under Chapter X of the Charter, exercises oversight of the Commission on Human Rights and must approve its decisions. In addition, human rights issues are debated in the General Assembly's specialized committee, the Third (Social, Humanitarian and Cultural) Committee, within whose jurisdiction they fall. Beyond that, such problems may arise interstitially in debates in the other specialized committees of the General Assembly having jurisdiction over other matters—for example, in the Special Political Committee, in the Fourth (Decolonization) Committee, and in the Sixth (Legal) Committee. Specialized agencies of the United Nations, most notably Unesco and the International Labor Organization, have always felt free to examine human rights aspects of their ordinary jurisdiction, which they have been disposed to define very broadly anyway. The judicial arena—to Western lawyers, and especially to those influenced by American constitutional experience, the prime legal arena for implementation and extension of human rights through judicial "legislation"—does not have a direct role in international law making on human rights within the United Nations legal system as a whole. In considerable measure, this is because of the limited, "consensual" jurisdiction of the International Court in *inter partes* matters, and the political failure, to date, to maximize the law-making potential of its advisory opinion jurisdiction; as well as the somewhat negative and restrictive "traditional" or "classical" view of the court's legislative role taken by many members of the United Nations up to date. The court can and does hear issues involving Charter principles of human rights when they are raised interstitially in the course of litigation on other issues, or in the much rarer instances when they reach the court in their own right, as in *South West Africa, Second Phase* in 1966[30] and in *Namibia* in 1971.[31] Neither the Universal Declaration of Human Rights of 1948 nor the subsequent, related United Nations law-making acts were conceived or designed as instruments for court-based interpretation and application. Reflecting some constitutional drafting models of the postwar era, and perhaps also intrinsic intellectual-legal attitudes and preconceptions of some, at least, of their political sponsors, they are documents addressed more to legislators (as canons of self-restraint), or to administrators (as counsels of prudence), and not to courts. There is also a didactic, hortatory quality, and a disposition to be prolix and to try to spell things out by enumeration. While a determined law-making group with a common consensus and some civil courage can certainly—whether court or legislature proper—draw comfort and support, and also technical-legal footnotes, from the Universal Declaration of 1948 and its companion United Nations acts, from the strictly technical constitutional law viewpoint there is not quite the same degree and intensity of psychological support as provided, for example, by the succinct, lapidarian-style American constitutional Bill of Rights, which seems well attuned to the needs of judicial activists bent on the progressive development of law.

Differing "Regional" Approaches: Eurocentrism and Human Rights

The proliferation of General Assembly specialist committees, United Nations commissions, and United Nations specialized agencies now actively engaged in human rights questions testifies, of course, to the degree to which such questions permeate all aspects of contemporary community decision making. But it also reveals a growing dissatisfaction and irritation on the part of many states about what they feel to be particularist, and not universal, philosophical and ideological assumptions present in the definition and application of human rights in the older, official United Nations arenas, and even some of the newer ones like the Helsinki review conferences. The irritation of states outside the two big blocs, Soviet and

Western (and even of some lesser, supporting members of those blocs), with the two superpowers' propensity for making revived Cold War issues out of what should today transcend the old Soviet-Western bipolar rivalry and be accepted as part of the "new" universal principles of international law is evident enough. An intellectually much more interesting and intriguing question, however, is that of the current state of the general (non–Cold War) United Nations human rights dialogue. At the annual meeting, in the summer of 1982, of the United Nations Commission on Human Rights in Geneva, the Iranian delegation roundly condemned certain other national delegations for their attacks on the then state of human rights in Iran, going beyond the more obvious (and valid) retort that those other national delegations had been strangely silent on the state of human rights in Iran during the regime of the deposed Shah. Certainly there was a strong element of subjectivity and special pleading in some of the latter-day criticisms of the Ayatollah's administration made by governments that had consciously and deliberately ignored the excesses of the earlier Iranian government, which had been militarily allied to them. What was raised now, however, was the issue of historical objectivity and impartiality in relation to a country that had recently undergone a major cultural, social, and economic revolution.[32] Is that valid as a general legal criticism?

In their ultimate historical origins, the United Nations Universal Declaration of 1948 and the three related acts of 1966 represent the flowering of Western liberal constitutional thought. But Western constitutionalism, as it emerged historically in Western national societies, tended to reject or downplay the idea of group or collective rights. It also stresses political and civil rights, but is correspondingly light on social and economic rights. Western constitutional thinking on human rights, indeed, reflects the "open society" values that characterized Western laissez-faire society in its political and economic heyday. There is an emphasis on mobility of persons and goods and ideas as a virtue in itself, and on the removal of all legal and other rules that might otherwise clog or fetter free economic development. In American constitutional history, the concept of "liberty of contract," applied as a philosophic absolute and abstract and attached to the legal category of fair constitutional procedures (due process of law), was successfully employed from the late nineteenth century right up to the era of President Franklin Roosevelt's New Deal, to outlaw social reform legislation—minimum wages and maximum hours laws, for example. It took the infusion of newer, social democratic ideas for this rather strange liberty-of-contract-in-the-abstract constitutional imperative to be overcome, and for a new imperative that emphasized substantive freedom and equality of bargaining power between the rival economic forces in Western society to take its place. But the older pre-1937 American constitutional experience with a Bill of Rights jurisprudence that equated political and civil rights with laissez-faire economic ideas and preservation of the special privileges of the economically most powerful segments of society is well known to jurists in other systems and usually taken as an example to be avoided and positively legislated against in their own new ventures in constitution making. It colors a great deal of the attitudes in United Nations arenas to Western espousals of human rights issues. Is Western legal thinking on human rights preoccupied with formal, procedural, political and civil rights, at the expense of substantive economic rights; and is the effect, if not the design, of such an exclusive *political* preoccupation, when projected in world community terms, to leave the door open to the most ruthless and predatory economic forces in international society, especially the great Western-owned and controlled multinational corporations?

Another criticism of Western, and by inference some United Nations approaches to human rights concerns an emphasis on *individual* as distinct from group or collective rights, producing, in critics' views, a certain lack of reality in the approach to contemporary society and its social conflicts.[33] It was only in the 1970s that the concept of reverse discrimination (or affirmative action) in favor of culturally, socially, or economically disadvantaged groups came to be considered, and to a limited degree accepted, as an imperative in Western municipal, national constitutional systems.[34] The old individualistic emphasis that the Western "open society" ideal enjoined gave free rein to aggressive, upwardly mobile groups in Western society, but, as a matter of history, seemed merely to facilitate the creation of further effective social and economic barriers to other, more passive ethnic-cultural communities. The awakening juridical conscience of American national society has now seen constitutional acceptance of the need for affirmative action on a group or collective basis,[35] to aid the effective social and economic integration of the nonwhite communities into American life. This attitude, as enforced in the 1970s by the United States Supreme Court, has meant replacing or diluting the older, purely individualist conception of human rights by recognition of the relevance of special constitutional protection qua group or collectivity. There was nothing in the American constitutional Bill of Rights preventing such a "progressive development" of law by judicial interpretation; and a fortiori there is nothing in the Universal Declaration of Human Rights of 1948 or the related United Nations law-making acts impeding full constitutional development of group and collective rights within the United Nations legal framework. There is a widespread feeling among very many Third World countries that the "new" international law involves group or collective rights—*peoples' rights*—in addition to purely individual rights; social and economic rights, in addition to political and civil rights *stricto sensu;* and affirmative action through world community interventions—going beyond past legal passivity and claimed "neutrality"—in order positively to redress the economic imbalance existing between the developed postindustrial societies and the rest of the world. It is this restlessness with the regular human rights arenas of the United Nations, which are widely perceived as dominated by outmoded, "classical" Western spatially and temporally limited conceptions of the ambit of human rights, that accounts for the recourse to so many other, different, varied United Nations law-making arenas[36] in the quest for a New International Economic Order, a New World Information and Communications Order, and other similar postulated goals of contemporary international law. For the developed, and especially the Western, countries, the correct response is not to give up on the "classical" individual political and civil rights, but to recognize that, even in municipal, national law systems of the main Western states, the jurisprudence has undergone its own "progressive development," through judge-made law and also parliamentary enactment, so as to encompass the newer social and economic rights, group rights, and affirmative action programs.[37] Why should this not apply to human rights at the international law level?

11. International Law Making for an Era of Transition

An era of transition such as we live in today, in the contemporary world community, involves, as we have seen, conflict and interaction of different ideological systems and of the different political, economic, and military groupings and associations of states in which they manifest themselves. This may mean not merely differences among key participants as to the basic values present in any given problem situation and as to the institutions and techniques to be used for its solution, but also differing conceptions of the movement and direction of world history and of the models of world public order that should be set up to influence or shape such historical development or unfolding. We have seen how the two superpowers, for different reasons, in their early reactions viewed the Ayatollah Khomeini's cultural revolution in Iran as antihistorical and not to be condoned or supported in long-range terms: the United States not only because it meant the overthrow of the Shah and his American-leaning military dictatorship, but also because it interrupted the trend toward an eventual Western-style, consumer-oriented society in Iran; the Soviet Union because it meant, in Soviet terms, an anachronistic revival of historically regressive religious forces in Iranian government. The shape that the Ayatollah was seeking to give to Iranian policy making for the future simply did not accord with the two superpowers' views of the rational, staged development of national societies within their own respective larger world conceptions.

Alternative World Order Constructs

For the two superpowers and their lesser, supporting states, the de facto political-military settlement at war's end in Europe and in Asia in 1945 represented a sufficiently satisfactory balance of power or accommodation between the different interests of the main states that had come together, in part by design and in part by accident of history, in that military alliance of convenience known as the wartime alliance against fascism. The United Nations, as the postwar venture in international organization decided upon and legally adopted by the wartime allies in their San Francisco Conference in 1945, reflected, in its special institutional arrangements—the constitutionally predominant role of the Security Council, balanced by the permanent members' (Big Power) veto on substantive issues—the wartime consensus of 1941–1945 continued and projected into the postwar era, with all its implications for the future of international relations. It is possible today, as it was not perhaps possible in 1945, publicly to question the political wisdom or basic morality of all the dispositions, territorial and other, made by the allied wartime leaders at Yalta and Potsdam in 1945;[1] and one may even call for a legal reexamination and revision of those 1945 accords, to the extent that time itself, on the principle *die normative Kraft des Faktischen,*[2] has not made its legal impact in either totally rewriting some of the original historical events or else simply confirming and legitimating them in their original sense through the sheer passage of the years. It is hardly possible, however, to deny that the Yalta and Potsdam accords constituted the fundamental political-military premise—that extralegal "political" fact or *Grundnorm*—from which the postwar world public order system flowed, with the United Nations at its core.

Within the United Nations itself, we have seen the differing doctrinal-legal positions taken by the two superpowers in their approach to the nature and character of international organization: the original and still-continuing Soviet position that the Charter constitutes only a limited treaty between states, derogating from or limiting those states' sovereignty and legal competences for certain purposes (but only for certain purposes), and to be strictly or restrictively construed for that reason; the original Western position, (formulated in the early postwar period of that "small" United Nations with Western majority voting coalition control of the General Assembly), that the Charter is a constitution, capable, as such, of continuing growth and adaptation to changing societal conditions in the world community and to be broadly and creatively interpreted on that account. The original Western "optimistic" or legally expansionist view of the Charter and of the General Assembly law-making mandate hardly survived the disappearance in the late 1950s of the automatic pro-Western voting majority in the General Assembly; and it has been left to the new Third World majority in the General Assembly to espouse in its turn the broad, "Charter as constitution" approach to the United Nations and its law making, now abandoned, in some embarrassment, by its original Western sponsors.

The Western-devised doctrinal-legal base for an expansion of General Assembly law-making powers under the Uniting for Peace resolution of 1950 remains as a constitutional precedent for the future; but it is possible, viewing Uniting for Peace now as an ad hoc Western response in 1950 to a specific Soviet political-military ploy at that time, to exaggerate its effects on long-term Soviet-Western relations within the United Nations and on the working of the main United Nations institutions. Once the Cold War was over, the two superpowers quickly moved to reestablish their wartime patterns of consultation, exchange, and cooperation on matters of common interest and concern. The Soviet-Western debates of the late 1950s and throughout the 1960s over peaceful coexistence and its codification in legal principles (eventually to be achieved in the friendly relations declarations adopted by United Nations General Assembly resolution of 1970) merely veiled the fact of the constant and continuing Soviet-Western discussions and negotiations, throughout all that period, over nuclear and general disarmament; security of frontiers and other territorial dispositions and respect for "spheres of influence"; and positive cooperation in such matters as scientific research and exploration, Antarctica, outer space, and the like. The era of Soviet-Western détente, beginning by the end of the 1950s certainly and lasting until the early or middle 1970s at least, was a very fruitful one in international peace keeping and also international law-making terms. The two superpowers, reverting perhaps to wartime habits but also reacting to events and doing what came naturally, preferred to reach their consensus and their agreements bilaterally, in summit meetings outside the main United Nations arenas and processes, and without the distracting presence of irrelevant third parties. There was nothing in this that was incompatible or in conflict with the United Nations Charter itself; but it was rather closer to the original Soviet limited or "holding operation" conception of the United Nations and its law making than to the earlier American "constitutional," expansionist view of the United Nations role and powers.

With the weakening and decline of the Soviet-Western détente process from the mid-1970s onward, the resultant gap in effective world peace keeping[3] and the critical lag in nuclear and general disarmament have led to a search for arenas and processes other than the Big Power summit meetings and their bilaterally agreed and drafted treaty texts as the source for subsequent multilateral conventions. This has meant, in fact, a return to the United Nations, and a return, in particular, to the General Assembly, where the permanent members' (Big Power) veto cannot legally operate to prevent or restrain collective action.

Parallel to the Big Powers' apparent effective abdication of responsibility as to general (non-Soviet-Western) peace keeping and disarmament has been their apparent lack of concern or interest in other areas of potential international law making—in particular, North-South relations and the correction of the extreme economic imbalance currently existing between developed postindustrial societies and the rest of the world. For the new social and economic law making challenges which, for Third World countries in contradistinction to the Soviet Union and the United States, seem to rank ahead even of peace-keeping and disarmament questions, this lack of concern means back to the General Assembly, and the use in particular of United Nations–based special law-making conferences. The successful completion and signature of the United Nations Convention on the Law of the Sea in December 1982, after more than a decade of negotiations, demonstrated that it was indeed possible to make "new" international law in United Nations–based arenas and through United Nations legal processes, in spite of dragging of feet or outright obstruction and opposition by the Big Powers. Even if the two superpowers were to reestablish the Soviet-Western détente process it would hardly be possible to reestablish, on the same basis of preeminence as yesterday, the particular legal-institutional patterns (summit meetings and bilateral Big Power action to the exclusion of multilateral United Nations action) that characterized the détente process in its heyday. The rediscovery of the United Nations and the demonstration of the law-making opportunities of the General Assembly and of United Nations specialized law-making conferences authorized by it have clearly initiated a constitutional trend that by now can hardly be reversed. With it comes a new and more optimistic vision of a world community—beyond the peace-keeping and security and disarmament preoccupations of today—in which attempts can be made to resolve new problems—social and economic this time—by legal means, by conscious acts of community legislation.

Evolving United Nations Constitutionalism

Meanwhile, if the way to change through formal amendment of the United Nations Charter seems blocked by the difficult constitutional amending machinery established under the Charter itself, United Nations constitutionalism continues to evolve nevertheless, as illustrated in a number of important areas.

United Nations Membership: The Credentials Issue

The biggest political battle at the thirty-seventh annual session of the General Assembly in the autumn of 1982 concerned the Charter-established legal criteria for United Nations membership (Chapter II, "Membership," Articles 3–6) and their relevance and applicability to the

General Assembly's rules of procedure (I, "Credentials," Rules 27–29). The occasion for the battle was the acceptance of the credentials of the Israeli delegation to the General Assembly; the legal precedent which some members sought to invoke was the non-event at the thirtieth annual session of the General Assembly in 1975. On that occasion the white minority government of the Republic of South Africa, fearing that its delegation's credentials would not be accepted by a majority in the General Assembly's nine-member Credentials Committee, or thereafter by the General Assembly in plenary, simply did not turn up at the General Assembly,[4] and it did not return in subsequent years. The white minority government of the Republic of South Africa suspected, with good reason, that the General Assembly and its Credentials Committee would take such action as a means of protesting against South Africa's systematic practice of racial discrimination toward its nonwhite majority, and also against its defiance of General Assembly Resolution 2145 (XXI) of 1966 (adopted after the 8–7 World Court judgment declining jurisdiction to rule in *South West Africa, Second Phase*),[5] which declared South Africa's old League of Nations mandate over Namibia (South West Africa) to be terminated, and of the World Court advisory opinion of 1971, which in effect confirmed that resolution on legal grounds. The General Assembly had already the previous year, by Resolution 3206 (XXIX) of September 30, 1974 (adopted by a vote of 98–23, with 14 abstentions), approved the Credentials Committee report of that year rejecting the South African representatives' credentials.

The debate over the South African credentials focused on its white minority government's failure to adhere to what we might call proper standards of United Nations behavior, as manifested in its grave and continuing defiance of the decisions of the main United Nations institutions, the General Assembly and the World Court, and its manifest flouting of the purposes and principles of the Charter as set out in Chapter I (Articles 1–2). Contrary to the assertions of some major Western countries rallying to the government of South Africa's defense, the United Nations Charter never, as a matter of its history or of its actual language and drafting, accepted the principle of universality of membership. Right from the outset the so-called enemy states were excluded, and the criteria of membership set out in Articles 4, 5, and 6, which are supposed to govern admission, suspension, and expulsion of states, require, in legal terms, the exercise of a conscious value judgment on the part of the United Nations collectivity. Otherwise, the stipulations as to being "peace-loving," and "accept[ing] the obligations contained in the present Charter and . . . able and willing to carry out these obligations" (Article 4), and as to respecting the principles contained in the Charter (Article 6), would become legally otiose or meaningless. On the other hand, Articles

4, 5, and 6 of the Charter supply their own institutionally based sanctions for ensuring respect for the Charter norms on membership: vote of the General Assembly, upon the prior recommendation of the Security Council (to which, of course, the permanent members' veto would apply). It was the certain threat of frustration of any Security Council–General Assembly legal initiative against South Africa by any one of its several Big Power friends' veto in the Security Council that caused the General Assembly to turn to the Credentials Committee action. Rather than seeking to reapply in its own special forum the substantive criteria for membership spelled out in Articles 4 to 6 of the charter, the Credentials Committee (and after it, if need be, the General Assembly sitting in plenary to confirm and adopt the committee report) might have been better advised, politically and legally, to tackle the problem head on; it is self-evident that a white minority government, elected on a franchise that is legally restricted to a tiny percentage of the whole population of a multiracial society, can by no legal color of right claim to be representative and thus entitled to be accredited to speak for its disfranchised nonwhite majority. The only political disadvantage from this, the most direct and forthright legal approach, might be that as a precedent it would become almost sui generis: there is no other example in the United Nations membership of a multiracial society where a tiny minority sect so flagrantly rejects its own majority's claims to political participation or so consistently flouts United Nations attempts legally to correct that situation.

The moves at the thirty-seventh session of the General Assembly in the autumn of 1982 to reject the Israeli delegation's credentials were related politically to a number of events. A letter addressed to the Secretary-General of the United Nations on October 22, 1982, signed by some fifty states,[6] charged Israel with flagrant and persistent violations of international law and the UN Charter; with defiance of UN resolutions on Palestine and the Middle East; with failure, in particular, to "implement Security Council and General Assembly resolutions concerning Jerusalem, which it has illegally annexed and claimed as its capital"; and with the "effective annexation of the Syrian Golan Heights" in defiance of Security Council and General Assembly resolutions. These were serious charges, of course, and, if found proven to the satisfaction of the UN community, might be seen as establishing a prima facie case for recourse to the rules on suspension of membership rights and privileges, or expulsion, under Articles 5 and 6 of the charter. But such charges, even if proven, would not in themselves, on ordinary legal interpretation, constitute legal grounds for a rejection of state credentials under the General Assembly rules of procedure. There might be a valid legal quarrel with the Israeli government's official issuance of its UN delegation's credentials from the city of Jerusalem, flying in the face of Security Council and

General Assembly resolutions on the legal status of that city; but this point could surely be corrected by simply reissuance of the letters of credence from another city. As for the issue of the "representativeness" of the Israeli delegation—the main (and ultimately successful) legal objection to the seating of the white minority government of South Africa in 1974 and 1975—the Israeli case was surely distinguishable from the earlier South African precedent, the allegedly illegal military occupation of Arab territories and their populations not militating against the preponderant representative quality of the Israeli delegation in regard to Israel itself (including occupied territories). The legal objections to Israel's "peace-loving" character in terms of Chapter 4 of the Charter should properly be addressed to a legal forum other than the Credentials Committee.

But the letter to the Secretary-General by the fifty-odd states on October 22, 1982, constituted a legal footnote to an event already resolved within the UN community by the Secretary-General with the full support of very many of those same states.[7] In a brilliant tour de force of behind-the-scenes executive "quiet diplomacy," UN Secretary-General Pérez de Cuéllar persuaded most of the Arab states, which had been at the core of the movement to reject Israel's credentials, to withhold their objections for the then current thirty-seventh annual session. And so, after a preliminary procedural vote on a Finnish motion to adjourn debate on the Israeli credentials issue (adopted by 74–9, with 32 abstentions), the General Assembly went on to endorse, without vote, the seating of Israel and 155 other national delegations (including Democratic Kampuchea, a motion to reject Democratic Kampuchea's credentials having already been defeated by 90–29, with 26 abstentions).[8]

That was the end of the credentials issue at the thirty-seventh session of the General Assembly; though the joint letter of the fifty-odd states to the Secretary-General, entered into the official record with its collective "reservation" (in place of a negative vote) as to Israel's conduct in relation to Security Council and General Assembly resolutions on the Palestine and Middle East questions generally, contains the implied suggestion of possible future General Assembly action, presumably using other legal processes than the approval of national delegations' credentials. The Arab states' consensus *not* to press the matter of rejection of the Israeli delegation's credentials had been preceded by a warning by American Secretary of State Shultz that the United States would withdraw from the General Assembly and withhold its financial dues to the United Nations, if the motion of rejection were passed.[9] Such a move, which might once have caused consternation in the General Assembly, was received at the thirty-seventh annual session with far more equanimity, perhaps because it had been suggested before during the course of the session and was thus deprived of its full psychological weight when a really important issue came along. An earlier decision in September 1982 by one of the United Nations specialized agencies, the International Atomic Energy Agency, in Vienna, to reject the Israeli delegation's credentials had seen a similar American move; adoption of the motion rejecting the Israeli credentials in the IAEA had been aided by some legally questionable rulings from the chair, though the suggestion was that less uncompromising American tactics, prior to the actual vote, might have saved the day by allowing passage of a resolution criticizing Israel's conduct but avoiding suspension or rejection of credentials. The subsequent report of the IAEA to the General Assembly, presented by its Director-General, Hans Blix, in November 1982, rightly pointed out that the credentials question was one of "international constitutional law and procedure, by no means limited to the IAEA, and by no means limited to the current events";[10] and he called for a more generalized United Nations consensus answer that could apply to the General Assembly and all the specialized agencies. Such a consensus formation seemed in process in the General Assembly at that time; for an identical credentials-based move to that in the IAEA, one month later in another specialized agency, the International Telecommunications Union (ITU), was successfully settled by compromise.[11] But, if need be, the International Court of Justice could be approached for a further, updated policy interpretation, building on its two early "membership" opinions of 1948[12] and 1950.[13]

General Assembly and Security Council

The increasing pragmatism of the General Assembly, as its new Third World members increasingly acquired the skills of problem solving and practical compromises to supplement their already well-known capacity to draft general codes of principles, promised a willingness to use the General Assembly's legal powers—on the Uniting for Peace precedent of 1950—to move affirmatively to fill the gap in the peace-keeping role when, by reason of the threat or actual use of the permanent members' veto, the Security Council processes should become clogged and incapable of functioning as they were originally intended to do.

Curiously enough at first sight, in the one case in which, on objective legal grounds, the General Assembly seemed perfectly placed to assume the Security Council's defaulted functions—the British-Argentinian dispute over the Falklands (Malvinas)—the General Assembly did not choose to act. The original Security Council Resolution 502 of April 3, 1982, calling for an immediate cessation of hostilities, for the immediate withdrawal of the Argentinian forces, and for the United Kingdom and Argentina to seek a diplomatic solution and fully to respect the purposes and principles of the Charter, had been adopted by a vote of 10–1

(Panama), with 4 abstentions (China, the Soviet Union, Poland, and Spain).[14] The further Security Council Resolution 505, adopted on May 26, 1982, was introduced by Uganda in cosponsorship with Guyana, Ireland, Jordan, Togo, and Zaire, and asked the Secretary-General to undertake "a renewed mission of good offices" in an endeavor to bring about a peaceful solution to the Falklands (Malvinas) conflict. This time the resolution was adopted unanimously, after withdrawal of an earlier Irish draft calling, as a first step, for a complete suspension of hostilities for seventy-two hours.[15] On June 4, 1982, a further Security Council resolution, cosponsored by Panama and Spain, calling for an immediate cease-fire in the conflict, along with implementation of the previous Security Council Resolutions 502 and 505, was supported in the Security Council by an affirmative vote of 9–2 (the United Kingdom and the United States), with 4 abstentions (France, Guyana, Jordan, and Togo), but it failed legally because two permanent members, the United Kingdom and the United States, used their veto.[16] Yet in both political and legal terms the defeat of this latest Security Council peace-keeping move was questionable. According to a strict reading of the Charter, the United Kingdom, as a party to the dispute, was legally disqualified from voting and hence from casting a veto.[17] And immediately after the vote the United States representative, Ambassador Kirkpatrick, announced that she had been requested by her government to state that, were it possible for her delegation to change its vote, it would have changed it from a veto to an abstention.[18] It was a bizarre episode, presumably related to the impending resignation of American Secretary of State Haig, who had from the beginning maintained a consistently pro-British position even while purporting to fill the neutral role of mediator between the United Kingdom and Argentina—a venture by Secretary Haig which, quite predictably under the circumstances, had ended in failure. With the Security Council attempt to order an immediate cease-fire blocked only by the legally contestable attempt at veto by one of the permanent members that was itself a party to the dispute, and by the politically equivocal and presumably retrievable veto by another permanent member in process of changing its Secretary of State and presumably then its foreign policy to a more consciously neutral position as between the two parties, all the conditions seemed ripe for a successful recourse to an emergency special session of the General Assembly, under the special rules of procedure (Rules 8, 9, 19) developed, as legal "gloss" on the Charter, after the Uniting for Peace precedent of 1950. That such action did not occur seems directly attributable to several factors, all of which testify to the increasing pluralism of the Third World majority in the General Assembly and its ability to make pragmatic judgments and to distinguish, on the particular facts, on a case-by-case basis where necessary. There was a clear perception that both parties to the dispute were at fault in United Nations constitutional terms: the United Kingdom by its persistent dragging of its feet through seventeen years of bilateral diplomatic negotiations and its failure to liquidate in timely fashion the last remnants of its colonial empire, and Argentina by its recourse to force and direct action in clear violation of charter principles, for which even the suspicion of British bad faith in the prolonged bilateral negotiations between the two countries hardly constituted a justification—in the absence, at least, of further compelling reasons.

In a contest between that imperative principle of the "new" international law—decolonization—and the Charter principle of interdiction of the use of force in settlement of disputes, the result, for many Third World and other countries naturally sympathetic to the Argentine position, was something of a standoff, discouraging the obvious legal remedy to Big Power frustration of Security Council action, of recourse to the General Assembly. Further, numbers of Third World countries, including several within the geographical confines of the Americas, had legally at least questionable territorial frontiers with politically and militarily more powerful neighbors, and every reason, therefore, to fear a new precedent that might justify recourse to force if diplomatic negotiations should break down. The former British colony Guyana was the latter-day beneficiary, on decolonization and state succession to imperial Britain, of extended boundaries which the original "parent" imperial power imposed on Venezuela in the late nineteenth century; hence the Guyana abstention to the Security Council resolution of June 4, 1982, calling for an immediate cease fire in the Falklands (Malvinas) conflict.[19] Finally, Secretary-General Pérez de Cuéllar, who in the first six months of his term of office had demonstrated a sturdy independence from Big Power pressures and a capacity for effective behind-the-scenes negotiations and "quiet diplomacy," was by that time fully engaged in his own Falklands (Malvinas) good offices mission; and action within the General Assembly at that time might prejudice his efforts, which indeed came very close to success in the end.[20]

That Big Power obstruction, through use of the veto power in the Security Council, of the peace-keeping mandate might not be tolerated indefinitely, and that there was a continuing expectation that former imperial states would complete, in timely fashion, the last, nearly forgotten parts of the decolonization process, was indicated at the thirty-seventh session of the General Assembly, when, in October 1982, twenty Latin American states submitted a resolution in the General Assembly calling on the United Kingdom and Argentina to resume negotiations on sovereignty over the Falklands (Malvinas) and asking the Secretary-General to undertake a new good offices mission. The resolution was adopted on

November 4, 1982, by a vote of 90–12, with 52 abstentions.[21] The twelve negative votes were cast by the United Kingdom, Antigua and Barbuda, Belize, Dominica, Fiji, Gambia, Malawi, New Zealand, Oman, Papua New Guinea, Solomon Islands, and Sri Lanka, with the United States this time breaking ranks with the United Kingdom to vote in favor of the resolution.[22]

Office of Secretary-General

The evident success of the new Secretary-General, Dr. Pérez de Cuéllar, in his first year of office in 1982, in gaining the confidence and trust of the Third World countries stemmed from a felicitous combination of personal qualities and objective political facts. The office of Secretary-General is, as already noted, cast in general terms only, in the Charter, thus possessing an open-ended quality that allows it to expand or contract, depending on the personality and judgment, and also the political opportunities, of the particular incumbent. The last activist Secretary-General had been Dag Hammarskjöld, and his affirmative use of his powers had put him on a collision course with the Soviet Union in the political line that he had adopted on the Congo and other questions, up to his own untimely death. Dr. Pérez de Cuéllar displayed the quieter virtues in the exercise of executive-based pragmatism. His intervention in the Falklands (Malvinas) conflict, and his more covert good offices offered in the Iran-Iraq, Venezuela-Guyana, Honduras-Nicaragua, and Ethiopia-Somalia disputes were always tactful and discreet, and well received on that account by both sides, even if not immediately successful. His decision to examine the issue of human rights in Poland, over the protests of the Polish government,[23] and his refusal to be browbeaten by recurring threats of a United States withholding of its financial dues to the United Nations or even a United States walkout from the General Assembly, indicated an ability and also a willingness to stand up to the superpowers in appropriate places. The times seemed ripe, and the necessary majority political support in the General Assembly was certainly there, for a prudent use of the Secretary-General's inherent or implied constitutional powers—good offices, fact finding, executive inquiry, direct initiation of matters before the Security Council, "quiet diplomacy" in the General Assembly—in pursuit of the peace-keeping and other main objectives of the Charter. Executive activism seems, indeed, one of the more fruitful possibilities for curing the latter-day malaise of the United Nations produced by the decline of Soviet-Western détente and the manifest breakdown in the exercise of the Security Council's primary, peace-keeping responsibilities.

International Court of Justice

The International Court continued to suffer, even in the early 1980s, from the reputation—widely held in the General Assembly after the political misfortune of its 8–7 judgment in *South West Africa, Second Phase* in 1966[24]—of being a "white man's tribunal" that was politically loaded and biased against the developing Third World countries. To the extent that that charge might still be warranted several decades after the much criticized decision on an issue involving clear conflict between the "old" and the "new" international law, some part of the responsibility must be attributed to the predominantly Third World critics in their failure effectively to utilize the regular triennial electoral processes for the court, and the failure in consequence to produce a judicial majority favorable to the "new" international law.[25] A certain lack of sophistication as to the creative policy-making possibilities of the World Court, and the fact that the role of a final judge today is recognized in contemporary legal science as inherently "political," has produced and maintained a somewhat mechanical deference to old "regional" rules and quotas as to the allocation between blocs of the five judicial posts up for election every three years.

The court today is one of the prime law-making arenas of the United Nations without any inconvenient political obstruction of a Big Power veto over its decisions. The fact that its decisions are not technically enforceable on the court's own initiative, or that its case/controversy jurisdiction is dependent on the prior consent of the parties to a dispute, should not militate against the use by the General Assembly and Secretary-General of the advisory opinion, reference jurisdiction, which cannot, again, be blocked by Big Power veto. An advisory opinion ruling, as the *Namibia (South West Africa)* ruling of 1971[26] demonstrated, can have political teeth, even if, from a strictly technical viewpoint, it is legally unenforceable. The advisory opinion jurisdiction would seem to offer excellent opportunities to the court for new judicial activism on behalf of new international law making.

The court's own judges could themselves help, of course, in correcting old images of the court. In spite of the new and welcome power of the court to control the number of counsel and advocates to be heard on behalf of each party (Rules of Court, Article 58)—itself a response to the court's conclusion that "new" Third World countries might well be intimidated by the batteries of expensive (Western) counsel that the developed Western countries were able to enlist for their own causes, and therefore psychologically deterred from having recourse to the court in their own right—the court has done little to dispel the basically Eurocentric character of the written and oral proceedings before it. There has been, in particular, a somewhat "mannered" style to the patterns of oral argument that have been allowed to develop before the court, deriving from one or two venerable European national tribunals that have never been particularly noted for their ability to admit, in their own jurisprudence, the interplay of law and policy and to accept the correlative law-making role and responsibilities of a final tribunal.

A multicultural, multisystemic tribunal such as the World Court is supposed to be—can afford to be—sui generis and to develop its own distinctive forms of written pleadings and oral argument. With the new emphasis on judicial policy making, is there any particular reason why the International Court should insist on any particular formality in either written or oral pleadings, beyond clarity, succinctness, and relevance in the adducing of law and policy? It says a great deal as to dead-hand control and influence today of old court habits and legal thinking that a major case like the *Continental Shelf (Tunisia/Libyan Arab Jamahiriya)* judgment of 1982[27]—a contest between two Third World countries—could be dominated, in the written and oral proceedings before the court, by the same *Western* legal counsel and expert advisers. It was a case that seemed to call out, for its rational solution in a contemporary international law context, for the imaginative judicial invocation of policy; but that is hardly present in the final judgment, which is barren in policy terms and another exercise in the old-fashioned jurisprudence-of-concepts. Is there not at least a chance that it would have been better if the two parties had felt encouraged, by the court's past practice and attitudes, to make some greater use of their own nationals as counsel or expert consultants?

The court might also, with advantage, take another look at its own practice as to the creation of special chambers "for dealing with a particular case" (Statute of the Court, Article 26[2]; Rules of Court, Article 17). It was surely never intended, and it is certainly not what is stipulated, by either the court statute or the Rules of Court, that the actual parties to a dispute should dictate to the court the actual choice of judges and be able to impose their own will on the court; or, for that matter, that a five-member chamber could include a national of one of the parties and so compel a balancing national (if need be, ad hoc) judge for the other party. What we have in such situations is a veritable arbitration tribunal, composed by the parties themselves, but seeking a vicarious prestige and authority, qua court—in this case qua International Court of Justice. The special declaration[28] and two dissenting opinions[29] filed in *Delimitation of the Maritime Boundary in the Gulf of Maine Area, Constitution of Chamber, Order of 20 January 1982* seem intellectually sounder than the official opinion of the Court[30] on this point, and the whole issue deserves re-examination. In this particular case the court majority left the choice of judges for their special chamber to the parties concerned. The parties chose an exclusively Western European and North American panel for a matter—the delimitation of a single maritime boundary dividing the continental shelf and fisheries zone of the two parties—that had profound implications for the practical application of the principles of the new United Nations Convention on the Law of the Sea (signed in December 1982) and for the progressive development of the New International Economic Order, of which the new Law of the Sea is now accepted as an integral part. This leads to the question of what authority, if any, should be accorded, either as *jurisprudence* or *doctrines,* in contemporary international law to a judgment eventually emerging from a special chamber of the Court as constituted in accord with the Parties' own choice of the judges, and also more generally.

International Law Commission, Sixth (Legal) Committee, Special Codifying Commissions and Conferences

The atrophy of the International Law Commission in modern times, it is clear, has been due principally to its own self-denying ordinance—a quest for an absolute "legal" purity, untainted by the exigent here and now of contemporary political needs and aspirations of the world community. As a result, the ILC has seen itself confined de facto to the petit-point needlework of international law making, and has developed work habits suited to such a very modest role, being inordinately painstaking and time-consuming in its approach to its allotted tasks. That being so, it hardly seems useful to expend more time on trying to "reform" the ILC or to increase the importance of its agenda. It is better, perhaps, to leave it to perform its highly technical, deliberately noncontroversial functions to the best of its collective abilities; though it may seriously be questioned whether the ILC should be regarded as an ideal training and recruitment center for the judges of the International Court of Justice, unless one wants more of the same thing on the court.

What is certain is that "new" international law will continue to be made, in spite of the ILC; and that in default of ILC initiatives it will be made in other UN arenas using other, intellectually more flexible, personnel and other legal techniques better adapted to the progressive development of international law. The Third United Nations Conference on the Law of the Sea, the Special Committee on Friendly Relations and Cooperation among States, and the Committee on the Peaceful Uses of Outer Space demonstrate what can be done with wit and imagination and civil courage. Once one is liberated from the duty of deference to old-established arenas and processes, and can develop one's own special staff and law-making techniques, the special ad hoc functionally based approach of concentrating on a single subject seems to develop a group dynamism and enthusiasm and independent momentum in its own right.

To this we might add the occasional specialized ad hoc, single-issue law-making initiative within standing General Assembly committees, such as the concentrated legal activity on behalf of regulation of direct broadcasting from satellites, within the Special Political Committee; and also the opportunities for action within specialized agencies, such as the movement on behalf of a new world information order, successfully launched by Unesco and aided also by the ITU. The point is that there is a plurality of possible arenas for new international law making today, and rather than risk being blocked altogether by limiting action to a single one, it is useful and sensible to try them all, leaving it to the accidents of personnel to determine in which arena one will first succeed, and to the executive-administrative skills of the Secretary-General and his specialized Secretariat to effect any necessary coordination or oversight.

United Nations Expenses: Financial Dues of Member States

The UN expenses issue, dormant since the Soviet and French governments' disputing of the special financial assessment levied on behalf of the Congo operation and the particular political solution favored by then Secretary-General Hammarskjöld, with which the Soviet Union and France both strongly disagreed, flared up again at the thirty-seventh annual session of the General Assembly in the autumn of 1982. In *Certain Expenses of the United Nations, Advisory Opinion,* of 1962,[31] the International Court reaffirmed Article 17(2) of the Charter and its stipulation that "the expenses of the United Nations shall be borne by the Members as apportioned by the General Assembly." After that 9–5 majority court ruling, the United States attempted, at the nineteenth annual session of the General Assembly in 1964, to apply Article 19 of the Charter and thereby deprive the Soviet Union and France of their votes in the General Assembly so long as their special dues remained unpaid. The sole result of this move by the United States was to bring the work of the General Assembly to a complete standstill, until the United States finally gave way a year later, at the twentieth annual session in 1965, and allowed the work of the General Assembly to proceed without any solution of the expenses issue. (France later made an "equivalent" contribution in lieu of the Congo operations special assessment, though the Soviet Union never did.) The United States' legal initiative of 1964, to apply Charter Article 19 in order to take away the Soviet and French votes in the General Assembly because of their nonpayment of special financial assessments, remains, however, as a legal precedent for the future, for possible application against any future delinquent states.

We are reminded here once again—as we were reminded with the Uniting for Peace resolution of 1950—of the old legal maxim to beware of the legal precedents that you create to aid your own present cases, lest they be quoted and used against you in future cases. In December 1982 the General Assembly approved overwhelmingly—by 135–2 (Turkey, United States), with 8 abstentions (Belgium, Ecuador, Federal Republic of Germany, Israel, Italy, Luxembourg, Spain, and the United Kingdom)[32]—a resolution calling on all states to sign and adopt the new United Nations Convention on the Law of the Sea. The General Assembly had earlier rejected a joint Turkish–United States amendment to the principal motion, which sought to direct that the financing of the expenses of the preparatory commission for the International Sea-Bed Authority, to be set up under the new convention, should be borne by the states signatory to the convention and not by the United Nations as a whole.[33] The United States had previously made it clear that it would not sign the new convention, and it now indicated that it would not pay the United Nations assessments for the preparatory commission (estimated as under $1 million per year, for the United States). The president of the United Nations Convention on the Law of the Sea, Tommy Koh, described the United States decision as "very unfortunate . . . a very important step backwards: if every state takes decisions on its own, that is the start of fiscal irresponsibility and we would never find the funds to balance the UN's budgets."[34] Although the American administration suggested that the present Law of the Sea case could be legally distinguished from the Congo case of the early 1960s, on which the United States had based its own attempt to apply Charter sanctions (suspension of right of vote in the General Assembly) against the Soviet Union and France,[35] the ultimate decision on legality would not be that of the United States but that of the General Assembly and the International Court if need be. The decision whether or not to move legally against the United States on the issue, on the basis of the 1960s Congo precedent, would be a political one, of course. It was a matter of record that the United States had, during the same thirty-seventh session of the General Assembly, threatened a possible cut off of its financial contributions to two specialized agencies, the IAEA and the ITU and to the United Nations proper, in the event of decisions that it might consider unfavorable on the credentials question; and that several Third World countries had offered, if need be, to fill the gap in United Nations expenses caused by any American financial default or shortfall.

The Axiological Problem: Value Conflicts, Value Antinomies

We have noted already that in an era of transition in the world community, values, even when identified in common by the different, competing ideological systems, may sometimes emerge in direct conflict in particular crisis situations, though often the answer will be provided in the value concretization process when the actual factual record is considered. Thus, in the Falklands (Malvinas) affair, Argentina invoked the principle of decolonization, the first among the imperative principles of the "new" international law, and ranking in practice almost as *jus cogens;* while the United Kingdom invoked the Charter principle of the interdiction of the use of force. The United Kingdom attempted to counter the Argentina-invoked principle of decolonization by itself invoking the principle of self-determination of peoples. On a *de minimis* basis, international law could hardly concede to the 1,800 inhabitants now remaining from the original British garrison and dependents what it had already refused to consider as a politically viable option in the case of the very much larger population (120,000 people) of the Turkish sector of Cyprus. A rational contemporary application of the principle of self-determination of peoples in the Falklands (Malvinas) case would seem to have implied consulting the British settlers concerned and then offering to repatriate, with generous financial compensation, any of them not wishing to remain in the islands under any new non-British international status—to the United Kingdom itself or to some other former British colony like New Zealand. As we have suggested, in the particular facts of the Falklands (Malvinas) crisis, the axiological problem (with the particular value antinomy involved) was viewed as something of a legal standoff. The emerging United Nations consensus, therefore, even after the final British-American Security Council vetos of United Nations peace-keeping action, was in favor of a negotiated settlement, to be achieved through the Secretary-General's "quiet diplomacy" rather than direct General Assembly legislation; though the latter solution remained available and open, in the event of a future diplomatic or negotiating impasse.

The Middle Eastern crisis on first sight might seem to involve a clear and uncomplicated issue of application of the imperative international law principle of self-determination of peoples—in this case, self-determination and reunification in one independent state of the presently geographically scattered and dispersed Palestinian people. But on examination the factual record reveals also a valid claim to selfdetermination of the Israeli people, flowing from an original, preindependence colonial situation—the British mandate over former Turkish Palestine, derived from the League of Nations, that legally subsisted from 1919 until the United Nations' recognition of the state of Israel in 1948. In a certain sense, the new state of Israel emerged from its own war of national liberation and frequent terrorist-style direct action against an original European "parent" imperial occupying power that had to be persuaded to leave by forceful means. In this regard, the various United Nations attempts to resolve, in the one geographically very limited and concentrated region, the historical contradiction of Israeli and Palestinian claims to self-determination of peoples by balancing self-determination against security of territorial frontiers become not so unreasonable or unfair an attempt at pragmatic solution of a hitherto irreconcilable conflict. In United Nations practice, not less than in national practice, some more substantial and imaginative experiments with new models of federalism and plural constitutionalism might provide a first step toward establishing long-range solutions. For multinational societies whose constituent populations are not conveniently divided into separate geographical regions, and therefore not open to the easy political corrective of voluntary resettlement and relocation and subsequent territorial partition, pluralistic federalism under adequate United Nations control and supervision in a first, transition period might seem the only potentially viable nonmilitary solution. It is at least worth scientific study in depth in the attempt to work out alternative models.

Operationalism in International Legal Problem Solving

Historical Contradictions in Space and Time

In an era of transition, the key players will often react differently to the rapid flow of events in the society in which they are living and for which they are making decisions, reflecting their ability to perceive those events and to come up with imaginative and timely solutions. In a world community undergoing fundamental political, social, economic, and technological change today, the key issues are perceived by Third World leaders as economic ones, and the range of preferred solutions as involving the correcting, as rapidly as possible, of the severe imbalance, in terms of access to wealth and the world's resources, currently existing between the privileged postindustrial societies on the one hand and all the rest of the world—in essence, the North-South conflict. There is perhaps a tendency on the part of Third World leaders to underestimate the extent to which their own current economic difficulties are part of a larger world economic crisis that has shaken the national economies of the postindustrial societies themselves and brought a genuine crisis of confidence in those same societies, as to basic economic and trading institutions and processes and also as to their own expert economic advising and long-range forecasting. But there is no question that there is a fundamental cleavage between Third World perceptions of economic issues as the priority issues for the world community for the last part of the century, and the perceptions of the two old political-military blocs, Soviet and Western, and their respective leaders. By some curious warp of the time machine, both superpowers still seem intellectually rooted in the immediate postwar, Cold War era, now past, and to be devoting their main energies and resources to preparing for the holy war between postulated rival (Communist and capitalist) ideologies that they did *not* wage in 1948 or 1950. How else can one explain the renewed Big Power nuclear armaments race of the early 1980s, whose crushing domestic economic burden must be satisfied at the expense of sacrificing domestic social welfare programs? The two superpowers had the intellectual challenge in the early 1970s, after ten or fifteen years of very successful, empirically based application of the détente process in a wide range of Soviet-Western wise, pragmatic accommodations in disarmament and security, scientific, and even economic matters, of permanently institutionalizing their coexistence and cooperation across the old political-military and ideological frontiers of 1945. This would have implied revising and updating the postwar public order system by removing some of its original inequities and attempting now to extend its benefits and protections to the new Third World countries not present at the creation of the United Nations and the postwar world public order system in 1945. Ideas such as the one in circulation in the early 1970s, of a nonaggression pact between NATO and the Warsaw Pact, as a first step toward phasing out the rival military alliances altogether as anachronistic survivals from the Cold War, seemed timely and worth serious study. The leitmotiv of the Brandt *Ostpolitik* of the late 1960s and early 1970s in the Federal Republic of Germany was to replace the ideological debates of the Cold War by trade, commerce, and intellectual and cultural exchange between Eastern and Western Europe as a method of ending the division imposed at Yalta and Potsdam; the settlement of the territorial frontiers question in Central and Eastern Europe through the series of complementary mini-treaties between the Federal Republic of Germany and its neighbors was an intermediate step in this whole process. In this view, the major tragedy in international relations of the mid- and late 1970s on through the early 1980s must be the "missed opportunity" of the superpowers finally to consummate the process of détente and to allow the world community, as a happy consequence, to move on from the nearly exclusive preoccupations of the postwar era with Big Power–related peace and security problems, to other, *post*-postwar world community problems not having the same Big Power fixation. As it is, both superpowers have been preoccupied with mutual and reciprocal defensive moves—involving reestablishment in old spheres of influence and probing and testing for new ones, and the initiation of ever more sophisticated and frightening weapon programs—that make sense only in a context of an artifically revived postwar, Cold War era. To the rest of the world, a renewed Soviet-Western Cold War appears irrelevant and distracting to the solution of the *post*-postwar social and economic problems of the world community of the last part of the century. For those who want to live in the present time dimension and to participate actively in the solution of its unique problems, the Big Power revival of the old interbloc rivalry of another and older time dimension offers the paradox of a further historical contradiction. Those same Big Powers seem to agree very well in private on the necessity of preserving the constitutional-institutional status quo and their own special legal privileges therein (especially the veto in the Security Council), for they combine in a sort of unholy alliance in the General Assembly and the other main United Nations arenas to block attempts at reform and revision of the United Nations Charter, as originally drafted in 1945, by way of extension of the General Assembly's peace-keeping role and opportunity.

The Skills of Legal Pragmatism: Problem Solving

The new Third World majority in the General Assembly, once excoriated as "immature" or irresponsible in its actions in the General Assembly, began to move with some confidence and judgment in the early 1980s to try to fill the gap in contemporary international law making. This meant a new pragmatism and disposition to compromise and not to press a partisan position to the breaking point. There was a recognition by the new General Assembly majority, varied and plural in its ethnic-cultural and ideological composition, that decision making within the United Nations is an exercise in the art of the possible, and that practical problem solving in concrete cases may be worth as much as drafting abstract codes of a priori principles.

In an era of transition in the world community, the skills of legal pragmatism involve not merely scientifically detached and objective problem characterization and awareness of the space-time dimension of particular problem situations, but also a sophisticated cost-benefit analysis and quantification of the differing social costs of different proposed solutions, including some attempt at projection, on an empirical basis, of their chances of success and of whether success, as such, is itself worth the effort in every case.[36] Lastly, if the lesson of the Sibylline Books—recognition that the art of problem solving consists in working out solutions while they are still timely, and *before* a problem situation has become pathological and politically out of hand—is something that the two old blocs, Soviet and Western, would seem, on actual performance at the end of the 1970s and the beginning of the 1980s, to need to relearn, the countries of the new Third World majority in the General Assembly should also accept that the essence of legal pragmatism is the spirit of moderation and not using one's majority in too absolutist a way in every available problem situation, irrespective of its social value in long-range historical terms. The "progressive development" of international law doctrine and practice to bring it into accord with radically new societal conditions and demands of the contemporary world community requires development of a strategy for legal action, involving determination of priority subjects and their ranking in order of community importance, and then careful choice of the arenas and processes best suited to their practical achievement—what Mr. Justice Felix Frankfurter of the United States Supreme Court used to call a feeling for legal "roles and missions." What is also involved therein is some sort of informed judgment as to the factor of intellectual leadership—the problem-solving capacities of the different decision-making elites in the different arenas (General Assembly, International Court, ILC) at any time, and their abilities to identify their own precise moment in history and its special challenges.

On Legal "Receptions" and Legal Eclecticism

The movement from an "old," classical international law to a "new" one need not, and obviously cannot, involve a wholesale rejection of all that has gone on before in terms of international legal *doctrines* and *jurisprudence*. This is one of the reasons why some legal text writers and diplomats prefer the more comprehensive term *contemporary* international law, to describe the desired result of the present process of rewriting and modernization of the corpus of existing legal principles and rules. It should not be thought of as a legal dichotomy between "old" and "new," but rather as a continuum or process whereby the progressive development and updating of international law is going on all the time, in all main law-making arenas. An excellent example of the dynamic of change, involving continuity between past and present for purposes of projection of future legal principles and rules, is provided by that major United Nations law-making project of the decade of the 1970s, the Third United Nations Conference on the Law of the Sea, and its Convention, signed in December 1982. A very great deal of the final convention is no more than a restatement of the preexisting classical customary international Law of the Sea, as those major Western countries that refused to sign the final text when it was first opened for signature in December 1982 admitted. Other parts of the final convention represented classical, customary international law that was updated, or extended incrementally, within the permissible limits of legal codification as conventionally (and conservatively) understood. The legal breakthrough in the convention, and where it certainly evoked the political opposition of the United States and the other major Western countries that did not sign, was in the sections devoted to the sea bed and the ocean floor beyond national limits, and to the mining and development of their mineral and other resources. But in dedicating these to the world community in general, as the "common heritage of mankind," it might be argued that the founding fathers of the modern Law of the Sea were acting in the full spirit of that original founding father, Grotius, who at the opening of the seventeenth century successfully proclaimed that the high seas, outside the narrow national three-mile territorial sea, were incapable of appropriation and belonged to everyone. Ambassador Pardo's thesis on the "common heritage of mankind," as adopted and concretized by the treaty makers for the new United Nations Convention on the Law of the Sea, is an imaginative generic extension of existing classical international law principles and, as such, within the ambit of the United Nations' Charter-based mandate for the "progressive development" of international law.

The objection of Eurocentrism,[37] rightly advanced in concrete instances when what is involved is the attempt at mechanical and unimaginative application, today, to new societal facts, of rules worked out in another era in response to entirely different societal facts would benefit from more critical and discerning examination. The history of legal science shows that it is frequently marked by the large-scale reception, from one society by another at a different stage of political, social, and economic development, of codes or bodies of legal rules and principles worked out, elaborated, and refined in the first society. Sometimes the reception will be an imposed one, brought about by force of arms or conquest, as with the introduction of Roman law into most of Northern Europe, or the arrival of the Code Napoléon in many parts of Western Europe in the baggage trains of the emperor's armies; but at other times the reception will be a fully conscious and voluntary one, as part of a deliberate, planned policy of national modernization and industrialization, as with the adoption of either one of the two great European civil codes, the French and the German, in a number of the emerging, non-European societies of the late nineteenth and early twentieth centuries. There is nothing offensive, in ethnic-cultural terms, in such a reception when it is fully consensual, and when the receiving state feels intellectually emancipated enough to continue to adapt and transform the received model to special local and national conditions and needs. The received law will thereby take on an independent legal life and being of its own in the new environment: in sociology of law terms, a new, symbiotic, law-and-society relation will soon emerge;[38] otherwise the original reception will have been demonstrated as a political failure and will be quickly rejected and replaced by something new again. And so it is with international law. Expanding in the last part of the twentieth century from an original, classical base developed by and in response to the special needs of predominantly Western, European societies founded on the rise of commerce, it has become by now a vastly more inclusive and, in ethnic-cultural terms, pluralistic corpus of principles and rules,[39] paralleling the expansion in the boundaries and membership of the world community over the period since 1945.[40] The transformation has been achieved through the dialectical processes and political give-and-take of the United Nations General Assembly and other main law-making arenas—the specialized committees and commissions, the specialized agencies, and certainly also the International Court. It is part of the "progressive development" mandate stipulated by the United Nations Charter for international law for the future; and with proper operational skills on the part of the General Assembly majority in the performance of its own law-making tasks and in the elections for the other law-making arenas, the process of transformation can be continued and completed, in peace, through the present era of transition in the world community.

Notes

CHAPTER 1

1. C. Sepúlveda, *Curso de derecho internacional publico* [Course of public international law], 2nd ed. (Mexico: Editorial Porrua, 1960), pp. 191–198; D. R. Shea, *The Calvo Clause* (Minneapolis: University of Minnesota Press, 1955); A. García Robles, *México et las Naciones Unidas,* 2 vols. (Mexico: UNAM, 1970).

2. And see generally R. P. Anand, ed., *Asian States and the Development of International Law* (Delhi: Vikas, 1972); A. K. Mensah-Brown, ed., *African International Legal History* (New York: UNITAR, 1975); and Walter Rudolf, "Neue Staaten und das Völkerrecht," *Archiv des Völkerrects* 17 (1976): 1.

3. The Soviet doctrinal-legal writing on "unequal treaties" is extensive: V. M. Shurshalov, *Sovetskii ezhegodnik mezhdunarodnogo prava* [Soviet yearbook of international law] (Moscow, 1958), p. 150; A. N. Talalayev, ibid. (1959), p. 144; I. I. Lukashuk, ibid., p. 16; N. V. Zakharova, ibid. (1960), p. 157; F. I. Kozhevnikov, ed., (1957), *International Law. A Textbook for Use in Law Schools* p. 280.

4. G. I. Tunkin, "XXII Sezd KPSS i zadachi sovetskoi nauki mezhdunarodnogo prava" [The 22nd Congress of the Communist Party of the Soviet Union and problems of the Soviet science of international law], *Sovetskoe gosudarstvo i pravo* [Soviet state and law] (Moscow, 1962), p. 3.

5. Ibid.

6. M. S. McDougal, "International Law, Power and Policy: A Contemporary Conception," *Recueil des cours (Académie de Droit International de la Haye)* 82 (1953): 137, 143.

7. G. I. Tunkin, "Coexistence and International Law," *Recueil des cours* 95 (1958): 59–60.

8. For some Western interpretations, see generally R. Schlesinger, *Soviet Legal Theory,* 2nd ed. (1951), p. 273 et seq; W. W. Kulski, "The Soviet Interpretation of International Law," *American Journal of International Law* 49 (1955): 518; L. Lipson, *Proceedings, American Society of International Law* (Washington, D.C.: 1959), p. 41.

9. Ibid.

10. John N. Hazard, "Pashukanis Is No Traitor," *American Journal of International Law* 51 (1957): 385, 387.

11. Schlesinger, *Soviet Legal Theory,* pp. 281–282.

12. Kulski, "Soviet Interpretation."

13. Tunkin, "Coexistence and International Law," pp. 1, 60.

14. Ibid.

15. Ibid., p. 74; and see also Tunkin, "Sorok Let sosushchestvovania i mezhdunarodnogo prava" [Forty years of coexistence and international law], *Sovetskii ezhegodnik mezhdunarodnogo prava* (1958), p. 15.

16. Tunkin, "Coexistence and International Law," p. 1.

17. Kozhevnikov, ed., *International Law,* p. 7.

18. There are strong links also to earlier definitions by Krylov and Korovin: O. Lissitzyn, *American Slavic and East European Review,* 11 (1952): 257, 258–259.

19. See the definition by S. A. Golunskii and M. S. Strogovich, "The Theory of the State and Law," in *Soviet Legal Philosophy,* trans. H. W. Babb (1951), p. 370; and see also A. Vyshinsky, ed., *The Law of the Soviet State,* (trans. H. W. Babb) (1954), p. 50.

20. S. B. Krylov, "Les notions principales du droit des gens (la doctrine soviétique du droit international)" [The principal ideas of the law of nations (The Soviet doctrine of international law], *Recueil des cours* 70 (1947): 407.

21. See, for example, *International Law Association. Report of the Forty-Seventh Conference, 1956,* pp. 17 et seq.; ibid., *Report of the Forty-Eighth Conference, 1958,* pp. 417 et seq; ibid., *Report of the Forty-Ninth Conference 1960,* pp. 332 et seq; ibid., *Report of the Fiftieth Conference, 1962,* pp. 260 et seq; ibid., *Report of the Fifty-First Conference, 1964,* pp. 777 et seq.

22. See generally John N. Hazard, "Coexistence Codification Reconsidered," *American Journal of International Law* 57 (1963): 88; Hazard, "The Sixth Committee and New Law," ibid. 57 (1963): 604; Hazard, "New Personalities to Create New Law", ibid. 58 (1964): 952; Edward McWhinney, *"Peaceful Coexistence" and Soviet-Western International Law* (Leyden: A. W. Sythoff, 1964).

23. Declaration on Principles of International Law Concerning Friendly Relations and Cooperation among States in Accordance with the Charter of the United Nations, UNGA Res. 2625 (XXV), October 24, 1970. And see Sir Ian Sinclair, "Principles of International Law Concerning Friendly Relations and Cooperation among States," in *Essays on International Law in Honour of Krishna Rao,* ed. M. Nawaz, (1975), p. 107; R. Rosenstock, "The Declaration of Principles of International Law Concerning Friendly Relations. A Survey," *American Journal of International Law* 65 (1971): 713.

24. G. Arangio-Ruiz, "The Normative Role of the General Assembly of the United Nations and the Declaration of Principles of Friendly Relations," *Recueil des cours* 137 (1972): 137; Graf zu Dohna, *Die Grundprinzipien des Völkerrechts über die freundschaftlichen Beziehungen und die Zusammenarbeit zwischen den Staaten* [The basic principles of international law of friendly relations and cooperation among states] (1973), p. 265; J. Frowein, "Freundschaft und Zusammenarbeit unter den Staaten. Die UN-Resolution über freundschaftliche Beziehungen" [Friendship and cooperation among states. The UN resolution on friendly relations], *Europa-Archiv* 28 (1973): 70; A. Remiro Brotons, *Derecho Internacional*

Publico [Public international law] (Madrid: Editorial Tecnos, 1982), vol. 1, pp. 51 et seq.

25. A. Pelt, ed., *The Legal Principles Governing Friendly Relations and Cooperation among States in the Spirit of the United Nations Charter* (1966), especially the essays by Bystricky (p. 99); Srnska (p. 115); Outrata (p. 131); and M. Sahović (ed.), *Principles of International Law concerning Friendly Relations and Cooperation* (Belgrade: Institute of International Politics and Economics, 1972).

26. See generally Edward McWhinney, *The International Law of Détente. Arms Control, European Security, and East-West Cooperation* (Alphen aan den Rijn: Sijthoff and Noordhoff, 1978).

27. Ibid., ch. 3, pp. 39 et seq; ch. 4, pp. 70 et seq.

28. Ibid., ch. 5, pp. 92 et seq.

Chapter 2

1. G. I. Tunkin, Letter to the Editor, *The Times* (London), February 25, 1963.

2. Ibid.; and see also Tunkin, "Le droit international de la coexistence pacifique" [The international law of peaceful coexistence], *Problèmes de droit des gens. Mélanges offerts à Henri Rolin* [Problems of the law of nations. Collection in honour of Henri Rolin] (1964).

3. Tribunal of the Permanent Court of Arbitration, 1928. Reprinted in Scott, *Hague Court Reports,* Second Series 84.

4. "Le problème dit du droit intertemporel dans l'ordre international" [The problem of intertemporal law in the international order], Institut de Droit International, Report of Eleventh Commission, Max Sørensen, *rapporteur, Annuaire* 55 (1973): 1–116.

5. Institut de Droit International, *Annuaire,* 56 (1975): 339–374, 536–541.

6. Institut, *Annuaire* 55 (1973): 108.

7. Institut, *Annuaire* 56 (1975): 345–346.

8. Ibid., pp. 536–537.

9. Ibid.

10. Ibid.

11. Ibid., pp. 538–539.

12. Ibid.

13. ICJ, *Legal Consequences for States of the Continued Presence of South Africa in Namibia (South West Africa) notwithstanding Security Council Resolution 276 (1970). Advisory Opinion, Reports,* 1971, p. 16.

14. ICJ, *South West Africa, Second Phase, Judgment, Reports,* 1966, p. 6.

15. ICJ, *South West Africa, Preliminary Objections, Judgment, Reports,* 1962, p. 319.

16. ICJ, *Reports,* 1971, pp. 27–28.

17. Ibid.

18. Ibid.

19. Ibid., pp. 31–32.

20. ICJ, *Western Sahara, Advisory Opinion, Reports,* 1975, p. 12.

21. Ibid., p. 38.
22. Ibid., p. 40.
23. PCIJ, Series A/B, no. 53.
24. ICJ, *Reports,* 1975, p. 42.
25. Ibid., p. 60.
26. Ibid., p. 61.
27. Ibid., p. 64.
28. Ibid., pp. 85–86.
29. Ibid., p. 86. And see, generally, M. Bedjaoui, *Terra nullius, "droits" historiques et autodétermination* (*Terra nullius,* historic "rights," and self-determination) (1975); Bedjaoui, "Non-alignment et droit international" [Non-alignment and international law], *Recueil des cours* 151 (1976): 408 et seq. And see also M. S. Rajan, *Non-Alignment, India, and the Future* (Mysore: University of Mysore, 1970).
30. Ibid., pp. 86–87.
31. Ibid., p. 103.
32. Ibid., pp. 173–174.
33. ICJ, *Continental Shelf (Tunisia/Libyan Arab Jamahiriya), Judgment, Reports,* 1982, p. 18.
34. Ibid., pp. 157–277.
35. ICJ, *North Sea Continental Shelf, Judgment, Reports,* 1969, p. 3.
36. Ibid., pp. 211–212.
37. Ibid., p. 217.
38. Ibid., p. 218.
39. Ibid., p. 222.
40. ICJ, *Reports,* 1969, p. 21; cited in ICJ, *Reports,* 1982, p. 253.
41. Ibid., p. 254.
42. Ibid., p. 255.
43. Ibid.
44. Ibid., p. 256.
45. Ibid., pp. 258–260.
46. K. Doehring, "Die Wirkung des Zeitablaufs auf den Bestand völkerrechtlicher Regeln" [The influence of passage of time on the continuance of international law rules], *Jahrbuch der Max-Planck-Gesellschaft* [Yearbook of the Max-Planck Institute] (Heidelberg, 1964), p. 70. And see also W.-D. Krause-Ablass, *Intertemporales Völkerrecht. Die zeitliche Anwendungsbereich von Völkerrechtsnormen* [Intertemporal law. The time application-zone of international law norms] (Frankfurt am Main: Alfred Metzner, 1970), pp. 31–33.
47. Institut de Droit International, *Annuaire* 56 (1975): 536–541.
48. Ibid., pp. 538–539.
49. Charles De Visscher, "Positivisme et 'jus cogens' " [Positivism and "jus cogens"], *Revue générale de droit international public* [General review of public international law] 75 (1971): 5–11.
50. Institut de Droit International, *Annuaire* 56 (1975): 538–539.
51. G. Jellinek, *Allgemeine Staatslehre* [General theory of the state], 3rd ed., (1922), p. 269, pp. 337–339; K. Doehring, "Die Wirkung des Zeitablaufs," pp. 71–72.
52. K. Doehring, "Die Wirkung des Zeitablaufs," pp. 72–73; M. Lachs, *The*

Polish-German Frontier. Law, Life and the Logic of History (1964), p. 73. For a critique of Jellinek's original formulation, see F. Münch, "Brauch und Missbrauch der normativen Kraft des Faktischen" [Use and misuse of the normative force of facts], *Jahrbuch der Albertus-Universität zu Königsberg/Pr.* [Yearbook of the Albert University of Königsberg/Pr.] 15 (1965): 29.

53. See, in this regard, Edward McWhinney, *The International Law of Détente* (Alphen aan den Rijn: Sijthoff and Noordhoff, 1978), pp. 92–115.

54. K. Doehring, "Die Wirkung des Zeitablaufs," p. 72.

55. Vienna Convention on the Law of Treaties, 1969, art. 62 (2) (a).

56. W. Schaumann, "Clausula rebus sic stantibus," *Wörterbuch des Völkerrechts* 1 (1960): 289.

57. Institut de Droit International, *Annuaire* 55 (1973): pp. 15–16.

58. A. von Verdross, *Annuaire de la Commission de Droit International* 1 (1964): 36.

59. Baade, "Intertemporales Völkerrecht," *Jahrbuch für internationales Recht* [Yearbook for international law], 1957, pp. 229–256.

60. Ibid.

61. Verdross, *Annuaire*.

62. Charles De Visscher, *Problèmes d'interprétation judiciaire en droit international public* [Problems of judicial interpretation in public international law] (1963), pp. 66–67; D. Bindschedler-Robert, "De la rétroactivité en droit international public" [On retroactivity in public international law], P. Lalive and J. Freymond, eds., *Recueil d'etudes de droit international. En hommage à Paul Guggenheim* [Collection of studies in international law in honour of Paul Guggenheim] (Geneva: La Tribune de Genève, 1968), pp. 188–189; T. O. Elias, "The Doctrine of Intertemporal Law," *American Journal of International Law* 74 (1980): 285.

63. Cited, with approval, Vice-President Ammoun (separate opinion), ICJ, *Western Sahara,* Advisory Opinion, *Reports,* 1975, pp. 85–86.

Chapter 3

1. Compare R. A. Falk, "On the Quasi-Legislative Competence of the General Assembly," *American Journal of International Law* 60 (1966): 784; A. Bleckman, "Die Praxis des Völkergewohnheitsrechts," R. Bernhardt *et al.,* eds.)., *Völkerrecht als Rechtsordnung, Festschrift für Hermann* Mosler (Berlin: Springer, 1983), p. 89.

2. ICJ, *North Sea Continental Shelf, Judgment, Reports,* 1969, pp. 228–229 (J. Lachs, dissenting opinion).

3. ICJ, *Nuclear Tests (Australia v. France), Judgment of 20 December 1974, Reports,* 1974, pp. 269–270. (Judgment).

4. Compare Alfred Rubin, "The International Legal Effects of Unilateral Declarations," *American Journal of International Law,* 71 (1977): 1; and the present writer's response, ibid., 747.

5. Compare G. I. Tunkin, "Coexistence and International Law," *Recueil des cours,* 95 (1958): 23; Tunkin, *Sovetskii ezhegodnik mezhdunarodnogo prava* (Moscow, 1958), p. 15; F. I. Kozhevnikov, ed., *International Law. A Textbook for Use in Law Schools* (1957), pp. 12 and 247; S. B. Krylov, "Les notions principales

du droit des gens," *Recueil des cours,* 70 (1947): 436; I. I. Lukashuk, "SSSR i mezhdunarodnie dogovori" [The Soviet Union and international treaties], *Sovetskii ezhegodnik mezhdunarodnogo prava* (Moscow, 1959), p. 16.

6. Krylov, "Les notions," pp. 433–437; Kozhevnikov, ed., *International Law,* pp. 280–281; Lukashuk, "SSR," p. 16.

7. Tunkin, "Remarks on the Juridical Nature of Customary Norms of International Law," *California Law Review,* 49 (1961): 428–429; Tunkin, *Sovetskii ezhegodnik mezhdunarodnogo prava* (Moscow, 1958), p. 15; Tunkin, "Coexistence and International Law," p. 20.

8. Tunkin, "Coexistence and International Law," p. 26; Tunkin, "Remarks," pp. 423 and 428; V. Pechota, "Valne shromazdeni OSN a projednavani pravnich zasad miroveho souziti," *Casopis pro mezinarodni pravo* 7 (Prague, 1963): 97.

9. R.-J. Dupuy, "Droit déclaratoire et droit programmatoire: de la coutume sauvage à la 'soft law' " [Declaratory law and programmatic law: from wild custom to "soft law"], Mourgeon, ed., *L'élaboration du droit international public* [International Law Making], (1975), p. 132; R. Monaco, "Observations sur la hiérarchie des sources," R. Bernhardt *et al.,* eds.) *Völkerrecht als Rechtsordnung. Festschrift für Hermann Mosler* (1983), p. 599.

10. H. Strebel, "Quellen des Völkerrechts als Rechtsordnung" [Sources of International law as legal classification], *Zeitschrift für ausländisches öffentliches Recht und Völkerrecht* [Journal of foreign public law and international law] (Heidelberg) 36 (1976): 301. And see generally C. Parry, *The Sources and Evidences of International Law* (1965); A. d'Amato, *The Concept of Custom in International Law* (1971); I. I. Lukashuk, *Istochniki mezhdunarodnogo prava* [Sources of international law] (Moscow, 1966).

11. Strebel, "Quellen," p. 302.

12. See, for example, V. M. Shurshalov, *Sovetskii ezhegodnik mezhdunarodnogo prava* (Moscow, 1958), p. 150; A. N. Talalaev, ibid. (1959), p. 144; N. V. Zakharova, ibid. (1960), p. 157.

13. Compare I. I. Lukashuk, ibid. (1959), F. I. Kozhevnikov, ed., *International Law* (1957), pp. 280–281.

14. N. V. Zakharova, "Otkaz sovetskogo gosudarstva ot dogovorov tsarskoi rossii, narushavshikh prava narodov vostochnikh stran" [Renunciation by the Soviet state of treaties of Czarist Russia which violated the rights of the peoples of eastern countries], *Sovetskii ezhegodnik mezhdunarodnogo prava* (Moscow, 1962), p. 126.

15. See the early (postrevolutionary) study by the distinguished Soviet jurist Eugene Korovin, "Soviet Treaties and International Law," *American Journal of International Law* 22 (1928): 763. And compare S. Krylov, "Les notions," p. 433; F. I. Kozhevnikov, ed., *International Law,* p. 281. And see also a latter-day reformulation by Korovin, *American Journal of International Law* 40 (1946): 752.

16. R. Jennings, "The Progressive Development of International Law and Its Codification," *British Yearbook of International Law* 24 (1947): 304; H. Lauterpacht, "Codification and Development of International Law," *American Journal of International Law* 49 (1955): 16; Julius Stone, "On the Vocation of the International Law Commission," *Columbia Law Review* 57 (1957): 16. And see also W. K. Geck, "Völkerrechtliche Verträge und Kodification" [International law treaties and codification], *Zeitschrift für ausländisches öffentliches Recht und Völkerrecht* 36 (1976): 96.

17. O. Schachter, M. Nawaz, and J. Fried, *Toward Wider Acceptance of UN Treaties* (New York: UNITAR, 1971); J. M. Ruda, *The Final Acceptance of International Conventions* (1976); Lord McNair, *The Law of Treaties* (Oxford: Clarendon Press, 1961), p. 129.

18. See, generally, Edward McWhinney, "The Illegal Diversion of Aircraft and International Law," *Recueil des cours* 138 (1973): 261; reprinted 1975.

19. ICJ, *Reports,* 1969, pp. 228–229.

20. ICJ, *Reports,* 1974, p. 253.

21. Developed more fully in Edward McWhinney, *The International Law of Détente. Arms Control, European Security, and East-West Cooperation* (Alphen aan den Rijn: Sijthoff and Noordhoff, 1978).

22. J. Castaneda, *Legal Effects of United Nations Resolutions* (1969); O. Asamoah, *The Legal Significance of the Declarations of the General Assembly of the United Nations* (1966); R. Higgins, *The Development of International Law through the Political Organs of the United Nations* (1963); K. Skubiszewski, "A New Source of the Law of Nations: Resolutions of International Organisations," *Recueil d'études de droit international.* P. Lalive and J. Freymond, eds., *En hommage à Paul Guggenheim,* (Geneva: La Tribune de Genève, 1968), p. 508; J. A. Frowein, "Der Beitrag der internationalen Organisationen zur Entwicklung des Völkerrechts" [The contribution of international organizations to the development of international law], *Zeitschrift für ausländisches öffentliches Recht und Völkerrecht* 36 (1976): 147; C. Schreuer, "Recommendations and the Traditional Sources of International Law," *Jahrbuch für Internationales Recht* 20 (1977): 103.

23. See, for example, the comments by V. Pechota, "Valne shromazdeni OSN."

24. Statute of the International Court of Justice, Articles 4, 8.

25. Ibid., Article 10 (2).

26. ICJ, *South West Africa, Second Phase, Judgment, Reports,* 1966, p. 6.

27. Ibid.

CHAPTER 4

1. Nielsen Rep. 203, 307 (1926).

2. PCIJ, Series A/B, no. 70 (1937), 76.

3. Trib. Arb. Mixtes 409, 413.

4. See, generally, Julius Stone, "*Non Liquet* and the Function of Law in the International Community," *British Yearbook of International Law* (London: 1959), p. 124; D. I. Feldman, V. V. Lazarev, and V. N. Likhachev, "O poniatii probelov v. sovremennom mezhdunarodnom prava" [On the notion of gaps (lacunae) in contemporary international law], *Sovetskii ezhegodnik mezhdunarodnogo prava* (Moscow, 1980), p. 127; B. Vitanyi, "Les positions doctrinales concernant le sens de la notion de 'principes généraux de droit reconnus par les nations civilisées,'" [Doctrinal positions concerning the meaning of the notion 'general principles of law recognized by civilized nations'], *Revue générale de droit international public* 86 (1982): 131; Shabtai Rosenne, "Equitable Principles and the Compulsory Jurisdiction of International Tribunals," *Festschrift für Rudolf Bindschedler* (1980), p. 407.

5. ICJ, *Reports,* 1966, p. 323.

6. *The Yearbook of World Affairs* (1972), p. 346.
7. PCIJ, Series A/B no. 53.
8. ICJ, *Reports,* 1951, p. 116.
9. ICJ, *Reports,* 1948, p. 71; ICJ, *Reports,* 1949, p. 48; ICJ, *Reports,* 1950, p. 14; ICJ, *Reports,* 1952, p. 128.
10. ICJ, *Reports,* 1969, p. 100.
11. Ibid., p. 132.
12. Ibid.
13. Ibid., pp. 132–134.
14. Ibid., p. 135.
15. Ibid., p. 136.
16. Ibid., p. 137.
17. Ibid., pp. 139–140.
18. Ibid., p. 150.
19. Ibid., p. 149.
20. ICJ, *Reports,* 1982, p. 18. And see, generally, K. Oellers-Frahm, *Zeitschrift für ausländisches öffentliches Recht un Völkerrecht* 42 (1982): 804; and E. Zoeller, *Revue générale de droit international public* 86 (1982): 645.
21. Ibid., p. 157.
22. Ibid., p. 253.
23. Ibid.
24. Ibid., p. 254.
25. Ibid., p. 255.
26. Ibid.
27. Ibid., p. 256.
28. See, generally, A. von Verdross, "Forbidden Treaties in International Law," *American Journal of International Law* 31 (1937): 571; Verdross, "*Jus dispositivum* and *Jus Cogens* in International Law," ibid., 60 (1966): 55; *The Concept of "Jus Cogens" in International Law* (Geneva: Carnegic Endowment, 1967); Erik Suy, "The Concept of *Jus Cogens* in Public International Law," ibid., 17; G. Schwarzenberger, "International *Jus Cogens?,*" ibid. 115 (reprinted *Texas Law Review* 43 [1965]: 455); Charles De Visscher, "Positivisme et 'Jus Cogens,' " *Revue générale de droit international public,* 75, (1971): 5; K. Marek, "Contribution à l'etude du *jus cogens* en droit international," [Contribution to the study of *Jus Cogens* in international law], P. Lalive and J. Freymond, eds., *Recueil d'études de droit international. En hommage à Paul Guggenheim* (Geneva: La Tribune de Genève, 1968), p. 426; G. Geamanu, "*Jus Cogens* en droit international contemporain" [*Jus Cogens* in contemporary international law], *Revue roumaine d'etudes internationales* [Roumanian Review of International Studies] (Bucharest, 1967), p. 87; L. N. Shestakov, "K voprosu opredelenia norm *jus cogens* v mezhdunarodnom prave" [On the definition of *jus Cogens* in international law], *Sovetskii ezhegodnik mezhdunarodnogo prava* (Moscow, 1980), p. 66; L. A. Aleksidze, ibid. (1969), p. 127; I. N. Karpenko, ibid. (1970), p. 204; M. Virally, "Réflexions sur le *'Jus Cogens'* " [Reflections on *'Jus Cogens'*], *Annuaire français du droit international* (1966), p. 5; S. E. Nahlik, "*Jus Cogens* and the Codified Law of Treaties," *Revista "Temis" (Facultad de Derecho de la Universidad de Zaragoza), "Symbolae García Arias"* [Review 'Temis' (Faculty of Law of the University of Zaragoza[(1973), p. 35; F. Münch, "Bemerkungen zum *ius cogens,*" R. Bernhardt *et al.,* eds. *Völkerrecht als Rechtsordnung, Festschrift für Hermann Mosler* (1983), p. 617.

29. Sir Ian Sinclair, "Vienna Conference on the Law of Treaties," *International and Comparative Law Quarterly* 19, (1969): 66–69; Schwarzenberger, "International *Jus Cogens?,*" pp. 138–140; Naklik, "*Jus Cogens* and the Codified Law of Treaties," pp. 88 et seq.

30. Nahlik, "*Jus Cogens,*" pp. 98–99 and 102; Sinclair, "Vienna Conference," p. 66.

31. Nahlik, "*Jus Cogens,*" p. 103; Sinclair, "Vienna Conference," p. 66.

32. Nahlik, "*Jus Cogens,*" p. 91; Suy, "The Concept of *Jus Cogens,*" pp. 45–48.

33. Nahlik, "*Jus Cogens,*" p. 90; Suy, "The Concept of *Jus Cogens,*" p. 50.

34. Suy, "The Concept of *Jus Cogens,*" pp. 53–55.

35. Sinclair, "Vienna Conference," p. 66.

36. Verdross, "*Jus Dispositirum* and *Jus Cogens,*" pp. 55, 59–60.

37. Suy, "The Concept of *Jus Cogens,*" p. 18.

38. Nahlik, "*Jus Cogens,*" 103.

39. Ibid.

40. Schwarzenberger, "International *Jus Cogens,*" pp. 139–140.

41. Nahlik, "*Jus Cogens,*" pp. 101–102.

42. Ibid., p. 102.

43. ICJ, *Reports,* 1969, pp. 132–133.

44. Vitanyi, "Les positions doctrinales," p. 48.

45. F. Münch, "Die Völkerrechtslehre als Völkerrechtsquelle," [International Law Teaching as International Law Source], *Die Friedenswarte* [The Peace Watch] 56 (1966): 349; M. Lachs, *The Teacher in International Law* (The Hague: Martinus Nighof, 1982).

46. W. G. Grewe, "Vom europäischen zum universellen Völkerrecht. Zur Frage der Revision des 'europazentrischen' Bildes der Völkerrechtsgeschichte" [From European to universal international law. On the question of the revision of the Eurocentric image of the history of international law], *Zeitschrift für ausländisches öffentliches Recht und Völkerrecht* 42 (1982): 449.

47. R.-J. Dupuy, "Droit déclaratoire et droit programmatoire: de la coûtume sauvage à la 'soft law'" [Declaratory law and programmatic law: from wild custom to "soft law"], Mourgeon, ed., *L'élaboration du droit international public* [The elaboration of public international law] (1975), p. 132; M. Lachs, "The Threshold in Law-Making," R. Bernhardt *et al.,* eds., *Völkerrecht als Rechtsordnung. Festschrift für Hermann Mosler* (1983), p. 493.

48. Rudolf Bernhardt, "Verfall and Neubildung von Gewohnheitsrecht im Meeresvölkerrecht" [Decay and Renewal of Customary Law in the International Law of the Sea], H. P. Ipsen and K.-H. Necker, eds., *Recht über See. Festschrift Rolf Stödter zum 70 Geburtstag* [Law of the Sea. *Festschrift* for Rolf Stödter on his 70th birthday] (1979), p. 155.

CHAPTER 5

1. Alf Ross, *The United Nations, Peace and Progress,* (1966), p. 93.

2. United Nations Doc.A/AC 24/SR 6–14; and see also draft resolution of Argentina, UN Doc. A/AC 24/15, November 23, 1948.

3. ICJ, *Conditions of Admission of a State to Membership in the United Nations, Advisory Opinion, Reports,* 1948, p. 57.

4. ICJ, *Competence of the General Assembly for the Admission of a State to the United Nations, Advisory Opinion, Reports,* 1950, p. 4.

5. A. Alvarez, *Le droit international nouveau dans ses rapports avec la vie actuelle des peuples* [The new international law in its relations with the real life of peoples] (1959).

6. M. S. McDougal and R. Gardner, "The Veto and the Charter: An Interpretation for Survival," *Yale Law Journal,* 60, (1951): 258; and compare Leo Gross, "Voting in the Security Council: Abstention from Voting and Absence from Meetings," ibid., p. 209.

7. Discussed more fully in Edward McWhinney, *The World Court and the Contemporary International Law-Making Process,* (1979), pp. 155–56.

8. ICJ, *Certain Expenses of the United Nations, Advisory Opinion, Reports,* 1962, p. 151.

9. Ibid., p. 230.

10. Ibid., p. 268.

11. Ibid., pp. 230–232.

12. United Nations, General Assembly, *Official Records: Report of the Secretary-General on the Work of the Organization,* Thirty-Seventh Session, Supplement No. 1 (A/37/1), 1982, pp. 3–4.

13. United Nations, General Assembly, *Official Records: Report of the Special Committee on the Charter of the United Nations and on the Strengthening of the Role of the Organization,* Thirty-Sixth Session, supp. no. 33 (A/36/33), p. 37.

14. Ibid., p. 40.

15. Ibid., pp. 29–35.

16. Ibid., p. 38.

17. Ibid., p. 37.

18. Ibid., p. 30.

19. Ibid.

20. United Nations, Security Council, S/1501; *SCOR,* V, *Resolutions and Decisions,* 1950 (S/INF/5/Rev. 1), pp. 4–5.

21. United Nations, Security Council, S/1511, ibid., p. 5.

22. United Nations, Security Council, S/1588, ibid.

23. United Nations, *SCOR,* V, no. 24, pp. 3, *et seq.*

24. Ibid., *GAOR,* V, supp. 20 (A/1775), pp. 10–12.

25. Ibid., *GAOR,* V, First C., pp. 63 *et seq.*

26. Leo Gross, "Voting in the Security Council," p. 209; and compare M. S. McDougal and R. Gardner, "The Veto and the Charter," p. 258. And see, generally, Davidson Nicol, *The United Nations Security Council* (New York: UNITAR, 1982); Marie-Françoise Labouz, *L'Organisation des Nations Unies et la Corée* (Paris: Les Publications Universitaires de Paris, 1983).

27. United Nations, SCOR, XI, Meeting 749, p. 31.

28. See, generally, United Nations, SCOR, XI, Meetings 748–751.

29. Ibid.

30. See United Nations, Security Council cease-fire resolution (presented by Panama and Spain) of June 4, 1982, vetoed by the United Kingdom and the United States. PR SC/4420.

31. See, for example, Julius Stone, *The Province and Function of Law* (1946), pp. 421 et seq.

32. A. F. J. Thibaut, *Über die Notwendigkeit eines allgemeinen bürgerlichen Rechts für Deutschland* [On the necessity of a universal civil law for Germany] (1814).

33. F. K. von Savigny, *Vom Beruf unsrer Zeit für Gesetzgebung und Rechtswissenschaft* [On the vocation of our time for law-making and legal science] (1814).

34. Julius Stone, "On the Vocation of the International Law Commission," *Columbia Law Review* 57 (1957): 16; W. K. Geck, "Völkerrechtliche Verträge und Kodification" [International law treaties and codification[, *Zeitschrift für ausländisches öffentliches Recht und Völkerrecht* 36 (1976): 96.

35. See, generally, H. Lauterpacht, "Codification and Development of International Law," *American Journal of International Law* 49 (1955): 16; Julius Stone, "On the Vocation of the International Law Commission" p. 16; S. Rosenne, "The International Law Commission, 1949–59," *British Yearbook of International Law* 36, (1960): 146; Herbert W. Briggs, *The International Law Commission* (1965); B. G. Ramcharan, *The International Law Commission. Its Approach to Codification and Progressive Development of International Law* (1977); *The Work of the International Law Commission* (United Nations, N.Y.: 1st ed., 1966; 3rd ed., 1980); Mohamed El Baradei, T. M. Franck, and R. Trachtenberg, *The International Law Commission. The Need for a New Direction* (N.Y.: UNITAR, 1981); T. M. Franck and Mohamed El Baradei, "The Codification and Progressive Development of International Law: A *UNITAR* Study of the Role and Use of the International Law Commission," *American Journal of International Law* 76 (1982): 630.

36. Briggs, *The International Law Commission,* pp. 175 *et seq.; The Work of the International Law Commission,* 3rd ed. (1980), pp. 36 et seq.; Sir Ian Sinclair, "Principles of International Law Concerning Friendly Relations and Cooperation among States," M. K. Nawaz, ed., *Essays on International Law in Honour of Krishna Rao* (1975), p. 109.

37. Sinclair, "Principles."

38. Ibid.

39. Ibid.

40. Ibid. And see Edward McWhinney, "The 'New' Countries and the 'New' International Law: The United Nations Special Conference on Friendly Relations and Cooperation among States," *American Journal of International Law* 60, (1966): 1; Luke T. Lee, "The Mexico City Conference of the United Nations Special Committee on Principles of International Law Concerning Friendly Relations and Cooperation among States," *International and Comparative Law Quarterly* 14, (1965): 1296.

41. Sinclair, "Principles"; R. Rosenstock, "The Declaration of Principles of International Law Concerning Friendly Relations: A Survey," *American Journal of International Law* 65 (1971): 713.

42. Sinclair, "Principles," p. 139.

43. Franck and El Baradei, "Codification," p. 634; Ramcharan, *The International Law Commission,* pp. 206 *et seq.;* and, more generally, see Briggs, *The International Law Commission,* pp. 54 *et seq.*

44. Ramcharan, *The International Law Commission,* pp. 38 et seq.; Franck and El Baradei, "Codification," p. 633; and, more generally, see Rosenne, "The International Law Commission," pp. 154 et seq.

45. See, generally, Briggs, *The International Law Commission,* pp. 54 *et seq.;* Rosenne, "The International Law Commission," pp. 122 et seq.

46. United Nations, General Assembly, Sixth Committee. Intervention by Guy de Lacharrière. (French Permanent Mission to the United Nations, New York, October 30, 1981.)

47. De Lacharrière, Intervention. These remarks were specially cited and adopted by the French representative in the Sixth Committee at the thirty-seventh session of the General Assembly in 1982; United Nations, Sixth Committee, General Assembly. Intervention by Noel Museux. (French Permanent Mission to the United Nations, New York, November 5, 1982.)

48. United Nations Sixth Committee, General Assembly (thirty-sixth session, 1981). Declaration by Doudou Thiam, president, International Law Commission.

49. United Nations, General Assembly, Sixth Committee. Intervention by Mohammed Bedjaoui. (Algerian Permanent Mission to the United Nations, New York, November 12, 1981.)

50. See Briggs, *The International Law Commission,* p. 33, for the arguments successfully advanced in 1956 for expanding the ILC's original fifteen members to twenty-one; identical arguments were advanced, in 1961, in expanding from twenty-one to twenty-five; and in 1981, in expanding from twenty-five to thirty-four. See also Briggs, *The Work of the International Law Commission* (3rd ed., 1980), p. 7.

51. United Nations, General Assembly (A/36/371 rev. 2), November 20, 1981.

52. United Nations, General Assembly, Resolution, "Enlargement of the International Law Commission: Amendments to Articles 2 and 9 of the Statute of the Commission" (A/RES/36/39), November 20, 1981.

53. El Baradei, Franck, and Trachtenberg, *The International Law Commission.*

54. Oscar Schachter, M. Nawaz, J. Fried, *Toward Wider Acceptance of UN Treaties* (New York: UNITAR, 1971.)

55. See, in this regard, Edward McWhinney, "The Illegal Diversion of Aircraft and International Law," *Recueil des cours,* 138 (1973): 261; reprinted 1975.

56. Sinclair "Principles" p. 139; Rosenne, "The International Law Commission," pp. 154 *et seq.*

57. Ramcharan, *The International Law Commission,* pp. 115 et seq.; Franck and El Baradei, "Codification," p. 632.

Chapter 6

1. United Nations, General Assembly, *Official Records: Report of the International Court of Justice, 1 August 1981–31 July 1982,* Thirty-Seventh Session, supp. Nov. 4 (A/37/4), 1982.

2. ICJ, *Certain Expenses of the United Nations, Advisory Opinion of 20 July 1962, Reports,* 1962, p. 151.

3. ICJ, *South West Africa, Second Phase, Judgment, Reports,* 1966, p. 6.

4. ICJ, *South West Africa, Preliminary Objections, Judgment, Reports,* 1962, p. 319.

5. ICJ, *Legal Consequences for States of the Continued Presence of South Africa in Namibia (South West Africa) Notwithstanding Security Council Resolution 276 (1970), Advisory Opinion, Reports,* 1971, p. 16.

6. United Nations, Department of Public Information, GA/6478, November 5, 1981; and see generally T. O. Elias, *New Horizons in International Law* (Alphen aan den Rijn: Sijhoff & Noordhoff, 1979), p. 78.

7. United Nations, General Assembly, Security Council (A/36/862; S/14886), March 4, 1982.

8. Ibid.

9. See T. O. Elias, *New Horizons in International Law,* p. 79.

10. ICJ, *Reports,* 1966, p. 6.

11. ICJ, *Reports,* 1966, p. 323.

12. ICJ, *Reports,* 1971, p. 16.

13. ICJ, *Reports,* 1971, pp. 31–32.

14. M. Hudson, *The Permanent Court of International Justice, 1920–1942,* p. 511.

15. ICJ, *Reports,* 1971, p. 303. And see also J. G. Merrills, "Sir Gerald Fitzmaurice's Contribution to the Jurisprudence of the International Court of Justice," *British Yearbook of International Law* (London: 1975–1976), p. 183.

16. ICJ, *Nuclear Tests (Australia v. France), Interim Protection, Order of 22 June 1973, Reports,* 1973, p. 99; ICJ, *Nuclear Tests (Australia v. France), Judgment of 20 December 1974, Reports,* 1974, p. 253.

17. *Livre blanc sur les expériences nucléaires* [White paper on Nuclear Tests] (Paris: Comité interministériel pour l'information, 1973). And see, generally, the comments by G. de Lacharrière, *Annuaire français de droit international* [French Yearbook of International Law] (Paris, 1973), p. 235; Edward McWhinney, *The World Court and the Contemporary International Law-Making Process,* (1979), pp. 34 et seq.

18. PCIJ, *The Mavrommatis Palestine Concessions Case* (Ser. A no. 2), p. 16.

19. See the comments by Judge Lachs: M. Lachs, "The Revised Procedure of the International Court of Justice," F. Kalshoven, P. J. Kuyper and J. G. Lammers, eds., *Essays on the Development of the International Legal Order in Memory of Haro F. van Panhuys,* (1980), p. 29; T. O. Elias, *The International Court of Justice and the Indication of Provisional Measures of Protection (Gilbert Amado Memorial Lecture)* (1978), p. 2. And see, generally, R. P. Anand, *Studies in International Adjudication* (New Delhi: Viking Publications, 1969).

20. ICJ, *Western Sahara, Advisory Opinion, Reports,* 1975, p. 12.

21. ICJ, *United States Diplomatic and Consular Staff in Tehran, Provisional Measures, Order of 15 December 1979, Reports,* 1979, p. 7; ICJ, *United States Diplomatic and Consular Staff in Tehran, (United States of America v. Iran), Judgment of 24 May 1980, Reports,* 1980.

22. ICJ, *Reports,* 1979, p. 11.

23. Ibid.

24. M. Lachs, "The Revised Procedure," p. 42.

25. Ibid., p. 43.

26. ICJ, *North Sea Continental Shelf, Judgment, Reports,* 1969, p. 3.

27. E. Jiménez de Aréchaga, "The Amendment to the Rules of Procedure of the International Court of Justice," *American Journal of International Law* 67

(1973): 2–3; H. Mosler, "Aktuelle Aspekte des Verfahrensrechts des Internationalen Gerichtshofes," [Actual aspects of procedural law of the International Court], P. Fischer, H. F. Köck, A. Verdross, eds., *Völkerrecht und Rechtsphilosophie (Internationale Festschrift für Stephan Verosta zum 70 Geburtstag)* (1980), pp. 249, 255.

28. Lachs, "The Revised Procedure," p. 43.

29. Ibid.

30. Ibid., p. 44.

31. ICJ, *Delimitation of the Maritime Boundary in the Gulf of Maine Area (Canada/United States of America), Constitution of Chamber, Order of 20 January 1982, Reports,* 1982, p. 3.

32. Compare, however, Jiménez de Aréchaga, "Amendment to the Rules," pp. 2–3.

33. ICJ, *Reports,* 1982, p. 10.

34. Ibid., p. 11.

35. Ibid., pp. 12–13.

36. Jiménez de Aréchaga, "Amendment to the Rules." And see, generally, E. Zoller, "La première constitution d'une chambre spéciale par la cour internationale de justice. Observations sur l'ordonnance du 20 janvier 1982" [The first constituting of a special chamber by the International Court of Justice], *Revue générale de droit international public,* 86 (1982): 305.

37. Jiménez de Aréchaga, "Amendment to the Rules," p. 3.

38. ICJ, *Reports,* 1982, p. 10.

39. Ibid., p. 11.

40. Ibid.

41. Ibid., p. 12.

42. L. Gross, "The International Court of Justice: Consideration of Requirements for Enhancing Its Role in the International Legal Order," *American Journal of International Law* 65 (1971): 286. Compare President T. O. Elias's views, *New Horizons in International Law,* p. 78: ". . . There does not appear to be any likelihood of a return to the old order in which Europe dominated the Bench. . . . Western European candidates in the future would stand a far better chance of being elected if they had or were thought to have liberal or progressive views *vis-à-vis* the problems of the Third World."

43. Gross, "The International Court of Justice," pp. 271–272.

44. ICJ, *Continental Shelf (Tunisia/Libyan Arab Jamahiriya), Judgment, Reports,* 1982, p. 18.

45. *Report of the International Court of Justice, 1 August 1981–31 July 1982* (1982), p. 2.

46. Lachs, "The Revised Procedure," p. 44. And see also Gross, "The International Court of Justice," pp. 320 et seq.

47. ICJ, *Reports,* 1949.

48. M. Lachs, "The Decision-Making Powers and the Judiciary within the United Nations," *Völkerrecht und Rechtsphilosophie* (1980), p. 389; Gross, "The International Court of Justice," p. 253; R.-J. Dupuy, "L'adaptation de la Cour internationale de Justice au monde d'aujourd'hui [The adaptation of the International Court of Justice to today's world], *Revue belge de droit international* (1966), p. 28.

49. ICJ, *Rules of Court* (as amended, 1972), Article 55; *Rules of Court*

(adopted April 14, 1978), Article 58. And see, generally, Jiménez de Aréchaga, "Amendment to the Rules," pp. 7–8; Lachs, "The Revised Procedure," pp. 37–38.

50. As to the inordinate length and documentation (and, hence, enormous expense) of the written pleadings and counterpleadings in certain past cases of the court, see Gross, "The International Court of Justice," pp. 301–302.

Chapter 7

1. ICJ, *Advisory Opinion, Reports,* 1962, p. 151.
2. United Nations, General Assembly, *Official Records: Report of the Special Committee on the Charter of the United Nations and on the Strengthening of the Role of the Organization,* Thirty-sixth Session, supp. no. 33 (A/36/33), 1981.
3. Ibid., *Official Records: Report . . . on the Charter. . . ,* Thirty-seventh Session, supp. no. 33 (A/37/33), 1982.
4. Ibid., *Official Records: Report on the Charter. . . ,* Thirty-sixth Session, 1981, p. 18.
5. Ibid., pp. 29–30.
6. Ibid., p. 18.
7. Ibid., pp. 12–61.
8. Ibid., pp. 29–30.
9. Ibid., p. 30.
10. Ibid., pp. 34–35.
11. Ibid., pp. 34, 40.
12. Ibid., p. 37.
13. Ibid., p. 38.
14. Ibid., p. 35.
15. *United Nations, General Assembly, Official Records: Report . . . on the Charter. . . ,* Thirty-seventh Session, 1982.
16. Ibid., pp. 58–78, 79–80. Draft recommendation presented by Egypt on behalf of Non-Aligned Countries of the Special Committee (document A/AC.182/L.29), and revised draft recommendation presented by Egypt (document A/AC.182/L.29/Rev.1). An earlier version of this document, on behalf of Egypt itself (document A/AC.182/WG/50), is included in the earlier, 1981 *Report,* Thirty-sixth Session, 1981, pp. 62–63.
17. United Nations, General Assembly, *Official Records: Report . . . on the Charter. . . ,* Thirty-seventh Session, 1982, p. 58.
18. Ibid., p. 59.
19. Ibid., p. 60.
20. Ibid.
21. Ibid., p. 68.
22. Ibid., p. 58.
23. Ibid., pp. 73–74.
24. Ibid., pp. 75–77.
25. Ibid., pp. 79–80.
26. Ibid., p. 79.
27. Ibid., pp. 80–83 (documents A/AC.182/L.25; A/AC.182/WG/51).
28. Ibid., p. 80.

29. Ibid., pp. 80–81.

30. Ibid., p. 81.

31. Ibid., pp. 81–82.

32. United Nations, General Assembly, *Official Records* (A/C.6/37/L.5/rev.1), November 24, 1982.

33. Ibid.

34. United Nations, General Assembly, *Official Records:* (A/C.6/37/L.19), November 26, 1982.

35. Draft Manila Declaration on the Peaceful Settlement of International Disputes, United Nations, General Assembly, *Official Records: Report . . . on the Charter. . .*, Thirty-seventh Session, 1982, pp. 9–14.

36. *United Nations Journal,* no. 82/221, November 16, 1982.

37. United Nations, General Assembly, *Official Records: Report of the Sixth Committee: Peaceful Settlement of Disputes between States,* (A/37/590), November 5, 1982.

38. United Nations, General Assembly, *Official Records* (SG/SM/3361, L/2450), November 15, 1982.

39. Preamble to Manila Declaration, para. 6.

40. Preamble to Manila Declaration, paras. 8, 9. The friendly relations declaration of 1970 is also cited in the substantive sections of the Manila Declaration: Part I, s. 12 (in the context, again, of self-determination), and Part II, s. 6 (in the context, again, of self-determination, freedom, and independence, particularly of "peoples under colonial and racist regimes or other forms of alien domination").

41. As perhaps suggested, in another context (the 1925 Geneva protocol on the prohibition of the use of poisonous gases and bacteriological warfare), in the debate in the First Committee of the General Assembly at the thirty-seventh annual session, 1982. United Nations, General Assembly, First Committee, Intervention by J. Alan Beesley. (Canadian Permanent Mission to the United Nations, New York, November 29, 1982.)

42. Manila Declaration on the Peaceful Settlement of International Disputes, Part I, s. 4: "States parties to a dispute shall continue to observe in their mutual relations their obligations under the fundamental principles of international law concerning the sovereignty, independence and territorial integrity of States, as well as other generally recognised principles and rules of *contemporary* international law."

43. Ibid., Part II, s. 4.

44. Ibid., Part II, s. 3.

45. Ibid., Part II, s. 6.

46. Ibid., Part I, s. 6.

47. Ibid., Part II, s. 5.

48. Ibid.

Chapter 8

1. United Nations General Assembly, *Official Records: Report of the Secretary-General on the Work of the Organisation,* Thirty-Seventh Session, Supplement no. 1 (A/37/1), 1982. And see, generally, Rahmatullah Khan, *Implied Powers of the United Nations* (Delhi: Vikas, 1970).

2. Ibid., pp. 3–4.
3. Ibid., p. 1.
4. Ibid., p. 2.
5. Ibid., p. 3.
6. *New York Times,* December 21, 1982.
7. United Nations, Office of the Secretary-General, SG/A/301, BIO/1938, November 16, 1982.
8. United Nations, Department of Public Information (WS/1105), December 10, 1982, p. 6.
9. United Nations, Department of Public Information (WS/1102), November 19, 1982, p. 7.
10. See the statement by Davidson Nicol, executive director of UNITAR, to the Sixth Committee, General Assembly, at the thirty-seventh annual session, 1982. (UNITAR, New York, 23 November, 1982).
11. United Nations, General Assembly, Sixth Committee, Intervention by Richard Saint-Martin. (Canadian Permanent Mission to the United Nations, New York, November 29, 1982.)
12. United Nations, Office of the Secretary-General, *Proposed Medium-Term Plan for the Period 1984–1989,* chap. 3, "International Justice and Law" (Future A/37/6, Chap. 3), pp. 6–7.
13. See United Nations, General Assembly, Sixth Committee, *Organization of Work, Note by the Secretariat,* Thirty-seventh Session (A/C.6/37/L.1), September 24, 1982.
14. See United Nations, General Assembly, Sixth Committee, *Programme of Work,* decisions adopted by the Sixth Committee at its second and ninth meetings, held on September 27, and October 5, 1982, Thirty-seventh Session, Sixth Committee), (A/C.6/37/2) October 5, 1982.
15. United Nations, General Assembly, Sixth Committee, Intervention by Shabtai Rosenne. (Israeli Permanent Mission to the United Nations, New York, November 4, 1982).
16. Ibid.
17. Ibid.
18. United Nations, General Assembly, *Official Records: Report of the International Law Commission on the Work of Its Thirty-fourth Session, 3 May–23 July 1982,* Thirty-seventh Session, supp. no. 10 (A/37/10), 1982, p. 278.
19. Rosenne, Intervention, November 4, 1982.
20. M. El Baradei, T. M. Franck, and R. Trachtenberg, *The International Law Commission. The Need for a New Direction* (New York: UNITAR, 1981).
21. United Nations, General Assembly, *Official Records: Report of the International Law Commission on the Work of Its Thirty-fourth Session,* pp. 272–273.
22. Ibid., p. 273.
23. Declaration by Paul Reuter, president, International Law Commission, to the Sixth Committee, General Assembly, thirty-seventh session, 1982.
24. United Nations, Department of Public Information, Press Section, Thirty-seventh General Assembly, Sixth Committee, 46th Meeting (PM), (GA/L/2242), November 16, 1982, p. 9. Closing statement of Paul Reuter, president, ILC.
25. Ibid.
26. Ibid.

27. Ibid.

28. United Nations, General Assembly, Sixth Committee, *Official Records: Agenda Item 125, Report of the International Law Commission* (A/C.6/37/L.27), Thirty-seventh Session, December 3, 1982.

29. Compare Rosenne, "The International Law Commission, 1949–59," *British Yearbook of International Law,* 36, (London: 1961), pp. 154 et seq.

30. B. G. Ramcȟaran, *The International Law Commission. Its Approach to the Codification and Progressive Development of International Law* (1977), pp. 115 *et seq.*

31. Ibid. M. El Baradei, T. M. Franck, and R. Trachtenberg, *The International Law Commission,* p. 6.

CHAPTER 9

1. See generally Roscoe Pound, *An Introduction to the Philosophy of Law* (New Haven: Yale University Press, 1922), pp. 169 *et seq.;* Julius Stone, *The Province and Function of Law* (Sydney: Associated General Publications, 1946), pp. 355 *et seq.*

2. J. Kohler, *Lehrbuch der Rechtsphilosophie* [Textbook of legal philosophy] (1909).

3. As to values in law (goal values), see generally Myres S. McDougal and Harold D. Lasswell, "The Identification and Appraisal of Diverse Systems of Public Order," *American Journal of International Law,* 53 (1959): 1, reprinted in Myres S. McDougal and Associates, *Studies in World Public Order* (New Haven: Yale University Press, 1960), p. 3. The term "value" is used hereafter as the more comprehensive generic classification.

4. Discussed generally in Edward McWhinney, *Constitution-Making. Principles, Process, Practice* (Toronto: University of Toronto Press, 1981, p. 52 *et seq.*

5. Ibid., p. 7.

6. Ibid., p. 86.

7. ICJ, *South West Africa. Preliminary Objections, Judgment, Reports,* 1962, p. 319; *South West Africa, Second Phase, Judgment, Reports,* 1966, p. 6.

8. ICJ, *Legal Consequences for States of the Continued Presence of South Africa in Namibia (South West Africa) Notwithstanding Security Council Resolution 276 (1970), Advisory Opinion, Reports,* 1971, p. 16.

9. Charles Rousseau, "Argentine et Grande-Bretagne: Guerrre des Falklands," *Revue générale de droit internationál public* 86 (1982): 724; T. M. Franck, *American Journal of International Law* 77 (1983): 109.

10. See generally, ICJ, *Western Sahara, Advisory Opinion, Reports,* 1975, p. 12.

11. The subsequent Convention on the Conservation of the Antarctic Marine Living Resources, signed in 1980 and concluded among the parties to the original Antarctic treaty, does not purport to rule, one way or another, on existing territorial claims in the region.

12. ICJ, *Reports,* 1975, p. 12.

13. Edward McWhinney, *The International Law of Détente* (Alphen aan den Rijn: Sijthoff and Noordhoff, 1978), pp. 92 *et seq.*

14. United Nations, General Assembly, *Official Records: Declaration on the Establishment of a New International Economic Order* (A/RES/3201 [S-VI]) May 9, 1974.

15. United Nations, General Assembly, *Official Records: Programme of Action on the Establishment of a New International Economic Order* (A/RES/3202 [S-VI]) May 16, 1974.

16. United Nations, General Assembly, *Official Records: Charter of Economic Rights and Duties of States* (A/RES/3281 [XXIX]) January 15, 1975.

17. See, generally, Mohammed Bedjaoui, *Pour un nouvel ordre économique international* (Paris: Unesco, 1979), English translation, *Towards a New International Economic Order* (Paris: Unesco; New York: Holmes & Meier, 1979); C. Tomuschat, "Die Charta der wirtschaftlichen Rechte und Pflichten der Staaten," [The charter of economic rights and duties of states]. *Zeitschrift für ausländisches öffentliches Recht und Völkerrecht* 36 (1976): 444; E. U. Petersmann, "Die Dritte Welt und das Wirtschaftsvölkerrecht" [The Third World and economic International Law], ibid., p. 492; *Towards a New International Economic Order. Report by a Commonwealth Experts Group* (London: Commonwealth Secretariat, 1975).

18. As to the "consensus rule," see generally C. W. Jenks, "Unanimity, the Veto, Weighted Voting, Special and Simplified Majorities and Consensus as Modes of Decision in International Law," *Cambridge Essays in International Law: Essays in Honour of Lord McNair* (London: Stevens and Sons, 1965), p. 488; G. de Lacharrière, "Consensus et Nations Unies" [Consensus and the United Nations], *Annuaire français de droit international* (Paris: 1968), p. 9; S. Bastid, "Observations sur la pratique de consensus" [Observations on the practice of consensus], J. Tittel, ed., *Multitudo Legum Ius Unum: Festschrift für Wilhelm Wengler,* (Berlin: Interrecht, 1973), 1: 11; W. Wengler, "Rechtsvertrag, Konsensus und Absichtserklärung im Völkerrecht" [Legal agreement, consensus, and intention-clarification in international law], *Juristenzeitung* 31 (1976): 193.

19. See, for example, the reservations expressly entered by the United States (United Nations Doc. A/PV. 2229, 1 May 1974), p. 41; West Germany, ibid., p. 51; France, ibid., p. 73; Japan (United Nations Doc. A/PV 2230, 2 May 1974), p. 17; United Kingdom (United Nations Doc. A/PV 2231, 2 May 1974), p. 12.

20. G. Feuer, "Réflexions sur la charte des droits et devoirs économiques des états" [Reflections on the charter of economic rights and duties of states], *Revue générale de droit international public* 79 (1975): 273.

21. More generally, see G. Schwarzenberger, "The Principles and Standards of International Economic Law," *Recueil des cours* 1 (1966): 1.

22. B. Boutros-Ghali, "Les fonds arabes pour le développement économique, *"Annuaire français de droit international* (1975), p. 6.

23. See generally D. Kebschull, *et al.,* eds., *Die neue Weltwirtschaftsordnung* [The new world economic order] (Hamburg: Weltarchiv, 1977); H. Besters, ed., *Eine neue Ordnung der Weltwirtschaft?* [A new order for the world economy.] (Baden-Baden: Nomos, 1975); *Justice économique international* [International Economic Justice] (Paris: Gallimard, 1976); "Report, Legal Aspects of a New International Economic Order, *International Law Association, Report of the Fifty-Ninth Conference, 1980* (London: International Law Association, 1982), pp. 263 *et seq.;* F. P. Feliciano, "International Law and the Establishment of a New International Economic Order," *Philippine Review of Business & Economics* (1976): 66.

24. *North-South: A Programme for Survival* (Brandt Commission Report) (London: Pan Books, 1980).

25. See letter dated September 7, 1982, from the president of the Third United Nations Conference on the Law of the Sea to the president of the General Assembly (United Nations Doc. A/37/441, September 14, 1982); letter dated October 8, 1982, from the president of the Third United Nations Conference on the Law of the Sea to the president of the General Assembly (United Nations Doc. A/37/441, add. 1, October 14, 1982). And see also R. P. Anand, ed., *Law of the Sea: Caracas and Beyond* (New Delhi: Radiant, 1978); Rahmatullah Khan, *The 200-Mile Economic Zone: Indian Ocean Fisheries* (Delhi: Ankur, 1977); Vladimir Kopal, *Problémy nové Kodifikace Mézinárodniho práva mořskéno* (Problems of the Law of the Sea) (Prague: Academia Praha, 1983).

26. United Nations, Department of Public Information (WS/1101), November 12, 1982; ibid., (WS/1105), December 10, 1982; ibid. (WS/1106), December 17, 1982; Draft Final Act (A/CONF.62/121), October 21, 1982; United Nations Convention (A/CONF.62/122), October 7, 1982.

27. United Nations, Department of Public Information, (WS/1106), December 17, 1982.

28. *New York Times,* December 11, 1982.

29. Ibid., December 10, 1982; December 17, 1982; December 31, 1982.

30. Ibid., December 10, 1982.

31. Ibid., December 11, 1982.

32. United Nations, Department of Public Information (WS/1106), December 17, 1982; *New York Times,* December 9, 1982.

33. United Nations Institute for Training and Research, Progressive Development of the Principles and Norms of International Law Relating to the New International Economic Order. Analytical Papers and Analysis of Texts of relevant Instruments (UNITAR/DS/5) August 15, 1982; and see also United Nations, Department of Public Information (UNITAR/479), September 29, 1982.

34. Ibid.; and see also United Nations, *Progressive Development . . . Report of the Secretary-General* (A/37/409), October 1, 1982, pp. 8 et seq.

35. Ibid.

36. United Nations, General Assembly, Sixth Committee, Intervention by Richard Saint-Martin. (Canadian Permanent Mission to the United Nations, New York, November 29, 1982).

37. Statement by Dr. Davidson Nicol, executive director of UNITAR, to the Sixth Committee, General Assembly, November 23, 1982.

38. United Nations, *Progressive Development . . . Report of the Secretary-General* (A/37/409), October 1, 1982, pp. 11 et seq.

39. UNITAR/DS/5, August 15, 1982, pp. 1–2.

Chapter 10

1. See generally United Nations General Assembly Resolution 3314 (XXIX), December 14, 1974, "Annex, Definition of Aggression"; Julius Stone, *Legal Controls of International Conflict* (New York: Rinehart, 1954), pp. 330 *et seq.;* Julius Stone, *Aggression and World Order* (Berkeley: University of California Press, 1958); B. B. Ferencz, *Defining International Aggression: The Search*

for World Peace (Dobbs Ferry, N.Y.: Oceana, 1975); P. Rambaud, "La définition de l'agression par l'O.N.U." [The definition of aggression by the UN], *Revue générale de droit international public* 80 (1976): 835; A. Randelzhofer, "Use of Force" *Encyclopaedia of Public International Law* (R. Bernhardt, dir. 1982) 4: 265.

2. Covey Oliver, "International Law and the Quarantine of Cuba," *American Journal of International Law* 57 (1963): 375; and see also Julius Stone, *Aggression and World Order,* pp. 99–100.

3. United Nations Department of Public Information (WS/1078), June 4, 1982; ibid. (WS/1079) June 11, 1982.

4. Ibid. (WS/1079), June 11, 1982.

5. *Le Monde,* Paris, May 5, 1982.

6. Ibid. As to the British proclamation of a two-hundred-mile "total exclusion zone" around the Falklands (Malvinas) in purported exercise of the legal right of self-defense, see United Nations Department of Public Information (WS/1073) April 30, 1982.

7. E. Klein, "Nationale Befreiungskämpfe und Dekolonisierungspolitik der Vereinten Nationen" [National liberation struggles and decolonization politics of the United Nations] *Zeitschrift für ausländisches öffentliches Recht und Völkerrecht* 36 (1976): 618; D. Schröder, *Die Dritte Welt und das Völkerrecht* [The Third World and international law] (Hamburg, Frankfurt: Alfred Metzner Verlag, 1970), pp. 49 et seq.; K. Doehring, *Das Selbstbestimmungsrecht der Völker als Grundsatz des Völkerrechts* [The self-determination right of peoples as principle of international law) (1974); K. Ginther, "Liberation Movements," *Encyclopaedia of Public International Law,* 3: 245.

8. United Nations, General Assembly, Resolution 147 (XXXII), December 16, 1977.

9. See, generally, United Nations, General Assembly, *Official Records: Report of the Ad Hoc Committee on International Terrorism,* Thirty-fourth Session, supp. no. 37 (A/34/37), 1979: United Nations, General Assembly, *Measures to Prevent International Terrorism Which Endangers or Takes Innocent Human Lives or Jeopardizes Fundamental Freedoms, and Study of the Underlying Causes. . . , Report of the Secretary-General* (A/36/425), September 21, 1981.

10. See, generally, Edward McWhinney, "The Illegal Diversion of Aircraft and International Law," *Recueil des cours* 138 (1973): 261; reprinted 1975; and see also "Report of the Committee on International Terrorism" (A. P. Rubin, *rapporteur), International Law Association, Report of the Sixtieth Conference, 1982* (London: International Law Association, 1983).

11. John F. Murphy, *The United Nations and the Control of International Violence,* (Totowa, N.J.: Allanheld, Osmun 1982); V. S. Mani, "International Terrorism," *Indian Journal of International Law* 18 (1978): 206.

12. See, generally, Edward McWhinney, *The International Law of Détente* (Alphen aan den Rijn: Sijthoff and Noordhoff, 1978), pp. 39–91; J. H. Kahan, *Security in the Nuclear Age. Developing U.S. Strategic Arms Policy* (Washington: The Brookings Institution, 1975); G. Delcoigne and G. Rubinstein, *Nonprolifération des armes nucléaires* [Nonproliferation of nuclear arms] (Brussels: Université Libre de Bruxelles, 1970); M.-F. Furet, *Le désarmement nucléaire* [Nuclear disarmament] (Paris: A. Pedone, 1973); D. Colard, *Le désarmement* [Disarmament] (Paris: Armand Colin, 1972); D. Schwarzkopf, *Atom-herrschaft* [Atomic command] (Stuttgart: Seewald Verlag, 1969).

13. See, generally, R. Boardman, *International Organization and the Conservation of Nature* (Bloomington: Indiana University Press, 1981).

14. See, generally, F. M. Auburn, *Antarctic Law and Politics* (Bloomington: Indiana University Press, 1982). And see also R. Wolfrum, "The Principal of the Common Heritage of Mankind," *Zeitschrift für ausländisches öffentliches Recht un Völkerrecht* 43 (1983): 312.

15. United Nations, General Assembly, Resolution 115 (XXXIII).

16. *New York Times,* November 2, 1982.

17. Ibid.

18. International Commission for the Study of Communication Problems, *Many Voices, One World: Communication and Society Today and Tomorrow* (Unesco, 1980).

19. See generally Carl Q. Christol, "Telecommunications, Outer Space, and the New International Information Order," *Syracuse Journal of International Law and Commerce* 8 (1981): 348; "A New World Information Order: The Developing World and the Free Flow of Information Controversy," ibid., p. 249.

20. Unesco, Press Release 2435, December 3, 1982; United Nations, Department of Public Information (WS/1105), December 10, 1982; *Le Monde,* Paris, December 6, 1982.

21. *New York Times,* November 28, 1982; ibid., December 4, 1982.

22. Ibid.

23. United Nations, General Assembly, Special Political Committee, *International Cooperation in the Peaceful Uses of Outer Space: Preparation of an International Convention on Principles Governing the Use by States of Artificial Earth Satellites for Direct Television Broadcasting.* Agenda items 62 and 63 (A/SPC/37/L.5/rev. 1), November 19, 1982.

24. United Nations, Department of Public Information (WS/1106), December 17, 1982.

25. *New York Times,* November 23, 1982; ibid., December 11, 1982.

26. See, generally, Carl Q. Christol, *The Modern International Law of Outer Space* (New York and Oxford: Pergamon Press, 1982), pp. 605 *et seq.;* Carl Q. Christol, "Telecommunications, Outer Space, and the New International Information Order," *Syracuse Journal of International Law and Commerce* 8 (1981): 343; Mustapha Masmoudi, "Le nouvel ordre mondial de l'information et les satellites de radio-diffusion directe," [The new world information order and satellites of direct radio-diffusion], *Syracuse Journal of International Law and Commerce* 8: 322; Gabriel Warren, "A Canadian Perspective on Direct Broadcast Satellites and the New World Information and Communication Order," ibid., p. 391.

27. See, for example, speech by Chancellor Helmut Schmidt to the *Bundestag,* March 23, 1977, *The Bulletin* (Bonn), April 13, 1977.

28. See, generally, Edward McWhinney, *The International Law of Détente,* pp. 162–164, pp. 243–244.

29. Statistics issued by the Greater New York Conference on Soviet Jewry and the National Conference on Soviet Jewry showed that 2,670 Soviet Jews were granted emigration visas in 1982, compared with 9,447 in 1981, and a high level of 51, 320 in 1979. *New York Times,* December 30, 1982.

30. ICJ, *Reports,* 1966, p. 6.

31. ICJ, *Reports,* 1971, p. 16.

32. *Globe and Mail,* Toronto, July 20, 1982.

33. T. O. Elias, *New Horizons in International Law* (1979), p. 159 *et seq.*

34. See, now, *Regents of the University of California* v. *Bakke,* 438 U.S. 265 (1978); and see also the Indian Supreme Court decision in *State of Kerala* v. *N. M. Thomas,* A.I.R. (1976) S.C. 490; discussed in Edward McWhinney, *Constitution-Making. Principles, Process, Practice* (Toronto: University of Toronto Press, 1981), p. 86 *et seq.*

35. *Regents of the University of California* v. *Bakke,* 438 U.S. 265 (1978).

36. For example, the recourse to Unesco in human rights and also in NWIO matters: see S. Bastid, "La mise en oeuvre d'un recours concernant les droits de l'homme dans le domaine relevant de la compétence de l' UNESCO" [The instituting of a resort concerning human rights in the domain flowing from Unesco's competence], R. Bernhardt, *et al.,* eds., *Völkerrecht als Rechtsordnung. Festschrift für Hermann Mosler,* (Berlin: Springer, 1983), p. 45.

37. See, for example, S. P. Marks, "The Peace–Human Rights–Development Dialectic," *Universitetsforlaget* (Stockholm) 4 (1980): 339; Diego Uribe Vargas, *La tercera generación de Derechos Humanos y la Paz* (Bogotá: Plaza Janes, 1983).

Chapter 11

1. Krystyna Marek, "Retour sur Yalta" [Return to Yalta] *Revue générale de droit international public* 86 (1982): 457.

2. F. Münch, "Brauch und Missbrauch der normativen Kraft des Faktischen" [Use and misuse of the normative force of facts] *Jahrbuch der Albertus-Universität zu Königsberg/Pr.* 15 (1965): 29.

3. Erik Suy, United Nations Peacekeeping System, *Encyclopaedia of Public International Law* (R. Bernhardt, dir. 1982), 4: 258.

4. United Nations, Department of Public Information (WS/728), September 19, 1975.

5. ICJ, *Reports,* 1966, p. 6.

6. Credentials of representatives to the thirty-seventh session of the General Assembly, letter dated October 22, 1982, addressed to the president of the General Assembly (A/37/563), October 22, 1982. And see letter dated October 25, 1982, from the Permanent Representative of Israel to the United Nations (A/37/565), October 25, 1982.

7. *New York Times,* October 21, 1982.

8. United Nations, Department of Public Information (WS/1099), October 29, 1982.

9. *New York Times,* October 20, 1982; ibid., October 21, 1982.

10. Statement by Hans Blix, Director-General of the International Atomic Energy Agency, to the thirty-seventh session, United Nations, General Assembly, November 18, 1982; United Nations, Department of Public Information (WS/1102), November 19, 1982; United Nations, General Assembly (A/37/PV.71) November 19, 1982.

11. *New York Times,* October 20, 1982.

12. ICJ, *Conditions of Admission of a State to Membership in the United Nations, Advisory Opinion, Reports,* 1948, p. 57.

13. ICJ, *Competence of the General Assembly for the Admission of a State to the United Nations, Advisory Opinion, Reports,* 1950, p. 4.

14. United Nations, Department of Public Information (WS/1070), April 8, 1982.

15. Ibid. (WS/1077), May 28, 1982.

16. Ibid. (WS/1079), June 11, 1982.

17. United Nations Charter, Article 27 (3) ("The Security Council, Voting").

18. United Nations, Department of Public Information (WS/1079), June 11, 1982.

19. Ibid.

20. United Nations, General Assembly, *Official Records: Report of the Secretary-General on the Work of the Organization,* Thirty-seventh Session, Supplement No. 1 (A/37/1), 1982, p. 2.

21. United Nations, Department of Public Information (WS/1100), November 5, 1982.

22. Ibid.

23. Ibid. (WS/1107), December 23, 1982.

24. ICJ, *Reports,* 1966, p. 6.

25. Compare T. O. Elias, *New Horizons in International Law* (1979), pp. 78–79.

26. ICJ, *Reports,* 1971, p. 16.

27. ICJ, *Reports,* 1982, p. 18.

28. ICJ, *Reports,* 1982, p. 10 (declaration of Judge Oda).

29. Ibid., p. 11 (dissenting opinion of Judge Morozov), and p. 12 (dissenting opinion of Judge El-Khani).

30. ICJ, *Reports,* 1982, p. 3.

31. ICJ, *Reports,* 1962, p. 151.

32. United Nations, Department of Public Information (WS/1105), December 10, 1982.

33. United Nations, Third United Nations Conference on the Law of the Sea: *Turkey and United States of America: Revised Amendment* (A/37/L.15/rev. 1), November 24, 1982.

34. *New York Times,* December 31, 1982.

35. Statement by Ambassador Kenneth L. Adelman, United States, to the thirty-seventh session of the General Assembly, December 3, 1982 (United States Mission to the United Nations); *New York Times,* December 31, 1982; ibid., January 2, 1983.

36. See, generally, Roger Fisher, *Improving Compliance with International Law* (Charlottesville: University Press of Virginia, 1981); Richard Bilder, *Managing the Risks of International Agreement* (Madison: University of Wisconsin Press, 1981).

37. W. G. Grewe, "Vom europäischen zum universellen Völkerrecht. Zur frage der Revision des 'europazentrischen' Bildes der Völkerrechtsgeschichte [From European to universal international law. On the question of the revision of the Eurocentric image of the history of international law], *Zeitschrift für ausländisches öffentliches Recht und Völkerrecht* 42 (1982): 449.

38. Julius Stone, *Of Law and Nations* (Buffalo: William S. Hein, 1974), pp. 119 *et seq.;* Manfred Lachs, *The Teacher in International Law* (The Hague: Martinus Nighoff, 1982).

39. Perspectives are offered variously by Myres S. McDougal, Harold D. Lasswell, and W. M. Reisman, "Theories about International Law: Prologue to a Configurative Jurisprudence," *Virginia Journal of International Law* 8: 189; R. A. Falk, "On the Recent Further Decline of International Law, A. R. Blackshield, ed., *Legal Change Essays in Honour of Julius Stone* (Sydney: Butterworth, 1983), p. 264; René-Jean Dupuy, *Leçon inaugurale (Chaire de Droit International), Collège de France,* (Paris: Collège de France, 1980); T. O. Elias, *New Horizons in International Law;* G. Abi-Saab, "The Third World and the Future of the International Legal Order," *Revue égyptienne de droit international* 29 (1983): 27; R. P. Anand, *New States and International Law* (Delhi: Vikas, 1972).

40. *North-South: A Programme for Survival* (Brandt Commission Report) (London: Pan Books, 1980).

Index

Activism, judicial, 114–16
Aerial piracy, 53–53, 103–4, 193
Affirmative action, 179, 211–12
Afro-Asian states, 10, 57, 108–9. *See also* specific countries
Aggression, U.N. definition, 191
Algeria, 102, 111–12
Alvarez, Judge (ICJ), 69, 83
Ammoun, Vice President (ICJ), 32–33, 69–71, 77, 119–20
Antarctic Conservation Treaty, 197
Antarctic Treaty (1959), 18, 174–75, 197
Argentina, 82–83
  Falklands crisis and, 9, 11, 89, 96, 173–74, 191–92, 220–23, 229
Australia, 44, 54, 117–20
Axiological problem, 228–30
Azevedo, Judge (ICJ), 69, 83

Bayona-Ba-Meya, 32–33, 40
Bedjaoui, Judge Mohammed (ICJ), 33, 40, 60, 102, 112
Belgium, 64
Berlin Conference (1885), 32–33, 175
Bipolarity (Soviet–U.S.), 16–20
Blix, Hans, 220
Boni, Judge (ICJ), 34, 119, 120
Brandeis, Louis, 177
Brandt, Willy, 176, 231
Brezhnev, Leonid, 5, 20, 194–95
Brierly, J. L., 101

Canada, 126–29, 172–73, 225–26
Carter, Jimmy, 195
Chambers, Special (ICJ), 123–29, 131, 225–26
Charter
  Special Committee (General Assembly), 87, 90, 91–92, 135–41, 143
  United Nations, 3–4, 56, 57, 74, 76, 206–9
    "gaps" in, 57, 61, 81, 91–96, 191–92
    International Court of Justice and, 105–6, 131–32
    membership and, 81–84, 216–20
    peace imperative and, 189–93
    reform of. *See* Charter reform
    superpower doctrinal-legal positions and, 214–15
    as treaty versus constitution, 84–87, 165–67
Charter of Economic Rights and Duties of States, 179–82

Charter reform, 133–41, 167
by direct amendment, 133–35
Manila Declaration, 141–44
Special Committee of General Assembly on, 87, 90, 91–92, 135–41, 143
China
People's Republic of, 50–51
International Court of Justice and, 110–11
Pancha Shila agreement and, 10, 17, 19
regional international law of, 10–11
Taiwan, 10, 88, 89, 92–93
Chinese Communist international law, 10–11
Chou En-Lai, 17
Civil law
codification, 96–104, 114
reasoning, 108
past judicial decisions and, 61
"Classical" international law, 21–24
human rights and, 212
Institut de Droit International and, 25–27, 38–41
International Court of Justice legislation and, 27–37
intertemporal law and, 24–25
Law of the Sea and, 184
limitations of, 37–41
sources of
formal, 43–44
ranking of, 44–45
synthesis of Soviet, socialist international law and, 16–19
Clausula rebus sic stantibus, 51, 75
Code Napoléon, 96–97, 108, 234
Codification, 96–104, 157–58
Law of the Sea. *See* Law of the Sea
Co-existence, peaceful
development of concept of, 16–19
historical critique of, 19–20
Commission on Transnational Corporations, 201–2
"Common heritage of mankind," 233–34
Common law, reasoning, 108
equity in, 64–65
judicial self-restraint versus activism in, 114
precedents in, 57, 61
Comparative international law, 96–97
Congo crisis, 146, 227, 228
Constitutionalism, United Nations, 84–85, 133–35, 165–68, 206–7, 210–11, 216–28
credentials of members and, 216–20
General Assembly and, 220–23
International Court of Justice and, 224–26
International Law Commission and, 226–27
Secretary-General and, 223
Security Council and, 220–23
Sixth (Legal) Committee and, 226–27
U.N. expenses and, 227–28
"Contemporary" international law, 142–43, 233
Continental Shelf Convention (1958), 35

Conventions, international, 49–55. *See also* specific conventions
Credentials
  General Assembly, 216–20
  International Atomic Energy Agency, 220
  International Telecommunications Union, 220
Credentials Committee, General Assembly, 216–19
Cuban missile crisis, 49
Cultural pluralism, 5–6
Custom, international, 47–49
  law based on, 101–2
Cyprus, 174

Declarations, General Assembly
  Friendly Relations, 19–20, 54, 65, 76, 90, 99–100, 141–42
  Human Rights, 150, 208–11
  Manila Declaration, 141–44
  New International Economic Order, 179, 180
Decolonization imperative, 170–77
  Falklands (Malvinas) crisis and. *See* Falklands (Malvinas)
  Fourth Committee and, 413
  intertemporal law and, 24–25
  Western Sahara (ICJ) case and, 29–34, 40, 60, 119–20, 177
Dédoublement fonctionnel, 12, 78, 100
de Gaulle, Charles, 3
de Lacharrière, Judge Guy (ICJ), 101
De-Stalinization, 13
Détente (East–West), 3–5, 22, 142, 215–16, 231–32
  key treaties in, 54–55, 194–95

Developing countries
  Latin American international law and, 9–10
  See also Third World and specific countries
Development, international law, 10–11, 19–20, 96–104, 232–35
Dicey, A. V., 158
Disarmament
  general, 193–95
  nuclear, 18, 54–55, 193–95
Doehring, Karl, 38, 39

Eclecticism, legal, 233–35
Economic rights, 177–88
Economic sovereignty, 177–88
Egypt, 95, 137, 139, 141
Elections
  of judges (ICJ), 59–60, 101–2, 109–12
  Security Council, 110
El-Erian, Judge (ICJ), 60, 111
El-Khani, Judge (ICJ), 128, 129
"Enemy states," U.N. Charter, 191
Enlightenment imperative, 197–205
Environmental protection, 125, 179, 195–97
Equity, 63–73, 78–79
  in Manila Declaration, 141
Ethiopia, 108, 170
Ethnocentricity, legal, 6–7, 27, 112–13
"Eurocentrism," 7, 8, 22, 108–9, 187–88, 234–35
  of "classical" international law, 37–38
  in environmental protection, 196

human rights and, 209–12
intertemporal law and, 24–25
in *Western Sahara* case (ICJ), 29–34
Evensen, Judge (ICJ), 34
Expenses, U.N. (ICJ), 85, 107, 133, 227–28

Faktischen, die normative Kraft des, 39, 41, 214
Falklands (Malvinas), 9, 11, 89, 96, 173–74, 191–92, 220–23, 229
Financing, United Nations, 85, 107, 133, 227–28
Fiore, Pasquale, 33
Fitzmaurice Judge Gerald (ICJ), 108, 115, 116
Fleischhauer, Carl-August, 150
Ford, Gerald R., 194–95
Forster, Judge (ICJ), 33, 119, 120
Fourteen Points, 178
Fourth Committee, General Assembly, 143, 174
France, 35, 88, 139–40, 176
expenses of United Nations and, 227, 228
Nuclear Tests Judgment (ICJ), 44, 54, 117–20
Suez crisis and, 95
François, J. P. A., 101
Frankfurter, Felix, 233
Friendly Relations, Declaration, 19, 54, 65, 76, 90, 99–100, 141–42
critique of, 19–20

"Gaps," United Nations Charter, 57, 61, 81, 91–96
"enemy states," 191
self defense, 191–92
General Assembly, United Nations
Charter amendment and. *See* Charter reform
codification of international law and, 98–104
Credentials Committee of, 216–19
ethnocentrism of, 27
Fourth Committee of, 143, 174
International Court of Justice and, 106, 109–12, 130
legal pragmatism and, 6, 232–33
membership in, 81–84, 216–20
peaceful coexistence and, 19
resolutions of. *See* Resolutions, General Assembly
Sixth (Legal) Committee of. *See* Sixth (Legal) Committee
Special Committee of, 87, 90–92, 135–41, 143
Special Political Committee of, 150, 204
Third World and legislation of, 56–58, 60–61, 79
U.N. constitutionalism and, 220–23
"Generalists," legal, 205–6
General principles of law, 48, 62–63, 64, 70, 77
Geneva Convention (1949), 150; (1958), 44, 54, 98
Gény, 108
Germany, 28, 29, 63, 77, 96–97
Democratic Republic, 89
Federal Republic of, 44, 89, 231
Ostpolitik and, 20, 39, 176, 231

Great Britain. *See* United Kingdom
"Green" movements, 196
Gros, Judge (ICJ), 34, 127
Gross, Leo, 130
Grotius, Hugo, 23, 234
Group of Seventy-Seven, 180
Gulf of Maine (Canada/U.S.), 126–29, 225–26
Guyana, 222

Hague Convention (1970), 52, 103–4, 193
Haig, Alexander, 221
Hammarskjöld, Dag, 146, 223, 227
"Hard" law, 78–79
Helsinki Final Act, 55, 206
Helsinki Review Conferences, 206
Historical relativism
  spatial dimension of international law and. *See* Spatial dimension, international law
  temporal dimension of international law and. *See* Temporal dimension, international law
Holmes, Oliver Wendell, 40, 177
Hong Kong, 11, 50
"Honoratiores," legal, 112–14
"Hot Line" Agreement, 194
Huber, Max, 24, 26, 38, 39
Hudson, Judge Manley (ICJ), 64, 101, 116
Hughes, Charles Evans, 108
Human dignity imperative, 205–12
  "specialists" and "generalists" in international legal negotiations, 205–6
  U.N. Charter-based principles and processes, 206–9
Human Rights, U.N. Declaration, 150, 208–11
Human rights imperative, 209–12

Ideological pluralism. *See* Pluralism, ideological
Ihering, Rudolf von, 113
Imperative principles, international law, 62–79
  categories, 62–76
    equity, 63–73, 78–79, 141
    general principles of law, 48, 62–64, 70, 77
  Jus cogens, 26–27, 58, 67–68, 73–76
  contemporary trends in sources, 76–79
    dédoublement fonctionnel, 78
    "soft" and "hard" law, 78–79
  as source of international law, 62–76
Imperialism
  Western Sahara (ICJ) case and, 29–34, 40, 60, 119–20, 177
India, 192
  constitutionalism of, 164–65
  Pancha Shila agreement and, 10, 17, 19
Indonesia, 192
Institut de Droit International, 25–27, 38–41
Intergovernmental Bureau for Information (IBI), 202
International Atomic Energy Agency, 220
International Court of Justice (ICJ), 7, 101, 105–32
  comparative "regional" attitudes to international ad-

judication and, 106–9
contradictions and conflicts in, 116–23
equity concept and, 64–73, 78–79
future of judicial settlement in, 129–32
General Assembly and, 106, 109–12, 130
judges in. *See* Judges (ICJ)
judicial decisions of, 27–37, 39–41, 58–61
Continental Shelf (Tunisia/Libya), 34–37, 71–72, 225
Expenses, U.N., 85, 107, 133, 227–28
Gulf of Maine (Canada/U.S.), 126–29, 225–26
Namibia (South West Africa), 27–29, 40, 109, 116, 130–31, 171–72, 224
North Sea Continental Shelf, 35–37, 44, 54, 69–71, 120, 124
Nuclear Tests (Australia/France), 44, 54, 117–20
South West Africa, Second Phase, 27, 40, 60–61, 68, 108–9, 114–16, 130–31, 171–72, 224
United States Diplomatic and Consular Staff in Tehran, 120–121
Western Sahara, 29–34, 40, 60, 119–20, 175, 177
jurisdiction of, 105–6
Manila Declaration and, 144
Security Council and, 106, 109–12, 130
special chambers for institutional reform in, 123–29, 131, 225–26
Third World and, 45–46, 113–114, 119–20, 125, 127, 130–32
U.N. Charter and, 105–6, 131–32
U.N. Constitutionalism and, 224–26
U.N. membership and, 82–84
International Law Commission (ILC), 39, 73–76, 98–104, 111, 123, 153, 184
formation of, 98–101
reform of, 101–4, 134–35, 155–61
Sixth (Legal) Committee of General Assembly and, 155–56, 158–59
U.N. constitutionalism and, 226–27
International Programme for the Development of Communication (IPDC), 201
International Telecommunications Union (ITU), 198, 203, 204, 220
Intertemporal law, 24–41
development of general rules of, 25–27
formulation of, 24–25, 38
legislation, 27–41
Iran, 120–23, 179, 210, 213
Ireland, Republic of, 174
Island of Palmas, 24–25, 38
Israel, 177, 217, 218–20, 229–30
Italy, 35

James, William, 6
Japan, 89
Jaurès, Jean, 40

Jellinek, G., 39
Jessup, Judge Philip (ICJ), 40, 68, 115
Jiménez de Aréchaga, President (ICJ), 128
Johnson, Lyndon B., 20, 195
Judges (ICJ)
activism of, 114–16
decisions of. *See* International Court of Justice, judicial decisions
election of, 59–60, 101–2, 130
political-legal factors in, 109–12
as legal "honoratiores," 112–14
Jural postulates, 162–64
concretization of, 168–70
Jus aequum, 68
Jus cogens, 26–27, 58, 67–68, 73–78
jus gentium, 7, 63, 68, 71, 77
Jus naturale, 63

Kennedy, John F., 20, 195
Khomeini, Ayatollah Ruholiah, 6, 210, 213
Khrushchev, Nikita, 13, 17, 20
Kirkpatrick, Ambassador Jeane, 221
Koh, Ambassador Tommy, 186, 228
Kohler, J., 6, 163
Korean War, 56–57, 92–94
Koretsky, Judge V. M. (ICJ), 101, 107
Korovin, Eugene, 14–17
Kozhevnikov, Judge F. I. (ICJ), 16
Krylov, Judge S. B., 16, 17, 82

Lachs, Judge Manfred (ICJ), 25, 44, 68, 122–23, 125–26, 130, 131
Laski, Harold, 115
Lasswell, Harold D., 22
Latin American international law, 9–10, 29
Law making process, international law
imperative principles in. *See* Imperative principles, international law
sources of law in. *See* Sources, international law
Law of the Sea, 23–24, 51, 71, 125, 182, 184–86
Geneva Convention (1958), 44, 54, 98
U.N. Conference on, 35–36, 101, 104, 142, 155, 158, 184, 195, 233–34
U.N. Treaty on, 49, 185–86, 195, 200, 216, 226, 228, 233–34
League of Nations, mandate, 15, 28–29, 58–59, 85, 106, 107
on Palestine, 177, 229
over South West Africa (Namibia), 108–9, 115–16, 171, 217
Legal Affairs Office (U.N.), 153
Legal Counsel (U.N.), 150–53
Legislation, international, 55–58. *See also* Resolutions, General Assembly
Liberation, wars of national, 192–93
Liberia, 108, 171
"Liberty of contract," United States, 178
Libya, 34–37, 71–72, 225
Lopatka, Adam, 150

MacBride Commission (Unesco), 199, 200
McDougal, Myres S., 13
Maine, Henry, 66, 68
Malik, Ambassador, 92–93
Mandate, League of Nations. *See* League of Nations, mandate
Manila Declaration, 141–44
Mankind, "common heritage of," 233–34
Mare liberium doctrine, 23, 184
Marshall, John, 84, 86
Marxist-Leninist theories
  in Chinese Communist international law, 10–11
  in Soviet Socialist international law, 11–20
Mauritania, 31–34, 40,60, 119–20, 175, 177
M'Bow, Amadou-Mahtar, 201
Membership, United Nations, 80–84
  credentials for, 216–20
  Security Council, 109–10, 136
Montreal Convention (1971), 52, 103–4, 193
Moon Treaty (1979), 197
Morocco, 31–34, 40, 60, 119–20, 175, 177
Morozov, Judge (ICJ), 122–23, 128, 129
Moscow Summit Meeting (1972), 5, 68, 194
Mossadegh, Muhammad, 179

Nahlik, Stanislaw E., 75, 76
Namibia (South West Africa) (ICJ), 27–29, 40, 109, 116, 130–31, 171–72, 224
Natural resources, 125, 179, 195–97. *See also* Law of the Sea
Nehru, Pandit Jawaharlal, 17
Netherlands, 23, 64, 192
  intertemporal law and, 24, 26, 38
"New" countries
  International Court of Justice and, 108–9
  international custom and, 47–48
  progressive development and codification of international law and, 99–100
New International Economic Order (NIEO), 46, 58
  Charter, 179, 180–82
  Declaration, 179, 180
  Programme of Action, 180, 186–88
"New" international law, 21–22
  "classical" international law compared with, 21–24, 37–41
  human rights and, 210–11
  Institut de Droit International and, 25–27, 38–41
  International Court of Justice decisions and, 27–37
  principles of, 142–43
New World Information Order, 197–205
NIEO. *See* New International Economic Order
Nixon, Richard M., 5, 20, 194, 195
Non-Aligned countries, 137–39, 141, 180
North Sea Continental Shelf (ICJ), 35–37, 44, 54, 69–71, 120, 124
North-South relations, 46, 230
Nuclear Arms on Seabed Treaty

(1971), 55
Nuclear Nonproliferation Treaty (1968), 55
Nuclear Tests (Australia/France) (ICJ), 44, 54, 117–20
Nuremberg War Crimes Tribunal, 63, 77

Oda, Judge (ICJ), 34–37, 71–72, 127–29
"One world" imperative, 195–97
OPEC. *See* Organization of Petroleum Exporting Countries
Operationalism, 230–35
  contradictions in space and time and, 230–31
  legal "receptions" and eclecticism in, 233–35
  skills of legal pragmatism and, 232–33
Organization of Petroleum Exporting Countries (OPEC), 183
Ostpolitik, 20, 39, 176, 231
Outer Space Treaty (1967), 43, 55, 194

Pacific Settlement of Disputes, 137
Palestinian people, 52–53, 150–51, 177, 218–19, 229–30
Pancha Shila Agreement (1954), 10, 17, 19
Pardo, Ambassador, 185, 195, 234
Partial Test Ban Treaty (1963), 18, 54–55, 194
Pashukanis, E. B., 14–15
Peaceful coexistence
  development of concept of, 16–19
  historical critique of, 19–20
Peaceful settlement of disputes, 141–44
Peace imperative, 87–91, 189–95
  nuclear and general disarmament in, 193–95
  outlawing use of force and, 189–93
"Peace-loving states," membership, 82–83
Peking summit meeting (1972), 68
People's rights, 211
Pérez de Cuéllar, Javier, 87, 147, 150, 199, 219, 222, 223
Permanent Court of International Justice, 31, 34, 58–59, 64–65, 69, 105–7, 114. *See also* International Court of Justice
Pescatore, Judge, 26
Pluralism
  cultural, 5–6
  ideological, 4–5, 162–212
    economic sovereignty imperative and, 177–88
  enlightenment imperative and, 197–205
  human dignity imperative and, 205–12
  jural postulates and, 162–63
  "one world" imperative and, 195–97
  peace imperative and, 189–95
  self-determination of peoples and, 170–77
  values and value choice in, 164–70
Poland, 81, 149–50
Popper, Karl Raimund, 66
Portugal, 23, 192
Postulates, jural, 162–64
  concretization of, 168–70

Potsdam Conference (1945), 3, 4, 20, 81, 176, 190–91, 214, 231
Pound, Roscoe, 162–63
Pragmatism, legal, 6, 232–33
Problem solving, legal, 232–33
Progressive development, international law, 98–104, 232–35
Publicist, legal, 12, 78, 100, 187–88

Quiet diplomacy, 149, 219, 229

Ratio decidendi, 30
"Reception," legal, 233–35
"Regional" international law, 8–20
  Chinese, 10–11
  human rights imperative and, 209–12
  International Court of Justice and, 106–9
  Latin American, 9–10
  Soviet, 11–20
  Western-based, 16–19
Relativism, historical
  spatial dimension of international law and. *See* Spatial dimension, international law
  temporal dimension of international law and. *See* Temporal dimension, international law
Resolutions, General Assembly, 45–46, 55–58
  on communication, 199, 200, 202
  on disarmament, 195
  on Falklands crisis, 220–23
  on granting independence to colonial countries, 170, 171
  on human rights, 208
  on New International Economic Order, 178–79, 182, 186–8
  on Sea-Bed Committee (1967), 35
  on terrorism, 193
  United for Peace, 57, 61, 87, 93–96, 139–41, 215, 227–28
Reuter, Paul, 158–60
Reverse discrimination, 179, 211–212
Revolution
  French, 22
  Russian, 22, 45, 50
Roman law, influence, 65, 71, 73, 74, 234
Roosevelt, Franklin D., ,210
Rosenne, Shabtai, 142, 154–56
Ross, Alf, 82
Rules of Court (ICJ), 224–25

SALT I, 55, 194–95
SALT II, 55, 194–95
San Francisco Conference, United Nations (1945), 81, 85, 142, 190, 214
Satellites, 202–4
Savigny, F. K. von, 97, 158
Scelle, Georges, 12, 78, 100, 101
Schwarzenberger, Georg, 68, 75
Secretary-General, United Nations, 138, 144, 145–50
  Palestinian people and, 219–20
  quiet diplomacy of, 149, 219, 229
  superpowers and, 146–47, 149
  U.N. constitutionalism and, 223
  U.N. Legal Counsel and, 150–53
Security Council
  United Nations Charter amendment and, 133–35
  elections of, 110

International Court of Justice
and, 106, 109–12, 130
permanent members of, 109–10,
136
South Africa/South West Africa
and, 27–28
U.N. constitutionalism and,
220–23
veto in, 56–57, 59, 81–84, 87–96,
136–37
Self defense, right of, 191–93
Self-determination of peoples, 6–7,
29, 119–20, 168, 169, 170–77
economic, 177–88
in Manila Declaration, 141
Palestinian, 52–53, 150–51, 177,
218–19, 229–30
Settlement, peaceful, 141–44
Sinclair, Ian, 74, 99, 100
Sixth (Legal) Committee (GA), 99–
102, 113, 140–41, 152, 153–
55, 184, 187, 204
International Law Commission
and, 155–56, 158–59
U.N. constitutionalism and,
226–27
Socialist international law, 11–20
unequal treaties and, 9–11, 45–
46, 49–51
"Soft" law, 78–79
Sørensen, Max, 25, 38, 40
Sources, international law, 42–61
closed categories of formal, 42–
44
contemporary trends in, 46–61,
76–79
dédoublement fonctionnel, 78,
international conventions, 49–
55
international custom, 47–49
international legislation, 55–58
judicial decisions, 58–61
"soft" and "hard" law, 78–79
hierarchical ranking of, 44–46
imperative principles as, 62–76
equity, 63–73
general principles of law, 62–
63
jus cogens, 73–76
South Africa, Republic of, 60, 61,
108–9, 115–16
South West Africa and, 27–29
U.N. membership and, 217–18
South Africa, Union of, 171
South West Africa
Namibia, 27–29, 40, 109, 116,
130–31, 171–72, 224
*South West Africa, Second
Phase,* 27, 40, 60–61, 68,
108–9, 114–16, 130–31, 171–
72, 224
Sovereignty
economic, 177–88
natural resource, 179
political
in *Namibia* case, 27–29
in *Western Sahara* case, 29–
34
Soviet-Chinese relations, 51, 92–93
Soviet international law, 11–20
unequal treaties and, 9–11, 45–
46, 49–51
Soviet Union, 3–5
bipolarity of United States and,
16–20
codification of international law
and, 99–100
doctrinal-legal position of, ver-
sus United States, 213–16
expenses of United Nations and,

227, 228
International Court of Justice and, 85–86, 107–8, 113
jus cogens limits on treaties and, 73, 75–76
Marxist-Leninist theories in People's Republic of China and, 10–11
New International Information Order and, 199–201
temporal dimension of international law and, 21–22
United Nations formation and, 85
United Nations position of, 56–57
Soviet-Western relations, 3
Cuban missile crisis, 49
human rights and, 209–12
Moscow Test Ban Treaty (1963), 18, 54–55, 194
peaceful coexistence and, 16–20
Secretary-General and, 146–50
Space Treaty (1967), 43, 55, 194
United Nations Charter and, 85–86
Uniting for Peace Resolution and, 140
Space Treaty (1967), 43, 55, 194
Spain
African colonization and, 29–34
influence of, on Latin American international law, 9, 29
Law of the Sea and, 23
Spanish Sahara, 29–34, 40, 60, 119–20, 175, 177
Spatial dimension, international law, 8–20, 124
defined, 8
historical critique of peaceful coexistence in, 19–20
international custom and, 48
in Latin American regional international law, 9–10
Marxist-Leninist theory in China, 10–11
versus Socialist international law, 13–16
in Soviet-bloc countries, 11–19
synthesis of Soviet, Socialist and Western-based international law, 16–19
Special Committee, General Assembly, 87, 90, 91–92, 135–41, 143
"Specialists," legal, 205–6
Special Political Committee, General Assembly, 150, 204
Spender, Percy, 108, 115
Spheres of influence, 215
Stalin, J. V., 17
State responsibility, 203–4
Stockholm Conference, Environment (1972), 196–97
Strategic Arms Limitation Talks. *See* SALT I; SALT II
Strebel, H., 46
Succession states, 176–78
Suez crisis (1956), 95
Summit meetings, 5, 68, 194, 215
Superpowers
détente and. *See* Détente
differing doctrinal-legal positions of, 213–16
Law of the Sea and. *See* Law of the Sea
New International Information Order and, 199–201
Secretary-General and, 146–47, 149

See also Soviet Union; United States
Supreme Court, United States, 27, 108, 114, 117–78, 211
Suy, Erik, 150, 185

Taiwan (Nationalist China). *See under* China
Tarazi, Judge (ICJ), 122–23
Temporal dimension, international law, 21–41
Institut de Droit International and, 25–27
international custom and, 48
intertemporal law and, 24–25
judicial decisions on (ICJ), 27–41
spatial dimension and, 8
Terra nullius, 30–33, 119–20
Terrorism, international, 52–53, 103–4, 193
Text writers, legal, 12, 78, 100
Thant, U, 146–47
Thatcher, Margaret, 11, 50, 173
Thiam, Doudou, 101
Thibaut, Anton, 96–97
Third World, 4
economic issues and, 230–31
election of judges and, 11–12
environmental protection and, 196–97
General Assembly legislation and, 56–58, 60–61, 79
International Court of Justice and, 45–46, 113–14, 119–20, 125, 127, 130–32
international development law and, 10–11
New International Information Order and, 198–201
"new" international law and, 22–23
Uniting for Peace Resolution and, 140–41
See also specific countries
Tokyo Convention (1963), 52–53, 103–4, 193
Transition, era of, 213–35
alternative world order constructs in, 213–16
evolving U.N. constitutionalism and, 216–28
operationalism in, 230–35
value conflicts and value antinomies in, 228–30
Treaties
bilateral, 40, 54–55. *See also* disarmament
drafting of, 73–76
law making based on, 101–4
multilateral, 40, 49–54
equity concept in, 66–67
U.N. Charter as, 85–86
unequal, 9–11, 45–46, 49–51, 67
Treaties Law, Vienna Convention, 26, 67, 73–76, 101
Treaty on the Manufacture and Stockpiling of Bacteriological Weapons (1972), 55
Tunisia, 34–37, 71–72, 225
Tunkin, Gregory, 12–17, 21, 47–48, 76

Unequal treaties doctrine, 9–11, 45–46, 49–51, 67
UNEP. *See* United Nations Environment Program
Unesco. *See* United Nations Educational, Scientific, and Cultural Organization

UNITAR. *See* United Nations Institute for Training and Research
United Kingdom, 88, 176
Canada and, 172–73
China and, 50
Falklands crisis and, 9, 11, 89, 96, 173–74, 191–92, 220–23, 229
Suez crisis and, 95
United Nations Educational, Scientific, and Cultural Organization (UNESCO)
New International Information Order and, 198–201, 204
United Nations Environment Program (UNEP), 197
United Nations Institute for Training and Research (UNITAR), 103, 152, 157, 187–88
United States 3–5
bipolarity of Soviet Union and, 16–20
doctrinal-legal position of, versus Soviet Union, 213–16
expenses of United Nations and, 228
Falklands crisis and, 9, 11, 89, 96, 173–74, 191–92, 220–23, 229
Gulf of Maine (Canada/U.S.), 126–29, 225–26
intertemporal law and, 24, 26, 38
Iran crisis and, 120–23
Latin American international law and, 9–10
Supreme Court of, 27, 108, 114, 117–18, 211
territorial disputes of, 126–29
Uniting for Peace Resolution (GA), 57, 61, 87, 93–96, 139–41, 215, 227–28
Uti possidetis doctrine, 9

Values, legal, 164–70
concretization of, 168–70
conflicts and antinomies of, 228–30
identification of, 164–68
ranking of, 168
Verdross, A. von, 40, 74
Versailles Treaty, 29, 59, 106, 123, 189
Veto, Security Council, 56–57, 59, 87–91, 136–37
Vienna Convention on Consular Relations (1963), 121–22
Vienna Convention on Diplomatic Relations (1961), 121–22
Vienna Convention on the Law of Treaties, 26, 67, 73–76, 101
Vyshinsky, Andrei, 16, 94

Waldheim, Kurt, 146–47, 151, 152
Waldock, President Humphrey (ICJ), 74, 126
"Watergate" crisis, 5, 194
Weber, Max, 42, 58, 145
Western Sahara (ICJ), 29–34, 40, 60, 119–20, 175, 177
Wilson, Woodrow, 178
Winiarski, Judge (ICJ), 86, 107, 108
World Court. *See* International Court of Justice; Permanent Court of International Justice

Yalta Conference (1944), 3, 4, 20, 81, 176, 190–91, 214, 231
Yugoslavia, 95